Embracing Risk

Embracing Risk
The Changing Culture of
Insurance and Responsibility

Edited by

Tom Baker *&* Jonathan Simon

The University of Chicago Press
Chicago *&* London

Tom Baker is professor of law and director of the Insurance Law Center at the University of Connecticut. Jonathan Simon is professor of law at the University of Miami and author of *Poor Discipline: Parole and the Social Control of the Underclass* (Chicago, 1993), which won the 1994 American Sociology Association's Sociology of Law Section Distinguished Book Award.

The University of Chicago Press, Chicago 60637
The University of Chicago Press, Ltd., London
© 2002 by The University of Chicago
All rights reserved. Published 2002
Printed in the United States of America

11 10 09 08 07 06 05 04 03 02   1 2 3 4 5
ISBN: 0-226-03518-2 (cloth)
ISBN: 0-226-03519-0 (paper)

Library of Congress Cataloging-in-Publication Data

Embracing risk : the changing culture of insurance and responsibility / edited by Tom Baker and Jonathan Simon.
    p. cm.
    Includes bibliographical references and index.
    ISBN 0-226-03518-2 (cloth : alk. paper)—ISBN 0-226-03519-0 (paper : alk. paper)
    1. Risk—Sociological aspects. 2. Risk (Insurance). 3. Responsibility. I. Baker, Tom, 1959– II. Simon, Jonathan.

HM1101 .E43 2002
302′.12—dc21

2001042733

♾ The paper used in this publication meets the minimum requirements of the American National Standard for Information Sciences—Permanence of Paper for Printed Library Materials, ANSI Z39.48-1992.

Contents

Acknowledgments

This book emerged out of an ongoing dialogue among a growing number of writers who are exploring questions of risk, insurance, and responsibility from a variety of cultural, historical, and sociological perspectives. We owe a debt to more people engaged in that project than is possible to acknowledge. Three institutions have played crucial roles: the Law and Society Association, the Insurance and Society Study Group, and the Insurance Law Center of the University of Connecticut. Most of our contributors met through the Law and Society Association, and many of the essays were first presented at Association meetings. The dialogue that began in the Association has continued in the Insurance and Society Study Group, which has been an incubator for ideas and research of the sort represented here. The Insurance Law Center has funded both the Study Group and a related conference on risk held in Hartford in April 1999. The Insurance Law Center also supports the work of Tom Baker. Professor Simon's work on this project has been supported by the University of Miami School of Law.

In addition to the contributors, a number of people from the Law and Society Association have been particularly supportive of the work that went into preparing this book; they include Richard Abel, Ross Cheit, Malcolm Feeley, Nancy Reichman, Robert Rosen, and Carol Weisbrod. Special mention should also go to Marianne Sadowski, University of Connecticut Ph.D. and J.D. 2002, who provided substantial assistance in the revision and compilation of the book, and Brian Glenn, Ph.D. candidate at Oxford, whose presence as Research Fellow at the Insurance Law Center advanced the project.

Contributors

Tom Baker is Connecticut Mutual Professor of Law and director of the Insurance Law Center of the University of Connecticut.

Geoffrey Clark is associate professor in the Department of History at the State University of New York, Pottsdam.

Richard Ericson is principal of Green College and professor of law and sociology at the University of British Columbia.

François Ewald is Insurance chair at the Conservatoire National des Arts et Métiers, and director of Research and Strategy for the Fédération Française des Sociétés d'Assurances.

Kevin Hagerty is assistant professor of sociology at the University of Alberta.

Carol Heimer is professor and chair of sociology at Northwestern University and senior research fellow at the American Bar Foundation.

Martha McCluskey is associate professor of law at the State University of New York, Buffalo.

Pat O'Malley is professor of law and legal studies and deputy dean of the Faculty of Law and Management at La Trobe University, Australia.

Nikolas Rose is professor of sociology at Goldsmiths College, University of London.

Jonathan Simon is professor of law at the University of Miami.

Deborah Stone is an independent scholar, a research professor at Dartmouth College, and a former professor of politics and social policy at Brandeis University.

Stephen Utz is professor of law at the University of Connecticut.

ONE

Embracing Risk

Tom Baker and Jonathan Simon

Centuries are too convenient not to be used for organizing historical developments. But as cognitive psychologists have discovered, people are so hard-wired for seeing patterns that we tend to see them where there are none. For this reason, historical patterns witnessed at the start of a new millennium may be sufficiently suspect members of an already highly suspicious class that they ought, perhaps, to be discounted entirely. With that said, however, a premise of this book is that we are, at the beginning of the twenty-first century, witnessing an important transformation in the approach to risk and responsibility, an approach that we call "embracing risk."

In coining the term *embracing risk,* we mean to both evoke and distinguish the idea of "spreading risk" that has been so influential over the last century. Embracing risk captures two related cultural trends. The first follows logically from efforts to spread risk and consists of a wide variety of efforts to conceive and address social problems in terms of risk. For example, money management, social services, policing, environmental policy, tort law, national defense, and a host of otherwise unrelated fields have all come to share a common vocabulary of risk. The second cultural trend is a reaction against spreading risk, and it consists of various efforts to make people more individually accountable for risk.

Together these two trends mean that, as more of life is understood in terms of risk, *taking* risks increasingly becomes what one does with risk. Once you begin to look, you can see these efforts almost everywhere: in transformations in the private insurance market, pensions, and social insurance; and in popular culture, where extreme sports, day trading, and the cult of the technology entrepreneur all exalt individuals who (at least seem to) spurn the safety nets of large institutions.

Ideas like embracing risk or spreading risk inevitably promise more than they can deliver, and they never capture more than a partial vision of a cultural moment. Yet that does not diminish their importance. The notion of insurance as risk spreading was a veritable genie from a bottle in the early twentieth century, as reformers sought to extend its logic from workplace accidents to automobile accidents, unemployment, poverty, disease, and nearly every other social problem, with wide-ranging consequences (Simon 1998). We see signs that embracing risk may become as symbolically powerful. Indeed, reformers today are recasting their approaches to many of those same problems in terms of embracing risk.

This embrace of risk creates new challenges, not only for those with risks to spread or embrace, but also for the study of risk and insurance. Historians, anthropologists, political scientists, and lawyers have all explored the emergence of modern approaches to risk and insurance. But the implicit background for much of this work has been the risk-spreading approach. For example, this work has almost always understood insurance as a mechanism of risk spreading, and risk itself in terms of future harms with measurable probabilities (Ewald 1986).

The two trends that come together in embracing risk challenge us to understand other aspects of both risk and insurance. Insurance institutions that embrace risk push us to recognize that insurance can be about much more than risk spreading. Looking back with this expanded vision, we see that insurance has always done much more than spread losses. Similarly, if risk is something to be embraced, it cannot only be about harm or danger. And, once we free risk from risk spreading, there is no longer a reason to confine risk to probability. Once again, looking back with expanded vision we see that risk was never completely tied up with either harm or probability.

The essays in this book are a variety of efforts to bring into view changes along two axes—changing ways of governing risk and changing ways of doing the sociology of insurance and risk. They represent the beginning of what we hope will be an important new area of thought and research. We have collected these essays together to invite and encourage further work along either of the above axes or between them. Toward that end, in the remainder of this introduction we consider each axis in a bit more detail. Introductory sections at the beginning of each of the two parts of the book describe the individual essays that follow them and how each essay contributes to the book's main themes.

From Spreading Risk to Embracing Risk

From the adoption of workers compensation laws in the early twentieth century through at least the late 1980s, the United States and other industrializing societies socialized, or spread, more and more risks. Over this period, ever-expanding public and private insurance pools assumed financial responsibility for significant risks faced by individuals, families, and organizations. On the private side, the twentieth century witnessed the dramatic growth of health insurance, tort liability insurance, workers compensation insurance, and private pensions (which typically have an annuity, and, hence, insurance character), as well as the slower but still steady rise in older forms of insurance such as life, property, and disability insurance. On the public side, there was the creation and perhaps even more dramatic expansion of an entirely new social insurance sector, beginning with the multifaceted Social Security program during the New Deal and followed by Medicare, Medicaid, and natural disaster insurance, as well as a host of public sector insurance ventures directed primarily at business risks.

During this era, insurance was widely understood as the science and art of spreading risks over populations. Indeed, some visionaries went so far as to claim that insurance embodied the superiority of science and technology over religion. Through insurance, science would be able to resolve social conflicts and produce forms of collective mutuality envisioned but unachieved by any of the major religions (see, e.g., Dawson 1895).

The trend was not always uniform, and significant risks and important segments of the population were always left out. Nevertheless, the overall picture during this period is one in which the steadily employed, as well as an expanding percentage of those outside the labor market, enjoyed increasing protection from the financial consequences of illness, injury, old age, premature death of the family breadwinner, fire, and natural disaster. Indeed, "more insurance for more people" might best describe the twentieth-century U.S. domestic social policy well into the Reagan/Bush years. Our focus is on the United States, but we think that experience is not unique. If anything, risk has been socialized to an even greater extent in Western Europe and Japan.[1]

More recently, there has been a series of developments in the United States and elsewhere that suggest the appeal of a domestic social policy of "more insurance for more people" has begun to fade in favor of policies that embrace risk as an incentive that can reduce individual claims on collective resources. Significantly, these developments are occurring in both public and private forms of insurance, so that they cannot be attributed solely to a reexamination of the role of the state in the distribution of risk and responsibility.

Above all, these developments reflect an increased concern about how people react to being protected from risk and a new emphasis on the need to manage incentives to curtail what is perceived as the runaway growth of public and private insurance programs. This focus on what Carol Heimer (1985) has called the "reactive" nature of risk has led to outright reductions in benefits in some social insurance programs, such as workers compensation and public welfare programs. It has also led to the increasing coordination of the finance and delivery of insured services, manifested most obviously in the United States by the shift to managed health care in both private and public health insurance, but also by related developments in property and liability insurance and workers compensation. Across a wide range of institutions, officials are now as concerned about the perverse effects of efforts at risk shifting as they are about the risks being shifted. For example, rather than seeking to eliminate poverty (a master goal of the "more insurance" era), current social policy aims at eliminating welfare.

While these changes are often seen as a shift against the poor in favor of the well off, and against consumers and in favor of business, they affect the middle class as well as the poor, and businesses as well as individuals. For example, private pensions, annuities, and life insurance are engaged in an historic shift of investment risk from broad pools (the classic structure of risk spreading through insurance) to individual (middle-class) consumers and employees in return for the possibility of greater return. Many annuities and pensions have moved from a "defined benefit" approach, in which the risk of sufficient revenues to pay the promised benefit is on the collective pool, to a "defined contribution" approach, in which the risk of sufficient revenues for a comfortable retirement remains on the individual. (Remarkably, this significant change in the circumstances facing an increasingly large proportion of U.S. families is taking place with almost no public discussion.) The claim is that embracing risk will provide workers with greater returns with which to enjoy their retirement.

Similar developments are also occurring in insurance products sold to large businesses. Since the 1980s there has been significant growth in alternative risk mechanisms addressing property and casualty risks. Many of these reward businesses for retaining risk. Examples include captive insurance companies, fronting, third-party administrators, and finite risk insurance; in each of these, the individual business retains most of the risk while obtaining the tax and risk management benefits of the insurance form. Similarly, employers increasingly are self-insuring for workers compensation and health insurance risks, and there is a related trend toward larger deductibles, retroactive premiums, and other similar ways of retaining risk by organizations that continue to use traditional insurance. In addition, although this is a controversial claim, there may be an increasing use of corporate structure to insulate assets from risky activities, with a corresponding reduction in the ability of the tort/liability insurance system to socialize risk (Lopucki 1996).

In the public arena, the most significant manifestation of this trend may have been the discussion of social security reform in the 2000 presidential campaign. Historically, the Social Security system has been the most visible example of the "spreading risk" approach. The government collects a fixed percentage of earned income (up to a salary cap) through a special payroll tax that functions as a social insurance premium. In return the government provides a guaranteed annual income beginning at retirement or disability, keyed to a person's earnings history and intended to keep the elderly and disabled above poverty. This system spreads the risk of physical inability to work among almost the entire working population.

The Republican candidate, George W. Bush, and the Democratic candidate, Al Gore, both proposed creating a market-linked segment of the Social Security retirement benefit that represented a significant move away from the spreading risk approach. Both plans would have placed on individuals the risk that market forces will result in disappointing or even zero returns. Although Bush proposed a more dramatic departure from tradition (under which participants could place as much as 2 percent of their income into an individualized private investment fund), the details of the respective plans are less important here than the fact that both represented a new emphasis on risk and reward.

Popular culture and consumer behavior also reflect the increasing attraction of risk-taking activities. Perhaps most significant is the dramatic expansion of stock market investing, particularly in its "extreme" version—day trading. Long considered of little value or interest to middle-class, wage-earning Americans, the stock market since the 1980s increasingly has become an object of intense mass appeal. By the end of the twentieth century, participation in the market reached extraordinary levels, and all manner of supporting activities proliferated as well—web sites, magazines, television and radio shows.

This broad focus on investing is often attributed to the bull market of the 1990s, and no doubt the repeated stories of success fueled the popular growth in investing (much as news of gold strikes in California helped set off that "rush"). But the appeal of investing was also enhanced because of its resonance with the larger cultural trend of embracing risk. This was particularly evident in day trading, in which ordinary individuals give up their day jobs to become full-time market players using the web and discount brokers. Here the objective evidence suggests that, even at the height of the market, most people lost money, and many lost badly. Thus the popular interest in day trading seems to us to reflect less the promise of easy wealth than the cultural attraction of embracing risk. It represents the possibility of attaining autonomy, leaving behind the frustrations of working for someone else, by risking your own capital.

Beyond the stock market, numerous other activities promising the possibility of wealth or thrills, or both, have moved from the illegal and tawdry to the legal and acceptable, including gambling (once illegal, now state sponsored in most parts of the United States), extreme sports, and adventure travel. As with the stock market, the influence of direct participation expands many times when one considers those caught up in reading, watching, listening, and thinking about all these ways of embracing risk.

Although the embrace of risk represents a systematic change in thinking about institutions, with the potential to transform the social contract, it is important to emphasize two kinds of limitations. One is the endurance of the risk-spreading infrastructure. As François Ewald notes in the final chapter of this volume, insurance institutions remain central even as the coherence and appeal of what he calls the "solidarity" paradigm (our risk spreading) decline. Just as individual fault and responsibility remained part of modern legal culture even with the growth of risk spreading and social insurance in the early twentieth century, so too will risk spreading survive the embrace of risk. For example, the middle classes of the United States have shown considerable resistance when faced with immediate reductions in their own safety nets, despite their enthusiasm for programs aimed at saving the poor from dependence on others. Indeed, we see the embrace of risk more as a recognition of the limits of risk spreading than as a wholesale replacement for it.

The second limitation relates to risk taking. While some kinds of risk taking have reached an expanded class base (such as investing) and others a newly upgraded cultural status (such as gambling and extreme sports), others have become subject to even greater anxiety and harsh repression (such as economic immigration, drug taking, and sexual experimentation). Moreover, as François Ewald suggests in his chapter, some kinds of risk taking accepted in the era of risk spreading, ranging from consumption of new technologies to the likelihood of casualties in military service, have become subject to inconsistent but often powerful public resistance and demands for "zero risk."[2] Clearly, taking risks is only one part of a complex emerging configuration of risk that also includes new demands for precaution and even abstinence. Significantly, however, "taking risks," "zero risk," and "just say no" all reject the more utopian claims of the risk-spreading evangelists in favor of a new responsibility for the risks imposed on oneself and others.

Risk and Insurance

Insurance is the paradigmatic risk-spreading institution, and most discussions of insurance focus, appropriately, on its risk-spreading features. Not surprisingly given our focus, risk spreading occupies a comparatively small place in the extensive discussion of insurance in this volume. Nevertheless, we would not want anyone to think that we ignore the risk-spreading aspects of insurance. After all, the growth of the "insurance state" was predicated on the ability of social insurance institutions to spread losses (Ewald 1986). Nevertheless, there are other, less often considered aspects of insurance that the embracing risk approach leads us to emphasize.

Because almost everyone, at least in the developed world, has so much experience with insurance—buying auto, life, and homeowners insurance; consuming medical services covered by health insurance; paying social insurance taxes; and so on—insurance is a category that people tend to believe they understand. Yet, as anyone who has thought deeply about insurance can report, identifying its core features for the purpose of clearly distinguishing it from what is not insurance is anything but a simple task. Spencer Kimball, one of the leading insurance law scholars of the twentieth century, began a textbook he wrote late in his career by writing: "There is no good definition of 'insurance,' for any purpose. This book will not seek to provide one" (Kimball 1992:xxv).

Following the French social theorist (and our contributor) François Ewald, though employing a somewhat different framework, we distinguish among four aspects of insurance: institutions, forms, technologies, and visions (Ewald 1991). We find these categories useful because they demonstrate the conceptual variety of the activities lumped under the label "insurance." For this reason, the precise definitions of the categories are less important than the sense of the multiple aspects of insurance that they capture.

The first two of these categories, insurance institutions and insurance forms, have intuitively obvious meanings. Insurance institutions are the various kinds of organizations that provide insurance. Federal social insurance agencies (such as the U.S. Social Security Administration) and stock insurance companies (such as Allstate Insurance Company) are two (very different) insurance institutions. Insurance forms are the various kinds of insurance provided by insurance institutions, as well as the variations in form among those kinds. Life and property insurance are two different forms of insurance. "Whole" life insurance (life insurance that builds a cash value and, thus, incorporates a savings element) and "term" life insurance (life insurance that does not include a savings element) are two different forms of life insurance. Fire insurance and flood insurance are two different forms of property insurance.

Insurance technology is the "how to" of insurance. Examples include the mortality tables, underwriting classifications, and inspection procedures of ordinary life insurance; the incentive-based medical provider contracts, retrospective review, and computerized claim processing procedures of managed health care companies; the payroll tax, disability schedules, and administrative review procedures of the social security program; and the standard-form insurance contracts used in almost all private insurance.

Insurance in this sense of insurance technology refers to a set of procedures for dealing with risk.[3] The concept of self-insurance may help illustrate what it means to understand insurance as a technology. An organization that self-insures with respect to a particular risk does not purchase insurance for that risk. Thus, at the risk of belaboring the obvious, that organization has no insurance for that risk. Yet self-insurance differs from no insurance in that an organization that self-insures does not simply forgo buying insurance, it also adopts (at least in theory) a set of self-insurance procedures. These procedures are similar to those an insurance company would apply—for example, keeping track of past losses and setting aside financial reserves to meet comparable losses in the future.

As a technology for managing risk, insurance extends far beyond what might ordinarily be understood as the insurance field. Insurance institutions have developed many ways of managing risk that other people and institutions have adopted. The great life insurance companies were pioneers in epidemiology and public health. The fire insurance industry formed Underwriters Laboratories, which tests and certifies the safety of household appliances and other electrical equipment. Insurance companies seeking to cut their fire losses formed the first fire departments. More recently, health insurance companies have been behind many efforts to compare, test, and measure the effectiveness of medical procedures. Focusing on insurance technology helps us to see that insurance not only spreads risk, it also does all the other things that these insurance technologies do.

Finally, insurance visions are ideas about and images of (or, alternatively, discursive practices regarding) insurance that animate the development of insurance technologies, institutions, and forms.[4] Insurance visions are the aspects of insurance that we are most interested in, yet they are less easily described than insurance technologies, institutions, and forms. The best way we know of explaining what we mean is by example.

The first example comes from work by the sociologist Viviana Zelizer (1979). As Zelizer has described, it was once commonly believed that life insurance was immoral, either because it represented a presumptuous interference with divine providence, because it was seen as a form of gambling, or because it impermissibly equated life and money. This vision of insurance has had important consequences for the development life insurance institutions in the West. It slowed the growth of life insurance in at least France and the United States, and it helps explain the intense preoccupation in the United States during the mid-nineteenth century with establishing the morality of all kinds of insurance (Zelizer 1979; Baker 1996). As discussed in chapter 2, related ideas about risk and insurance more generally affect Islamic institutions today.

A second example comes from earlier work by Tom Baker (1994) addressing the role of insurance visions in insurance contract law. Because the primary benefit of insurance is a sense of security that for most people is never tested by a catastrophic loss, the value of insurance rests, in an important sense, in the imagination. Courts have recognized the importance of imagination to insurance by placing great emphasis on the "reasonable expectation of the insured" and by holding that insurance advertising is relevant evidence for determining that expectation. In that advertising, insurance companies evoke a vision of insurance that differs from the vision of insurance they employ when denying claims. (See also Stone 1994.) Their "sales" vision is the promise "to be there," and it is dominated by narratives of family and the need to protect the individual against sudden misfortune. Their "claims" vision is a complicated amalgam of tough love and protecting the insurance fund, and it is dominated by narratives of institutional ethics and the need to protect ratepayers against fraud and abuse. As described by Baker, courts first decide which of these visions to employ in resolving insurance contract disputes. Who wins a dispute often depends as much on which vision the court adopts as on how the court applies that vision.

A third example is the actuarial vision of insurance that we and others have described (Simon 1988; Baker 2000; Pal 1986). In the actuarial vision, the ideal type of insurance involves premiums paid in advance, guaranteed indemnity in the event of a covered loss, and risk-based premiums based on the best available information regarding the expected losses of the individuals insured. This vision of insurance has had enormous consequences. It helps explain the decline of fraternal insurance in Britain and the Unites States over the nineteenth and early twentieth centuries, as actuarial expectations overcame the values of "friendship, brotherly-love and charity" (Doran 1994). It helps explain the decision to model unemployment insurance on private insurance, and the related effort to tightly link benefits to premiums (Pal 1986). And it helps to explain the intensity of the popular belief that Social Security retirement benefits have been earned by the people who collect them, as well as the corresponding expert belief that Social Security is not really insurance (because the money to pay today's retirees comes from the contributions made by today's workers and not from the contributions of the retirees themselves). Indeed, the actuarial vision of insurance has been so successful that many well-informed people would deny that it is a vision at all and assert, instead, that it is *the* model of insurance.

Finally, conceptions about risk in general, and the embrace of risk in particular, are also examples of insurance visions. The idea that some amount of risk is good for people and that too much protection is harmful has important consequences for the development of insurance technologies, institutions, and forms, as well as the development of personal identity and social institutions other than insurance. Many of the essays in this book explore these consequences.

As we hope this brief discussion illustrates, this framework of insurance institution, form, technology, and vision opens a more expansive view on the workings of insurance than the relatively simple (but very important) concept of risk spreading. We will not in this book ignore risk spreading. The fact that insurance spreads some losses and not others is an essential feature of the distributional concerns addressed in many of the chapters. But even there it is not the risk spreading per se that we find notable. Rather it is the visions of insurance that animate decisions about whose and which losses to spread.

Risk(s) beyond Insurance

The essays in this book also address risk(s) beyond insurance in three senses. First, they consider the use of insurance technologies and visions to govern risk outside of insurance institutions. Second, they address the role of other kinds of institutions and practices in developing technologies and visions for dealing with risk (some of which in turn may influence insurance). And, third, they address risks that are beyond insurance in the sense that they cannot or, perhaps should not, be governed by insurance. The first two we think of as addressing risk beyond insurance, and the third as addressing risks beyond insurance. Hence the heading "risk(s) beyond insurance."

From our opening description, it might seem that the vision of embracing risk refers only to the latter idea: that, for the benefit of individual or social welfare, some risks cannot or should not be transferred to insurance institutions. Yet we think embracing risk also encompasses a broader idea of *governing through risk*. Though it can hardly be summed up in a single sentence, the core idea of governing through risk is the use of formal considerations about risk to direct organizational strategy and resources. Indeed, for those who equate risk with insurance (Ewald 1991), this is one way that insurance produces a change in the culture.

There are many contemporary examples of governing through risk. Money managers develop portfolios at the risk–reward frontier (Bernstein 1992, 1996). Social service agencies target at-risk children (see, e.g., Health and Human Services 1994). Community policing efforts are targeted at high-risk areas (Ericson and Haggerty 1997). Environmental engineers conduct risk assessments of hazardous waste sites and other sources of environmental concern (Graham and Weiner 1995). Mountain climbers rate peaks and climbs according to risk and climbers according to the risks they are qualified to take (Simon, chapter 8 this volume). Fraternities redefine gender relations in response to the risk of sexual harassment (Simon 1994). Judges and law reformers debate accident law in terms of the allocation and spreading of risk (Calabresi 1970). And presidents and prime ministers alike now define themselves by the risks they would have the state lift from the shoulders of the populations (criminal victimization, poverty in old age) and the risks they would not (poverty in childhood, economic security, health care) (Giddens 1999).

Admittedly, thinking of risk or risks as beyond insurance reflects a very insurance-centered view of the world. The world is full of risks and only some are handled by insurance. Why isn't the more appropriate question, "Which few of the many risks in the world are handled by insurance and why?" Surely that is a more coherent, manageable set of risks to identify and discuss. After all, insurable risks are by definition susceptible to the insurance technologies, forms, and institutions that the study of risk and insurance aims to explore.

Yet thinking about risks as *beyond* insurance does add something to understanding. Insurance institutions and technologies gather risks, concentrate and contain ("pool") them, shape and package them for resale on the secondary market, or, alternatively, plug them directly into the distributional circuits of the state. In the process, they spread and thereby, in an important sense, eliminate (or at the very least reduce the importance of) those risks from the day-to-day concern of people who are exposed to them. Risks that are beyond insurance are not spread and eliminated in this way, with consequences for the people exposed. A risk beyond insurance is experienced in a very different way than a risk that is insured.

In a society in which "more insurance for more people" has been so strongly encouraged, thinking of a risk as beyond insurance leads to an obvious question: Why? What distinguishes this risk from the other risks turned over to insurance? Is it uninsurable in some technical or practical sense and, if so, according to what logic and compared to what other risks that are insurable? Or, is it uninsurable in a normative sense—meaning that it should not be insured? If so, according to what logic, for whose benefit and, once again, compared to what other risks that are insurable?

Because of the crucial role of insurance institutions in socializing risk and responsibility (a role that Tom Baker explores in chapter 2), studying risks beyond insurance opens a window on the limits of social responsibility and the role of ideas about individual responsibility in the shaping of insurance institutions and forms. For example, when Jonathan Simon describes in chapter 8 the competition between the climbing ethic of summiteering and the climbing ethic of mountaineering, he is quite consciously developing a metaphor for application in the flatlands below.

Toward a Sociology of Insurance and Risk

Although there is a significant research literature on insurance and risk, it remains relatively small compared to the importance of insurance to society. Given the enormous size of insurance institutions relative to contemporary Western economies, it is surprising that most social scientists and historians have paid so little attention to insurance. Indeed, looking at twentieth-century governance, it is tempting to see insurance as the sleeping giant of power.

Consider just the following two examples of insurance setting social standards in the United States. First, as Carol Heimer discusses in chapter 6, insurance acts as a gatekeeper to homeownership. Homeownership is rightly taken to be one of the constitutive features of the American economy, with all its attendant influences on both consumption (more of it) and political preferences (more conservative). Not surprisingly, the availability of mortgages at an affordable rate is widely regarded as an important economic indicator. The role of homeowner's insurance as a vital ingredient in the availability of mortgages is much less widely recognized, however. Obtaining homeowners' insurance is mandatory for standard mortgages, and homeowners' insurers employ their own underwriting concerns that are independent from the screening procedures implemented by the lender (Squires 1997).

Second, private insurance can be a crucial form of delegated state power. Rather than set its own criteria for access to vital economic freedoms like operating an automobile or a business (which would be politically controversial and even, perhaps, unconstitutional), the state mandates that a person wishing to engage in any such activity first obtain some form of insurance. Examples include liability insurance for automobile owners, workers compensation insurance for employers, and surety bonds for companies engaged in business with the state. In most cases, the state avoids providing the insurance and thereby asks the private market—typically property-casualty insurance companies—to set the underwriting criteria that will determine access to these privileges and immunities. Motivated by controlling losses they have contracted to pay, the companies set up their own norms of conduct, which they enforce by contract terms and pricing (and, ultimately, through the state judicial system).

Whether obtained as a result of compulsion or simple prudence, insurance is a form of regulation. Specific exclusions and conditions written into coverage for property, life, and health amount to a form of private legislation as binding as any the state legislature enacts. Significantly, this "legislation" acts inside the home or business, where the sovereignty of the king was traditionally expected to stop (O'Malley 1991). Indeed, within a regime of liberal governance, insurance is one of the greatest sources of regulatory authority over private life.

Despite this central role, insurance has been almost completely ignored by the traditional humanities and social sciences, at least outside of economics departments and business schools. As a result, neoclassical economics is now the dominant paradigm for the analysis of insurance and risk. The leading insurance journals and academic departments (at least in the United States) are populated by economists. Policy debates over the nature and extent of public insurance and the regulation of private insurance are almost always framed in economic terms. Yet, although economic analysis has produced significant, insightful work on insurance (Baker 1996), that work has largely ignored institutions, history, and culture—precisely what we would emphasize.

There has been significant sociological work on some insurance institutions, most significantly social insurance and, more recently, private health insurance. With some important exceptions in the area of economic sociology, however, most of this research operates at different levels and with different purposes than we envision for a sociology of insurance and risk. The work on social insurance roughly breaks down into three groups: work on the origins and political trajectory of the welfare state (see, e.g., Nonet 1969; Skocpol 1992); work on the interaction of social insurance organizations with their clients (see, e.g., Lipsky 1980); and work on the limits of social insurance in achieving redistributive ends (see, e.g., Piven and Cloward 1971). None of this work focuses broadly on insurance. Similarly, nearly all the work on private health insurance is focused exclusively on the effect of insurance on medicine and health (see, e.g., Starr 1982) and, thus, falls within the sociology of medicine rather than the sociology of insurance and risk.

Governmentality and Economic Sociology

The immediate intellectual roots for this project lie in two traditions: economic sociology and the "governmentality" literature stimulated by the later work of Michel Foucault. Because both of these traditions are relatively unfamiliar ones, and few people have read broadly in both, it is worth spending some time reviewing them. In the process, we describe how they contribute to the development of a sociology of risk and insurance. Our goal is not to set out a definitive statement or program of research, but rather to provide a sense of an emerging field of inquiry.

Economic sociology is a branch of sociology that shares many of the goals and concerns, and some of the methods, of institutional economics. In briefest terms, it involves the application of empirical and conceptual sociological methods to economic phenomena, and it dates back to the giants of classical sociology: Marx, Weber, and Durkheim (Smelser and Swedborg 1994). Economic sociology has largely neglected insurance and risk as demonstrated, for example, by *The Handbook of Economic Sociology* (Smelser and Swedborg 1994), which contains no significant discussion of insurance and only a brief discussion of risk. Nevertheless, the framework and methods of that tradition can be readily applied to insurance and risk. Indeed, Viviana Zelizer's (1979, 1985) and Carol Heimer's (1985) work on insurance and risk are directly within that tradition. Both played an important role in promoting the work that appears in this volume.

Zelizer's study of nineteenth-century life insurance documented the role of religious and other cultural ideas and practices in the development of the U.S. life-insurance market. In her first book, *Morals and Markets*, she explained the dramatic expansion of the life-insurance market in the mid-nineteenth century as the result of ideological work by insurance entrepreneurs. The entrepreneurs successfully overcame profound moral and religious objections to insurance (objections that delayed the growth of the French life-insurance market even longer) by inventing and then promoting a vision of life insurance as a form of moral responsibility. In a chapter in her second book, *Pricing the Priceless Child,* she charted the growth of the market for life insurance for children as a cultural battleground. On the one side were insurance companies offering the poor security from the shame and fear of burying a child in a pauper's grave. On the other side were middle-class reformers who saw child insurance as an invitation to murder. By demonstrating the importance of culture to the development of the market, Zelizer helped reinvigorate economic sociology and began an important conversation with economists that the essays in this book hope to continue. By focusing on the role of culture in the development of insurance (and the role of insurance institutions in changing culture), she put insurance on the map of economic sociology.

Heimer's study of insurance contracting, *Reactive Risk and Rational Action,* also engaged a topic of great interest to economists: the moral hazard of insurance. A term with a very rich history (Baker 1996, 2000), "moral hazard" refers to the effect of insurance on incentives. If not properly managed, insurance can reduce the incentive to be careful to avoid a loss and it can reduce the incentive to manage the costs of recovering from loss. As Heimer put it, risk is reactive, not static. Working within a rational choice framework that she shares with economics, she explored empirically how insurance companies manage reactive risk through the use of insurance contracts.

Heimer's research on the contracting behavior of insurance companies provided the first detailed sociological study of private insurance as a form of social control. As her research revealed, control is the fulcrum for managing moral hazard. Losses over which the insured has no control do not present a moral hazard problem, because the reaction of the insured to being freed from risk does not affect the odds of loss. The less control the insured has over loss, the more willing insurance companies are to sell insurance, and the more complete that insurance will be. Where the insured has substantial control, however, the price for buying insurance often includes giving up a measure of that control. Insurance companies may demand that the insured institute safety procedures, undergo periodic inspections, or allow the insurance company to control the efforts taken to recover from loss. Examples include sprinkler requirements in commercial fire insurance contracts, inspection clauses in workers compensation insurance contracts, and hospitalization precertification clauses in health insurance contracts. When insurance companies manage moral hazard, they are regulating behavior, not simply spreading risk.

Along with demonstrating that insurance is a form of regulation, Heimer's research also provided a historical, conceptual, and empirical framework for understanding the embrace of risk. The claim that embracing risk is good for individuals and society rests on the assertion that, in her terms, the reaction to being freed from risk can be as harmful as the insecurity that insurance aims to prevent. Heimer's study explored in a detailed, convincing fashion the circumstances in which insurance companies have required their policyholders to retain some risk, which creates what Heimer called a "community of fate" between the insurance company and the policyholder. This community of fate lessens the policyholder's incentive to react to insurance by reducing care. By documenting the extent to which many different kinds of insurance contracts create communities of fate, Heimer's research helps us see that insurance companies have always required people to embrace some risks.

Research inspired by Foucault's late work on governmentality also provides an important foundation for our project. The word *governmentality* is his neologism for "governmental rationality." For Foucault, government is a much broader concept than the government of a political system. Indeed, rather than a noun referring to a set of institutions, he understood the word *government* to refer to a set of practices that are engaged in by individuals and institutions at every level of society. Think of the governor on a motor vehicle—a device that prevents the vehicle from going faster than a set speed—or the self-government of one's own behavior. "Governmental rationality" is "a way or system of thinking about the nature of the practice of government (who can govern; what governing is; what or who is governed), capable of making some form of that activity thinkable and practicable both to its practitioners and to those upon whom it was practiced" (Gordon 1991:3). The clearest illustration of the concept of governmental rationality in this book appears in chapter 5.

Our earlier description of insurance as a form of regulation already suggests the appeal of the governmentality literature to the study of insurance and risk. That literature provides a set of concepts and contexts for investigating governmental practices across a wide range of social fields and institutions. Within the governmentality literature, insurance is simply one of many forms of knowledge and practices that operate in the space between the individual and the state.

In his lectures on governmentality, Foucault called attention to the gap between studies of power at the level of the individual (as in his *History of Sexuality*) and studies of power at the level of the state (Gordon 1991). The governmentality literature has begun to fill that gap. Our contributors François Ewald and Nikolas Rose have been perhaps the most important French and English language contributors to this line of research generally.

Ewald's framework of insurance technologies, institutions, forms, and visions is directly in this tradition, helping to explain how insurance functions as a form of government. His 1986 book, *L'Etat Providence* traced the history of the welfare state by focusing on the emergence of risk as a dominant way of knowing and intervening in the world beginning in the nineteenth century. For Ewald, risk is the product of insurance technologies that bring probabilistic methods to bear on aggregated data, producing actuarial representations of risk as an object that can be known and distributed. Ewald's paradigm case was workers compensation, which aimed to rationalize industrial accidents by preventing harm where possible and then spreading the costs of accidents that could not be prevented. (See also Ewald 1991; Burchell, Gordon, and Miller 1991; Rose 1999.) Put in terms of our project, Ewald offered a genealogy of the paradigm of "more insurance for more people."

Recent work by Rose (1999) has explored the breakdown of this social logic of governance and the emergence of other approaches that emphasize the individual. (See also Stenson and Watt 1999; Simon 1999.) Rose describes these approaches as "advanced liberalism," linking them to the tradition of liberal thought that arose in the nineteenth century. The cultural trend we identify as embracing risk fits closely with the advanced liberal emphasis on the individual. Many of the policies Rose links to advanced liberalism seek to place more risk on the individual and to dismantle the large risk pools that socialized risk under the mandate of more insurance for more people.

Embracing risk is a strategy of government—a governmental rationality—that applies to many levels of society. As Jonathan Simon explores in chapter 8, embracing risk can be a strategy of individual self-government. Pat O'Malley and Martha McCluskey find in chapters 5 and 7, respectively, that embracing risk can be a strategy of government by or through the state. And as Tom Baker, Carol Heimer, Martha McCluskey, and Nikolas Rose explore respectively in chapters 2, 6, 7, and 9, embracing risk can be a strategy of government by such intermediate social institutions as insurance companies, employers, banks, and health care institutions.

The Risk Literature

The subject of risk has received more widespread scholarly attention than insurance. Yet most of the research on risk focuses on the needs and opportunities of existing insurance institutions, rather than on the social and cultural role of risk and insurance more broadly conceived.[5] Notwithstanding that common orientation, risk studies is far from a unified field. Indeed, there are at least as many approaches to studying risk as there are academic disciplines (Krimsky and Golding 1992; Burger 1993). As a result, reading the risk literature across disciplines reveals almost as much about those disciplines as it reveals about risk. In that sense, the risk literature is as much a window on academic disciplines as risk management is a window on organizations, and as visions of insurance (and risk) are windows on social change.

At the risk of oversimplification, we lump much of the risk literature into the broad category of risk assessment and management and sharply distinguish the methods and purposes of that literature from our own. The risk assessment and management literature is concerned with identifying, measuring, reducing, and otherwise managing risk. This includes not only the approaches to risk assessment and perception represented by risk researchers at Chicago, Wharton, Harvard, Colorado, Tufts, and other mainstream research institutions, but also work in the "normal accident" tradition of sociology epitomized by the sociologist Charles Perrow (Perrow 1999).

Across all the disciplines, the risk assessment and management literature has instrumental purposes that the essays in this book do not share. In other aspects of our lives, we applaud many of the efforts and goals of this literature. But our purposes in this book are very different. We are interested here less in what *is* a risk than we are in the social construction of risk.[6] And, in truth, we are less interested in the social construction of risk per se than we are in the use of risk in the social construction of reality. Put perhaps more intelligibly, we are less interested in what *is* a risk than we are in what is done *in the name of* risk.

Although the essays in this book differ from one another in many ways, each explores how risk institutions and visions shape the social world. From an opening chapter by Tom Baker analyzing the role of insurance institutions in the distribution of responsibility, through a concluding chapter by François Ewald suggesting that the logic of government may be moving beyond insurance to precaution, each contributor treats the current technologies, forms, and visions of risk and insurance as problems in their own right.

Our focus on the use of risk is similar in some ways to work by Mary Douglas and others in what has been described as a cultural approach to risk (Rayner 1992). That work has persuasively argued that what is a risk differs across time and space, not according to an objective, scientific process, but rather according to the logic and influence of institutions: "Whatever objective dangers may exist in the world, social organizations will emphasize those that reinforce the moral, political or religious order that holds the group together" (Rayner 1992:87). In other words, people in organizations actively select among and then use risks to further goals that bear at best a very loose connection to their expressed purpose of assessing and managing the objective danger that exists in the world. For example, in their well-known study of environmentalism, Douglas and Wildavsky (1982) argued that the shift in public concern from national security to environmental risk did not result from a change in the objective risks at issue. Instead, it resulted from a shift in influence from traditional center institutions dominated by markets and bureaucracies (such as large corporations, the military, and government agencies) to sectarian organizations (such as environmental movements and peace groups). The center had placed a higher priority on risks to prosperity and national security, while sectarian organizations emphasized environmental risk.

The contributors to this volume undoubtedly would all ascribe to the core cultural construction of risk insight of this literature. Fundamentally, however, the cultural risk analysts are engaged in a very different project than ours, one that lies much closer to the risk assessment and management project. Particularly in her later work, Douglas and her collaborators are engaged in advising policy makers about how to understand public perceptions of and reactions to the potential dangers that exist in the world (see, e.g., Douglas 1985; Rayner 1992). Our work lies more distant from the "pull of the policy audience" and more focused on social change (Sarat and Silbey 1988).

In addition, we take issue with the exclusive focus of even the cultural risk literature on the avoidance of "risk as danger." In one of her more recent essays, Mary Douglas states that what is "new" about risk is that it has become a synonym for danger: "Whereas originally a high risk meant a game in which a throw of the die had a strong probability of bringing great gain or great loss, now risk refers only to negative outcomes. The word has been preempted to mean bad risks" (Douglas 1990:3). Risk in this view is something to be avoided, spread, or otherwise managed, not something to be encouraged or embraced. Yet this account leaves out the extraordinary amount of risk-seeking behavior in our culture—the stock market, lotteries, sports betting pools, extreme sports, recreational drug use (including tobacco—teens smoke in part because it's dangerous [Ponton 1998])— and the equally significant phenomena of vicarious risk seeking epitomized by what the *New York Times* called "explornography" (Tierney 1998; Simon, chapter 8 this volume).

We think that risk today is not only about bad risks, but also about opportunity. Many of the phenomena we describe as embracing risk proceed from an implicit belief that risk is a positive force that can be directed toward socially useful ends. Indeed, an awareness that risk can be (and currently is being) socially constructed as a good as well as a bad is among the things that most distinguishes the essays in this volume from much of the earlier risk literature.

Embracing Risk and the Risk Society

Like much of the work collected in this book, scholarship in the "risk society" tradition of Ulrich Beck takes a more encompassing sociological perspective (Beck 1992; Giddens 1990; Ericson and Haggerty 1997). This scholarship chronicles the emergence of a "world risk society" in which exposure to risk becomes a defining characteristic for social groups. Written in a post-Marxist tradition with greater immediate resonance for European than U.S. readers, the risk society scholarship focuses on the emergence of new risks that transcend traditional social boundaries like class and nation. Examples include mad cow disease, acid rain, nuclear power, and the risks that may accompany genetically modified organisms. These differ from many risks of an earlier era because they are global, they threaten the privileged as well as the underprivileged, and they challenge the capacity of traditional insurance institutions.

We share Beck's sense that recent years have witnessed an important change in the way risk is articulated and deployed. Our theme of embracing risk parallels in some ways his argument that concerns about risk are reshaping the dominant strategies of security. Indeed, many of the specific practices described in this volume—new ways of managing mental illness (chapter 9), new forms of sport and recreation (chapter 8), and new uses for insurance technologies (chapter 6)—can be seen as ways of responding to a crisis of governance that Beck's risk society is one account of.

Yet we part ways with Beck in what might seem to be contradictory fashion. On the one hand, we find his concept of risk unduly narrow. It parallels the "risk as danger" approach of the risk and culture literature, and misses the appeal of embracing risk.[7] On the other hand, we find the scope of his sociological ambition too grand: an example of the "one size fits all" standardization that epitomizes the modernist approach whose decline he chronicles. It is an irony that we are all vulnerable to as well. The Risk Society remains deeply anchored in the sociological tradition of grand theorizing. Yet that tradition is a good example of the modernism that Beck critiques in his work.

We mean our concept of embracing risk to be more provisional. Indeed, as the concluding essay by François Ewald demonstrates, there are competing paradigms at work. The essays in this book explore and challenge the embrace of risk, its historical development, and its contemporary meaning. In the process, they sketch the outline of what we almost hesitate to call (for fear of interrupting a remarkable discussion across the usual lines of academic disciplines and divisions) a sociology of insurance and risk, which would be concerned with an important and underexamined set of institutions and practices that address risk. It would develop a vocabulary to define and describe insurance institutions and their development over time. It would explore their historical and social contexts, their initial purposes, and the process through which they developed purposes and intended and unintended effects of their own. It would also explore how these insurance institutions and practices affected other institutions and practices.

We are not going to set out here *the* or even *a* sociology of insurance and risk, because we believe the field requires further mapping before a definitive framework or method can be adequately defended. Rather, this book represents the first collection of essays that can be united under the banner of the sociology of insurance and risk and only the third book in English in the field. (The first two are Zelizer's *Morals and Markets* [1979] and Heimer's *Reactive Risk and Rational Action* [1985].) Our aim is to foster, and in some cases, further conversations across disciplines, institutions, and continents. Toward that end, our efforts here are avowedly exploratory and tentative. The best evidence of the promise of a sociology of insurance and risk lies in the chapters written by our twelve contributors. Thus, we encourage you to read on.

NOTES

1. Our primary focus in this introduction is on the developments in the United States, but the trends we describe, both past and present, apply with some differences to other postindustrial societies. A number of the essays in this book examine other countries, including France, the United Kingdom, and Canada. While the dif-

ferences among these societies are worthy of separate treatment, for now we want
to stress the commonalities.

2. Ewald's assertion that contemporary culture is becoming more "riskphob[ic]"
(Ewald, chapter 11 this volume) might seem to contradict the embracing risk thesis.
Yet, our views in fact are largely consistent, differing perhaps most in the national
mood about these changes in our two respective countries (France and the United
States). We agree with Ewald that the risk-spreading (or solidarity) paradigm is on the
wane, though we differ in the emphasis we place on the various responses to that
trend. Ewald mainly focuses on catastrophic risks, for which a new mandate of precaution may be replacing the previous emphasis on prevention and compensation.
Much of what we have described as embracing risk operates in the arena of noncat-
astrophic risk. Indeed, many of the private insurance market adaptations to the embrace of risk encourage individuals and institutions to maintain catastrophic insurance coverage. In an important sense our "embracing risk" and Ewald's "precaution"
operate at two different ends of the probability spectrum. Embracing risk makes
most sense for risks that are relatively predictable and capable of being managed by
individuals and organizations. On the other hand, precaution makes most sense for
risks that are unpredictable (indeed, in that sense would not be regarded as "risks"
at all within the traditional, and not always sustainable, distinction between risk
and uncertainty). At the same time Ewalds's essay may also reflect a genuine difference in atmosphere between France and the United States. In Europe, with a stronger
environmental movement and less hostility toward state regulation, there does
seem to be a more pronounced shift toward precaution than in the United States.
(Though the public aversion to low-probability, high-consequence risks explored by
Margolis (1986), for example, may be the U.S. version of the move to precaution.)

3. This is one of the places where we have varied Ewald's framework. He appears
to have a more fixed notion of insurance technology than we wish to adopt. In his
1991 essay, he identifies "the" technology of insurance as the art of combining risks,
using the term *risk* in a somewhat technical sense of future harms that can be addressed through the language of probability. We regard insurance technology as both
a larger and a smaller category than that. Insurance technology is a larger category
in the sense that it can address nonprobabilistic risks (which would not be "risks"
at all within Ewald's definition of risk). Insurance technology is a smaller category
in the sense that we are at least as interested in the individual components involved
in combining risks, which differ among insurance institutions and forms and over
time and place, as we are in what Ewald calls the "art of combinations," which most
insurance institutions share.

4. This is another place where we have varied Ewald's framework. The English
translation of his work uses the word *imaginary* to refer to this category. We decided
against adopting that term because of its well-entrenched, somewhat negative con-
notation of "counterfactual." Although the word has some appeal because it emphasizes the role of imagination in culture, we substituted a term that we believe
will be less likely to confound understanding: "vision." Regardless whether "imaginary" or "vision" is the better term, your thought process at this moment justifies
our disagreement with Ewald, because you have stopped to consider the role of imagination in constructing social meaning.

5. We must be clear from the very start that this in itself is not a criticism. Following Foucault (1977) we take for granted that all ways of gathering knowledge require access to the channels and flows that exercises of power create, and that all
ways of exercising power require methods for producing knowledge about the subjects of power.

6. For that reason, we deliberately have almost nothing to say about the low-

probability, high-consequence risks that have received so much attention in the risk studies literature (see, e.g., Margolis 1996) and, thus, leave aside the interesting and important psychometric and social cognition issues raised by those risks.

7. One difference here, paralleling some of our differences with Ewald, may be cultural. It may be in this regard that national differences in interpreting these developments are particularly pronounced. France, Germany, and Japan, among other nations, remain more politically committed to risk spreading while the United States, the United Kingdom, Australia, and New Zealand have been most enthusiastic in embracing risk. For example, concerns about high technology and biomedical risks have been far more prominent on the European political agenda then in the United States.

REFERENCES

Baker, Tom. 1994. "Constructing the Insurance Relationship: Sales Stories, Claims Stories and Insurance Contract Damages." *Texas Law Review* 72:1395–1433.

———. 1996. "On the Genealogy of Moral Hazard." *Texas Law Review* 75:237–92.

———. 2000. "Insuring Morality." *Economy and Society* 29:559–77.

Beck, Ulrich. 1992. *Risk Society.* London: Sage.

Bernstein, Peter L. 1992. *Capital Ideas.* New York: Free Press.

———. 1996. *Against the Gods.* New York: John Wiley.

Burchell, Graham, Colin Gordon, and Peter Miller, eds. 1991. *The Foucault Effect: Studies in Governmentality.* Chicago: University of Chicago Press.

Burger, Edward J., ed. 1993. *Risk.* Ann Arbor: University of Michigan Press.

Calabresi, Guido. 1970. *The Cost of Accidents.* New Haven: Yale University Press.

Dawson, Miles M. 1895. *The Principles of Insurance Legislation.* New York: Hamboldt Library.

Doran, Nob. 1994. "Risky Business: Codifying Embodied Experience in the Manchester Unity of Oddfellows." *Journal of Historical Sociology* 7:131–54.

Douglas, Mary. 1985. *Risk Acceptability according to the Social Sciences.* New York: Russell Sage.

———. 1990. "Risk as a Forensic Resource." In *Risk*, ed. E. J. Burger. Ann Arbor: University of Michigan.

Douglas, Mary, and Aaron Wildavsky. 1982. *Risk and Culture.* Berkeley: University of California Press.

Ericson, Richard V., and Kevin D. Haggerty. 1997. *Policing the Risk Society.* New York: Oxford University Press.

Ewald, François. 1986. *L'Etat Providence.* Paris: Grasset.

———. 1991. "Insurance and Risk." In *The Foucalt Effect: Studies in Governmentality*, ed. G. Burchell, C. Gordon, and P. Miller. Chicago: University of Chicago Press.

Foucault, Michel. 1977. *Discipline and Punish.* New York: Pantheon Books.

———. 1978. *The History of Sexuality.* New York: Pantheon Books.

Giddens, Anthony. 1990. *The Consequences of Modernity.* Stanford: Stanford University Press.

———. 1999. "Risk and Responsibility." *Modern Law Review* 62:1–10.

Gordon, Colin. 1991. "Governmental Rationality: An Introduction." In *The Foucalt Effect: Studies in Governmentality*, ed. G. Burchell, C. Gordon, and P. Miller. Chicago: University of Chicago Press.

Graham, John D., and Jonathan Baert Weiner, eds. 1995. *Risk vs Risk*. Cambridge: Harvard University Press.

Hacking, Ian. 1990. *The Taming of Chance*. Cambridge: Cambridge University Press.

Heimer, Carol A. 1985. *Reactive Risk and Rational Action: Managing Moral Hazard in Insurance Contracts*. Berkeley: University of California Press.

Kimball, Spencer. 1992. *Cases and Materials on Insurance Law*. Boston: Little, Brown.

Krakauer, John. 1997. *Into Thin Air*. New York: Vintage.

Krimsky, Sheldon, and Dominic Golding. 1992. *Social Theories of Risk*. Westport, Conn.: Praeger.

Lipsky, Michael. 1980. *Street Level Bureaucracy: Dilemmas of the Individual in Public Services*. New York: Russell Sage Foundation.

LoPucki, Lynn M. 1996. "The Death of Liability." *Yale Law Journal* 106:1–92

Lowi, Theodore J. 1990. "Risk and Rights in the History of American Governments." In *Risk*, ed. E. J. Burger. Ann Arbor: University of Michigan Press.

Margolis, Howard. 1996. *Dealing with Risk*. Chicago: University of Chicago Press.

Nonet, Philippe. 1969. *Administrative Justice: Advocacy and Change in a Government Agency*. New York: Russell Sage Foundation.

O'Malley, Pat. 1991. "Legal Networks and Domestic Security." *Studies in Law, Policy and Society* 11:171–90.

———. 2000. "Uncertain Subjects: Risks, Liberalism and Contract." *Economy and Society* (forthcoming).

Pal, Leslie A. 1986. "Relative Autonomy Revisited: The Origins of Canadian Unemployment Insurance." *Canadian Journal of Political Science* 19:71–92.

Perrow, Charles. 1999. *Normal Accidents: Living with High-Risk Technologies*. New York: Basic Books.

Piven, Francis Fox, and Richard Cloward. 1971. *Regulating the Poor: The Functions of Public Welfare*. New York: Pantheon Books.

Ponton, Lynn E. 1998. *The Romance of Risk: Why Teenagers Do the Things They Do*. [[Au: city?]]: Perseus Books.

Rayner, Steve. 1992. "Cultural Theory and Risk Analysis." In *Social Theories of Risk*, ed. S. Krimsky and D. Golding. Westport, Conn.: Praeger.

Reichman, Nancy. 1986. "Managing Crime Risks: Toward an Insurance-Based Model of Social Control." *Research in Law, Deviance and Social Control* 8:151–72.

Rees, Joseph. 1994. *Hostages of Each Other: The Transformation of Nuclear Safety since Three-Mile Island*. Chicago: University of Chicago Press.

Rose, Nikolas. 1999. *Powers of Freedom*. Cambridge: Cambridge Univeristy Press.

Russo, Richard. 1988. *The Risk Pool*. New York: Random House.

Sarat, Austin, and Susan Silbey. 1988. "The Pull of the Policy Audience." *Law and Policy* 10:97–166.

Simon, Jonathan. 1988. "The Ideological Effects of Actuarial Practices." *Law and Society Review* 22:771–800.

———. 1993. *Poor Discipline: Parole and the Social Control of the Underclass, 1890–1990.* Chicago: University of Chicago Press.

———. 1994. "In the Place of the Parent: Risk Management and the Government of Campus Life." *Social and Legal Studies* 3:14–45.

———. 1998. "Driving Governmentality: Automobile Accidents, Insurance and the Challenge to Social Order in the Inter-War Years, 1919–1941." *Connecticut Insurance Law Journal* 4:521–88.

———. 1999. "Law after Society." *Law and Social Inquiry* 24:143–94.

Skocpol, Theda. 1992. *Protecting Soldiers and Mothers: The Political Origins of Social Policy in the United States.* Cambridge: Belknap Press, Harvard University Press.

Smelser, Neil J., and Richard Swedborg, eds. 1994. *The Handbook of Economic Sociology.* Princeton: Princeton University Press.

Squires, Gregory, ed. 1997. *Insurance Redlining.* Washington: Urban Institute Press.

Starr, Paul. 1982. *The Social Transformation of American Medicine.* New York: Basic Books.

Stenson, Kevin, and Paul Watt. 1999. "Governmentality and 'the Death of the Social'?: A Discourse Analysis of Local Government Texts in South-east England." *Urban Studies* 36:189–201.

Stone, Deborah. 1994. "Promises and Public Trust: Rethinking Insurance Law through Stories." *Texas Law Review* 72:1435–46.

Tierney, John. 1998. "Explornography: The Vicarious Thrill of Exploring When There's Nothing Left to Explore." *New York Times Magazine,* 26 July, 18.

U.S. Department of Health and Human Services. 1994. "Availability of Funds for School Health Services and Health Education/Promotion for Homeless and At Risk Children and Youth." *Federal Register* 59:24171.

Zelizer, Viviana A. 1979. *Morals and Markets: The Development of Life Insurance in the United States.* New York: Columbia University Press.

———. 1985. Pricing the Priceless Child: The Changing Social Value of Children. Princeton: Princeton University Press.

PART ONE

Toward a Sociology of Insurance and Risk

The book's first part focuses on the interplay between risk and insurance in various historical and social contexts. Although insurance is not the only field organized by risk, there is no other field in which risk has for so long been such a central organizing principle. Indeed, at least since the eighteenth century, the insurance field has been an incubator for ideas and technologies of risk that have had great influence well beyond its boundaries. Particularly because insurance has received surprisingly little attention in recent scholarship outside economics, these essays represent an important contribution to the study of risk.

As these essays illustrate, insurance is not a unified institution. Nor is risk is a monolithic concept. Insurance institutions, forms, and technologies depend on shifting cultural conceptions of risk, security, and responsibility—the visions discussed in the first chapter. Far from a natural progression tracing a mathematical or historical imperative, insurance in all its forms is a social and cultural product.

Chapter Two

The essay by Tom Baker, "Risk, Insurance, and the Social Construction of Responsibility," explores the shifting relationships among these three terms. Baker describes how ideas about responsibility shape understandings of insurance—in particular by obscuring in the United States the social and collective nature of private insurance—and how insurance institutions in turn shape ideas about responsibility. The way we go about deciding who is responsible for what depends in important ways on the risks assumed by insurance.

Baker addresses various perceptions of insurance, arguing that how we understand it affects how we perceive and reproduce our social reality. He also explores the complex meaning of "responsibility," dissecting five analytically distinct meanings to explain how insurance distributes responsibility. His essay reminds us that individuals do not have to passively accept individual self-interest as the primary legitimate goal of insurance. The dominant insurance vision that Baker analyzes is only one way of conceiving the complex relation between insurance, risk, and responsibility, and Baker offers alternative visions, such as the Islamic mode of communal social insurance. Insurance is neither just about the rote and automatic spreading of loss nor the passive reflection of a preexisting social and economic reality, but also involves the production of social reality and modes of classification and governance.

Chapter Three

Deborah Stone's essay, "Beyond Moral Hazard: Insurance as Moral Opportunity," introduces the important new concept of the "moral opportunity" of insurance. Stone coined this term to identify an expansionary social dynamic that counters the individual-based forces of moral hazard and adverse selection that traditionally concern insurance and economic analysts. The moral opportunity of insurance is a social dynamic that "tends to increase what gets perceived as insurable and deserving of collective support." Stone identifies six distinct mechanisms underlying this expansionary dynamic of insurance. She argues that the dynamic is appropriately thought of as *moral* opportunity, because it is powered by beliefs that insurance is a way to help others and to be helped. Like Baker's analysis of insurance and the social construction of responsibility, Stone's discussion of the moral opportunity of insurance reveals the influence that insurance institutions and technologies have on how we imagine individual and social responsibility.

Chapter Four

Geoffrey Clark's essay, "Embracing Fatality through Life Insurance in Eighteenth-Century England," takes a rigorous historical look at the role of gambling and virtue in the development of the modern insurance regime. Clark examines how insurance grew hand-in-hand with gambling, arguing that the business of insurance—seemingly the epitome of Enlightenment reason and sober self-possession—actually stimulated the speculative passions as much as it depressed risk taking. Clark demonstrates that "the culture of risk management epitomized by life insurance emerged not so much from an attempt to banish risks as to play with them."

In the process, Clark analyzes how risk sometimes is both individualized *and* socialized. He discusses how life insurance simultaneously enabled families to protect themselves against financial disaster, and promoted continuity and autonomy in the larger commercial society. In this sense, the notion of embracing risk exposes a paradox: individuals sometimes were convinced to purchase life insurance to preserve their family or business's security; in the meantime, insurers invested the premiums in risky enterprises that were arguably necessary for the progress of the nation. All of these activities embraced risk in hopes of improving English society, by expanding commerce, extending credit, and giving more security to the growing "virtuous" middle classes.

Chapter Five

Pat O'Malley's essay, "Imagining Insurance: Risk, Thrift, and Life Insurance in Britain," begins where the preceding essay leaves off. O'Malley analyzes insurance visions among the working class in nineteenth- and twentieth-century Britain. He describes how insurance actively constructed individual and social responsibility during this period, tracing how the governance of insurance organizations reflected changing ideas about the moral development of the working poor. In the process, he links what he and François Ewald call insurance "imaginaries" (what we call insurance "visions") to political rationalities. Shifting ideas about thrift, risk, and insurance correspond to broader political transformations: from the classical liberalism of Gladstone, to the welfare liberalism of Beveridge, and finally to contemporary neoliberalism as illustrated by Thatcher's politics.

O'Malley charts a remarkable transformation in the triangular relationship between thrift, risk, and insurance. As he usefully emphasizes, that transformation took place through the working out of insurantial imagination, not "simply class interest, market pressures or actuarial techniques." Thrift and speculation, polar opposites in Victorian England, come together in the voluntary thrift of the worker-entrepreneurs hitching their pensions to a roaring market. All is well and good while the market prospers. But what happens when the economy sours, and the social security system is no longer there to pick up the pieces?

Chapter Six

Carol Heimer's essay, "Insuring More, Ensuring Less: The Costs and Benefits of Private Regulation through Insurance," investigates the institutional and distributional consequences of insurance as a technology for managing risk (not simply spreading it). Using the language of economic sociology, Heimer conceptualizes insurance gatekeeping as a form of institutional embeddedness (links between institutions—here insurance and other institutions) that has replaced individual embeddedness (links between individuals).

Heimer contends that this expansion of insurance poses a moral hazard threat, but not for the reasons commonly discussed in the economics literature. Where most moral hazard analyses consider the insured as the threat, Heimer contends that *insurers* also constitute a moral hazard threat because they seek to minimize what gets classified as a loss in order to maximize financial profits. On the one hand, insurance is a loss-spreading device and works best when the risk pool is large and diverse. On the other hand, insurers can offer better premium rates to policyholders and profits for themselves and their shareholders by decreasing the pool's diversity and excluding those most likely to experience loss. Thus, Stone and Heimer offer two different perspectives on insurance's expansionary tendencies. Stone sees expanding insurance as a critical tool to legitimate social aid and to ultimately produce new modes of collective aid. Heimer perceives expanding insurance regimes as a coercive force that reinforces social class differences by restricting the choices available to those who cannot access insurance, and for whom alternative modes of risk management are no longer available.

Chapter Seven

Martha McCluskey explores the social construction of risk in the context of contemporary social insurance debates in "Rhetoric of Risk and the Redistribution of Social Insurance." Consistent with Heimer, McCluskey emphasizes the relationship between insurance visions and the increasing inequality within and among societies. Instead of guaranteeing security, contemporary social insurance regimes entice people to take personal responsibility in return for potentially higher payoffs. Yet, as McCluskey emphasizes, popular culture's celebration of risk (as described by Jonathon Simon in chapter 8 of the book) significantly depends on security. Thus, McCluskey reveals a double standard: whether we embrace risk depends on who takes the risk and who gets the security. Risk and security depend on a morally based social vision—at some point, we must ask who *deserves* the risks and security.

McCluskey first analyzes this double standard by looking at workers compensation, which is often considered the founding social insurance program in the United States. McCluskey then explores two examples of social insurance aimed at protecting capital, both of which share the double standard of risk taking. First, the International Monetary Fund (IMF) socializes global investors' risks through taxpayer-backed loans used to bail out debts of countries facing financial collapse. Second, the U.S. Federal Reserve Bank has taken a newly expanded social insurance role by protecting creditors against the risk that high levels of employment from economic growth will increase inflation.

McCluskey challenges us to recognize that security and risk are not naturally antithetical; how we perceive security, risk taking, responsibility, and insurance is part of a complex social, political, cultural, and economic value system. Ultimately, she states that "recent embrace of risk taking represents not a rejection of security but a moral judgment affirming and strengthening systems of inequality and subordination." Thus, McCluskey leaves us with provocative questions about the social meaning of risk, security, responsibility, and insurance. Who do insurance institutions protect, and how do they protect? How do insurance forms and technologies affect how citizens, as well as nations, perceive their roles in our contemporary global economy?

Themes and Connections

A number of themes connect these essays. The theme that unites the essays at the highest level is, of course, the socially constructed nature of risk and responsibility. Emphasized most directly by Baker, this theme features prominently in each of the essays in both this and the second part. A related theme is the problematic relationship between risk and security. Emphasized most directly by McCluskey, it is also developed by Clark in relation to insurance and gambling, by Stone in relation to insurance's moral opportunity, and by Heimer in relation to insurance gatekeeping. O'Malley also addresses risk and security as he discusses thrift (one road to security) and British working class moral values. As McCluskey and Heimer describe, one person's security can promote another's risk. In addition, as McCluskey, Stone, and O'Malley each illustrate, what we are conditioned to perceive as security and risk affects (and is affected by) political and social values.

A third theme may well seem obvious to readers unaccustomed to the thin air of rational choice theory (and its close cousins, risk–benefit analysis and much of neoclassical economics). This theme is the significance of history, institutions, and culture—in short, the importance of units of analysis larger than individuals and their preferences. Addressed most directly by Stone's fundamentally social concept of moral opportunity, larger units of analysis figure prominently in each of the essays in this part: from Heimer's analysis of institutional embeddedness, to McCluskey's exposure of the double standard of risk and security, to Baker's exploration of insurance as social responsibility, and to Clark's and O'Malley's description of the role of moral and cultural forces in the definition of insurance institutions.

In addition, these essays recognize that embracing risk has distributional consequences. As Heimer discusses most directly, insurance transactions are embedded in a larger network of social relations. Insurance is not equally available to all people. This (lack of) availability does not merely reflect power structures, but also helps to construct and reproduce social hierarchies. Once again, insurance technologies, institutions, and forms are not simply rote mechanisms to spread risk and compensate loss. Instead, they actively shape social reality.

The final and perhaps most important theme that unites these essays is the significance of insurance visions to the development of insurance and other institutions of risk and responsibility. Conceptions of specific insurance forms and technologies help to construct ways of viewing the world that are then taken for granted and, thus, not questioned. It is not that material conditions and scientific principles are irrelevant, simply that any account that focuses only on the interests of the powerful or on developments in demographics, probability theory, or actuarial science is incomplete.

Why in America do we marvel at the productivity of genetically enhanced food that fills our tables at lower cost, while in Europe mass movements mobilize to keep that food out? The difference is clearly not in any objective reality or fundamental scientific principle, and it is not exclusively in the predominantly American ownership of property rights to genetic innovation. As our authors' visions and imaginaries reveal, there have been and can be diverse kinds of risk societies. There is not simply an inevitable historical march toward a utopia of either risk spreading or Green Power. Collectively, these essays invite readers to re-imagine their understanding of risk, insurance, and responsibility in light of the diverse possibilities of the past and the present.

> [G]overnment is not just a power needing to be tamed or an authority needing to be legitimized. It is an activity and an art which concerns all and which touches each. And it is an art which presupposes thought. The sense and object of governmental acts do not fall from the sky or emerge ready formed from social practice. They are things which have had to be—and which have been—invented. Foucault observed that there is a parcel of thought in even the crassest and most obtuse parts of social reality, which is why criticism can be a real power for social change.—Graham Burchell, Colin Gordon, and Peter Miller, *The Foucault Effect: Studies in Governmentality.*

TWO

Risk, Insurance, and the Social Construction of Responsibility

Tom Baker

Insurance, we all know, transfers risk. Yet, what we usually think of as a transfer of risk is also a transfer of responsibility. Without health insurance, I am responsible for my medical bills, my choice of doctor, and, in consultation with my doctor, my course of treatment. With health insurance, the insurer assumes some of that responsibility. Insurance, then, not only distributes risk (Abraham 1986), it also distributes responsibility.

This relationship between insurance, risk, and responsibility has great significance for the embrace of risk that is the main subject of this volume. In an important sense, the proliferation of risks produces a proliferation of responsibilities. Put perhaps more controversially, risk *creates* responsibility, and not only through the risk taking Jonathan Simon explores in chapter 8.

Without knowledge of the potential for something good or bad to happen, we have no occasion to assume or assign responsibility for it. Once we have that knowledge—once we become aware of a risk—that risk becomes each individual's responsibility unless or until it is assumed or assigned elsewhere. The identification of a new risk of harm is unlikely to be experienced as a thrill or as an occasion for building character, but rather as an added burden, and, if there is no obvious new benefit that accompanies becoming aware of the new risk, with a destabilizing sense of losing control. The promise of insurance and other forms of risk management is gaining a measure of control over an uncertain world. Indeed, it was just this promise of control that led some Calvinists to denounce insurance as a presumptuous interference with Providence (Zelizer 1979). Yet, as we will see,

reaching out to insurance institutions for protection cedes responsibility
to them. Thus risk not only *creates* responsibility, but also, through the
means explored in this chapter, *socializes* that responsibility. If we understand the embrace of risk to include the embrace of insurance and other aspects of risk management, then we might wonder whether the embrace of
risk is really about individual responsibility, and we might think more
about social control—which sometimes might take the shape of enforced
individual responsibility.

A COMPARISON OF TWO FAMILIES in quite different circumstances
begins to illustrate the relationship between insurance and responsibility.
Imagine first a professional couple living in Avon, Connecticut, a small
town outside of Hartford. If they are typical of others in their class, we can
easily identify over sixteen forms of insurance that address various risks in
their lives. Through payroll taxes, they have rights to a basic level of unemployment and disability insurance, as well as a modest retirement annuity, some life insurance, and generous health insurance for their old age
or upon disability (all of which are provided under the Social Security and
Medicare Acts). From the private insurance market, they have homeowners' insurance, automobile insurance, term life insurance, and an annuity.
Through employment, they have health insurance, sick leave, life insurance, workers compensation, additional disability insurance, pension plans
with significant annuity features, and, possibly, employment severance arrangements that we can understand as a form of supplemental unemployment insurance.

All of this insurance transfers risk from the couple to an insurance fund
and, therefore, changes the financial consequences of the events to which
the insurance applies. A house fire remains a tragedy to the couple even
with insurance (because of the risk to life and the loss of the irreplaceable)
but the tragedy is not financial (at least as long as the insurance company
comes through on its promise). Similarly, an extended illness remains an
unhappy event for all the obvious reasons, but once again the financial effect is muted: sick leave provides short-term income, disability insurance
provides income over the longer term, and health insurance covers the
medical expenses. Whether living beyond working age is a blessing or a
bane depends on many circumstances, but financial need is unlikely to be
one of them: the couple will have an income and health insurance for life.

Now imagine a second couple living in the nearby Hartford neighborhood of Frog Hollow. The wife cleans houses in the first couple's neighborhood, and the husband works for a painting contractor. What insurance

pads the sharp corners in their lives? Like the Avon couple, the husband has rights to basic social insurance financed by payroll taxes (unemployment insurance, disability insurance, health insurance in old age or disability, an annuity, and a limited form of life insurance). The wife, however, is paid "under the table," so her only forms of social insurance are means-tested, noncontributory programs that provide a very low level of disability insurance and, in old age or disability, health insurance. As long as her husband works, she is unlikely to qualify for these income-based benefits. Neither the husband nor the wife receive any private insurance through employment. They have purchased automobile and life insurance, but their life insurance would pay only enough to cover the cost of a funeral and a few months of rent, and their auto insurance provides the mandatory minimum coverage, which does not cover losses to their own car. They don't own their home, nor do they have renters' insurance, which is an extravagance few among their neighbors can afford.

It takes little imagination to contrast the meaning that illness has for the two couples. Unwelcome in both places, it is a financial disaster only in Frog Hollow. Because that couple has less insurance, they bear more responsibility for the consequences of illness and other unfortunate events. They have no health insurance, no sick leave, and no private disability insurance. All medical costs are their responsibility, as are the rent, the groceries, and the other routine expenses that must be paid in sickness and in health. In the Avon household, in contrast, health insurance, sick leave, and, depending on how long the illness persists, private disability insurance relieve the couple of much of that responsibility. Sickness, along with house fires, disabling injuries, old age, and perhaps even death have different meanings in the two households, according to the presence or absence of a collective—insurance—that assumes responsibility for the financial consequences of those events.

Insurance as *Social* Responsibility

All these forms of insurance depend on the participation of many to share the burden of those with a qualifying need. Thus, extending insurance asserts a degree of social responsibility over the insured against events.

Thinking about insurance as a form of "social responsibility" often founders on the use of the term *social*. One impediment—an amorphous and confused notion of "the social"—is readily dealt with by understanding that term not to refer to an abstract entity but rather to the group of participants in any particular insurance arrangement. A second, more serious im-

pediment is a vision of insurance as a series of independent, bilateral contracts that leaves out the collective dimension of insurance.

So hidden is this collective dimension in the American perspective toward insurance that many, perhaps the majority, in the United States never
realize that, if they are lucky, most of their premiums for most forms of insurance will go to pay other people's claims. (For an exception, see Stone
1993.) For example, in years of teaching law students about insurance, I
have learned that one of their most common assumptions about insurance
is that it is similar to a savings account. The students recognize that many
forms of insurance differ from savings accounts in the degree of flexibility
allowed in the timing of insurance withdrawals. Nevertheless, they often
expect that over the course of a lifetime the deposits made by each person
should roughly equal the withdrawals on that person's insurance account.
But unless the insurance truly is a form of savings (as in the case of annuities and accumulating life insurance) or a very close substitute (as in the
case of Social Security retirement benefits), it rarely is desirable for the
"withdrawals" to equal the "deposits." Indeed, when it comes to health,
disability, property, liability, and term life insurance, if your withdrawals
equal your deposits, you have had, in at least some respects, a very unfortunate life.

A discussion of insurance in a recent book on Islamic finance law nicely
illustrates, by way of contrast, the absence of the social in the typical American understanding of insurance. Frank Vogel begins by describing the
"problem" that insurance appeared to present under traditional Islamic
law: "As a single contract, insurance violates *riba* ['interest'] and *gharar*
['gambling'] rules. One party pays cash premiums in return for the promise
of the other party to pay a cash sum on the occurrence of a contigent future
event. So viewed, it resembles a bet. Moreover, most insurance companies
invest their premiums in forbidden interest-bearing investments" (Vogel
and Hayes 1998:151). In other words, Western insurance, at least as understood from a Western perspective, appears to violate the Islamic prohibition
of gambling and other contracts based on chance as well as the Islamic prohibition of usury.[1]

As Professor Vogel describes, recent Islamic scholars have provided a legal solution to this problem by rethinking the nature of insurance. Their solution reveals an Islamic perspective on insurance that highlights the social
in ordinary insurance arrangements. The first step was to recognize that
"through the law of large numbers, insurance contracts in the aggregate involve very little uncertainty. The parties are transacting in something—
coverage for a certain risk—which can be known and valued quite pre-

cisely" (1998:152). Although this defense of insurance overstates the certainty involved in at least some forms of insurance (witness the recent troubles of Lloyd's), it accurately describes the inherently collective nature of any form of insurance that is based on the law of large numbers.

As Vogel observes, "[t]his defense, *interestingly*, shifts the focus from any particular contract and bilateral relationship to insurance viewed in the aggregate and as an institutional form. While individual contracts appear to lead to gross disparities of consideration determined by random events, in the aggregate they involve no unfairness, gambling, excess risk, or contention" (id.). This defense is "interesting" from an American perspective, because the typical American perspective focuses on individual bilateral relationships, not the collective. Yet, as the Islamic scholars recognized, insurance is inherently collective because it depends on the existence of a large group through which the risks of unfortunate events are dispersed. Thus the "bilateral contract" of the American vision of insurance rests on the participation of many others in the insurance institution.[2]

The second step in the legal solution to the Islamic prohibition of insurance points even more directly toward the collective aspect of insurance: "In the 1970's, another tack was found, which also involves viewing insurance as an institution, but with an added twist. Proponents of a new 'Islamic insurance' proposed that insurance be offered, not as a bilateral contract transferring a known risk, but as a charitable collective enterprise by which Muslims pool resources to aid each other in the event of casualty or loss" (Vogel and Hayes 1998:152). In form, this new Islamic insurance differs from American insurance:

> Employing this new justification, a new form of insurance company called *takaful* (lit., "solidarity") has been devised, offering a "*takaful* contract." By this contract, members in the company promise to make periodic payments, which the company maintains in accounts in their names and invests Islamically. Members agree that if one of their number should suffer a covered loss, each will make a proportionate gift from his account to cover that loss. The legality of this contract seems to depend on the general principle that gratuitous acts tolerate relative high degrees of *gharar* ["risk"], and also on a [ ] view that gift promises can be binding. (Id.)

Within the framework of Islamic law, the formal differences Vogel describes are crucial. But within the framework of policy analysis employed by Vogel and other Western analysts they are far less so.

The basic difference between the Islamic and American conceptions of insurance is one of perspective, not economics.[3] From a secular American perspective, insurance appears as a set of bilateral contracts that transfer risk for the benefit of the individuals who choose to make those contracts. From an Islamic perspective, however, insurance appears as an institution that reduces or eliminates risk for the benefit of the social group. Importantly, the institutions that result from either the American or the Islamic conception can also be described within the framework of the other: an Islamic insurance company is an institution that individuals use to shed risk, just as an American insurance company is a way that a group shares risk.

Insurance and the *Distribution* of Responsibility

The image of insurance as a bilateral contract tells us that individuals obtain insurance to lighten their responsibilities. Seen in this way, insurance can appear only to *re*distribute responsibility, and in only one direction: from individuals to insurance funds. Insurance institutions, in other words, only remove responsibility; they do not create it.

This is, of course, a baseline fallacy (Hale 1923). At least in developed countries, there is no world without insurance on which insurance institutions subsequently act. There is, instead, a world that includes insurance institutions that assume some (but rarely all) financial responsibility for the consequences of some events (but not others), and for some people (but not others). A decision within an insurance institution about how much financial responsibility to assume for what and for whom parcels out the rest of that responsibility to individuals and other institutions.

Moreover, even if we were to imagine a world without insurance on which insurance institutions act, those institutions would "remove" responsibility from individuals in the same sense that a sculptor "removes" stone from a block. In the case of insurance and responsibility, there is no single artist with a grand design, nor is the medium a lifeless block of stone. There is, instead, an uncoordinated set of insurance institutions that act on and through individuals and other institutions that do not always do what is expected. Uncoordinated and imperfect though they may be, however, these institutions structure the risk transfer choices that we can make and, through those choices, the distribution of responsibility.

A second, more important stumbling block to understanding how insurance institutions distribute responsibility is the complexity of the set of ideas bound up in the concept of responsibility itself. We can begin with the commonsense notion that insurance is something that responsible people arrange to have. The link between insurance and this sense of responsibility was forged in the nineteenth century in response to strong moral and religious objections to insurance (Baker 1996; Zelizer 1979). If this history means that obtaining insurance is the responsible thing to do, then people with insurance should be *more* responsible than people without insurance, not less.

Part of what is going on here is word play: "responsible" in the sense of "trustworthy, loyal, helpful, . . . " and the rest of the Boy Scout code, being played off against "responsible" in the sense of obligated to pay or accountable. It is responsible in the first sense to get insurance precisely because not having insurance makes one responsible—in the financial accountability sense—for any number of bad things that can happen. The linking of these two meanings in the context of insurance, however, extends beyond word play. Historically, insurance institutions have tried to become responsible (accountable) primarily for people who are responsible (trustworthy) and to keep the irresponsible out. In the private insurance arena, that effort is manifested in admonitions to agents and underwriters, and in opposition to efforts to curtail character underwriting (the latest being opposition to the use of credit scores in insurance underwriting). In the social insurance arena, that concern is manifested in the concept of the deserving poor—the notion that children, the disabled, and the elderly poor deserve public support because their present need is not the result of irresponsibility on their part (Handler and Hasenfeld 1991).

As this social insurance example suggests, there is a third, causal meaning to the word *responsible.* The able-bodied poor are excluded from noncontributory social insurance programs in part because of a social judgment that they are responsible in this causal sense for their poverty, whether because of lack of effort or poor choices made earlier in life.

"Responsible" also has a fourth meaning: free, self-determining, or autonomous. "I'm responsible for *X*" means that *X* is my turf—an area in which I am free to act or not. Admittedly this meaning is difficult to tease out from the first three. Self-determination can be an important element of what it takes to be a trustworthy person, and it can be hard to hold someone accountable for an act that was not self-determined. Yet we do find self-determining people who are not trustworthy and we do at times hold people accountable for their acts that involved no autonomy or free choice. So, freedom is a distinct, if related, sense of the term.

Finally, there is a relational sense to the word *responsible* that is captured in the social insurance concept of solidarity. Although this relational dimension may also be implicit in some of the other meanings of "responsible," it too is distinct. I can be responsible in this relational sense (solid with), whether I am trustworthy or not, for things that I did not cause, and this solidarity is not necessarily coextensive with my moral or legal ac-

countability or my degree of self-determination. Indeed, a mismatch between popular understandings of accountability and solidarity can be a
strong social force pushing accountability in a broader or narrower direction (see, e.g., Simon 1988).

From these five meanings of the adjective "responsible" we derive five
corresponding meanings of the noun "responsibility": trustworthiness, accountability, causality, freedom, and solidarity.[4] Can insurance be said to
distribute all five types of responsibility?

Insurance and Accountability

My imprecise use of the word *responsibility* so far has focused
on its accountability sense, and the kind of accountability I have addressed is financial. Admittedly, that is because I find the idea that insurance institutions distribute financial responsibility the easiest to understand.

Health insurance coverage for abortion provides a useful example.
When we understand insurance as a form of social responsibility, it is perfectly plain why someone who is morally opposed to abortion would object
to being included in a health plan that pays for abortions. A decision to include abortion assigns the financial responsibility to the insurance institution and, through the institution, to all the members of the institution. It is
similarly plain why a person who regards access to abortion as a necessary
element of women's emancipation would object to health plans that refuse
to pay for abortions. A decision to exclude abortion from the coverage offered by health insurance institutions assigns the financial responsibility
for the procedure to individuals who have abortions, which not only makes
abortion more expensive for individuals but also stigmatizes the procedure
as outside the realm of ordinary health care.

The health insurance context also helps us see that insurance institutions distribute accountability in a broader sense than who pays for health
care. As leading U.S. health insurance companies transform themselves
into managed care organizations, they assert more control over medical
care and they become more accountable—certainly in a moral sense and
possibly also in a legal sense—for adverse medical outcomes.[5]

Other forms of insurance also assume significant accountability in an
effort to control their financial obligations. For example, along with the
growth of workers compensation insurance has come a proliferation of
knowledge workers—workers compensation claims, benefits, and risk
managers—who assume responsibility for preventing losses and for controlling the costs of recovering from loss. These new professions represent

"accountability centers" that would not exist in the form they do in the absence of workers compensation insurance.

At least potentially, these new professions distribute responsibility in all five senses of that term. They identify the locations of causal agents in organizational structures or networks; they assume accountability for monitoring the behavior of those causal agents; they define what behavior marks those agents as trustworthy, loyal, and so on; they limit the freedom of those agents to act in undesirable ways; and they establish organizational procedures that may increase or decrease solidarity among members of the organization.

Insurance and Trustworthiness

Insurance institutions also mark people or organizations as responsible in the trustworthy sense. For example, it is nearly impossible in the United States to obtain financing for a home, a car, or other property without first obtaining insurance covering that property. Having insurance marks a potential borrower as responsible in a sense that is very important to lenders: the borrower can be trusted to repay the loan even if disaster strikes.[6] This is the reason insurance "redlining" (the practice of identifying geographic regions in which an insurance company prefers not to issue policies) is of such concern (Squires 1997). A neighborhood redlined by insurance companies is a more risky place for banks to lend. Without good financing opportunities, fewer people invest in the neighborhood, and without investment the neighborhood becomes an even more risky place for banks, causing further decline.

Insurance also marks people as trustworthy in such seemingly unexpected fields as major league sports and the movie business. When so much depends on the health of stars, sports teams and producers manage that risk by securing life and disability insurance that protect some of their profits in the event of death or disability. Too public a relationship with illegal drugs, for example, may render a star "irresponsible," and, hence, uninsurable, and an uninsurable star may become a former star, or at least a less highly compensated one (Hubbard 1997).

Insurance institutions also mark people as trustworthy (or not) at the claims end of the insurance relationship. In nearly any claim decision, deciding whether to pay involves a moral evaluation of the claimant. For example, the question "Does this worker have a repetitive stress injury?" invariably involves the question "Can this worker's story be trusted?" If the answer to the second question is "yes," the claim will be paid with less investigation than if the answer is "no" (Baker and McElrath 1996; O'Malley 1991).

Finally, and perhaps most important, insurance institutions distribute trustworthiness by structuring situations so that people act in a more or less responsible—in the Scout code—manner. Erving Goffman (1961) touched on this power of institutions (and the limits of that power) in his study of total institutions such as asylums and prisons, and Carol Heimer and Lisa Staffen (1998) have studied this explicitly in their effort to understand "the social organization of responsibility in the hospital and the home."

Workers compensation insurance provides a number of useful examples of how insurance institutions structure situations in this manner. One common approach is designing and maintaining workplaces so that it is difficult for workers to behave in an unsafe manner, thus making it easier to practice safety. Workers compensation insurance achieves this in a direct, command-and-control manner through teams of inspectors employed by insurance companies and consulting firms. It also achieves this in an indirect manner through experience-based premiums that give employers an incentive to prevent injuries.

A second common approach to fostering responsible behavior focuses on injured workers and their return to work (see, e.g., Holland 1988). Here, the responsible behavior being fostered is following through with the doctor's or therapist's orders and returning to work as soon as it is physically safe to do so. Toward these ends, workers compensation develops rehabilitation regimes and surveillance techniques that make it easier for the injured worker to complete the therapy needed to recover from the injury (and harder to avoid it).

A third, more difficult to document, approach to fostering responsible behavior is suppressing workers compensation claims (McCluskey 1998). From the perspective of the workers compensation regime, an accident is a problem only if it produces a claim, and the size of the problem turns on the amount of benefits paid on the claim. Accordingly, suppressing claims may be the "responsible" thing to do. As this suggests—and this is a very important point—the responsibility fostered by an insurance regime is defined with respect to the internal logic of that regime and not according to an external perspective. In other words, insurance institutions not only structure situations so that people behave in a responsible manner, they also define what behavior is (and is not) responsible. This is not to suggest that insurance institutions can define responsibility in a mechanistic, clockwork-like manner. Any given definition of responsibility can be contested in a multitude of ways. For example, the line between discouraging frivolous claims and suppressing legitimate claims is contested on a daily basis in workers compensation hearings across the country (McCluskey 1998).

A final approach to encouraging people to act in a responsible (trust-worthy, loyal, helpful, and so on) manner is making those who are injured share the responsibility (financial accountability) for their injuries. A detailed examination of this approach would take us deep into the economics and rhetoric of moral hazard, but the underlying idea is that insurance encourages people to behave less responsibly because it relieves them of some of the negative consequences of their actions, leading them to take greater risks on the job and discouraging them from returning to work after injury in a timely fashion (Baker 1996). Three ways to address this moral hazard were just considered: designing safe workplaces, adopting back to work programs, and suppressing claims. Another way is to reduce workers compensation benefits. Of course, this approach undercuts the primary *compensation* purpose of workers compensation and, for that reason, it is contested.

Insurance and Causation

Insurance institutions can also mark people or organizations as "responsible" in the causal sense of the word. Liability insurance, like the tort system upon which it depends, is of course inextricably bound up with questions of causation (Hart and Honoré 1985). In deciding when and whether to defend and pay claims, liability insurance claims personnel regularly decide who or what caused the event or situation out of which the claim has emerged. Workers compensation insurance also illustrates this dynamic. Each compensation payment reflects a judgment that an illness or injury was caused by the worker's employment. These judgments are affected by the nature of workers compensation benefits and the availability of other forms of compensation.

One demonstration of this comes from a study of doctors' judgements about whether an injury or illness resulted from employment (Butler et al. 1997). The study compared doctors in health maintenance organizations (HMOs) with those in private practice. The compensation incentives of the two groups differed in a crucial respect: private health insurance paid more for a given illness or injury than workers compensation insurance, but workers compensation insurance paid more than the HMOs. This meant that, if the illness or injury was work related, doctors in HMOs were paid more for treating the patient, while doctors in private practice were paid less than they would have been paid if the condition was not work related. Not surprisingly, the study showed that the HMO doctors were more likely than the doctors in private practice to diagnose an injury or illness as work related.

Of course the study tells us nothing about which doctors were right.

What it shows is that payment systems affect judgements about causation. When the payment system favored the work-related diagnosis, more injuries were deemed work related. When the payment system favored a contrary diagnosis, fewer injuries were deemed work related. Absent workers compensation, even fewer injuries would be understood to be caused by employment because there would be even less occasion to link employment to work. Thus workers compensation produces injuries at work, not because of moral hazard (or at least not *only* because of moral hazard), but rather because it gives us a reason to link an event (injury) with a cause (work) where otherwise that event might never have been linked to that cause.

Similar causation decisions must be made with respect to potential overlaps among workers compensation and other payment systems, such as automobile insurance, disability insurance, and tort liability. In each situation, the compensation decisions depend on judgments about who or what caused the particular event, and those judgments will be affected by the way that the compensation systems are designed.

In addition to such case-by-case approaches to causation, insurance institutions are also involved in shaping public opinion regarding causation. Beliefs about who or what tends to cause some event or situation can have a significant impact on political decisions allocating financial accountability. For example, much of the rhetoric of moral hazard identifies people as "responsible" in a causal sense for their condition, and thus not deserving of insurance support (Baker 1996; McCluskey 1998). We can see this at work in such diverse fields as social insurance, workers compensation, and products liability.

Insurance and Freedom

Insurance can also affect responsibility in the freedom or self-determination sense. As Carol Heimer documented in *Reactive Risk and Rational Action*, insurance is intimately tied up with social control. The more that the insured loss lies within the control of the individual insured, the more strings an insurance company attaches to the promise to insure (Heimer 1985). What I described earlier as "structuring situations so that people act in a more or less responsible—in the Scout code sense—manner" is a form of social control.

Insurance-based limits on freedom/autonomy/self-determination (none of these terms is exactly right) affect not only insurance beneficiaries but also people and institutions that provide insured services, such as doctors and lawyers. Indeed, both the medical and legal professions currently are engaged in a struggle to maintain their professional autonomy in the face of cost control efforts by insurers (see, e.g., Frankford 1994; American Bar Association 2001). Doctors and managed health care receive the most public attention, but the same dynamic affects tort defense lawyers and liability insurance. Liability insurance companies instruct defense lawyers whether and when to take depositions, whether and when to settle, whether and when to hire experts, and so on. Moreover, the legal expense accounting systems used by some U.S. liability insurance companies allow them to tell their law firms which lawyers within the firm are the most effective (from a cost efficiency perspective), thereby affecting compensation and promotion within the firms.

The connection between responsibility, freedom and insurance is also illustrated by the way that both professions have embraced their legal liability in response to insurance-based social control. One of the little known aspects of the initial Clinton health care proposal was to eliminate doctor's liability for medical malpractice and to replace it with liability of managed care organizations (Sage 1997). Organized medicine protested vigorously, recognizing that legal responsibility would help preserve their autonomy. "I can't do that or I will be sued for malpractice," is a powerful response to a cost-cutting effort by an insurance company. Because accountability in our legal culture is often based on the freedom of an agent to make a choice, removing accountability can easily be seen as a step toward the loss of the freedom to make the choice.

As Carol Heimer's (1985) research suggests, almost all of these social control efforts can be traced to the effect of insurance on incentives, commonly referred to as the problem of moral hazard. Although the rhetoric of moral hazard can be turned to selfish ends (Baker 1996), the core insight—that, all other things being equal, people behave differently when they bear the costs of their misfortune than when they do not—cannot seriously be questioned. Of course, all things usually are not equal, and insurance-based social control is one of the factors why insurance does not necessarily lead to an explosion of costs. Indeed, as I have argued earlier, "the success of insurers in managing insurance incentives may well mean that the most important 'moral hazard' effect is not increased loss, but rather increased social control" (Baker 1996:282).

Insurance and Solidarity

Depending on the degree to which the premiums or benefits are linked to individual characteristics or choices, the fortunes of the members of an insurance group can be linked together to a greater or lesser extent. As the differences between individual life insurance and U.S. Social Security benefits show, there are great variations in the degree of solidarity insurance institutions embody. Individual life insurance, with its underwriting guidelines and risk classifications, epitomizes the individualistic end of the insurance spectrum; Social Security, with its mandatory participation and income-based premiums and benefits, the solidaristic end. A health care plan with community rating (everyone pays the same premium) and open enrollment (no one is turned away) is more solidaristic than a plan that charges the sick more than the healthy and turns the riskiest applicants away.

The choices we make among available insurance institutions reveal the limits of our sense of solidarity with others, as the current debate over the U.S. Social Security retirement system reflects. A choice to change Social Security from a guaranteed-benefit, one-size-fits-all program to something that looks like an individual retirement account (IRA)—in which contributions are earmarked for, and invested according to the directions of, individual contributors—would signal that we understand Social Security to be more about self-protection (and less about solidarity) than we once did, and that we feel less responsibility for those who fall behind under the IRA approach.

Of course, the exercise of such choices does more than reveal preferences. It also shapes the further development of insurance institutions. The more our choices reveal that we understand insurance to be about self-protection, the more that insurance institutions will adapt to provide us the best individualized protection at the cheapest individualized price. For private insurance, this adaptation is relatively straightforward, as illustrated by the market-driven shift in the United States from a largely community-rated health insurance system to a more heavily risk-rated health insurance system (Jacobi 1997). But even social insurance programs respond to preferences, albeit through the political process. The proponents of the proposal to add the IRA-like component to Social Security clearly hope (and maybe even expect) that this self-protection intervention into a currently solidaristic domain will teach people to demand more of the same.

The development of insurance institutions shapes, in turn, what is imaginable about the meaning of participation in insurance institutions. The more that insurance institutions adapt to satisfy self-interest, the more the satisfaction of self interest will seem to be the natural role of insurance institutions and the more far-fetched the idea of using insurance to achieve solidarity. The U.S. health care situation illustrates this point well. The debate over the government's role in U.S. health insurance is, in significant part, a debate over the nature of health insurance: does it exist to protect me and mine, or does it serve a greater good? This debate does not take place in a policy vacuum, but rather in a rapidly changing health care marketplace. The more that commercial insurance companies, HMOs, and third-party administrators erode the market share of Blue Cross organizations (by offering lower-risk groups lower prices and broader service), the more difficult it becomes for the Blues to maintain their historic policies of community pricing and open enrollment. The greater the competitive pressure on community pricing and open enrollment, the more natural an individualist conception of self-interest appears as the foundation of health insurance, and the more that government efforts to promote affordable health insurance for everyone appear to be interventions in an otherwise neutral health care marketplace.

The development of our ideas about the meaning of participating in insurance institutions affects, in turn, the choices we make among available insurance institutions. If community pricing and open enrollment seem doomed to failure, why waste precious resources propping them up? If openly linking insurance and solidarity is a vain hope, why not amend the Social Security Act to allow segregated, IRA-type accounts? In this manner, insurance ideas and insurance institutions engage in the elaborate dance that is the social construction of responsibility.

Of course, it is possible to imagine different steps to this dance. If, like the organizers of Islamic *takafuls*, we understood insurance to be about solidarity, we might work to find ways of organizing insurance institutions around groups of people who feel some degree of responsibility for each other. If insurance institutions grouped together people who felt responsible for each other, it might become easier to imagine insurance as being about solidarity. And if, in turn, we understood insurance to be about solidarity, we might choose the best group over the best individualized protection at the cheapest price.

Might this be the trajectory of Islamic insurance? Only time will tell. The important point here is not to predict the future or idealize Islamic insurance, but rather to emphasize the interaction of insurance ideas and institutions in the social construction of responsibility.

Conclusion

My argument is that insurance is a form of social responsibility and that insurance institutions shape responsibility in five analytically distinct senses of that term—accountability, trustworthiness, causation, freedom, and solidarity. Insurance shapes accountability through decisions about premiums and benefits, through subrogation and coordination of benefits, and through risk-management techniques designed to reduce the exposure of insurance institutions to loss. Insurance shapes trustworthiness through decisions about whom to insure, what premiums to charge, and whose claims to pay, as well as through risk-management techniques designed to foster responsible behavior. Insurance shapes causation through decisions about whose claims to pay and what kinds of benefits will be offered to cover what kinds of events, and, once again, through risk-management techniques that identify who or what causes loss in order to minimize losses in the future. Insurance shapes freedom through many of the efforts to control moral hazard. Finally, insurance shapes solidarity through decisions about risk classification and underwriting, and through risk-management techniques that alter the structure of organizations. Seen in this way, insurance institutions cease to play only a passive, loss-spreading role and, instead, actively construct (and are constructed by) the world they inhabit.

NOTES

1. The link between insurance and gambling is not unique to Islamic law. The mathematical underpinnings of insurance are often attributed to encounters between mathemeticians and eighteenth-century nobles who wished to improve their odds at the gaming tables. (Hacking 1975). Moreover, gambling and insurance were intertwined institutionally in England well into the eighteenth century, as reflected in a lively literature debating the "prudential" and "speculative" origins of insurance (Pearson 1990; Clark 1999).

2. Although this is true for contracts generally, which rest on shared understandings and the existence of a state willing and able to enforce them (Isaacs 1934; Nietsche 1967; Durkheim 1933), the bilateral contract vision of insurance rests on a collectivity in a more specific sense as well. Insurance requires a formal group through which risks and responsibilities are shared.

3. Keeping separate accounts is an accounting exercise that would be tedious, but certainly possible with the use of computers, to arrange in a Western insurance company. Under American contract law, the promises made by *takaful* members would appear to be binding contracts, whether called "gifts" or not. Although the *takaful* ownership structure appears to differ from that of American insurance companies "owned" by shareholders, there are analogous corporate structures in the American insurance industry. Some American insurance companies are run on a nonprofit basis in which the company is formally understood to exist for the benefit of the class of people eligible to obtain insurance from the company (for example, Teachers Insurance Annuity Company and the original Blue Cross companies); others are "mutuals" in which all profits are returned to the policyholders (for example, State Farm Mutual Insurance Company, Prudential Insurance Company). Indeed, Vogel notes that "[s]ome proponents of [the *takaful*] approach also approve of conventional mutual insurance, since it is also based on mutual self-help" (Vogel and Hayes 1998:151). The investment limits in the *takaful* do differ in kind from the investment limits on an American insurance company, which are supposed to be di-

rected solely at solvency concerns. These investment limits, however, do not implicate Vogel's bilateral versus collective distinction.

4. In an essay brought to my attention by Carol Heimer, the philosopher Richard McKeon develops a somewhat different analysis of the meaning of responsibility, which he describes as embodying three aspects: "accountability," "imputability," and "freedom and rationality" (McKeon 1957). His sense of responsibility as accountability is similar to mine, although he appears to confine accountability to the realm of law and punishment. By "imputability," he means that results can be imputed to causes and causal agents—which is analogous to my "causality" sense of responsibility—but within "imputability" he links causality with what I would call ethical or moral accountability. He argues that people are responsible in a moral or ethical sense only for harm that they voluntarily cause and includes this sense of moral responsibility as part of the imputation of a causal relationship. McKeon's sense of responsibility as embodying freedom and rationality is intended to perform a quite different task than my sense of responsibility as a character trait (trustworthy, loyal, helpful, and so on). Although it is quite possible he would have said I am hopelessly confused, he might also have said that freedom and a shared rationality are necessary to the development of a world in which people can be judged to have the character trait of responsibility. (Interestingly, Nietzsche would have said that the opposite was true—that the freedom to contract required, first, the development of a responsible person (Nietzsche 1967, Essay 2.) Finally, although I first thought to think of responsibility as freedom because of McKeon, I am not taking the position here that freedom and rationality are linked. These important philosophical details aside, it is clear that McKeon agreed with the fundamental point that responsibility involves a social judgment in a social context and, accordingly, that the concept of responsibility provides a useful lens through which to view social relations:

> The concept of responsibility relates actions to agents by a causal tie and applies a judgment of value to both. It involves assumptions, therefore, about the agent and about the social context in which he acts. The agent may be an individual or a group acting in the context of a society or a political state, or an individual, group, or community acting in the looser association of free individuals or independent communities or states whose actions affect each other. In either situation, responsibility is a reflexive relation: the responsibility of the individual and the responsibility of the community of which he is a member are interdependent . . . . (McKeon 1957:82)

5. Here, because McKeon (1957) assigns moral accountability to his "imputation" sense of responsibility, his account might differ. He might say that as organizations assert greater control they become responsible in the "imputation" sense of that word, but not necessarily in the "accountable" sense.

6. It may be more accurate to say that the insurance does not mark the borrower as "trustworthy" so much as provide an institutional replacement for an earlier requirement that the borrower (or a personal guarantor) be such. The replacement of informal networks with institutional commitments is the subject of Carol Heimer's essay in chapter 6 of this volume. Indeed, she suggests that "trustworthiness" may sometimes be too moralistic a term.

REFERENCES

Abraham, Kenneth. 1986. *Distributing Risk.* New Haven: Yale University Press.

American Bar Association. 2001. *Ethical Obligations of a Lawyer Working under Insurance Company Guidelines and Other Restrictions.* Standing Committee on Ethics and Professional Responsibility Formal Opinion 01–421.

Baker, Tom. 1994. "Constructing the Insurance Relationship: Sales Stories, Claims Stories and Insurance Contract Damages." *Texas Law Review* 72:1395–1433.

———. 1996. "On the Genealogy of Moral Hazard." *Texas Law Review* 75:237–92.

Baker, Tom, and Karen McElrath. 1996. "Whose Safety Net?: Home Insurance and Inequality." *Law and Social Inquiry* 21:229–64.

Butler, Richard J., et al. 1997. "HMOs, Moral Hazard and Cost Shifting in Workers Compensation." *Journal of Health and Economics* 16:191–206.

Clark, Geoffrey. 1999. *Betting on Lives.* Manchester: Manchester University Press.

Durkheim, Emile. 1933. *The Division of Labor in Society,* trans. G. Simpson. Glenroe, Ill.: Free Press.

Frankford, David. 1994. "Managing Medical Clinicians' Work through the Use of Financial Incentives." *Wake Forest Law Review* 29:71.

Goffman, Erving. 1961. *Asylums.* New York: Doubleday.

Hacking, Ian. 1975. *The Emergence of Probability: A Philosophical Study of Early Ideas about Probability, Induction and Statistics.* London: Cambridge University Press.

Hale, Robert. 1923. "Coercion and Distribution in a Supposedly Non-Coercive State." *Political Science Quarterly* 38:470.

Handler, Joel F., and Yeheskel Hasenfeld. 1991. *The Moral Construction of Poverty: Welfare Reform in America.* Newbury Park, Calif.: Sage.

Hart, H. L. A., and Tony Honoré. 1985. *Causation in the Law.* 2d ed. Oxford: Clarendon Press.

Heimer, Carol A. 1985. *Reactive Risk and Rational Action: Managing Moral Hazard in Insurance Contracts.* Berkeley: University of California Press.

Heimer, Carol A., and Lisa R. Staffen. 1998. *For the Sake of the Children: The Social Organization of Responsibility in the Hospital and the Home.* Chicago: University of Chicago Press.

Holland, Vicki. 1988. "Steps to Return to Work." *Risk Management* November: 25.

Hubbard, Elizabeth. 1997. "When Worlds Collide: The Intersection of Insurance and Motion Pictures." *Connecticut Insurance Law Journal* 3:267–304.

Isaacs, Nathan. 1939. "Contracts, Torts and Trusts." Vol. 6, pt. 1, p. 1 of *National Law Library,* ed. Roscoe Pound et al. New York: Collier.

Jacobi, John. 1997. "The Ends of Health Insurance." *University of California at Davis Law Review* 30:311–404.

McCluskey, Martha T. 1998. "The Illusion of Efficiency in Workers Compensation "Reform." *Rutgers Law Review* 50:657–941.

McKeon, Richard. 1957. "The Development and the Significance of the Concept of Responsibility." Reprinted in Richard McKeon, *Freedom and History and Other Essays* (Chicago: University of Chicago Press, 1990).

Nietzsche, Friedrich. 1967. *On the Genealogy of Morals,* essay 2, sections 1–2, trans. W. Kaufmann and Hollingdale. New York: Random House.

O'Malley, Pat. 1991. "Legal Networks and Domestic Security." *Studies in Law, Policy and Society* 11:171–99.

Pearson, Robin. 1990. "Thrift or Dissipation: The Business of Life Insurance in the Early Nineteenth Century." *Economic History* 43:236.

Rothschild, Michael, and Joseph Stiglitz. 1976. "Equilibrium in Competitive Insurance Markets: An Essay on the Economics of Imperfect Information." *Quarterly Journal of Economics* 90:629.

Sage, W. M. 1997. "Enterprise Liability and the Emerging Managed Health Care System." *Law and Contemporary Problems* 60 (2): 159–210.

Simon, Jonathan. 1988. "The Ideological Effects of Actuarial Practices." *Law and Society Review* 22:772–800.

Smith, Barry D., James S. Trieschman, Eric A. Wiening. 1987. *Property & Liability Insurance Principles.* Malvern, Penn.: Insurance Institute of America.

Squires, Gregory, ed. 1997. *Insurance Redlining.* Washington, D.C.: Urban Institute Press.

Stone, Deborah. 1993. "The Struggle for the Soul of Health Insurance." *Journal of Health, Politics, Policy and Law* 18:287–317.

Vogel, Frank E., and Samuel L. Hayes III. 1998. *Islamic Law and Finance: Religions, Risk and Return.* Boston: Kluwer Law International.

Zelizer, Viviana. 1979. *Morals and Markets: The Development of Life Insurance in the United States.* New York: Columbia University Press.

Beyond Moral Hazard: Insurance as Moral Opportunity

Deborah Stone

A basic dictum about insurance is that it does not change the probability of an adverse event—it can only mitigate the financial consequences of the event. However, a long and influential tradition of economic thought holds that insurance may indeed change the likelihood of adverse events through a phenomenon known as "moral hazard" (Baker 1996; Heimer 1985). According to the moral hazard argument, insurance actually increases the occurrence of adverse events through its incentives to people who have insurance. When people are insured (the argument goes), they are less careful to avoid or prevent accidents, diseases, thefts and other losses, and thus insurance indirectly increases the number of losses. Insurance also operates directly to increase adverse events by giving insured people an incentive to bring about the very harms and damages for which they are insured so they can collect financial proceeds. In this view, insurance works like a pawnshop; it enables people to get cash for their possessions.

In this essay, I turn both parts of the conventional wisdom upside down. I argue that insurance *does* change the likelihood of adverse events, but not through its influence on individual behavior. Rather, through its effects on political culture and collective political action, insurance increases the number and kinds of events that we consider adverse and worthy of collective responsibility. Insurance thus has an inherent expansionary dynamic: insurance tends to beget more insurance.

At first blush, this argument may seem to be just a variant of the moral hazard argument, so I want to make three important distinctions. First, the moral hazard argument holds that insurance creates *individual incentives* at least to be lax about avoiding harms and maybe even actively to cause them. Moral hazard works through the individual psyche. By contrast, I argue that insurance creates *social mechanisms* that tend to increase what gets perceived as insurable and deserving of collective support. Both phenomena could be said to lead to an increasing reliance on insurance, but I argue that complex institutional and cultural forces, rather than simple rational calculations by individuals, are the engines driving this expansion.

Second, the moral hazard argument regards the kind of individual behavior it describes as immoral—hence the name. Insurance creates a temptation into evil, though evil runs the gamut from mere carelessness and indifference through intentional failure to prevent loss, all the way to deliberate and active destruction. In the literature of insurance and economics, moral hazard is sometimes treated as a matter of "bad character," and sometimes as a matter of rational decisionmaking in response to incentives, and presumably therefore morally neutral (Heimer 1985). However, even when economists describe moral hazard as a phenomenon of purely rational behavior, there is usually a pejorative undertone. After all, rational behavior is always self-interested, so even this form of moral hazard is motivated by greed, selfishness, and personal gain at the expense of others. In short, moral hazard describes immoral motives.

In contrast, I believe the act of participating in insurance can be and often is a highly moral choice, because (following another long line of thought) insurance is a form of mutual aid and collective responsibility (Stone 1993). To participate in a risk-pooling scheme is to agree to tax yourself not only for your own benefit should you incur a loss, but also for the benefit of others who might suffer from loss when you do not. Insurance thus creates what might be called "moral opportunity," the opportunity to cooperate with and help others. The political mechanisms of insurance expansion I describe call forth moral motives—motives of charity, compassion, civic responsibility, and justice.

Third, the moral hazard argument is often used to denigrate the value of insurance as a social institution and to limit its development. The argument is a form of conservative, anti-reform, anti-redistributive thinking that economist Albert Hirschman (1991) dubbed "the perversity thesis." In this form of argument, opponents of a reform claim that although the reform is intended to ameliorate a social problem, it will in fact make the problem worse. Insurers, of course, promote the social value of insurance, but they too use the idea of moral hazard to justify limits on the amounts and conditions of coverage they offer, the kinds of people and risks they are willing to insure, and the amount of cross-subsidy they build into their pricing (Heimer 1985; Baker 1996). Many economists and policy analysts use the concept of moral hazard to argue against broad social provisions of insurance and any kind of assistance to the needy (Epstein 1997a, 1997b). The general lesson of moral hazard, as Tom Baker has shown (1996: 238–40), is "less is more": less insurance and less social assistance mean more security, welfare, safety, productivity, well-being, and general social good.

By contrast, I see the expansionary effect of insurance as a social welfare gain rather than a loss. The social and political dynamic I describe fosters social policies that improve both the well-being of individual citizens and the democratic health of the polity. Insurance is one of the principal mechanisms by which modern societies define problems as amenable to human agency and collective action. It is not only an institution of repair, but also of social progress, and is a major way for communities to make life better for their individual members.

Much could be said about the empirical and normative validity of the moral hazard argument, but the purpose of this essay is not to analyze moral hazard. Instead, I ask why insurance, once introduced, has a tendency to expand in society. What mechanisms operate to enlarge the range of different kinds of losses that people believe *ought* to be brought under the umbrella of insurance? This essay explores six mechanisms underlying the expansionary dynamic I call the "moral opportunity" of insurance.

Insurance as a Forum for Discourse about Mutual Aid

Political institutions resolve conflicts and make policies, but they also play another more fundamental role. They shape public discourse about deep moral questions: What is justice? What is fairness? What causes bad or harmful events? What kinds of detriments are "natural"—what we call accidents of nature, God, or fate—and what kinds are humanly caused or at least humanly preventable?

Insurance is a social institution that particularly invites moral contemplation about suffering, compassion, and responsibility. In so doing, it enlarges the public conception of social responsibility. Insurance serves as an arena for this kind of reflection and deliberation because it is kept in the public consciousness by the private marketing activities of commercial insurers, the bargaining activities of unions and workplaces, and the public debates over social insurance. The basic premise of insurance is collective responsibility for harms that befall individuals, because insurance pools people's savings to pay for individuals' future losses (Jerry 1996:17). Thus whenever insurance is discussed, questions of allocating responsibility between individuals and society are barely beneath the surface (Baker, chapter 2 this volume).

Much of the collective nature of insurance is disguised, or at least not readily obvious to the policyholders, especially in private insurance (Stone 1994:19). Unlike the fraternal organizations and mutual aid societies of the late nineteenth and early twentieth centuries, the modern insurance company is so huge that individuals rarely have any face-to-face contact with managers and virtually never have any contact with other policyholders. Much like transformations elsewhere in American civic life (Skocpol 1999), insurance organizations are no longer primarily membership associations where people actually interact and work toward common goals. They are instead highly centralized and professionally managed bureaucracies that provide no opportunity to get to know and cooperate with one's fellow citizens.

Nevertheless, several factors highlight the collective, mutual-aid aspects of insurance and promote conversation about the contours of moral responsibility in a community. Private insurers market their policies chiefly by trying to induce a sense of vulnerability in their target audiences. Therefore, much insurance advertising portrays or alludes to some kind of terrible harm that can befall people. For example, Blue Cross/Blue Shield ran a series of advertisements for health insurance with the theme of "What if?" One ad in the series pictures the face of a middle-aged woman, surrounded by smaller images of problems, as if she were imagining each of them in a cartoon bubble. Each image has a "What if?" caption, such as "What if I need a new heart?" or "What if I get sick when I'm away on business?" (Blue Cross/Blue Shield 1996b). Another ad in the same series pictures a man, presumably an executive, asking "What if I want low premiums?" and "What if our welder needs prenatal care?" (Blue Cross/Blue Shield 1996a). An Equitable advertisement for life insurance aimed at healthy older people pictures a couple standing on a beach, dressed for rugged weather. The caption reads: "We can finally be relaxed about life. But can you ever be relaxed about money?" (Equitable 1996). One Allstate advertisement pictures a lone house struck by a giant lightning bolt (Allstate 1997); another features an ambulance speeding down a highway late at night, with the caption, "Who's picking your kid up after the prom?" (Allstate 1999). An AIG advertisement for commercial insurance pictures a disheveled, worried man behind bars; the large caption reads, "Your foreign export manager is in a foreign jail. No one knows where. Or Why? . . . Who Insures You?" (AIG 1999b). This advertisement is one of a series, all featuring a story in which a business experiences some unanticipated trouble. In another ad of the series, a construction worker is lying on the ground holding his head. The text reads: "On time. On budget. Then the crane collapsed. Who Insures You?" (AIG 1999a).

This kind of advertising that highlights vulnerability has several subtexts. It is designed to make people feel they need help even if they are perfectly fine. It tells people that even when we think we are self-sufficient, strong, and successful, we are vulnerable to severe harms and losses, and we need to line up help while we still can.

Another implicit but very important message of these advertisements is that insurance is a helping institution—it will be there when you need it, and it is a reliable and effective place to turn for help (Baker 1994). For example, the text of the AIG ad with the executive in prison reads: "You sent him halfway around the world to mine opportunity. He's a valuable employee. He's in trouble. What should you do? Do you know the laws? The culture? The courts? . . . [W]e have people who bring a local understanding to your business, who grasp the intricacies of a foreign culture, who can negotiate foreign law" (AIG 1999b). Indeed, many insurance advertisements explicitly portray their company's main purpose as helping people. In 1993, CIGNA adopted the motto "a business of caring" (CIGNA 1993). Some advertisements for its property and casualty, international, and personal lines feature the word *Help* in large print over photographs of people giving help.[1] An advertisement for long-term care insurance suggests that the company is like a warm, nurturing grandmother. It pictures a classic grandmotherly woman in a printed house dress, sitting at her kitchen table, peering out over her reading glasses and stirring a cup of tea. The text alongside reads, "If you think she was overprotective, you should see our long-term care insurance" (CIGNA 1993). An advertisement for Prudential Insurance Company tells overwhelmed young parents that the company can help them get through parenthood (Prudential 1994).

Still another message of insurance marketing is that it is legitimate to need and get help in many situations and that insurance is a form of help that does not rob you of your dignity and independence. That message is explicit in an advertisement of Lincoln Financial Group showing a young man kayaking in the wilderness: "I have a MOTHER. I have a FATHER. I even have a BIG BROTHER. I DON'T need someone else looking out for me. I NEED someone who can help me look out for myself" (Lincoln Financial Group 1999). An ad for The Hartford shows a young woman in a wheelchair, dressed in hiking gear. She has just wheeled across a wooden bridge over a river rapids, and is holding her arms outstretched, embracing the joy of the outdoors. The text reads: "Careers happen. Accidents happen. Second careers happen.

Life happens," and goes on to say the company offers programs to "help you take on what life has to offer" and to "help people get back to work again" (Hartford 1997).

This last message is particularly important, since so much of American political culture valorizes independence and self-sufficiency and teaches that needing and accepting help is shameful (Fraser and Gordon 1994). Insurance, even private insurance for businesses and for professional, well-off classes, legitimates the very idea of help and mutual interdependence. The insurance industry's need to expand their markets is, subtly, a strong cultural force inculcating the value of mutual aid.

Insurance's legitimization of mutual aid and dependence is not unambiguous, however. Most insurance marketing is aimed at elites: those at the upper end of the income and status scales are encouraged to lean on others through insurance, while the poor are told that needing and getting assistance is shameful and degrading (McCluskey 2001). Moreover, insurance legitimates the idea of help in part because we construct it as "self-help," distinct from welfare and other means-tested assistance, which we construct as "handouts" and "dependence" (Fraser and Gordon 1994). For example, many insurers market life insurance by appealing to a professional man's or woman's obligation to provide for his or her family. A long-running advertisement series by Massachusetts Mutual Life Insurance Company ("Mass-Mutual") typically lists three poignant promises the parent makes to his or her child—for example, "A promise never to say, 'Chris, I mean Bobby, I mean Tim.' A promise matching sailor suits will never come near your closet. A promise to be there for you. And you. And you" (MassMutual 1992a). The tag line of these ads is "MassMutual—We help you keep your promises." One message of such advertisements is that each person is no longer responsible for the economic well-being of his or her own nuclear family. Nothing in these promises, or in most life insurance advertising, suggests that one is responsible for the well-being of one's friends and neighbors, much less one's larger social community or those less fortunate.

Yet even the family-responsibility theme so prevalent in life insurance advertising promotes a message of altruism. Solomon Huebner, perhaps the leading and most influential scholar of life insurance in the first half of the twentieth century, framed life insurance as an act of altruism and a moral obligation. "Failure of a head of family to insure his life . . . amounts to gambling . . . and the gamble is a particularly mean one since in case of loss, the dependent family and not the gambler must suffer the consequences" (Huebner [1915] 1935:15). "Emphasis should be laid on the 'crime of not insuring,' and the finger of scorn should be pointed at any man who, although he has provided well while he was alive, has not seen fit to discount the uncertain future for the benefit of a dependent household" (id. at 26, emphasis added). Huebner, in essence, reversed the moral hazard argument: the moral wrong of insurance consisted not in the temptation to bad behavior created by insurance, but rather in the temptation to avoid insurance and squander one's money on immediate pleasures.

In contemporary marketing, life insurance is still often portrayed as a way of meeting one's family obligations and even as a way of strengthening family ties. "Another way to say 'I love you' is with good insurance protection," declares one of the Metropolitan Life Insurance Company ads, showing Lucy (from Charles Schulz's *Peanuts* comic strip) knitting a pair of baby booties (Metropolitan 1998). Husbands and fathers, and more recently wives and mothers, are exhorted to provide for their loved ones if they should die. "Life insurance isn't for the people who die. It's for the people who live," explains an advertisement sponsored by the Life and Health Insurance Foundation for Education (Life and Health 1999). The MassMutual series mentioned above extols the role of "promises" in maintaining social cohesion (MassMutual 1992b). Each MassMutual ad, no matter what the specific family situation and promise it portrays, concludes: "Nothing binds us one to the other like a promise kept. Nothing divides us like a promise broken. At MassMutual we believe in keeping our promises. That way all the families and businesses that rely on us can keep theirs."

Thus private insurance marketing is a cultural force that legitimates social obligation and mutual aid. To be sure, it also weaves in a strong strand of individual responsibility and self-help (Lincoln Financial Group 1999). For example, a Prudential advertisement extols self-reliance with the motto "Be Your Own Rock" and a genial-looking man saying, "I worked long hours. I never turned down overtime. And I invested in the future. I want my children to remember me as the man who sort of inspired them to stand on their own two feet" (Prudential 1996). Nevertheless, the subtexts of insurance advertising necessarily legitimate help, portray insurance as a helping institution, and teach the virtue of providing assistance to others. Thus, the Prudential ad, after encouraging the reader to "be your own rock," says that Prudential offers a variety of products that "can *help you* manage your life" (emphasis added).

Social insurance plays a similar role in legitimating collective responsibility and mutual aid, though there are big differences in how legitimation occurs and in the relative emphases on the themes of self-help and helping others. Importantly, American social policy is molded on an insurance model. As Jonathan Simon and others have argued, the replacement of tort liability with insurance (workers compensation) as a regime for governing work accidents in the early twentieth century became the "blueprint for the governing of mature industrial society" (Simon 1997–98:524). According to some scholars, the American welfare state should really be known as an "insurance-opportunity state" (Marmor, Mashaw, and Harvey 1990) or a "security state" (Moss 1996:4) because its overwhelming mode of providing for citizens' well-being is through insurance programs rather than through means-tested assistance programs. As David Moss notes, workers' compensation, unemployment insurance, old age and disability insurance "have much more in common with deposit insurance and pension insurance" than they do with Aid to Families with Dependent Children, the archetypal welfare program. Insurance has a different purpose and targets a different population than welfare. The goal of insurance is to "offer security to individuals who have something to lose [e.g., a job, savings, earning potential] rather than assistance to the needy, who have little or nothing to lose" (id.).

One measure of the importance of insurance in social policy is the fact that public spending on social insurance is about two-and-a-half times spending on assistance (id. at 179). Another measure is that private insurance analogies were central to the design, promotion, and ultimate passage of New Deal social insurance (Cates 1983), and the imagery of personal contributions, individual accounts, and earned entitlements is crucial to the vigorous public support Social Security programs continue to enjoy in the face of strong efforts to scale them back. Through these analogies, social insurance, like private, is cast as "self-help," as providing for oneself and one's family by contributing to insurance while one is working (id. at 57). Even though beneficiaries' payments into the system rarely, if ever, cover the costs of their benefits, there is a widely sustained public belief that social insurance benefits are earned and are not "handouts."

Even while proponents of social insurance portray it as self-help, however, they, like the marketers of private insurance, inevitably rely on and appeal to notions of altruism, collective responsibility, and mutual aid. Just as early promoters of private life insurance had to overcome the stigma of insurance as gambling and the fear that insurance would tempt people into irresponsible dependence (Clark 2000; Zelizer 1979), early advocates of social insurance had to overcome the stigma of social insurance as the paternalistic invention of an autocratic state (Germany) and the fear that social insurance would undermine workers' initiative, effort, and productivity (Lubove 1968). Old-age pensions, warned Prudential Life Insurance Company's chief actuary, by removing the prospect of poverty in old age, would abolish "the most powerful incentive which makes for character and growth in a democracy" and strike a blow at the "root of national life and character" (Hoffman 1909:368, 389).

In promoting social insurance, the early advocates set forth two arguments that continue to undergird social insurance today. First was the argument that industrial society creates risks that the individual cannot possibly ameliorate or compensate for himself. If the individual cannot mitigate these risks, then he cannot and should not be held responsible for them (Eastman [1910] 1969). Isaac Rubinow, one of the leading Progressive social insurance advocates, set forth this argument in his 1913 classic book, *Social Insurance:* "For social insurance, when properly developed, is nothing if not a well-defined effort of the organized state to come to the assistance of the wage-earner and furnish him with something he individually is quite unable to attain for himself." Social insurance, he said, represented "a new concept of the state as an instrument of organized collective action, rather than of class oppression" (Rubinow [1913] 1969:500). The paternalistic and authoritarian state became the ethical and rational state.

Second was the argument that social insurance, properly structured, far from inducing people to be lazy, careless, or dependent, could actually motivate them to be careful and enable them to work (Moss 1996:60–61). John Commons, who might be considered the intellectual father of social insurance, put it thus: "I wanted all employers to be compelled by law to pay accident compensation as an inducement to accident prevention" (Commons 1934:141). These early proponents believed that individual workers did not have the ability to prevent the common hazards of industrial economies—work accidents and injuries, involuntary unemployment, and sickness—but that employers *did* have it within their powers to prevent many of these ills. As David Moss says, they reasoned that "an employer required to compensate all workers who were injured on the job, fell sick, or were laid off would take great pains to prevent the occurrence of such contingencies" (Moss 1996:60–61).

Just as Solomon Huebner flipped the moral argument in life insurance, casting as morally suspect the person who failed to buy insurance rather than the one who did buy it, early social insurance advocates flipped the moral argument as well. Opponents of social insurance (and of public charitable aid more generally) typically depicted the poor and needy as "social dependents" or "social parasites," and worried that the mere prospect of aid would induce even the working poor into lazy reliance on aid, thus dragging them down into pauperism. The advocates, instead, cast those who resisted social insurance as the real social parasites: "[A] business which does not make good, as far as indemnity in money can do it, the losses of human energy as well as of broken and worn out machinery, is parasitic and socially bankrupt," wrote Charles Henderson (1909:243–44), another leading figure of the social insurance movement.

One could trace similar themes in the discussion of most new forms of social and private insurance. The important point is that in promoting either private or social insurance, advocates frame it as a legitimate helping institution. Of course, marketing, promotion, and advocacy serve the direct purposes of those who conduct these activities, but indirectly they also serve as a kind of moral education of the citizenry.

Insurance as a Norm Giver

The existence of insurance as a fundamental and ubiquitous aspect of both commercial and personal life means that an organized system of help is also something people take for granted, even if they do not think terribly hard about or even understand the way insurance is organized. Social insurance programs—workers compensation, old age, survivors, and disability insurance—because they are government-run, have an *obvious* public character and appear transparently as communal forms of assistance. Private insurance, especially those segments that are marketed and organized as individual policies instead of group policies, may appear more as bilateral market contracts rather than any kind of community-sponsored aid system. But even the marketing of private insurance emphasizes to consumers that in buying insurance, they are buying the promise of help from a large organization with the fiscal capacity to remedy even huge losses (Baker 1994).

Perhaps the aspect of insurance that most strongly establishes a public expectation of community aid is liability or "third-party" insurance, that is, insurance that one party carries for the express purpose of paying for injuries and losses that he or she causes to others. In life insurance, most property insurance, or the old-age, medical care, and disability components of Social Security, people contribute to insurance in order to protect themselves and their families. In third-party coverage, they purchase insurance for the express benefit of strangers—anyone who might happen to be injured by the insured's activities. Of course, liability coverage protects the insured person against financial loss from adverse tort judgments, and in that sense, third-party insurance is self-protection. But third-party insurance can also be seen as a way of organizing and ensuring responsibility to others. Liability in the absence of insurance would mean that many people would be unable to pay the full costs of damage awards against them, so that their responsibility would be formal but hollow. Liability insurance, especially when it is mandatory, is thus a social mechanism for enforcing common-law obligations to others.

Workers compensation was the first such insurance, and it spread rapidly as a social innovation in the period from 1910 to 1920 (Witt 1998:1467). Workers compensation replaced an uncertain regime of tort liability for workplace accidents with a regime in which employers were made financially responsible for their employees' injuries and medical costs (Friedman and Ladinsky 1967:71). Crucially for my argument, workers compensation was, and often still is, justified as a moral obligation of one powerful and financially strong sector (employers) to help a less powerful and financially weaker sector (workers) through the intermediate institution of insurance (McCluskey 1998). Workers compensation set forth a model of social relations in which certain hazards of modernity were deemed to be beyond the control of individuals, while the activities in which these hazards occurred—in this case, factory work—were considered eminently beneficial to society. The solution was to establish a system of compulsory insurance by which the costs of losses could be spread among the larger society that benefited from the activities that produced the losses. At the same time, the people who suffered losses in the course of socially beneficial activities would be helped by the community they had served (Moss 1996).

This model of insurance as a system to underwrite the unavoidable costs of socially worthy activities and to share the losses had an enormous impact on American governance. Most notably, insurance came to be regarded as an alternative to other forms of regulating hazardous activities (Simon 1997–98:563–67).

Insurance is a form of what Foucauldian scholars call "discipline," that is, a system of inculcating norms, supervising behavior, and enforcing compliance with norms (Foucault 1995; Simon 1988). Those who view insurance through the lens of moral hazard do not see this disciplinary or regulatory power. Indeed, they see insurance as undermining individual self-restraint and even inciting people to destructive behavior. Thus, for example, in early debates about making liability insurance compulsory for automobile owners, opponents claimed that insurance stimulated irresponsible behavior (Simon 1997–98:566). It would be an inducement to fraudulent claims and malingering, and worse, it would insulate drivers from the costs of their carelessness and thus give them "licenses to do harm with impunity." Proponents of mandatory automobile liability insurance viewed the same situation through the lens of moral opportunity. Mandatory insurance, they believed, was a way of inculcating a sense of responsibility toward others, teaching the importance of careful driving, and compelling automobile owners to assume financial responsibility for the consequences of their driving (id. at 565–66, 584).

Even though the early proposal for mandatory automobile liability insurance failed on a national scale, most states now require car owners to carry liability insurance (Rice 1998:1134). Every time a person buys and registers a car, he or she has an encounter with a state agency that, by insisting on proof of insurance, teaches a moral lesson about mutual aid: you may not drive your car unless you participate in a system of helping people who might be injured by your car. At the same time, the car registrant absorbs another lesson: if you are injured by anyone else's automobile, you have a right to expect help from that person through his or her insurance. These are potent lessons about interdependence and reciprocal obligation.

Because virtually every adult citizen participates in various forms of mandatory insurance, from automobile liability insurance to unemployment insurance, old-age pensions, and disability insurance, everyone is exposed to two of the moral assumptions of these programs: collective responsibility for the well-being of individuals and individual responsibility for the well-being of others. Not everyone accepts these norms—many would opt out of some mandatory insurance if they could, and many scholars and policymakers, believing that individuals should be responsible for themselves, think insurance should never be mandatory (Epstein 1997b; Skidmore 1999). Nevertheless, insurance is deeply embedded in the social ordering of modern society and citizens cannot escape its implicit moral lessons, no matter how much they chafe under mandatory participation.

Insurance as a Standard Setter

Insurance often pays for services to alleviate harms, rather than paying cash to compensate for losses. By funding services, it stimulates the development of harm-alleviating technologies and occupations that then become part of the societal standard of care. Once these technologies and services are part of the societal standard of care, they also may come to be seen as legitimate, if not morally essential, collective aid. Lack of the services necessary to provide the standard of care then becomes, in effect, an adverse event against which people believe they are, or ought to be, insured.

This process is most evident in health insurance. Simply by paying for medical care, insurance stimulates the development of medicine because it directs financial resources to that sector. Arguably, the modern hospital is a creature of health insurance (Starr 1982:290–334). But insurance also fosters medical innovation more directly: insofar as Medicare includes reimbursement for medical training and research as components of its pay-ments for patients, it stimulates innovation. And insofar as any health in-surance pays for patients to receive treatment through clinical research trials, it pays for innovation (Rosenblatt, Law, and Rosenbaum 1997:211–15, 534–41).

In-hospital births illustrate how insurance coverage creates a new stan-dard of care that then becomes an object of political demand. Health insur-ance made in-hospital births possible for most women; without health in-surance, births never would have moved to the hospital because most families could not have afforded the cost (Leavitt 1986). With the growth of maternity coverage, in-hospital births became standard medical practice, and indeed, births at home came to be regarded as dangerous and medically substandard. This coverage led women (and their husbands and doctors) to expect a few nights in the hospital following childbirth. When, in the 1990s, managed care plans restricted payments for overnight stays and "kicked mothers out" (as was the perception of many), there was such a public out-cry that many states, and eventually Congress, legislated mandatory cover-age of at least forty-eight hours in the hospital for new mothers in the New-borns' and Mothers Health Protection Act of 1996 (Seaman 1997:499; Freudenheim 1996:A1).

Bone marrow transplants for women with breast cancer illustrate an even more complex set of political dynamics by which insurance can ex-pand the public understanding and organizational practice surrounding a standard of care (Rosenblatt, Law, and Rosenbaum 1997:281–82). We might hypothesize a social process something like this: physicians and clinical re-searchers develop a new treatment protocol and begin to use it. The new treatment is still experimental and yet to be proven effective, but more and more doctors begin to offer it to their terminally ill patients, as it offers some hope. Some insurance companies and plans agree to cover the treat-ment for their policyholders, and others deny coverage. Through the posi-tive coverage decisions of some insurers, the treatment becomes more com-mon, stimulating greater demand for it. Patients whose insurers deny coverage sue their insurers (or their families sue after they die). Through re-ports in the media, the suits create public awareness of the treatment and the controversy, and adverse publicity for insurers. As more plaintiffs are successful, insurers become fearful of future litigation should they deny coverage for the treatment. They begin to cover the treatment for more and more patients. Gradually, the new treatment, still unproven in scientific studies, becomes standard practice.

A General Accounting Office (GAO) study of insurance coverage of bone marrow transplants for breast cancer suggests that a scenario quite like the one just sketched does in fact operate. The GAO interviewed medical directors or other officials responsible for coverage decisions in twelve large, national health insurance companies. All said that they did not normally cover experimental or unproven treatments, that they believed bone marrow transplants for breast cancer were still unproven, but that they nonetheless covered this treatment. To explain this discrepancy, the insurers said the primary influence on their decisions to cover the treatment was the fact that the treatment was already widely used and there was suggestive evidence that it might also be beneficial to patients. The insurers also said the threat of litigation and the adverse publicity about their coverage policies were also very important factors in their decisions to cover the treatment (GAO 1996). One highly publicized suit, *Fox v. Health Net of California*, 29 Trials Digest 54 (Cal. Super. Ct., 1993), was particularly damaging and threatening to insurers, they said, because it focused on the insurer's economic self-interest as the reason for denial.. The case also received wide publicity because the jury awarded an $89 million verdict to the plaintiff (GAO 1996).

The political dynamic for expanding insurance coverage often does not stop even once major insurers begin to cover the treatment. The publicity surrounding coverage denials, deaths, suits, and plaintiffs' victories stirs public outrage and fuels activist mobilization. Popular culture can vastly amplify widespread media coverage of insurance coverage controversies, as evidenced in John Grisham's 1995 novel *The Rainmaker*, the story of a young lawyer who helps a family fight their health insurer to cover a bone marrow transplant for their dying son. As happens frequently in health insurance, advocacy groups for a particular disease or treatment propose state legislation to require insurers to cover their disease or particular treatments. In the case of bone marrow transplants for breast cancer, by 1995 seven states had enacted such mandates (GAO 1996:11). Sometimes these state-level populist movements rise to the national level, where advocates seek federal legislation to universalize the benefits they have won in some states (Tumulty 1988:28–32; Morone 1999; Sorian and Feder 1999). The expansion of state-level mandates for forty-eight-hour maternity coverage to federal legislation exemplifies this phenomenon.

The expansionary dynamic has still another phase. Once insurance coverage for a new treatment becomes relatively standard, even though the treatment itself may still be unproven and may be highly aggressive and risky to the patient, the very existence of insurance coverage may "normalize" the treatment. Insurance coverage, particularly state mandates requiring health insurers to cover a treatment, can subtly impose a moral pressure on people who have a disease or problem for which a treatment is covered. They might be pressured by their doctors, families, and friends to "try anything" as long as money is not an obstacle, to be "good patients," to use every available means to fight the disease, to stay in the battle until the end. Not accepting treatment that insurance would cover becomes defined as personal failure (Britt 1999:58–78).

Still another mechanism of enlarging the concept of insurable adverse events is far broader and more elusive than the redefinition of standards of care and well-being according to evolving technologies. Insurance and the remedial services it provides can change the cultural meaning of an entire social concept. For example, in thirty years of providing medical services for the elderly, a panel of the National Academy of Social Insurance wrote, "Medicare has helped to redefine the normal expectation of aging in America as a dignified, actively independent stage of life . . . rather than economically deprived dependency" (National Academy of Social Insurance 1999). By financing medical care as well as health services in nursing homes and private homes, Medicare essentially did away with the poor houses of yore (though some might say many nursing homes are the modern-day equivalent) (Rollins 1994; Vladeck 1980).

Home health services in particular have created an expectation that even people who need help with basic tasks of daily living—such as bathing, dressing, or eating—can aspire to remain in their own homes. Home health services were fostered by Medicare because they are cheaper than either nursing homes or hospitals (Szasz 1990:194–97). But in promoting these services and in denying hospital coverage, Medicare touted the advantages of remaining independent and staying in one's own home and community. These are goals to which most elderly people aspire anyway; being forced into a nursing home is often feared by the elderly as the worst possible fate. So when Congress tries to cut back home health benefits, as it did in the 1997 Balanced Budget Act, there is new political resistance and a heightened sense that going to a nursing home is an adverse event against which Medicare should insure.

To summarize, much of insurance, private and social, now provides services instead of or in addition to income to alleviate the consequences of adverse events. The perceived entitlements are to services, not cash; or to put it another way, the absence of services becomes perceived as the adverse advent against which people think they are insured. These services also become part of the general social expectation about what ought to be insured. Thus insurance for services expands cultural perceptions of the basic standard of care and well-being and the professional standard of care. These expanded standards effectively expand the definition of perceived adverse events.

Insurance as an Instrument of Social Reform

Because insurance is constructed by its advocates (including insurers themselves) as a source of help for people in trouble, people turn to it when they need help. Susan Daniels says that while she was Associate Commissioner of Disability, she was always asked why so many people come to the Social Security Administration's disability programs looking for disability benefits. "Because we have money and they don't," she always quipped (1995). That is the story of insurance. It is, or at least appears to be, pots of money waiting to be spent on people who need it.

Of course, people seeking help from insurance must prove that they and their specific troubles are covered. Insurers have a strong interest in minimizing their claims payments, and so every claim becomes something of a contest between the two sides (Baker 1994). Insurance policies are virtually the national metaphor for fine-print specificity and trick exclusions in contractual relationships. Yet even though the cards seem to be stacked in favor of insurers, the contests between claimants and their insurers are two-sided, and claimants often win.

Claimants' power comes in no small part from the leverage of ambiguity: insurance contracts are written in words, and words can never cover every possible situation. Like all legal contests, disputes over coverage become a matter of interpretation and persuasion. People who stand to benefit from an expanded interpretation use grievances, administrative channels, lawsuits and appeals, and legislative politics to get their situations read or written into a verbal formula. Ultimately, these contests are conducted like other political contests—people organize, form alliances, draw new groups into the contest, and try to mobilize elite and popular support for their side (Schattschneider 1960). They use existing rules and programs as an entering wedge, and try to expand their turf, their power, their resources incrementally.

Workers compensation illustrates these mechanisms of expansion well. State workers compensation programs were founded on the image of industrial accidents and injuries. The dominant image was a physical injury caused by a one-time, sudden, discrete event in the workplace. From the beginning however, some advocates thought occupational diseases should be included, and eventually the definition of a compensable injury was broadened to include more diffuse physiological and mental illnesses that might occur gradually over decades. Hence workers compensation came to include diseases caused by toxic exposures, injuries caused by cumulative, repetitive motions, and mental diseases or stress disorders. Through a variety of political actions, including union-sponsored research and advocacy, individual and class-action suits, advocacy of the scientific community, and in some cases employer and insurer efforts to end tort liability for occupational disease, these new kinds of harms were incorporated within workers compensation as legitimate adverse events for which workers deserved and would receive collective assistance (McCluskey 1998:767–87).

The evolution of workers compensation presents a very different picture of insurance expansion than the moral hazard framework would suggest. In the moral hazard model, insurance growth is driven by individuals who are, in turn, induced by the possibility of material assistance to become needy (in the workers compensation example, they get careless on the job) or to see themselves (illegitimately) as deserving help they do not really need (McCluskey 1998:742–44). In the moral opportunity model, insurance growth is driven by collective political action, and comes about through coalitions of beneficiaries and advocates who change the cultural understanding of a problem and use judicial and legislative channels to restructure the rules of insurance.

Claimants and potential claimants are not the only interests who stand to gain from insurance expansion, and not the only political actors who seek its expansion. "Career altruists," people whose jobs are centrally about helping other people (doctors, nurses, other health workers, many plaintiffs' lawyers, many scientists and social scientists, social activists), regard insurance plans and programs as potential tools for helping their clients. Many of these people devote some of their energies to helping make their clients eligible for the collective aid available in insurance pools. And they do so by using their professional skills to demonstrate how new problems fit within the old rubrics of insurance. Those whose careers are dedicated to helping others will turn, as people in trouble themselves do, to the best available source of help, and that is frequently insurance. Only in the narrowest sense could these helping professions be said to act in their own self-interest as they try to expand insurance coverage. Expanded coverage may help them get paid for the services they provide or the jobs they do, but the essence of their work is helping others.

In sum, because insurance is culturally constructed as a helping institution, people who need help and people who are professional helpers look to insurance as a source of help. In asking for insurance to cover their losses, people in trouble are in essence asking a collectivity to make good on its promises. And in fighting for insurance coverage on behalf of clients or groups of citizens, advocates and reformers are seeking to enlarge the sphere of collective moral responsibility for the well-being of individual members of their community.

Insurance as a Political Mobilizer

Insurance coverage for new services and technologies stimulates development of occupations and industries based on those technologies. These occupations and industries then acquire a vested interest in preserving and expanding insurance coverage for the services and products they provide. Again, health insurance provides a good example. Congress, when it decided to expand Medicare coverage for home health care after 1980, created a new demand for home care and essentially capitalized the industry (Szasz 1990:194). Congress deliberately encouraged home care expansion as a way to stem Medicare's expenditures on hospital and nursing home care. In the 1980 Omnibus Budget Reconciliation Act, two changes stimulated the home care industry. First, the Act liberalized eligibility requirements for home care services and expanded the number of visits Medicare would cover. These changes in effect boosted market demand for home care. Second, the Act changed agency certification requirements to make it easier for proprietary (for-profit) home care agencies to provide services for Medicare clientele. The number of Medicare-certified agencies almost doubled between 1980 and 1985, and predictably Medicare's home health expenditures more than tripled in the same period (from $662 million to $2,233 million) (id. at 196). By 1995, Medicare had become the source of payment for almost half of all home care services, and Medicaid for another quarter (National Association for Home Care 1997:4).

By the mid-1990s, home health care had become the new "cost crisis" in health (Kenney and Moon 1997). But when, in 1997, the federal government tried to cut back home health expenditures, two obstacles arose: first, an industry of home health agencies with well-developed trade and lobbying organizations, and second, a public expectation that ongoing home health care for chronic problems is necessary to a decent standard of living. Both of these obstacles to retrenchment are creatures of the social insurance program itself.

The phenomenon of vested interests might seem to be a close cousin to moral hazard in the sense that occupation groups and industries come to rely on insurance, just as individuals are said to rely on their insurance coverage in deciding how careful to be. The two phenomena—moral hazard and vested interests—differ in important respects, however. In economic theory, moral hazard is a psychological construct that describes the way insurance affects individual thinking and behavior. Insurance is believed to encourage an insured person to behave in a way that creates a greater likelihood of loss and, eventually, of the person's making an insurance claim (Baker 1996; Heimer 1985). The pejorative overtones of moral hazard are clear: insurance (according to the theory) induces behavior that is less than virtuous; it brings out or encourages the weaker side of human character, notably a failure to act carefully and responsibly.

By contrast, the mechanism by which insurance creates vested interests is a social phenomenon. It concerns the way insurance affects group behavior and character. The effect of insurance on occupations and industries is mediated through markets rather than through the individual psyche. By paying for policyholders to receive goods and services, insurance effectively creates paying customers and economic demand. This demand in turn sustains growth of an occupation or industry; the industry's survival and people's jobs depend on the continued flow of insurance payments. There is nothing particularly moral or immoral about a firm's reliance on its customers or its sources of revenue. When an enterprise takes action to maintain its customers or to increase its sources of revenue, we do not think it is behaving "carelessly." On the contrary, it is acting carefully and judiciously.

Moreover, insofar as an industry's product or service is socially beneficial, the industry's political efforts to maintain or expand insurance coverage might well be seen as efforts to broaden the distribution of a socially valuable and worthwhile commodity. Of course, the moral assessment here is ambiguous, since the providers of insured goods and services obviously benefit directly from third-party revenue sources. Nevertheless, the fact that they get paid to provide socially beneficial goods and services does not obviate the contribution they make to collective well-being. It is in this sense that the phenomenon of vested interests in insurance exemplifies moral opportunity.

Insurance as Equalizer

Equality is one of the great rallying cries in American politics. It is perhaps the strongest and most effective way to cast political demands. Equality is not an objective criterion, but an interpretation of distributive justice that depends on particular definitions of what is being distributed and the identity of the relevant recipients (Stone 1997). Obviously, not all inequalities are remedied by insurance or by other political means. The inequalities that affect organized political constituencies are the most likely to be remedied, and likewise, constituencies are often organized by leaders who define and publicize some version of inequality, making it politically visible and intolerable.

Equality thus sometimes functions as a "meta value" that directs insurance programs to remedy certain inequalities in the distribution of the other things insurance covers. Insurance coverage of mental illness illustrates how the drive to equalize serves as an expansive force in insurance. Mental health advocates have successfully invoked equality to improve coverage of mental illness by calling for "parity" between mental and physical illness, and by using the language and symbolism of discrimination and disparate treatment to characterize insurance coverage of mental disease (Gold 1997–98:771–82). Advocates for parity are united under the umbrella of equality in the Coalition for Fairness in Mental Illness Coverage, which includes the National Alliance for the Mentally Ill (a patient organization) as well as several provider organizations such as the American Psychiatric Association and the National Association of Psychiatric Health Systems. The coalition has won federal legislation that prohibits employer-sponsored plans from capping mental health benefits at lower levels than physical health benefits (Gold 1997–98:775–87).

Equality is the key symbolic resource in this movement. Like almost every current insurance movement, the coalition includes itself as part of the broader civil rights movement by analogizing its demands to those of the black struggle against racial discrimination. The Coalition for Fairness in Mental Illness Coverage has called mental illness "the last bastion of open discrimination in health insurance in this country" (Gold 1997–98:775–76). At a White House conference on mental illness in 1999, Tipper Gore implicitly joined mental illness to the civil rights movement when she characterized it as "the last great stigma of the 20th century," and President Clinton tapped into the theme by exhorting, "It's high time our health plans treat all Americans equally" (Scharfstein and Satel 1999:A18).

A similar strategy is being pursued by women's health and reproductive rights advocates. They are calling for parity in insurance coverage of prescription contraceptives and publicizing the fact that most insurance plans that cover prescription drugs and devices do not cover contraceptives. These groups have also seized on some recent insurer decisions to cover Viagra (the anti-impotence drug for men) to exemplify the differential treatment of men's and women's sexual and reproductive medical needs (Kilborn 1998:A1). A state representative introduced a contraceptive parity bill in the Washington state legislature by asking, "Women pay for contraceptives and insurance companies pay for Viagra. What's wrong with this picture?" (*Seattle Post-Intelligencer* 1999:A1). Though federal legislation on this issue has stalled, many states are discussing legislation to require insurance plans to cover contraceptives if they cover other prescription drugs, and eleven states have passed such laws (Center for Reproductive Law and Policy 1999:2). "Parity" has become the insurance term-of-art for equality.

In addition to claiming equality in the coverage of similar kinds of losses, advocates might claim equal treatment of policyholders across different insurance plans. Advocates of broad federal regulation of managed care are using this strategy in the current congressional debates over what has come to be called a "Patient Bill of Rights." These (mostly Democratic) advocates criticize the Republican proposals for not granting the same protections to members of private insurance plans that they grant to members of employer-sponsored plans. Thus inequality among plans is another rallying cry for regulations that will liberalize and expand health insurance coverage (Mitchell 1999:A1).

Equality is also the major force for reform in property and casualty insurance. Under the banner of "redlining," homeowners' insurance, commercial insurance, and automobile insurance have all come under attack for their differential and disadvantageous treatment of low-income, inner-city communities and ethnic and racial minorities (Squires 1997). The term *redlining* comes from an old industry practice of drawing red lines on maps around geographic areas where the companies would not sell or write insurance. The term is now used metaphorically to mean any unfavorable treatment of applicants or policyholders on the basis of the economic, racial, or ethnic make-up of their neighborhood, and even more broadly to mean unfair discrimination on the basis of stereotypes. "Redlining" is now used as a pejorative epithet to describe insurer practices of charging higher rates to some policyholders than to others, refusing to insure some applicants altogether, or refusing to cover some kinds of losses. (Murray 1997–98:736, 743–56).

As in health insurance politics, housing and community development advocates have used the imagery and legal tools of the civil rights movement to expand access to insurance. Coalitions for "fair housing" or "fair insurance" portray insurance classification decisions as "discriminatory," based on stereotypes rather than objective, empirical data. They use disparate impact analysis from Title VII jurisprudence to litigate insurance claims under the Fair Housing Act (Murray 1997–98:761). In Massachusetts, the first state to pass a law prohibiting redlining in homeowners insurance, the insurance statute reads like a grand civil rights declaration, prohibiting discrimination against every imaginable social category: "No insurer licensed to write and engaged in the writing of homeowners insurance in this commonwealth ... shall take into consideration when deciding whether to provide, renew, or cancel homeowners insurance the race, color, religious creed, national origin, sex, age, ancestry, sexual orientation, children, marital status, veteran status, the receipt of public assistance or disability of the applicant or insured" (id., citing H. B. 5649, 1996 Reg. Sess. §3 (Mass. 1996)).

Political demands for equality in insurance challenge the fundamental principle of actuarial fairness upon which most insurance operates (Stone 1993, 1990). The most basic principle of insurance is risk classification. Insurers assess and classify risks in order to price coverage as closely as possible to the risk presented by an applicant—in other words, they seek to collect revenues from each policyholder that will cover the costs of that person's probable losses. In political contests over insurance, insurers usually argue that their practices of charging differential rates or excluding certain categories of people and losses are simply reflections of economic reality (Treaster 1996:D1, D6). The people who appear to be discriminated against are treated differently because they pose objectively greater risks of loss (Murray 1997–98:738).

If we were to interpret this broad expansionary movement in insurance through the lens of moral hazard, we might say that groups seeking coverage of their problems or seeking coverage on equal terms with other groups are pursuing their self-interest and exemplifying the moral hazard problem. They would happily transfer their personal responsibilities to the collective society, and the very prospect of insurance induces them to shed personal responsibility and rely on outside help instead.

The lens of moral opportunity, however, focuses the same movement differently. Those seeking insurance expansion are making the quintessential democratic claim: they are asserting their membership in a community, their right to representation in its collective decisions, and their right to equal treatment vis-à-vis other citizens. The community of insureds is a group of people who share risks and who put some of their resources at the disposal of the community for the purpose of helping individual members who suffer losses. Groups and their advocates who make claims for inclusion are asking to have their problems recognized by one of the most important institutions for providing security. When they seek various kinds of mandates that require insurers to treat them and their problems in certain ways, they are in effect asking for a permanent seat at the table of community governance. They are unwilling to let insurers decide who should be included in the collective mutual aid system that insurance represents.

They use democratic political channels to open up insurance decisions to broader participation. In this view, security and its pursuit are genuine matters of civil rights.

Conclusion

Economics is the dominant paradigm for analyzing insurance. Within that paradigm, all social processes are understood to be the aggregate result of individuals' rational, self-interested, interest-maximizing behavior. Insurance is seen as an institution that modifies the incentives facing individuals, and offers them possibilities of gain (or loss alleviation) without their having to bear the full cost of their gains. This opportunity to gain without paying the full price is thought to create a temptation to immoral behavior, known as moral hazard. Moral hazard is, in this paradigm, an inescapable effect of insurance, and it means that insurance slowly, constantly, and inevitably creates more reliance on insurance and therefore ever more insurance.

Political science offers a very different interpretation of the steady long-term growth of insurance in modern industrial societies. Insurance is a social institution that helps define norms and values in political culture, and ultimately shapes how citizens think about issues of membership, community, responsibility, and moral obligation. Insurance influences how individuals behave, not so much by dangling incentives in front of them one by one, but rather by offering arenas for collective moral deliberation and political action. Insurance may also be regarded as a system of governance, and controversies over the design and operation of insurance plans as political struggles over the allocation of power and resources. Like any political authority, an insurance organization appears to citizens as an authority with the power and resources to improve or worsen their lives.

I have identified five broad political mechanisms by which insurance expands to cover more kinds of problems and more groups of people in more kinds of mutual aid arrangements. First, because it is a system of collective risk sharing, insurance invites public discussion of the appropriate boundaries of individual and social responsibility. Wherever it operates, whether in the private or public sector, insurance perpetuates itself and ensures its survival in part by defending the legitimacy of mutual aid. Second, insurance teaches citizens that they have an obligation to help others and the right to receive aid when they suffer certain kinds of losses. Third, insurance funds the development of helping technologies, services, and occupations, which in turn creates new and enlarged societal standards of well-being that alter public ideas about what adverse events ought to be insured and what standards of life quality ought to be provided through insurance remedies. Fourth, insurance policies and regulations offer ambiguity as a political resource to three sets of political actors who all have stakes in the expansion of insurance: claimants who want help with new kinds of problems, career altruists who see insurance as a tool for helping their clients, and service providers who depend on insurance reimbursement for their revenues. Finally, because equality is an overarching value in American political culture, claims of inequality and discrimination are powerful political tools for groups seeking inclusion of themselves and their problems in insurance plans. American political culture almost defines inequality as an adverse event itself, something that must be remedied as soon as it is revealed.

A political paradigm enables a different normative interpretation of insurance expansion. In the moral hazard model, insurance leads the individual to engage in immoral behavior; in the moral opportunity model, insurance alters societal ideas about responsibility and obligation. If individuals come to believe that getting help for their problems is legitimate, they do so out of changed cultural perceptions about the causes and possible remedies for their problems, not out of a character weakness or an insufficient determination to be self-reliant. And when individuals who share common problems join together to seek help from private or public insurance plans, they are acting not as a band of brigands, raiding the common wealth for their narrow gains, but are acting the role of virtuous citizens, using democratic means to make their voices heard and their needs understood.

That we have insurance for more and more needs and that we expand the scope of public responsibility for many kinds of losses does not signal a moral decline in the citizenry, as opponents of insurance claim. Insurance growth is a social response to the Enlightenment faith that much of what happens to humans is not a matter of fate and that many of our problems are within our control.

NOTES

This essay originally appeared in *Connecticut Insurance Law Journal* 6, no. 1 (1999): 11–46, and is reprinted here by permission of *Connecticut Insurance Law Journal*.

1. For example, an ad for CIGNA Property and Casualty portrays a fireman covered with soot, and says "Fire Departments, Ambulances, Rescue Squads. . . . Do you ever wonder who protects them? (CIGNA 1997). An ad for CIGNA International shows apparently Asian men in hard hats crouched around some dangerous-looking industrial equipment, and says "Moving your business away from home opens a world of new opportunities. . . . CIGNA can help you feel like you're not so far from

home" (CIGNA 1997b). Also, an ad for CIGNA Group Insurance shows a man snuggling twin little girls, one in each arm, saying "You never thought you'd have kids. Now you have two. . . . Keeping [their future] safe is what CIGNA Group Insurance is about." (CIGNA 1996).

REFERENCES

1980 Omnibus Budget Reconciliation Act , Pub. L. No. 96–499, 94 Stat. 2599 (1996).

AIG. 1999a. "Crane" advertisement. *Atlantic Monthly*, October, 2–3.

———. 1999b. "Foreign Jail" advertisement. *Atlantic Monthly*, August, 2–3.

Allstate. 1997. "Ambulance" advertisement. *U.S. News & World Report*, 12 May, 26.

———. 1997. "Lightning" advertisement. *Business Week*, 12 May, 9.

Bailey, Herman T., Theodore M. Hutchinson, and Gregg R. Narber. 1976. "The Regulatory Challenge to Life Insurance Classification." *Drake Law Review* 25:779.

Baker, Tom. 1994. "Constructing the Insurance Relationship: Sales Stories, Claims Stories, and Insurance Contract Damages." *Texas Law Review* 72:1395.

———. 1996. "On the Genealogy of Moral Hazard." 75 *Texas Law Review* 237.

———. 1999. "Insurance, Risk & Responsibility: Toward a New Paradigm?" Paper read at University of Connecticut School of Law Symposium, 11–12 April, Hartford, Connecticut.

Blue Cross/Blue Shield. 1996a. "Low Premiums" advertisement. *Business Week*, 6 May, 21.

———. 1996b. "New Heart" advertisement. *Time*, 29 April, 104.

Britt, Elizabeth C. 1999. "Conceiving Normalcy: Law, Rhetoric, and the Double-Binds of Infertility." Unpublished manuscript on file with author.

Cates, Jerry. 1983. *Insuring Inequality*. Ann Arbor: University of Michigan Press.

Center for Reproductive Law and Policy. 1999. "Contraceptive Equity Bills Gain Momentum in State Legislatures." 30 September, 2.

CIGNA. 1993a. "Caring" advertisement. *U.S. News & World Report*, 11 October, 39.

———. 1993b. "Overprotective" advertisement. *National Underwriter*, 15 November, 9.

———. 1996. "Group" advertisement. *Inc.*, May, 19.

———. 1997a. "Fire" advertisement. *Inc.*, May, back cover.

———. 1997b. "International" advertisement. *U.S. News & World Report*, 19 May, back cover.

Clark, Geoffrey. 2000. "Reckoning with Death: Virtue, Gambling and Life Insurance in Eighteenth-Century England." Unpublished manuscript on file with the Law Library at the University of Connecticut School of Law, 48.

Commons, John R. 1934. *Myself*. New York: Macmillan. Quoted in David Moss, *Socializing Security: Progressive Era Economists and the Origins of American Social Policy* 69 (Cambridge: Harvard University Press, 1996).

Daniels, Susan. 1995. Telephone conversation with the author, 15 March.

Eastman, Crystal. [1910] 1969. *Work Accidents and the Law.* Reprint, New York: Arno Press.

Epstein, Richard A. 1997a. "Health Care Law Shows Big Government Lives." Letter to the editor. *New York Times,* 10 August.

———. 1997b. *Mortal Peril: Our Inalienable Right to Health Care.* Reading, Mass.: Addison-Wesley.

Equitable. 1996. "Relaxed" advertisement. *Newsweek,* 13 May, 48–49.

Foucault, Michel. 1995. *Discipline and Punish.* 2d ed. Translated by Alan Sheridan. New York: Vintage Books.

Fraser, Nancy, and Linda Gordon. 1994. "A Genealogy of Dependency: Tracing a Keyword of the U.S. Welfare State." *Signs* 19 (winter): 309–36.

Freudenheim, Milt. 1996. "HMO's Cope with a Backlash on Cost Cutting." *New York Times,* 19 May.

Friedman, Lawrence M., and Jack Ladinsky. 1967. "Social Change and the Law of Industrial Accidents." *Columbia Law Review* 67:50.

GAO. 1996. *Health Insurance Coverage of Autologous Bone Marrow Transplantation for Breast Cancer.* Washington, D.C.: GAO.

Gold, Maggie D. 1997–98. "Must Insurers Treat All Illnesses Equally?—Mental vs. Physical Illness." *Connecticut Insurance Law Journal* 4:767.

Grisham, John. 1995. *The Rainmaker.* New York: Doubleday.

Handler, Joel F., and Yeheskel Hasenfield. 1997. *We The Poor People: A Social History in Welfare in America.* New Haven: Yale University Press.

Hartford. 1997. "Life Happens" advertisement. *Inc.,* May, 30.

Heimer, Carol. 1985. *Reactive Risk and Rational Action: Managing Moral Hazard in Insurance Contracts.* Berkeley: University of California Press.

Henderson, Charles Richmond. 1909. *Industrial Insurance in the United States,* 244. Quoted in David Moss, *Socializing Security: Progressive Era Economists and the Origins of American Social Policy* 61–62 (Cambridge: Harvard University Press, 1996).

Hirschman, Albert O. 1991. *The Rhetoric of Reaction.* Cambridge: Harvard University Press, Belknap Press.

Hoffman, Frederick L. 1909. "State Pensions and Annuities in Old Age." *American Statistical Association* 11:363. Quoted in Roy Lubove, *The Struggle for Social Security, 1900–1935* at 117 (Cambridge: Harvard University Press, 1968).

Huebner, Solomon S. [1915] 1935. *Life Insurance.* 3d ed. Reprint, New York: Appleton.

Jerry, Robert H., II. 1996. *Understanding Insurance Law.* 2d ed. New York: Bender.

Kenney, Genevieve, and Marilyn Moon. 1997. *Reigning in the Growth in Home Health Services under Medicare.* New York: Commonwealth Fund.

Kilborn, Peter T. "Pressure Growing to Cover the Cost of Birth Control." *New York Times,* 2 August.

Leavitt, Judith Walzer. 1986. *Brought to Bed: Childbearing in America 1750–1950.* New York: Oxford University Press.

Life and Health. 1999. "Live" advertisement. *Newsweek,* 18 October, 58.

Lincoln Financial Group. 1999. "Need and Responsibility" advertisement. *Time*, 8 November, 82–83.

Lubove, Roy. 1968. *The Struggle for Social Security, 1900–1935*. Cambridge: Harvard University Press.

Marmor, Theodore R., Jerry L. Mashaw, and Philip L. Harvey. 1990. *America's Misunderstood Welfare State*. New York: Basic Books.

MassMutual 1992a. "Keeping Promises" advertisement. *Business Week*, 16 November, 122.

———. 1992b. "Promise" advertisement. *Family Fun*, November/December, 4–5.

McCluskey, Martha T. 1998. "The Illusion of Efficiency in Workers' Compensation 'Reform.'" *Rutgers Law Review* 50:657.

———. 2001. "Rhetoric of Risk and the Redistribution of Social Insurance." Chapter 7 this volume.

Metropolitan. 1998. « Lucy » advertisement. *Parents*, January, 222.

Mitchell, Alison. 1999. "Senate Approves Republican Plan for Health Care." *New York Times*, 16 July.

Morone, James A. 1999. "Populists in a Global Market." *Journal of Health Politics, Policy and Law* 24:887.

Moss, David. 1996. *Socializing Security: Progressive Era Economists and the Origins of American Social Policy*. Cambridge: Harvard University Press.

Murray, William E. 1997–98. "Homeowners Insurance Redlining: The Inadequacy of Federal Remedies and the Future of the Property Insurance War." *Connecticut Insurance Law Journal* 4:735.

National Academy of Social Insurance. 1999. *Medicare and the American Social Contract*. Washington, D.C.: National Academy of Social Insurance.

National Association for Home Care. 1997. *Basic Statistics about Home Care*. Washington, D.C.: National Association for Home Care.

Prudential. 1994. "Overwhelmed" advertisement. *Family Life*, March/April.

———. 1996. "Rock" advertisement. *U.S. News & World Report*, 6 May, 26.

Rice, Willy E. 1998. "Insurance Contracts and Judicial Discord over Whether Liability Insurers Must Defend Insureds' Allegedly Intentional and Immoral Conduct: A Historical and Empirical Review of Federal and State Courts' Declaratory Judgments—1900–1997." *American University Law Review* 47:1131.

Rollins, Mary Richards. 1994. *Patients, Pain and Politics: Nursing Home Inspector's Shocking True Story and Expert Advice for You and Your Family*. New York: New Century.

Rosenblatt, Rand E., Sylvia A. Law, and Sara Rosenbaum. 1997. *Law and the American Health Care System*. New York: Foundation.

Rubinow, M. [1913] 1969. *Social Insurance, with Special Reference to American Conditions*. Edited by Leon Stein and Philip Taft. New York: Arno Press. Quoted in Theda Skocpol, "Associations without members," *American Prospect* 45 (July/August): 174–75.

Scharfstein, Steve, and Sally Satel. 1999. "'Parity' Isn't Charity." *Wall Street Journal*, 11 June, A18.

Schattschneider, E. E. 1960. *The Semi-Sovereign People.* Hinsdale, Ill.: Dryden Press.

Seaman, Suzanne. 1997. Comment. "Putting the Brakes on Drive-Through Deliveries." *Journal of Contemporary Health Law and Policy* 13:497.

Seattle Post-Intelligencer. 1999. "Time for Parity on Contraceptives." Editorial. 22 June.

Simon, Jonathan. 1988. "Ideological Effects of Actuarial Practices." *Law and Society Review* 22:771.

———. 1997–98. "Driving Governmentality: Automobile Accidents, Insurance, and the Challenge of Social Order in the Inter-War Years, 1919–1941." *Connecticut Insurance Law Journal* 4:521.

Skidmore, Max. 1999. *Social Security and Its Enemies.* Boulder: Westview Press.

Skocpol, Theda. 1999. "Associations without members." *American Prospect* 45 (July/August): 66–73.

Sorian , Richard, and Judith Feder. 1999. "Why We Need a Patients' Bill of Rights." *Journal of Health Politics, Policy and Law* 24:1137.

Squires, Gregory, ed. 1997. *Insurance Redlining: Disinvestment, Reinvestment, and the Evolving Role of Financial Institutions.* Washington, D.C: Urban Institute Press.

Starr, Paul. 1982. *The Social Transformation of Modern Medicine.* New York: Basic Books.

Stone, Deborah A. 1990. "The Rhetoric of Insurance Law: The Debate over AIDS Testing." *Law and Social Inquiry* 15 (spring): 385.

———. 1993. "The Struggle for the Soul of Health Insurance." *Journal of Health Politics, Policy and Law* 18:287–317.

———. 1994. Ad missions: how insurance companies sell ideology. *The American Prospect* 16 (Winter): 19–25.

———. 1997. *Policy Paradox: The Art of Political Decision Making.* New York: Norton.

Szasz, Andrew. 1990. "The Labor Impacts of Policy Change in Health Care: How Federal Policy Transformed Home Health Organizations and their Labor Practices." *Journal of Health Politics, Policy and Law* 15:191.

Treaster, Joseph B. 1996. "Writing Policies in Cities Once Written Off." *New York Times,* 30 October.

Tumulty, Karen. 1998. "Let's Play Doctor." *Time,* 13 July, 28–32.

Vladeck, Bruce C. 1980. *Unloving Care: The Nursing Home Tragedy.* New York: Basic Books.

Witt, John Fabian. 1998. "The Transformation of Work and the Law of Workplace Accidents." *Yale Law Journal* 107:1467.

Zelizer, Viviana. 1979. *Morals and Markets: The Development of Life Insurance in the United States.* New York: Columbia University Press.

Embracing Fatality through Life Insurance in Eighteenth-Century England

GEOFFREY CLARK

Today speculation and prudence are assumed to derive from opposing psychological impulses toward risk. This antithetical relationship is most conventionally reflected in economic analysis, which treats risk-loving and risk-averse behaviors as mathematical negatives of each other. Consequently gambling and insurance—as the respective incarnations of these risk-taking and risk-avoiding spirits—appear as discontinuous characteristics of *homo economicus.* Yet the complex topology of human psychology can hardly be captured by reference to a handful of equations purporting to describe an individual's preference for work or leisure, or for security versus adventure. The point was made long ago by Johan Huizinga, who observed that only a "hazy border-line" separates serious business from play, giving as prime examples the stock market and the life insurance business (1949:52–53).

Viewing the stock market as a field of play will surprise no one, but we are much less accustomed to thinking about the playful dimension of life insurance, which is universally advertised as the very epitome of prudence and sobriety. This carefully cultivated image of restraint and security, however, masks a past in which life insurance served as a vehicle for gaming. Though ostensibly devoted to risk avoidance, life insurance arose from and drew much of its initial popularity in eighteenth-century England from people's taste for gambling on others' lives.

If the speculative roots of the life insurance business are now so obscure, that can be attributed to sustained governmental attempts (at both the private and public levels) from the late eighteenth century to impose a new mental schema out of which various insurance practices and strategies could be formulated, what François Ewald has termed an "insurance imaginary" (1991:198). This new imaginary severed the long-standing mental and legal association of insurance with gambling and instead made them polar opposites, thereby redirecting insurance projects away from the speculative possibilities and grand designs characteristic of the insurance market of the early eighteenth century (Daston 1987, 1988:138). This procedure can most clearly be detected in the 1774 passage of the Gambling Act, which suppressed wagering by means of life insurance by requiring that a capacity for financial loss, a so-called insurable interest, be shown by purchasers of insurance policies in the lives they sought to insure.[1] The imposition of this new standard of economic motivation demarcated a legally sanctioned sphere of life insurance contracts from an illicit sphere of speculative life insurance wagers.

The boundary separating these newly fashioned legal categories, however, was by no means a clear one. How was one to monetize emotional loss, for example? And so long as there existed no technique for calculating the present discounted value of a life, how could the monetary equivalents of people's lives be scaled according to their age and projected future earnings? More fundamentally, the eighteenth century only gradually acquired the requisite confidence in statistical demography that made those monetary equivalents conceivable in the first place. We must recognize, therefore, that in the absence of these standardized measures the task of distinguishing between "speculative" and "prudential" motives in the context of life insurance was itself problematic. Since these categories are themselves the intellectual products of demographic calculation, they cannot be treated as inverses in the manner specified by economistic descriptions of risk-averse and risk-loving behaviors, and require instead a broader analytical framework.

Historically, the culture of risk management emerged not so much from an attempt to banish risks as to embrace them. The early life insurance business, as a matrix both of statistical calculation and rampant speculation, provides insight into the aleatory foundations of an industry whose techniques of risk management eventually bequeathed to the societies of the industrialized West unprecedented security in life, health, and property. It also furnishes a means to historicize the moral and rational calculus of economic action, which is too often regarded as naturally given rather than as socially constructed. In addition, the history of life insurance offers an opportunity to plumb the mental and cultural associations of risk management in the late seventeenth and early eighteenth centuries, a period during which life insurance was integrally connected not just to gambling but also to movements for moral reform, social improvement, and political liberty.

Gambling on Fatality

Life insurance was itself nothing new to the century of the Enlightenment, having been invented toward the close of the Middle Ages in the port cities of the western Mediterranean (Clark 1999:13–32). By the mid-sixteenth century Italian merchants had begun to underwrite lives in England. A wave of legal bans placed on the practice nearly everywhere else in Europe from the fifteenth to the seventeenth centuries transferred the business by default into the hands of English merchants, whose business centered on the lives of ship captains or of debtors seeking collateral to raise loans. Life insurance underwritten in the sixteenth and seventeenth centuries was issued for quite limited periods of time, typically ranging from a few months to a couple of years. This short-term coverage corresponded to the use of life insurance for discrete periods (the length of a sea voyage or the repayment of a loan, for example), as well as to the ad hoc nature of the associations of the merchant/insurers who underwrote marketed risks.

A decisive transformation in the life insurance market occurred at the very end of the seventeenth century, with the birth of permanent life insurance collectives. These collectives ushered in a twenty-five-year boom in life insurance promotions because they allowed the term of insurance coverage to be extended for the whole duration of life. This arrangement opened life insurance to a much wider market of people seeking long-term security in exchange for moderate periodic fees. The memberships of life insurance societies typically governed themselves by electing boards of directors, and members self-consciously came to each other's aid. Thus the cooperation entailed by the purchase of life insurance created a social and mental solidarity quite unlike the obscure affiliation that previously had linked the constituents of the risk pools drawn together merely through the business operations of individual underwriters.

These insurance societies differed significantly from the actuarially based premium insurance with which we are familiar today. Rather than relating a series of fixed premiums to a predetermined death benefit, they periodically redistributed membership fees in favor of the beneficiaries of dying members, share and share alike. This design imposed the financial risk of projecting the future level of their members' mortality upon the individual members themselves. As a consequence, the societies were never obliged to pay out in death benefits more than they received in fees.

Since Europe in the early eighteenth century still lived under threat of demographic calamities like the plague, forecasts of future mortality could not be made with great confidence. This limitation of the societies' obligations with respect to sharply fluctuating levels of mortality must be seen as a highly prudent measure quite at odds with the critical view of some scholars that early life insurance societies catered especially to clients with a taste for gambling on the longevity of third parties (Daston 1988:167, 170).

The Prevalence of Insurance Gambling

Whatever motivations insurance society promoters might have intended to draw upon, they undoubtedly did attract many customers whose primary interest in insurance lay in its speculative value. The prospect of profiting from a life insurance policy provided a strong incentive for third-party insurers to select persons whom they reckoned would die quickly, thus maximizing the expected return on their investment. Until it was outlawed by the passage of the Gambling Act in 1774, this sort of insurance gambling was quite prevalent both within insurance societies and in the life insurance industry at large. For example, in eighteenth-century England policies were issued on the lives of the Pretender and of the rebel lords during the Jacobite rebellion of 1745, as well as on the life of the unfortunate Admiral Byng during his trial for dereliction of duty (he was ultimately found guilty and executed much to the satisfaction of those who had insured his life). Even the lives of kings were not beyond the reach of the speculative insurance market: underwriters offered 25 percent against George II's returning alive from the Battle of Dettingen (Francis 1853:140; Mortimer 1761:103; Halperin 1946:64). But it wasn't only celebrities whose lives were insured willy-nilly. According to Nicholas Magens, a one-time director of the London Assurance Corporation who had a long and distinguished career in the insurance business, "in London People take the Liberty to make Insurances on any one's Life without Exception; and the Insurers seldom enquire much if there are good or bad Reasons for such an Insurance" (1755:32).

Life insurance provided in fact just the most institutionalized setting for what was in eighteenth-century England a rampant habit of gambling on life contingencies. Voltaire for one regarded the taste for betting on lives as peculiarly English, remarking that when the Sun King fell ill in 1715 the English ambassador, Lord Stair, could not forbear betting, "according to the genius of his nation, that the king would not live beyond September" (1754:87–88; Bensa 1897:xiii n.2). To be sure, the prevailing enthusiasm for betting on lives occasioned some worried comment. The members of White's, the famous gentlemen's club of St. James', were sometimes depicted as gambling maniacs who had abandoned civilized standards of charity and decency. In 1750 Horace Walpole picked up a story then circulating in the newspapers about a scandalous incident at White's in which a man collapsed at the door to the club and was carried in. The members of the club immediately made bets whether he was dead or not, and when the surgeon prepared to bleed him, the wagerers for his death interposed, objecting that the provision of medical care would affect the fairness of their bets (Ashton 1898:155–56).

Of course, the opportunity to bet on human life might lead gamblers not only into immoral behavior but into actual criminality. John Richardson, a member of one insurance cooperative called the Amicable Society, feared that some unscrupulous policyholder, "prompted by the Instigation of the Devil, and Hopes of a Temporary Reward," might "by some secret Means endeavour to hasten a Claim," as indeed happened in 1737 when a Southwark apothecary insured the life of his wife with the London Assurance Corporation and then poisoned her (Richardson 1732:8–9; London Assurance 1737).

Apart from such qualms occasionally expressed in the first half of the eighteenth century about the possible deleterious effects of gambling on lives, it is hard to detect voices condemning insurance gambling as inherently wrong. Life insurance societies commonly tolerated the holding of gambling policies—indeed, they sometimes encouraged them in order to boost business—provided that gamblers acted fairly. John Richardson worried less, for example, about the rare cases of life insurance leading to murder than the chronic problem of gamblers foisting "bad lives" on the Amicable, resulting in a larger number of annual claims and hence in unfairly small sums being paid to beneficiaries (1732:5). Another Amicable member, William Whiston, the famous mathematician and religious radical, agreed with Richardson that the Amicable experienced a rate of mortality significantly above its "naturally expected" level due to the purposive selection of unhealthy lives by life insurance speculators (Whiston 1732:5).

Yet strikingly, neither Whiston nor Richardson advocated the prohibition of speculative policyholding on third parties. Although Richardson suggested that prospective policy purchasers show cause why they wanted to insure a particular life, there is no indication that either he or Whiston believed that gambling on lives was wrong in and of itself. For them, gambling became problematic only if it involved fraud, which put other policyholders at a comparative disadvantage and depressed the value of all claims. In fact, far from attempting to suppress wagering, Whiston proposed as a remedy to the prevalence of bad lives that the Amicable Society choose two or three hundred healthy people between twelve and seventy years of age living in the vicinity of its office and require that speculative insurers select a person from this vetted pool. Whiston's plan sought not to root out gambling but to regulate it so that each life insured by the Amicable stood a roughly equal chance of dropping (1732:9). It was the fairness of the gamble, not the gamble itself, that was the overriding concern.

A Midcentury Shift

While during the first half of the eighteenth century objections to life insurance gambling concentrated on fraud and crime (not on the moral illegitimacy of the practice itself), after midcentury all forms of betting on life contingencies encountered a rapidly mounting chorus of hostility. Writers on commerce and business began to complain that the "spirit of gaming" had disgraced the insurance business, and they deplored the fact that gambling policies were "often set on foot, and promoted, for many thousands of pounds, even by merchants, insurers, and brokers, who in other respects stand fair in the eye of the mercantile world, as men of rank and reputation" (Weskett 1781:lv–lvi); see also Mortimer 1761:103; Marshall 1808:774).

But the reality was not that gambling had invaded legitimate business; rather, legitimate business was now being defined against the long-established practice of speculation on the continuance of human life. The new mood is evidenced by the defection in 1769 of a group of Lloyd's brokers and underwriters who superceded the older Lloyd's by reconstituting themselves as a more tightly controlled body that refused to issue gambling policies of insurance (Gibb 1957:46). Just why English society suddenly found gambling insurance unacceptable is a question that has usually been answered by reference to the rise of a sober middle-class culture that refused to countenance the use of a prudential institution for speculative ends. The invocation of this deus ex machina fails to explain with sufficient force or particularity, however, why intolerance of insurance gambling should have suddenly grown strong around the year 1770.

The real reasons behind this attitudinal shift can be detected in the evolving legal treatment of the ownership of human capital, a development manifest in three superficially unrelated cases from the early 1770s. The first stems from the rampant speculation that broke out in 1771 on the true

sex of Charles de Beaumont, the Chevalier D'Eon—a French soldier, diplo-
mat, and secret agent then living in London. The second concerned two
heirs who agreed to "run their fathers against each other," with the intended result being that the first to inherit would support the other. The
third concerned the rights of the slave Thomas Lewis.

The D'Eon Case

In late 1770 rumors regarding the sex of the Chevalier D'Eon
began to circulate around London, and by March of the next year books
had been opened at Lloyd's and other places in the city on the truth of the
reports (London Magazine 1777:445; Dictionary of National Biography,
s.n. "D'Eon"). Offering premiums of fifteen to sixty guineas per cent.
(varying with the prevailing degree of uncertainty about the case), underwriters issued policies reputedly totaling upwards of sixty thousand
pounds, payable upon proof that D'Eon was in fact a woman (Weskett
1781:584–85).[2]

The matter finally came to a head in 1777 when D'Eon quarreled with
his friend and confidante, M. De Morande, who then publicly disclosed that
D'Eon had three years before privately confessed to being a woman (London
Magazine 1777:445). Armed with De Morande's allegation, those who had
wagered on D'Eon's being female brought suit against the underwriters to
pay on policies that by then had been pending for several years. In July a suit
brought by a London surgeon, Mr. Hayes, against an underwriter and broker
known to posterity only as Jacques, was heard before Lord Mansfield at
Guildhall. The testimony offered at trial by De Morande and Mr. Le Goux,
a surgeon who claimed to have examined D'Eon's genitals, seemed to provide solid evidence of D'Eon's female sex. Although Lord Mansfield expressed grave reservations about the propriety of such bets, he did not hold
the contract to be illegal and directed the jury to determine a winner to the
bet, and it found in favor of the plaintiff (Gentlemen's Magazine
1777:346–47). In Da Costa v. Jones (Weskett 1781:584–85), a similar suit
brought to court the following year, Mansfield's patience for these irksome
disputes came to an end. Upon the jury's announcement of its verdict in favor of the plaintiff, Mansfield ordered an arrest of judgment and later overturned the verdict based on the impropriety of submitting matters of a
private and delicate nature to a public legal test. All wagers on D'Eon's sex
were thereby rendered invalid (Dictionary of National Biography, s.n.
"D'Eon").

The permissibility of the policies issued on the Chevalier's sex boiled down to a question of what limits could be placed on the creation of commercial property, and of how far the law would go to enforce speculative contracts made out of the fabric of other people's lives. D'Eon always refused to demean himself by providing the court with the proof necessary to decide the numerous bets on his true sex. He maintained that his honor as a nobleman had been violated by his person having become the subject of degrading commercial contracts (Kates 1997). Nevertheless, although Mansfield threw out all law suits arising from wagers on D'Eon's sex, he left D'Eon's aristocratic sensibilities behind. Mansfield ruled on more general terms that all subjects of the Crown possessed a certain property in their private persons that others could not freely appropriate.

The Pigot Case

Many of the same issues were raised by another Mansfield case, this one arising out of a notorious bet contracted in 1770 between two young aristocrats at a Newmarket soirée. William Pigot and the son of Sir William Codrington each expected to inherit fortunes upon the deaths of their respective fathers, and they therefore agreed to "run their fathers against each other," that is to bet on who lived longer. The idea was that the heir who first succeeded to his father's estate could afford to discharge the debts of his friend. Since Codrington's father was fifty years old and Pigot's over seventy, the bettors had Lord Ossory set odds to make the wager fair. When Ossory gave Codrington's father a better than three-to-one chance of surviving Pigot's, Codrington objected to the size of the handicap and withdrew from the wager. At this point another dinner guest, the Earl of March, offered to stand in Codrington's stead, and an agreement was therefore concluded between Pigot and March. Unbeknown to the parties at the time, however, Pigot's father had by a remarkable coincidence died earlier that same day 150 miles away in Shropshire. Upon learning of his father's death, Pigot refused to concede that he had lost the wager, claiming that because the bet was a contract *in futuro,* it was invalid since one of the lives had already terminated by the time the bet was made. March then brought suit before the King's Bench to compel Pigot's payment. Lord Mansfield left the case to the jury, which returned a verdict in favor of March.[3]

Although the wager between March and Pigot was held to be legally valid, the public outcry against two men wantonly betting on the lives of their fathers contributed significantly to the landmark passage of the Gambling Act. Thereafter all betting on human life was illegal, and gambling perforce was expelled from the business of life insurance. No longer could a proprietary interest in another person's life be created simply through the issuance of life insurance or the contracting of a wager. Simply put, the Gambling Act limited the extent to which the substance of human life could be converted into a commodity.

The Lewis Case

The commodification of human life was even more dramatically at issue in a justly famous case that came before the Chief Justice the same year as the Pigot case. Thomas Lewis was an enslaved black man who asked the court to rule that he had the right not to be removed from the kingdom against his will. When the jury returned a verdict declaring Lewis to be outside his master's power to compel his return to the West Indies, the public gallery rang to cheers of "No Property! No Property!" (Walvin 1992:14–15). As this chant suggests, the institution of slavery and unfettered gambling on lives shared an abstract identity. Each entailed the creation of property in human lives, coercively in the case of slavery, gratuitously in the case of speculative life insurance or gambling. Each transposed the profane calculus of the marketplace into the sacred and invaluable sphere of human life. Moreover, by treating not just human labor but human life itself as an object of commerce, both slavery and gambling on lives denied to their subjects the primary article of ownership assumed in any Lockean political compact: possession of the self. It was therefore to an emerging consciousness of the problematic relationship between economic and political liberty that the eighteenth-century insurance "imaginary"owed its demise.

Life Insurance and Virtue

The Gambling Act and the legal decisions that followed removed from the life insurance business its speculative aspects, but in doing so they also stripped life insurance of many of the imaginative aims and mental associations that had proved crucial to its marked growth from the late seventeenth century. The institutional forms and functions of insurance in its pre-actuarial phase expressed a distinctive consciousness about the possibilities of establishing civic virtue in a commercial society by protecting private fortunes, fostering social fellowship for mutual support, and promoting Christian ideals.

The habit of insurance was first inculcated among thousands of households throughout London and the provinces primarily by voluntary insurance associations, not the proprietary companies that later came to dominate the industry. These innovative bodies typically organized themselves as self-governing associations of policyholders, and therefore possessed characteristics both of businesses and clubs. Here individual responsibility was fused with a communitarian ideal, and in common with many other voluntary movements of the time with public-spirited aims, life insurance societies announced their intentions not only to indemnify their policyholders against loss, they also sought to contribute to the nation's moral, social, and economic improvement.

Life insurance societies routinely advertised themselves using the language of enlightenment and virtue, appealing to "wise and judicious persons" or "considering men" to join in a "pious and Charitable Undertaking" (Paternal Society for the Provision of Children 1710; Adams 1714; Amicable Society 1706:7). The societies advised prospective policyholders that through a variety of means they could contribute to the propagation of Christianity in foreign parts, help finance charity schools, augment the incomes of impoverished clergymen, and come to the relief of distressed debtors (Amicable Society 1706:7).

But the ambitions of life insurance projectors went beyond charitable benefaction and the support of kith and kin. Charles Povey, for example, designed his life insurance society in such a way that members automatically received his newspaper, *The General Remark on Trade*, so they could better "understand Trade and Business" (Povey 1706:1). Then, out of the profits of his newspaper and insurance society, Povey planned to build a hospital for up to one hundred society members who had fallen on hard times.

Although Povey's elaborate scheme entailed an unusual degree of socialized risk, other projectors were no less visionary. Richard Carter's projected life insurance society of 1712 was designed to help buoy the price of government lottery tickets (Carter 1712). Daniel Cholmondeley planned to sell contingent annuities for widows as a means for advancing the fisheries of Britain (Cholmondeley 1713, 1714). Sir James Hallet and others petitioned for a charter to grant contingent annuities, stressing the benefits that would accrue to the nation's trade by relieving commercial men of financial worry about bankruptcy or death (and thereby encouraging them to invest more of their capital to the nation's advantage) (*Special Report* 1720:67). Thinking along the same lines, a number of life insurance societies loaned their members money against the security of their policies, thereby introducing banking facilities to the life insurance business (Friendly Society for Insurance on Lives 1708, 1715[?]a, 1715b:15; Adams 1714; Perpetual Assurance Office 1709[?]). All of these insurance projects variously aimed at improving English society and morals by extending credit, expanding trade, and awakening people to the ways commerce could reform society.

Insurance during the Augustan period therefore attempted to forge a social alliance among people drawn together not just through enlightened self-interest but also through a dedication to the reformation of English society through charity and the increase of commerce. Ironically, by convincing individuals that life insurance enhances family security, these institutions expanded the national fund of investment capital, which enabled entrepreneurs and state ministers alike to embark upon more and greater speculative ventures, simultaneously advancing the wealth of the nation and the power of the state. Risk taking and avoidance were thus made a ferrogilt alloy in the service of British military and commercial ambition during the eighteenth century.

The attractiveness of these schemes lay in their combining the private advantage afforded by insurance with the public benefit that could be achieved by the investment of a large capital fund, what insurance promoters referred to as a "joint-stock." The terminology was telling, for most life insurance companies, unlike charitable foundations or friendly societies, were also profit-making ventures modeled after the joint-stock company, a type of business organization whose accessibility to smaller investors and ease of investment and disinvestment led to its rapidly growing importance in the finance of English industry from the 1680s (Dubois 1938:230; Scott 1911:441, 447). By investing in a joint-stock venture, members of life insurance societies not only acquired ownership of their policies but also gained title, like shareholders, to a fixed portion of their societies' assets. This fact is highly important for appreciating the dynamics of the early life insurance market and the particular moral regime under which they operated.

The proprietary nature of policyholding meant that, in common with the conventions followed in other sorts of joint-stock companies, the membership convened once or twice a year at a General Court to consider and vote upon general matters put to them by the directors. The boards of directors were in turn elected from among eligible society members. A substantial degree of control over life insurance companies was therefore vested in the policyholders themselves. Although they ceded direct oversight to an elected board and quotidian management of the office to the "register" (usually the projector himself), they collectively controlled their respective societies. Within the boundaries of these little commonwealths, policyholders gathered in an egalitarian fashion to protect one another from outrageous fortune. Inside this social shelter, the risks of falling into a demeaning social dependence on relations, neighbors, or the parish could be reduced, and the continued respectability of people of middling fortunes thereby assured. Life insurance seemed therefore to provide a means to preserve the independency of commercial families in the face of mortal disaster, and consequently to contribute to the continuity and autonomy of commercial society and, by extension, of the nation as a whole.

Of course, indemnification against loss was only one side of the allure of these early insurance schemes. As one insurance office acknowledged, the "[t]hings generally desired by the people . . . in undertakings of this nature, are security and advantage" (Perpetual Assurance Office 1709[?]). Accordingly, many societies spiced their offerings of insurance against mortal misfortune with plans for low-risk avenues to positive wealth. Some offices promised for instance to abate their fees as interest income from the joint-stock accumulated, until such time as the society became financially self-sufficient and could do away with members' contributions altogether. Members would then hold heritable title to stated death benefits free of charge. Other offices intended to invest their joint-stocks in real estate or in fisheries, the revenue from which would provide supplemental income to members or their heirs. Whatever the precise formula, the underlying idea was to settle upon the membership a perpetual estate to be held in common. Typically, the Amicable Society declared at its inception in 1706 that annual fees were expected to cease after thirty years, after which time the society "will settle a growing estate in each family for ever, by a better tenure than most are held in England" (Amicable Society 1706:5).

Given the long-term investment contemplated here, these are not the sort of enticements calculated to lure the gambling set. Rather, participants in early life insurance schemes seem to have responded in part to the promise of conservative management and a security of investment rivaling even estates in land, normally the safest and most highly esteemed of assets. Indeed, insurance societies aspired to fulfill the role played by land in securing the fortunes of grandee families by furnishing a durable vehicle for the transmission of commercial fortunes down the generations, thus satisfying, as J. G. A. Pocock has noted, a crucial requirement for the exercise of political virtue and the establishment of moral legitimacy in English society (1975:463).

That early life insurance societies were conceived of by their members as both collective estates and as agents of moral reform explains an otherwise puzzling feature of their operations. It seems at first strange that busi-

nesses based on at least a modicum of probabilistic expectation should not
have sought to increase their memberships indefinitely, given the increased
reliability of probabilistic forecasting implied by the law of large numbers.
Why, in other words, did life insurance societies always limit their sizes,
thereby leaving themselves more exposed to variance in the rate of mortality experienced by their members, presumably rendering membership less
attractive to their prospective clientele? The answer is not that promoters
of life insurance societies possessed an antiprobabilistic attitude that
blinded them to the risk-reducing benefits of an amplified membership
(Daston 1988:115), but rather that the calculus of mortality carried out by
the promoters and members was subordinated to other social and ethical
calculations.

The memberships of life insurance societies had no interest in growing
indefinitely because they comprised a moral as well as a proprietorial so-
dality. The common ownership of a private estate made policyholders dis-
inclined to dilute their own financial interest in the insurance society
through the admission of additional members, while the common moral
purpose that brought them together in the first place also segregated them
from society at large. Within the preserve of this civil society, the acquisitive impulses of the marketplace could be reconciled with the Christian
ideal of selfless benefaction, an aspiration embodied in the very design of insurance societies. Since in these redistributive schemes the size of death
benefits was largest when mortality was low, the continuing vitality of
one's fellows redounded to the pecuniary benefit of oneself or one's heirs.
Referring to this fact, the Second Society of Assurance boasted: "Here, in
our SOCIETY, is a world of good nature: We pray for the lives of others,
though we die our selves" (1709:25). Part reforming society, part joint-stock
company, the insurance society of the early eighteenth century may thus be
seen as a Janus-faced response to the moral and financial imperatives of the
Augustan age, and which united the apparently contradictory impulses for
assurance and adventure, for morality and money, into a coherent institutional form.

Conclusion

Historians have often noted that the organization and operation
of eighteenth-century life insurance offices corresponded to the limited actuarial techniques and mortality data available to insurance promoters
prior to the 1760s. A closer examination of the early life insurance movement reveals that its forms and practices were also shaped by strong ideo-

logical and cultural currents running through Augustan society and politics. Life insurance was conceived as a vehicle for the amplification of British power abroad, for the stimulation of undercapitalized industries, for social security, moral improvement, the propagation of Christianity, *and* for turning the uncertainties of life into opportunities for enrichment. While today we conceptually oppose security to speculation, the insurance market of the eighteenth century grew out of imagined outcomes that were all in some sense speculative or hopeful.

In giving substance to these imaginings, life insurance helped to propel a broad-based movement in early-eighteenth-century England for collective self-reliance, self-governance, and public benefaction—all characteristics associated with the emerging civil society of the Enlightenment. Yet insurance societies were especially vulnerable to predatory uses of life insurance policies precisely because of their constitutional commitment to the proprietary interest conferred by policyholding. In the face of insurance gambling and the danger that bad lives posed to their memberships, life societies attempted to maintain a uniform level of risk among the lives they insured in order to ensure an ideal of fair play. By the 1770s, however, a new governmental strategy was being honed to suppress the speculative uses of life insurance. Company directors no longer rested content simply to judge whether a proposed life met the minimum standards of insurability, but went further to judge the policyholder's *motive* for purchasing the insurance in the first place.

The implementation of this new moral criterion was accomplished on two fronts. First, insurance companies of the later eighteenth century assumed greater corporate authority over their policyholders, in part by removing the proprietary aspects of policyholding, as the Amicable Society did in 1771 (Amicable Society 1776:31). Once the characteristics of equity disappeared from life insurance policies, so too could the control by policyholders over the affairs of the society be diminished. Policyholders were thus reduced from being equal and self-governing proprietors of their societies to being corporate customers. On the second front, the hands of insurance firms were strengthened by parliament's determination to confine risk taking within specified moral parameters, a goal finally accomplished in 1774 by passage of the Gambling Act. With this legal rationale in place, both the state and insurance companies acquired the statutory authority as well as the categorical means to segregate existing life insurance practices into "licit" and "illicit" behaviors as defined by the emerging moral and rational calculus of economic action. In its essence, insurance might always be a gamble, but it was to become a legally sanctioned expression of a moral interest, insulated from the acquisitive passions that threatened to disrupt the virtuous operation of a propertied civil society.

NOTES

1. 14 Geo. 3, c. 48.

2. Gary Kates (1995:231) has noted that French financiers alone wagered some £100,000 on D'Eon's sex, suggesting that the total amount of money wagered in insurance offices, betting shops, and between individuals was much higher than Weskett's figure.

3. Earl of March v. Pigot, 98 Eng. Rep. 471–73 (1909); see also Weskett 1781: 582–84.

REFERENCES

Adams, William. 1714. *The Company of London Insurers on the Lives of Men, Women, and Children.* London: n.p.

Amicable Society. 1706. *A Letter from a Member of the Amicable Society for a Perpetual Assurance.* London: n.p.

———. 1776. Terms, Methods, and Advantages of Insuring Lives in the Office of the Amicable Society, contained in a List of the Members of the Corporation of the Amicable Society. London: n.p.

Ashton, John. 1898. *History of Gambling in England.* London: Duckworth.

Bensa, Enrico. 1897. *Histoire du contract d'assurrance au moven age.* Paris: Thorin et Fils.

Carter, Richard. 1712. *A Proposal for Settling a Perpetual Assurance on Lives, and for Advancing the Credit of 10 l. Lottery-Tickets.* London: n.p.

Cholmondeley, Daniel. 1713. *A Proposal for Granting Annuities to Raise a Stock for Improving the Fishery of Great-Britain.* London: n.p.

———. 1714. *The Articles of Settlement of the Benevolent Society, for Granting Annuities to Raise a Stock for Improving the Fishery of Great-Britain.* London: n.p.

Clark, Geoffrey. 1999. *Betting on Lives: The Culture of Life Insurance in England, 1695–1775.* Manchester: Manchester University Press.

Daston, Lorraine J. 1988. *Classical Probability in the Enlightenment.* Princeton: Princeton University Press.

———. 1987. "The Domestication of Risk: Mathematical Probability and Insurance, 1650–1830." In *The Probabilistic Revolution,* ed. L. Kruger, L. J. Daston, and M. Heidelberger. Vol. 1: *Ideas in History.* Cambridge: MIT Press.

Dictionary of National Biography. 1917. Oxford: Oxford University Press.

Dubois, Armand Budington. 1938. *The English Business Company after the Bubble Act 1720–1800.* New York: Commonwealth Fund.

Ewald, François. 1991. "Insurance and Risk." In *The Foucault Effect: Studies in*

Governmentality, ed. G. Burchell, C. Gordon, and P. Miller. Chicago: University of Chicago Press.

Francis, John. 1853. *Annals, Anecdotes, and Legends: A Chronicle of Life Assurance*. London: Longman, Brown, Green, and Longmans.

Friendly Society. 1708. *The Friendly Society for Assurance of Money upon Lives*. London: n.p.

Friendly Society. 1715[?]a. *Proposals for the Better Establishing and Perpetuating the Friendly Society, for Assurance on Lives, and for Raising a Joint-Stock*. London: n.p.

Friendly Society. 1715b. *Land Security for Establishing a Perpetual Insurance on Lives of Men, Women, and Children*. London: n.p.

Gentlemen's Magazine. 1777. July.

Gibb, D. E. W. 1957. *Lloyd's of London*. London: MacMillan.

Halperin, Jean. 1946. *Les assurances en Suisse et dans le monde*. Neuchatel: Éditions de la Baconnière.

Huizinga, Johan. 1949. *Homo Ludens*. London: Routledge and Kegan Paul.

Kates, Gary. 1995. *Monsieur D'Eon Is a Woman*. New York: Basic Books.

———. 1997. Personal communication with author. 11 August.

London Assurance. 1737. "Court of Directors Minutes." 30 November. London Guildhall MS 8728, vol. 4.

London Magazine. 1777. September.

Magens, Nicholas. 1755. *An Essay on Insurances*. Vol. 1. London: J. Habercorn.

Marshall, Samuel. 1808. *A Treatise on the Law of Insurance*. Vol. 2. London: A. Strahan.

Mortimer, Thomas. 1761. *Every Man His Own Broker*. 2d ed. London: S. Hooper.

Paternal Society for Provision of Children. 1710. PRO SP44/244, ff.72–3.

Perpetual Assurance Office. 1709[?]. *Proposals for Establishing a Perpetual Assurance Office*. London: n.p.

Pocock, J. G. A. 1975. *The Machiavellian Moment*. Princeton: Princeton University Press.

Povey, Charles. 1706. *Proposals for Raising a Fund of Two Thousands Pounds per Annum by an Amicable Contribution of Four Thousand Persons*. London: n.p.

Richardson, John. 1732. *Some Remarks and Consideration on the Original and Supplemental Charters, which Incorporate the Amicable Society for a Perpetual Assurance Office*. London: J. Roberts.

Scott, W. R. 1911. *The Constitution and Finance of English, Scottish, and Irish Joint Stock Companies to 1720*. Vol. 1. Cambridge: Cambridge University Press.

Second Society of Assurance. 1709. *The Articles of the Second Society of Assurance, for the Support of Widows and Orphans*. Dublin: n.p.

Special Report [Great Britain], from the Committee Appointed to Inquire into and Examine the Several Subscriptions for Fisheries, Insurances, Annuities for Lives, and All Other Projects. . . . 1720. London: Jacob Tonson.

Voltaire. 1754. Quoted in *Connoisseur*, 9 May.

Walvin, James. 1992. *Black Ivory: A History of British Slavery.* London: Fontana Press.

Weskett, John. 1781. *A Complete Digest of the Theory, Laws and Practices of Insurance.* London: Frys, Coachman, and Collier.

Whiston, William. 1732. *An Account of the Past and Present State of the Amicable Society for a Perpetual Assurance Office.* London: n.p.

Imagining Insurance: Risk, Thrift, and Life Insurance in Britain

PAT O'MALLEY

Recent developments in French social theory (see, e.g., Defert 1991; Ewald 1991) suggest that rather than thinking of the nature of insurance as driven primarily by actuarial advances, by "what the market demands," or by the narrow interests of pressure groups, emphasis needs to be placed on the role of "insurantial imaginaries." These are ways in which abstract techniques of insurance are given novel institutional forms by imaginatively linking them to practicable projects of government (incorporating but not restricted to government by the state). Such an approach does not deny the value of other ways of investigation, but focuses attention onto the intellectual and imaginative work done in rendering problems "thinkable and governable" in new ways (Miller and Rose 1990). For example, rather than understanding the emergence of an insurance category such as moral hazard in terms of the ways it reflects the interests of the powerful (Cuneo 1986), or as "naturally" arising out of the development of actuarialism (Pal 1986), we might ask such questions as the following: What assumptions were made about human nature and action in its formulation? What understandings about the nature of insurance, and of the problems it was to govern, were taken for granted or given shape by this idea? What intellectual and technical materials were assembled together—or had to be created—in order to translate the idea into practice? How, in short, did it come to be that such an *invention* could be thought of as possible, necessary, and practicable?

Such questions also tend to disrupt the naturalness of the development of insurance. Viewed from the present, it may seem that the rise of certain forms or elements of insurance was more or less inevitable, or had taken the only possible and effective route. But those who formulated insurance technologies had no such benefit of hindsight. True, the course they took was partly constrained, for inventions must be made using the intellectual and material resources at hand. Thus, for example, the successes of actuaries in managing lotteries on behalf of the state in the eighteenth century provided a fairly secure platform from which to launch popular, actuarially based life insurance in the nineteenth century (Dalton 1986). But each development was to some degree a foray into the unknown and followed no prescribed course. It is precisely for this reason that terms such as *imagination* and *invention* are deployed in this account—in order to stress the open and contingent development of that which may be taken for granted today.

This essay examines the history of British working class life insurance (and especially the form known as Industrial Life Assurance) through such a lens.[1] In this history, the category of "thrift" takes a central role. In the nineteenth century, thrift appears as a moral attribute of the individual, associated with what would now be thought of as risk avoiding and risk spreading. It was thought to be indispensable for working people, for governing their autonomy and security. Insurance techniques and politics at the time were never able to break free from its intellectual hold, but thrift was later distinguished by welfare liberal planners into two forms—"compulsory" and "voluntary"—a distinction that might very well have been meaningless within the moral discourse of nineteenth-century liberals.

Each of these constructs subsequently was used to rethink working class security and to invent specific forms of social (compulsory) and individually based (voluntary) life insurance. Later still, and paradoxically under the umbrella of restoring the Victorian virtues, thrift was turned on its head. People came to be imagined as *too* cautious and risk averse, rather than insufficiently so. In this environment, working class life insurance was reinvented as a fully commodified "investment product" with a strong speculative, *risk-taking*, element.

As this suggests, thrift, risk, and insurance are governmental constructs whose nature and form vary through time, but which exist in a triangular relationship such that variations in each has had implications for how the others are imagined and practised. This essay argues that these processes, in turn, are strongly influenced by the prevailing political rationality, in such a manner that *rethinking the meaning, nature, and place of thrift and risk in terms of changing political rationalities has been central to the process of imagining insurance.* Broadly speaking, this history divides into three phases, each characterised by the dominance of a different form of political rationality: classical liberalism, welfare liberalism, and neoliberalism.

Classical Liberalism: Policing Thrift

In Britain, insurance for the working classes emerged during the late eighteenth century century with the activities of the Friendly Societies—fraternal and benevolent insurance arrangements formed among skilled artisans. During the early part of the nineteenth century, successive political administrations legislated to encourage the Societies' role in providing life, burial, and sickness insurance for the working class. This was regarded not only as fostering self-help and industry but also as alleviating pressure on the poor rates.[2] There was nothing necessary about this way of thinking about insurance. In the previous century, major forms of insurance had involved wagers on the lives of others, until proscribed by the Life Insurance Act of 1774—known more widely as the "Gambling Act." The principal commentators of the day regarded gambling as "an offence of the most alarming nature; tending by necessary consequence to promote public idleness, theft and debauchery among those of the lower class" (Holdsworth 1969, xi:539, quoting Blackstone), a view retained through into the present century (Dixon 1991). Distinguishing insurance from gambling and rendering it an instrument of thrift was thus a significant process, and the place of *risk taking* in the genealogy of insurance therefore should not be forgotten. While the story of this process cannot be provided here, it is also important to note for later reference that maintaining this distinction remained a constant concern of legislators and of the judiciary until well into the twentieth century (Merkin 1980; Zelizer 1979).

While the Friendly Societies had never been associated with gambling insurance, in order to facilitate thrift and self-help, legislation encouraged them to replace their traditional emphasis on fraternalism and benevolence with actuarially based principles of fund management. The benevolent principles of the early Societies delivered benefits to members according to need rather than in proportion to their premiums or levels of risk, often leading to funds becoming insolvent (Select Committee 1825). From 1819 onward statutes required that the tables and rules of societies applying for registration be approved by "two persons at least, known to be professional actuaries or persons skilled in calculation" (59 Geo. III c.128). In the medium term, the effect of this shift was that control of the business of insurance was taken from the hands of policyholders and delivered to larger, actuarially based organizations (Select Committee 1889:ix).

As graduated contributions were imposed, actuarial techniques of government eroded benevolent organization, and members became divided and ordered according to their levels of contribution and risk categories. In the fraternally organized Societies, premiums had been paid either at the monthly meetings or had been collected by members themselves in their spare time. The larger, actuarially based Societies, however, substituted a model based on salaried or commission-funded collectors. By the 1870s, the Royal Commission into Friendly and Benefit Building Societies reported that full-time paid collectors were the "pivot of the whole system" (Royal Commission 1874). Life insurance for the working class had thus changed dramatically under the impact of actuarial governance for, as Doran (1994) argues, a new *disciplinary* regime had been ushered into the government of working class security: a regime of regulated contributions that were subject to the "policing" of collecting agents.

Significantly, such disciplinary relations were extended to a much wider market by the rise of industrial life insurance companies, which made a commercial principle out of this form of insurance relation. Industrial life insurance—dominated throughout the next hundred years by firms such as Prudential—focused on the poorer sections of the working class, whereas the Friendly Societies had been the providers for the "aristocracy of labour" (Gilbert 1965). The development of the commercial industrial insurances thus extended the reach of life insurance to the "the poor." By the early part of this century, industrial life insurance had become the principal institution for governing working class thrift, and few households were not enlisted in this regime.[3]

Part of the success of these rising companies was that, while they retained endowment policies (which were to grow again in importance in the next century), they increasingly emphasised burial insurance—exploiting the working class fear and shame associated with the pauper's funeral (Morrah 1955; Johnson 1985). Equally vital to their success was the disciplinary nature of the collecting strategies of industrial life insurance. Sale of policies and collection of premiums was characterized by the deployment of an army of agents who collected small weekly premiums, normally of only a few pence, at the home of the policyholder. The detailed reviews of the collectors' techniques undertaken by a series of governmental inquiries and committees from the mid-nineteenth to the mid-twentieth centuries map out a strategy of infiltration into the fabric of working class domestic life, aimed at maximizing the sale of insurance (Royal Commission 1874; Passfield 1915; Departmental Committee 1920; Select Committee 1933). The collector's regular call was timed to coincide with pay day, for it was recognized that the "thriftlessness" of the poor and the unpredictable pressures on their vulnerable domestic economy meant that available cash may have been spent within twenty-four hours. Collectors were instructed to pay detailed attention to the state of the home and its contents, to look for additions to household furnishings that would indicate an ability to purchase increased insurance, or to watch for the disappearance of items of furniture, indicating sale or pawn to tide over hard times. (Johnson 1985; Wilson and Levy 1937).

From the industry's point of view, this form and level of intrusion was not exploitative. Rather, it represented both a necessary way of doing business and a disciplinary strategy for ensuring the thrift and prudence of the poor policyholders in their own interests. Without such interventions, it was argued, the poor would not take out life insurance or would grossly underinsure themselves. It was claimed that they did not have the social and moral resources to sustain, unassisted, the long-term commitment required to maintain insurance policies. The industry represented its activity in terms of providing a necessary discipline of thrift, in which its roles were said to include those of educating people about the need to insure for the future, ensuring payments, generating security for the family, and providing moral support when other temptations were more alluring or competing necessities more demanding. But while there can be little doubt that the practices were disciplinary, and bordered on compulsion, from an early date the question of their role in inculcating thrift among the poor became the center of political contestation between the insurance industry and the government.

The State versus Business: The Critique of "Useless Thrift"

While the moral role of insurance in promoting thrift and reducing reliance on the Poor Law had dominated early British debates on life insurance, by the 1860s new issues were arising, concerned with the efficiency and the justice of governing thrift through Industrial Life Insurance. It was argued, most notably by government commissions and parliamentary leaders, that two major *systematic* problems involved in this model of insurance undermined its privileged status as a moral technology.

First and most significant was the problem of the *expense ratio.* For the middle classes, life insurance premiums were paid once or twice yearly at the office of the company. Making large individual outlays of this sort was beyond the capacity of most working people, who relied instead on frequent small payments. Such collection procedures were labor intensive and costly, and the payment of commissions to the army of collectors generated a drain of between 25 and 50 percent of the value of premiums collected. Accordingly the rate of return for poor people's thrift was recognised by all to be much lower than for the middle classes, and effectively involved "use-less thift" on the part of the poor. This was linked to a criticism that be-cause useless thrift represented a disincentive to thrift among the poor, and because the collectors were required to bear upon the poor in order to make them save, industrial life insurance did not work in practice to instill a moral virtue—a free-willed embracing—of thrift.

Second were the twinned problems of *lapses* and *overselling.* As the col-lectors benefited directly from the value of premiums collected, there were systematic pressures to increase sales. Overselling was held responsible for a high rate of lapsed policies among the poor. As early as the 1860s, the rate of lapses was seen by government officials as a *deterrent* to thrift among the poor, for holders of lapsing industrial insurance policies received nothing by way of return from their savings (House of Commons Debates 1864, vol. 173:1575). Ten years later Northcote's Royal Commission made the claim that it was in the agents' and companies' interests to sell policies to people whom they knew were unlikely to be able to sustain them, because the lapsing of policies amounted to windfall profits through "confiscation of the premiums of its members" (Royal Commission 1874:cx–cxxxiii). Thus while the importance of thrift as a means for governing the poor was never brought into question, and indeed was the driving concern of parliamentary critics, a contest emerged that focused on whether the lack of adequate pro-vision for security was the result of the absence of thrift among the poor, or the unsatisfactory institutional means for instilling thrift or for converting any such thrift into security.

The government's concerns about the need to encourage habits of self-reliance and to make the poor less reliant on poor relief brought it to chal-lenge the inadequacies of industrial insurance. In 1865, Prime Minister Gladstone set up a state-run fully contributory life insurance system de-signed to drive the industrial insurance companies from the market. In the Government Annuities Act of that year, a scheme was introduced that re-tained the practice of small premiums paid weekly, but dispensed with col-lectors. Instead, it required contributions to be made at the local post office. The expectation was that the thrifty poor would be attracted away from the industrial insurance companies because the post-office scheme's reduced collecting costs would result in a much higher rate of return to the policy-holder. Moreover, because the officials of the post office would have no fi-nancial interest in overselling policies, the plan would eliminate another of evils afflicting life insurance for the poor.

Within a decade, however, post office insurance appeared to have failed, with few people entering the scheme or sustaining payment of their premiums. The Northcote Royal Commission concluded from such evidence that the insurance industry, after all, was correct in its view that the poor would not practice thrift unless "specially invited and urged to do so by personal application from the collectors; nor will they keep up their payments unless the collector calls for them" (Royal Commission 1874). Accordingly, the Commission recommended that for any scheme of life insurance directed at the poor, "house to house collection will be required." Otherwise, it supported the continued operation of the post office scheme. Because this model worked through the fair "competition of the government," it was felt by the Commission that insurance companies could not claim state interference in the market. Moreover, as the post office scheme was fully contributory, it "did not carry with it something of the appearance of a relief system" (id.). The unanimous recommendation of the Commissioners, therefore, was that the system of government insurance, newly armed with insurance collectors, should be extended to more effectively compete in the field of industrial insurance.

By implication, government collectors would now enter the field in direct competition with those of the companies and societies. However, this proposal was never enacted, not because of liberal fears about the state entering the market, but because it created the image of government postal agents—or "special postmen"—acting inappropriately. In particular it was felt unacceptable that officers of the state would be constrained to act like common commercial salesmen. As Sir Edward Brabrook, the Chief Registrar of Friendly Societies noted, if the private insurance collector supports himself "by the arts of persuasion which he uses upon poor mothers to induce them to effect insurances; . . . (then) the special postman, if he is to be a success, would have to learn to use the same arts of persuasion, and would thus become as unlike the ordinary Government Officer as could be" (Brabrook 1898:78–79).

There was also concern that the commercial nature of such "special postmen" would blur the distinction between private and public, taking the government into private homes in a way that was still a concern to classical liberalism. Indeed, Gladstone had adverted to this very danger when setting up the post office scheme in 1864, stressing that "the House of Commons is not going to vote money to enable us to go into every cottage in the country" (House of Commons Debates 1864, vol. 173:1566). Finally, as Brabrook pressed, if an army of state collectors entered the field, then this would eliminate one of the main justifications for state involvement—the lowering of expense ratios.[4]

Available technologies of insurance for the poor thus appeared to be intrinsically compromised: first because the volitional basis of moral virtues such as thrift (which, under the regime of moral virtue, had to be exercised freely and habitually) was compromised by the necessity for some form compulsion; and second because the apparent impossibility of avoiding high collection costs meant that the institution of industrial life insurance generated wasted thrift. Thrift, as a moral virtue, was thus *problematically* embodied in specific institutional forms of insurance. The tensions set up were to transform thrift itself as a way of thinking about and governing working class security.

Welfare Liberalism: Social Insurance and "the Consumer"

Into the twentieth century, continuing critiques of industrial life insurance condemned its failures and injustices. Despite this, Prime Minister Lloyd George decided against incorporating industrial life insurance into his nationalized insurance scheme in 1911. Ostensibly this was because "there is hardly a household in this country where there is not a policy of insurance against death . . . (and) the ground has been very thoroughly covered" (House of Commons Debates 1911, vol. 31:1181). Almost certainly, this decision was made to minimize industry resistance to other developments (notably social health insurance), and reflected a pragmatic desire to deploy the insurance companies and their collectors as convenient agents for state insurances. But the upshot nevertheless was that industrial insurance survived, albeit to remain the target of repeated and severe criticisms, first by Sydney Webb (Passfield 1915) and later by further government reviews—the Parmoor Report (Departmental Committee 1920) and the Cohen Report (Select Committee 1933). None of these did very much more than reiterate and painstakingly document the problems already identified in the nineteenth century. During World War II, however, developments that foreshadowed the formation of the postwar welfare state not only brought to bear new pressures on industrial life insurance, but reconceptualized the whole framework of governing security through thrift, discipline, and insurance on which it was founded.

The Invention of "Socially Desirable Thrift"

The proposals of successive inquiries between 1879 and 1930 had more or less taken for granted the market-based delivery of life insurance. Northcote had recommended that the state enter as a competing supplier, Cohen urged that it expand its role as a competitor, and Parmoor had advised increasing regulation of the industry. However, in his report on *So-*

cial Insurance and Allied Services—in many ways the blueprint for post-war British welfare institutions—William Beveridge shifted the debate into the realm of welfare liberalism. He argued, in short, that "[t]he criticisms made upon life assurance in the past have not been met, and cannot be met while the system remains, as at present, a competitive business" (1942: 274). While the problems with industrial insurance noted by Beveridge were virtually identical to those located by each of the previous inquiries, Beveridge bypassed their inability to resolve the problems of industrial insurance by arguing that

> life assurance is not like other commodities because those who insure make their choice once for all when they take out a policy. They cannot buy less insurance or another form of insurance next day or change their assurance company without loss, as next day they can substitute bacon for beef or change their grocer without loss. Industrial assurance, that is to say *life assurance among people of limited means, is so different from most other commodities that it cannot be safely treated as an article of commerce.* (Beveridge 1942:275, emphasis added)

Beveridge achieved this position not by focusing on the moral problematic of thrift, but by imagining insurance in terms of the nature and behavior of commodities and consumers. He then moved on to distinguish two kinds of insurance commodity, those that behave like normal commodities ("luxuries") and those that behave like exceptional commodities ("necessities," which were in their turn defined by the fact that people with less than the means of subsistence continue to purchase them). In the case of the latter, market distribution presents "special dangers to the consumer." For the moment, we must pass by the highly significant reimagining of people as "consumers," for at this point, Beveridge reintroduced the idea of thrift. But it is a thrift transformed, for he argued that in the light of this analysis it is necessary for the state to create new *"socially desirable forms of insurance and thrift"* (id.).

The first of these forms, which he labelled "compulsory thrift," referred to the provision of necessities. Necessities have a common characteristic, namely, that they correspond to universal needs, and can thus be provided to all, and in a universal form. This being the case, the state could provide insurance for such commodities, via compulsory premiums extracted at source, providing all subjects with the same level of benefit. In the case of such universal needs, Beveridge suggested, personal practices of thrift were inappropriate or inadequate, for where personal thrift did not provide for them, the public purse would have to. Thereby, Beveridge took the element of compulsion that had always been mixed up in industrial life insurance, restricted it to provision for necessities, removed it from the "voluntary" market sector (where it had ever been problematic), and assigned it to the state where—even according to the tenets of classical liberalism—coercive power belongs.

Having evacuated compulsion to the realm of necessities, Beveridge could now articulate the second novel category: "voluntary thrift."[5] If compulsory thrift was to deal with "necessities" that could become a charge on the public purse, voluntary thrift was assigned to the sphere of "luxuries"— the provision of which, even if not provided for by the individual, could not legitimately become a responsibility of the state. Moreover, as luxuries relate to needs that are "less uniform and less universal," they were deemed by Beveridge to be appropriate subjects for "voluntary action rather than compulsion." In this way, the creation of two socially desirable forms of thrift, especially of voluntary thrift, allowed elements of working class insurance to become fully commodified for the first time since the passage of the Gambling Act.[6] The model is well illustrated with respect to burial insurance, once the mainstay of industrial life insurance. Beveridge (1942:271–75) proposed the introduction of compulsory burial insurance for "the essential universal need for direct funeral expenses." Expenses for luxuries, that is, items over and above those needed for the provision of what he referred to as "a decent burial," being less uniform and less universal, were assigned to the action of voluntary thrift.

Some of the old concerns upon which governing through the morality of thrift had focused, particularly those relating to the proper expenditure on necessities, were thus still to be governed. But they were to be governed "scientifically" rather than "morally" by state technocrats who would decide levels of need and determine the premiums required to fund them. In the process, Beveridge almost defined out of existence the nineteenth-century moral virtue of thrift, together with its disciplinary regime enforcing habits of frugality and saving. "Compulsory thrift," taking the form of contributions extracted at source, required no such moral compulsion. "Voluntary thrift," on the other hand, clearly implied that saving and insurance were matters of personal choice and discretion rather than moral pressure (Beveridge 1942:275).

Commodifying Insurance under Welfare Liberalism

In analyses of insurance under welfare liberalism, the compulsory and state-based nature of social insurances has normally monopolized the attention of theorists of insurance (see, e.g., Defert 1991; Ewald 1990,

1994). However, with respect to life insurance in this period Beveridge's focus on voluntarism and choice, and his analytical starting point of commodities and consumption, are equally fundamental issues. The economic discourse that shaped and provided the foundation for Beveridge's thinking was that of John Maynard Keynes, which may be distinguished from the classical economics of the previous century, inter alia, by its focus on consumption rather than production (Cutler, Williams, and Williams 1986; Waine 1991).

Beveridge was quite clear about the fact that the reforms he was proposing were to be understood in this framework, as being an expression of this shift in focus away from a framework of production:

> [C]orrect distribution does not mean what it has often been taken to mean in the past—distribution between the different agents of production, between land, capital, management and labour. Better distribution of *purchasing power* is required among wage earners themselves, as between times of earning and not earning and between times of heavy family responsibilities and times of light or no family responsibilities. (Beveridge 1942:167, emphasis added)

The full implications of this observation only emerge when a second matter is considered. Beveridge had observed that compared with the situation prevailing at the turn of the century, real living standards had increased by 30 percent and, still more important, the surplus income of those workers above the poverty line was eight times as great as the deficiency of those below it. Viewing authoritative predictions of postwar growth, he was confident that this trend would continue for the foreseeable future (Harris 1977). His first conclusion was that poverty could be eliminated by redistributing incomes within the working class—seemingly dispelling the lingering "Poor Law" concern that support for the poor represents a charge on the wealthy. This was to be the role of compulsory insurance. His second conclusion was that industrial life insurance would be obsolete in this new environment. The real incomes of workers would be such that door-to-door collection of insurance premiums, together with the problem of the expense ratio that it created, could be dispensed with. Workers would be able to pay insurance premiums in the same manner as the middle classes, and reap the benefits of increased returns on their investment.

This set of observations underlay his linking of voluntary thrift to the category of discretionary income, and to the notion that a sector of working class insurance could now be more completely commodified than had previously been thought possible.[7] As Zelizer (1994) has noted, thinking of income as "surplus" to necessities is a very specific way of thinking about money. If nothing necessary has to be gone without, personal expenditure is far less subject to moral constraint: it is rendered, as Beveridge termed it, "voluntary" in a sense that could not readily have been applied fifty years before. More generally, the rethinking of insurance, thrift, and surplus in this way took its place in what May and Cooper (1995) regard as part of a broader "reconstitution of citizenship" in which individuals and groups increasingly are seen not as *citizens* but as *consumers*.

As seen above, this rethinking of the subjects of insurance as consumers was quite explicit in Beveridge's work. While this is partly explained by his focus on Keynesian economics, it is also linked to new ways of thinking about liberalism that Beveridge saw emerging. In the liberal political discourses surviving into the 1940s, "choice," "freedom," and "liberty" scarcely appeared, while concepts such as "frugality," "thrift," and "savings" continued to hold center stage (Brett 1993). Accordingly, individualism "took its primary meaning from Protestantism and its ethic of hard work, personal responsibility, thrift and community service." By contrast, in the coming years, while the key characteristic of the individual was thus *independence*, "(t)oday it is *freedom*, most generally understood as freedom of choice in everything ranging from the colour of a new stove to sexuality" (Brett 1993:30, emphasis in original; see also Rose 1990).

Neoliberalism: Putting the Risk Back into Insurance

Beveridge proposed that the only way to rid the life insurance industry of its coercive and expensive collectors was to nationalize industrial life insurance, and displace it with a state Industrial Insurance Board that "would work steadily to substitute direct payment of premiums for collection" (1942:275). However, while social insurance on this model subsequently absorbed such areas as burial insurance soon after the war (in 1948), the political muscle of the industry, and failures of political will by the Labour Party, meant that the field allocated to voluntary thrift remained in the hands of industrial life insurance and its collectors. Nevertheless, writing in 1955, still in the shadow of Beveridge's threat of nationalization of industrial life insurance, one of the last apologists of industrial life insurance foresaw the conditions of its demise. It was possible, but unlikely, Daniel Morrah argued, that industrial life insurance could be ousted by the victory of a more determined socialist regime. In practice, however, a

> slighter revolution than that would suffice to make it superfluous. If the
> great mass of the people possessed bank accounts, and could habitually

maintain credit balances substantially exceeding the annual amount they thought reasonable to set aside for future needs, then they could provide against emergency by the methods of ordinary life assurance with its premiums paid at long intervals, and industrial assurance (paid) by weekly or monthly contributions, which is necessarily less economical, could not compete. (Morrah 1955:171)

In Morrah's view, however, the survival of industrial life insurance was assured because it was still the case that the mass of the populace "have neither bank accounts nor substantial capital resources," and that "weekly wages . . . so little exceed the necessary domestic outgoings of the week that thrift is always an effort." In such a setting, echoing his Victorian predecessors, Morrah saw that *"pressure and even strong pressure is therefore essential"* to effect adequate insurance against emergencies (1955:174, emphasis added). Yet within a decade, industrial life insurance had become a minor aspect of the life insurance industry (Dunning 1971), and it continued declining by degrees until by the late 1980s it accounted for less that 3 percent of new life insurance business. As far as the insurance industry and its commentators are concerned, Beveridge and Morrah had made correct predictions: the long boom of the 1950s and 1960s created the surplus income that made ordinary life insurance feasible for the working class, and the better return that this offered attracted the market away (id.).

In these years of postwar consumer prosperity, the mass of the population came to be viewed as *positively enlisted* rather than needing to be *morally coerced* into the institutions of fiscal security. Insurance no longer is imagined to be about preventing poverty through regular little acts of sacrifice. Rather, it is envisioned as the creation of wealth through the active ("voluntary") investment of disposable ("surplus") income—a vision of life insurance as fully commodified. This insurance language now speaks of "investment and pension products." Life insurance is "viewed as an alternative investment vehicle" that "no longer sits alone but forms part of the retail services sector" (Price Waterhouse 1990). Current discourses of "freedom of service"—that contrast so vividly with the nineteenth-century imagery of moral compulsion—reflect a valorization of the sovereign consumer that is associated with neoliberalism and the "enterprise culture" (Keat 1991). As Clayton (1985) indicates, the insurance commodity now is provided, in its own understanding at least, not in terms of what "is good for" the insured party, but in terms of "what the consumer wants."

If "thrift" gives way to "investment," it is in part because risk itself is being more positively evaluated in contemporary liberal political rationality. Previous generations of classical liberals and welfare liberals regarded the minimization of future risk as essential for the security of working people. The former fostered thrift and frugality, and the latter established social insurances to achieve this end. To neoliberals, however, risk is not only a negative thing related to harms and to be minimized, but also has its *positive* side that must be valued and made salient, as the source of profit and the root of enterprise and self-reliance (O'Malley 1994). It is also, in the postwelfare era, seen as a potent weapon against the "welfare dependency" that Beveridge's social insurances are now believed to have created (Thatcher 1993).[8]

This positive vision of risk is now beginning to generate a further restructuring of insurance regimes for the working classes. Increasingly, the "voluntary," commodified sector of insurance is being expanded into the "compulsory" field of social insurances. Successive regimes of government in Britain have been involved in a program of restricting access to, and diminishing the attractiveness of, welfare and compulsory social insurances, and of regulating and encouraging their substitution by "private welfare" (Alcock 1989). In this environment, life insurance takes on a changing role. "Encouraged" by legislation such as the Social Security Act of 1986, consumers are exhorted to purchase "investment products which allow the public to gain additional benefits to supplement those gained from the state" or to "contract out of the state scheme altogether in exchange for incentives." Rather than being thought as a contraction of social insurances and welfare, this process is represented as an "expanding market for pension products" (Price Waterhouse 1990).

In practice, the development of the "personal pension" scheme in the wake of the 1986 legislation represents an even more far-reaching development than these commentaries imply. In many respects, the commodification of insurance for workers that occurred during the 1960s and 1970s was no more than the extension of Beveridge and Labour's version of consumerism, in which consumers exercised freedom of choice among the offerings of the market. Thatcher's neoliberalism, however, attempted to establish a program of "worker capitalism" in which it was imagined that "[m]aking every adult a shareholder would serve as a specific antidote to the passivity and lassitude that overcome dependents of a welfare state" (Letwin and Letwin 1986:11). The "activated" worker thus moves beyond being a mere consumer to becoming an entrepreneur: "[T]he vast majority of British adults own investments in bank accounts, life insurance, unit trusts, and pension funds; and they thereby, though unknowingly, possess indirect claims on shares owned by such financial intermediaries. But . . .

however rewarding such investments are financially, they do not and cannot give their owners a sense of enjoying a rightful and potentially active voice in determining the policies of the nation's enterprises" (Letwin and Letwin 1986).

In the personal pension schemes this "defect" is remedied. While the contribution levels still are set at the time of the contract, instead of this delivering a fixed and actuarially calculated benefit upon realization, the final amount of the benefit will depend upon the performance of the individual investment portfolio or the preferred level-of-risk (high, medium, or low) policy package selected by the investor. This insurance, then, is not about "the taming of chance," the term that has come to be so familiar in risk-minimizing or risk-spreading readings of insurance. Rather, risk is to be given its head. Insurances now are to exploit risk and to expose the policyholder to the risk that is imagined to be the source of enterprise and gain. Ironically, the Prudential Corporation, formerly the doyen of industrial life insurance, is the leading company in the personal pensions market (Waine 1992).

Conclusion: Transforming Insurance?

For François Ewald, risk is understood as having two elements:

> Rather than with the notions of danger and peril, the notion of risk goes together with those of chance, hazard, probability, eventuality or randomness on the one hand, and those of loss or damage on the other—the two series coming together in the notion of accident. One insures against accident, against the probability of loss of some good. Insurance, through the category of risk, objectifies every event as an accident. Insurance's general model is the game of chance: a risk, an accident, comes up like a roulette number, a card pulled out of the pack. With insurance, gaming becomes the symbol of the world. (Ewald 1991:199)

What is remarkable about this passage is that insurance is defined as risk related to loss or damage, while simultaneously it is defined as a *game of chance*, with its clear connotations of the possibility of speculative gain. This latter imagery, of course, was precisely that potential element of insurance that successive generations of industry and government had attempted to stifle since the Gambling Act of 1774. While endowment policies certainly came to represent an investment for the future, it was always the solid security of actuarially known and guaranteed levels of benefit that were emphasised: *investment devoid of speculation* (Zelizer 1979). Life insurance thus retained its faith with the Victorian virtues of thrift and frugality into the last quarter of the twentieth century.

Ironically, despite the fact that welfarism is often assailed for eroding these virtues, the welfare liberal reforms developed by William Beveridge preserved them, albeit in a transformed state. Beveridge adhered to the idea that saving to cover future risks with respect to life's necessities, and for insurance to provide assured benefits, was absolutely crucial. So much so that it could not be left to inefficient mechanisms such as industrial life assurance, and certainly not to be vagaries of the market, but would be assigned to the scientific governance of state technocrats expert in risk spreading and risk minimization. Viewed in this way, the welfare state can be seen to be a profoundly conservative institution. While it transformed thrift from a personal moral virtue to an administrative procedure of the state, by making saving for individual security compulsory and rigorously predictable, it moved poles apart from the gaming model that was the skeleton in the closet of life insurance. Neoliberals, however, by encouraging insurance policyholders to expose their investments to the speculative hazards of the stock market, effectively restored the old sense of *gaming* to insurance— just as simultaneously they were transforming gambling itself into an acceptable "industry" (Dixon 1991).

Thus while leaders such as Margaret Thatcher (1993) have made much of the idea that neoliberals are restoring such Victorian virtues as thrift, in some ways nothing could be further from the truth. Thrift and financial speculation, at least in the lives of working class people, were at polar ends of the Victorian moral spectrum. There is thus little that is Victorian, albeit much that is held to be "virtuous" about current promotion of the gambling industry, mass participation in stock and futures markets, and the speculative life insurance market. If these are now institutions of thrift, then indeed the meaning of this term meaning has changed radically since Victorian times.

With these transformations, the triangular relationship between thrift, risk, and insurance also shifted dramatically. Each of these terms has undergone a change in meaning and evaluation, in ways that are articulated with underlying political rationalities. Nevertheless this articulation is rarely so straightforward that such changes can simply be translated directly from political discourse. Much depends on how insurance and its possible applications are imagined within these broad frameworks: the new terms and concepts that are invented to capture these in thought; the ways in which the meanings of these terms drift and are transformed; and the ways in which they come to be "translated" into institutional shape. While more traditional forms of analysis would interpret these processes as the working out of changes determined at another level such as class or the economy, the specific forms of insurance that exist within such determinations are often immensely diverse, and these diversities are highly consequential. It is the work of "insurantial imagination," rather than simply class interest, market pressures, or actuarial technique, that gives insurance its diversity.

NOTES

Research support for this paper was provided by the School of Law and Legal Studies, La Trobe University. Thanks to the staff of the British Library for assistance obtaining many documents. Thanks also to my colleagues for their comments and advice, especially Tom Baker, Kathy Laster, Nikolas Rose, Clifford Shearing, Jonathan Simon, Mariana Valverde, and Gary Wickham. An expanded version of this essay was published in *Connecticut Insurance Law Journal* 5, no. 2 (1999): 675–706, and is reprinted here by permission of *Connecticut Insurance Law Journal.*

1. The term *assurance* here is synonymous with the term *insurance.* While the former is strictly the correct term in this history, for ease of comprehension I will refer throughout to "industrial life insurance"—except of course in direct quotations using the original term. "Industrial Life Insurance" is the American name for the equivalent institution.

2. For example, the Friendly Societies Act of 1819, and the Acts of 1793, 1829, and 1834 (33 Geo. III c.54; 10 Geo. IV c.56; and 5 Wm. IV c.40). The preamble of the Act of 1793 for example referred approvingly to the Societies' role in "diminishing the public burthens."

3. By 1911, Lloyd George estimated that there existed in excess of 40 million industrial life insurance policies, and that "(t)here is scarcely a household in this country where there is not a policy of insurance against death" (House of Commons Debates 1911: vol. 31:1181). The Parmoor Committee estimated that close to three-fourths of the British population contributed to some form of industrial life insurance (Departmental Committee 1920).

4. Without collectors, the post office scheme continued to function in a marginal fashion. In 1920 it was again dismissed as ineffectual by a government inquiry—this time the Parmoor Report (Departmental Committee 1920)—largely on the basis of its inability to attract life insurance business without deploying collectors. It eventually closed in 1928.

5. Voluntary thrift was given formal party policy status in the Labour Party platform of 1949 (Labour Party 1949, 1950)

6. By "fully commodified," I refer specifically to the removal of moral compulsion, and the release of these aspects of insurance to what will now become matters of a new kind of liberty: "freedom of choice."

7. However, it needs to be noted that many critics challenged Beveridge's views on the "reality" of this surplus. See, e.g., Abel-Smith and Townsend 1965.

8. For the most recent political expression of such a view, see Prime Minister John Major's eulogizing of "the risk takers of Great Britain," whom he contrasts with those who take the prudent, cautious line. The latter, by implication, are at the root of any instance of economic underperformance (reported in *The Guardian,* 21–25 October 1995). Earlier views of a similar nature have been expressed throughout the literature of the New Right. See, in particular, Aharoni's (1981) deriding of the welfare state as the "No-Risk Society."

REFERENCES

Abel-Smith, B., and P. Townsend. 1965. *Poor and Poorest*. Harmondsworth: Penguin Books.

Aharoni, Y. 1981. *The No-Risk Society*. New York: Basic Books.

Alcock, P. 1989. "A Better Partnership between the State and Individual Provision: Social Security into the 1990s. *Journal of Law and Society* 16 (1): 97–111.

Beveridge, William. 1942. *Social Insurance and Allied Services*. London: HMSO (Cmd 6404).

Brabrook, Sir Edward. 1898. *Provident Societies and Industrial Welfare*. London: Robinson.

Brett, J. 1993. "The Party on the Road to Nowhere." *The Age* (Melbourne), 17 July.

Clayton, G. 1985. *British Insurance*. London: Elek Books.

Cuneo, C. 1986. "Comment: Restoring Class to State Unemployment Insurance." *Canadian Journal of Political Science* 19:93–98.

Cutler, T., K. Williams, and J. Williams. 1986. *Keynes, Beveridge and Beyond*. London: Routledge and Kegan Paul.

Dalton, B. 1986. *Classical Probability in the Enlightenment*. Princeton: Princeton University Press.

Defert, D. 1991. "Popular Life and Insurance Technology." In *The Foucault Effect: Studies in Governmentality*, ed. G. Burchell, C. Gordon, and P. Miller. London: Harvester Press.

Departmental Committee. 1920. *Report of the Departmental Committee on the Business of Industrial Assurance Companies (Parmoor Report)*. London: HMSO.

Dixon, D. 1991. *From Prohibition to Regulation*. Oxford: Clarendon Press

Doran, N. 1994. "Risky Business: Codifying Embodied Experience in the Manchester Unity of Oddfellows." *Journal of Historical Sociology* 7:131–54.

Dunning, J. 1971. *Insurance in the Economy*. London: Institute of Economic Affairs.

Ewald, F. 1990. "Norms, Discipline and the Law." *Representations* 30:138–61.

———. 1991 "Insurance and Risks." In *The Foucault Effect: Studies in Governmentality*, ed. G. Burchell, C. Gordon, and P. Miller. London: Harvester Press.

———. 1994 "Two Infinities of Risk." In *The Politics of Everyday Fear*, ed. B. Massumi. St. Paul: University of Minnesota Press.

Gilbert, B. 1965. "The Decay of Nineteenth Century Provident Institutions and the Coming of Old Age Pensions in Great Britain." *Economic History Review* (Series 2) 17 (4): 550–63.

Harris, J. 1977. *William Beveridge. A Biography*. Oxford: Clarendon Press.

Holdsworth, Sir W. (1969). *A History of English Law*. Vol. 3. London: Methuen; Sweet and Maxwell.

Johnson, P. 1985. *Saving and Spending. The Working Class Economy in Britain 1870–1939*. Oxford: Clarendon Press.

Keat, R. 1991. "Introduction. Starship Britain or Universal Enterprise?" In *Enterprise Culture*, ed. R. Keat and N. Abercromby. London: Routledge.

Labour Party. 1949. *Labour Believes in Britain.* London: British Labour Party.

———. 1950. *The Future of Industrial Insurance.* London: British Labour Party.

Letwin, S., and W. Letwin. 1986. *Every Adult a Shareowner.* London: Centre for Policy Studies.

May, C., and A. Cooper. 1995. "Personal Identity and Social Change." *Acta Sociologica* 38 (1): 75–85.

Merkin, R. 1980. "Gambling by Insurance. A Study of the Life Assurance Act 1774." *Anglo-American Law Review* 9:331–63.

Miller, P., and N. Rose. 1990. "Governing Economic Life." *Economy and Society* 19:1–27.

Morrah, D. 1955. *A History of Industrial Life Assurance.* London: Allen and Unwin.

O'Malley, P. 1994. "Regulating Enterprise Culture." *Canadian Journal of Law and Society* 9:205–15.

———. 1996. "Risk and Responsibility." In *Foucault and Political Rationality,* ed. A. Barry, T. Osborne, and N. Rose. London: UCL Press.

Pal, L. 1986. "Relative Autonomy Revisited: The Origins of Canadian Unemployment Insurance." *Canadian Journal of Political Science* 19:71–92.

Passfield, Lord. 1915. "Special Supplement on Industrial Insurance." *New Statesman,* 13 March, 1–32.

Price Waterhouse. 1990. *A Guide to the UK Insurance Industry.* London: Graham and Trotman.

Rose, N. 1990. *Governing the Soul.* London: Routledge.

Royal Commission. 1874. *Royal Commission to Inquire into Friendly and Benefit Building Societies. Fourth Report (Northcote Report).* London: HMSO (Cmd 961).

Select Committee. 1825. *Report of the Select Committee of the House of Commons on Laws Respecting Friendly Societies.* London: British Parliamentary Papers.

———. 1889. *Report from the Select Committee on the Friendly Societies Act 1875.* London: British Parliamentary Papers.

———. 1933 *Committee on Industrial Assurance and Assurance on the Lives of Children under Ten Years of Age (Cohen Report).* London: HMSO (Cmd 4376).

Thatcher, M. 1993. *The Downing Street Years.* London: Macmillan.

Wilson, A. and H. Levy 1937 *Industrial Life Assurance. An Historical and Critical Study,* London: Oxford University Press.

Waine, B. 1991. *The Rhetoric of Independence. The Ideology and Practice of Social Policy in Thatcher's Britain.* Oxford: Berg.

———. 1992. "Workers as Owners. The Ideology and Practice of Personal Pensions." *Economy and Society* 21: 27–44.

Zelizer, V. 1979. *Morals and Markets: The Development of Life Insurance in the United States.* New York: Columbia University Press.

———. 1994. *The Social Meaning of Money.* New York: Basic Books.

SIX

Insuring More, Ensuring Less: The Costs and Benefits of Private Regulation through Insurance

CAROL A. HEIMER

Introduction

Insurance, often credited with spreading risks and therefore fa-cilitating activities, may sometimes make some activities impossible be-cause insurance mechanisms have supplanted other risk-spreading devices. These days one must first acquire a surety bond before getting a loan to start a business, arrange for fire insurance before securing a mortgage to purchase a home, and offer proof of auto insurance to register a car or get a license to drive. But not everyone is able to secure insurance.[1] Some forms of insur-ance are more easily (and economically) available through employers and are therefore in practice unavailable to those who are unemployed or self-employed. For other forms of insurance, redlining is well documented (see the essays in Squires 1997). It is more difficult to purchase homeowner's insurance for an inexpensive or old home or for a home in a minority-dominated neighborhood.[2] Further, although it is fire insurance rather than homeowner's insurance that typically is required for securing a mortgage, insurers do not always offer them separately. The profits are higher on the combined policies.

Similarly, without insurance coverage such as fidelity bonds and surety bonds, it is difficult to secure a loan to start some kinds of businesses. People who lack a track record may be unable to get such insurance coverage. In the past, personal guarantees served the same functions. But personal suretyship has gone out of fashion. With the transformation of suretyship into a busi-ness, personal suretyship ceased to provide the link needed to secure capital. Banks equipped to assess credit ratings and process insurance forms are not equipped to evaluate a person's connections and personal guarantees. Thus those "outside the system" have more difficulty gaining a toehold with contemporary insurance arrangements than they might have had when nonmarket institutions offered alternatives to commercial forms. Indeed, some of these devices have been made more or less illegal. Worried that downpayments on property come from illegal activities or that there may not be a steady income to cover future payments, banks attempt to determine whether potential buyers have recently received the money for the downpayment rather than accumulating it steadily. A potential homeowner must be prepared to explain where the money came from and to assure the bank that the funds were given freely rather than borrowed.

This essay explores the displacement of other informal risk-management devices by formal insurance. It argues that this displacement has occurred in a process analogous to the displacement of firms that occurs with increasing concentration in an industry. But here it is a displacement of competing forms of risk management as institutional forms of embeddedness have replaced individual embeddedness and guarantees based on social relations. One result is that the management of some kinds of risk has probably increased the prevalence of other kinds of risk—at least for those who do not have access to formal insurance.

Let me frame my argument somewhat differently. Some have argued that the American domestic policy of "more insurance for more people" is now being reconsidered as insurers and government bodies become more concerned about the reactivity of risk (Baker and Simon, chapter 1 this volume). Insurers and risk-management institutions (broadly conceived to include both private and "social" insurance), now more concerned about how to manage the reactivity of risk, may be becoming more selective about what risks they are willing to cover. The balance between insurers and policyholders is thus shifting with fewer risks being assumed by insurers and more left to be covered by individuals themselves.[3] If the old regime was one of "more insurance," the new may be a "less insurance" regime.

But such a claim about the retreat of insurance seems to me incomplete and quite misleading for three reasons. First, it is misleading because the retreat affects different population groups differently. It probably is not even fair to characterize the new regime as offering "less insurance for fewer people." Instead it is a "more insurance for some, less for others" regime. Insurers have not backed off offering insurance to the "haves." Recent increases in income inequality are instead mirrored in inequalities in access to insurance. The safety nets of the rich (which of course include insurance policies) may be a fine, resilient mesh, but it is all too easy to fall through the much larger holes of the loosely woven safety nets of the poor.

Second, any retreat must be understood in the context of contemporary institutional arrangements. A story about the retreat of insurance is incomplete if it fails to include an account of the interdependence of insurance and other institutions. Although compensation of losses may be a core function of insurance, insurers serve other functions as well. Insurers are gatekeepers who can provide or withhold the calling card that gives people access to other goods and services. Like certification societies, standard-setting bodies, and credit inspectors, insurers make evaluations of who is worthy and who is not and other bodies rely both on these assessments and on the indemnity offered by insurers. Insurance assessments carry considerable weight because insurers are willing to put their money behind them. As long as other institutions look to insurers to set the conditions of eligibility as well as to compensate losses, less insurance coverage will not mean less social control by insurers. I know of no evidence that this dependence on insurers as gatekeepers has been discontinued.

Finally, those concerned about the reactivity of risk presumably advocate a shift to less insurance and more of something else. But what is that something else, and is it still possible in a world so shaped by insurance? An "end to welfare as we know it" cannot presage a return to the forms of self-reliance of past generations. Most families not covered by TANF (or its predecessor AFDC) cannot compensate for their low incomes with kitchen gardens; those without health insurance cannot offer to pay hospitals and physicians "in kind." Personal suretyship is no longer a substitute for surety or fidelity bonds—we no longer have a culture of patronage to sustain and regulate such guarantees and, in any case, governments and businesses are not willing to accept such personal guarantees. The objective of "less insurance" is presumably "more responsibility," but more responsibility may depend on the existence of alternative forms of risk management. I argue that these alternative forms have been displaced and discredited by formal insurance. When alternative forms of risk management either do not exist or are discredited, a concern with the proliferation of risk need not lead to decreases in insurance. As everyone seeks to pass losses to someone else, organizations may be unwilling to accept policyholder responsibility as an alternative to insurer guarantees. People, organizations, or activities deemed uninsurable come to be viewed as untrustworthy and undesirable interaction partners; in such a regime, "more responsibility" may mean only "more insurance" and "more opportunities for the insurable."

As important as risk spreading is, it is by no means the only accomplishment of insurance. Equally important is insurance's role as one of the main regulatory institutions of contemporary societies. As a regulator, insurance operates by stealth. Rather than being publicly debated as are regulations that originate with the state, insurance regulations are largely imposed. Moreover, they are less likely to be uniquely negotiated than are other contracts because insurance pools require standardization. The public may debate whether or not to require insurance as a precondition for participation in some activity, but it does not participate in decisionmaking about the conditions under which insurance is granted. Moreover, because organizations do not distinguish between their own rules and those imposed by insurers, people may be blissfully ignorant of the extent to which they are governed by insurers. As a covert regulator, insurance even exerts control in denying coverage. Although there may be technical reasons for denying insurance, activities or people deemed uninsurable are likely to find themselves excluded from more than just insurance. To be "beyond insurance" is often seen as a moral assessment that a person is imprudent or even irresponsible.[4] Rather than finding that they simply have to bear more risk than others, those who are unable to gain insurance coverage may instead find that technical and normative assessments are conflated and they are unable to get loans, run for office, drive a car, or operate a business.

In exploring this Foucauldian reality, I argue that government by insurers has arisen through a two-stage process. By refusing to take up contentious questions about which activities should be encouraged, permitted, and proscribed, and under what conditions, governments and organizations have created a regulatory vacuum. In embracing insurance, they have invited insurers to regulate in their stead. But the resulting alliance between insurers and the state, on the one hand, and insurers and other organizations, on the other, has led to the demise of informal regulatory mechanisms that once regulated and managed risk alongside formal insurance. With the strengthening of ties between insurers and other organizations, informal insurance arrangements may continue to work as a secondary safety net, but they are little help in gaining access to the resources controlled by large organizations. Even as insurers become more selective about the risks they are willing to assume, their reach expands as they regulate by excluding some and mandating the conditions of inclusion for others.

Social Relations as By-Products of Institutional Arrangements

To understand the peculiar character of insurance as a regulatory institution, we need to compare it with other institutional arrangements that also manage some forms of risk and uncertainty. As we see from examining discussions of the risk-management functions of hierarchy and embeddedness, the key point of difference is in the kinds of relationships that arise as a by-product of actions taken for other purposes.

Criticizing both the under- and the oversocialized conceptions of human action, Granovetter (1985) argues that economic action is much more embedded in structures of social relations than other social thinkers have imagined. The oversocialized conception assumes that people are so deeply affected by the social and normative systems whose rules they have internalized that obedience to norms is unthinking and essentially automatic. Once we know the rules of a particular social system, we will be able to predict what course of action its members will follow. In the undersocialized conception, people are very little affected by continuing relationships and norms of the social worlds they inhabit, making decisions for themselves as completely autonomous beings. Granovetter takes both conceptions to task, noting that they "have in common a conception of action and decision carried out by atomized actors. In the undersocialized account, atomization results from narrow utilitarian pursuit of self-interest; in the oversocialized one, from the fact that behavioral patterns have been internalized and ongoing social relations thus have only peripheral effects on behavior" (1985:485).

Granovetter then argues that "social relations, rather than institutional arrangements or generalized morality, are mainly responsible for the production of trust in economic life" (1985:491), although he is careful to remind readers that distrust, opportunism, and disorder are still present on a large scale. But this, he claims, is because economic sectors vary in the extent to which they are penetrated by networks of social relations and because some kinds of social relations create opportunities for malfeasance (particularly collective malfeasance). Social relations are therefore a necessary, but by no means sufficient, condition for trust. Using this argument about the importance of social relations, Granovetter examines the assertions of institutional economists (such as Williamson 1975, 1981) about the conditions under which transactions will occur inside a firm rather than in a market. Williamson argues that firms have the advantage over markets when uncertainties make it difficult to write contracts because people are unsure exactly what they will need and when control of the opportunism of interaction partners is especially important. Both problems, Williamson suggests, can be managed more effectively by the governance structures of firms than by the market. Granovetter questions Williamson's conclusions about both the nature of the market and the nature of the firm. He argues that authority relations are less efficacious in firms than Williamson suggests, and that market transactions are much more shaped by variations in the power of the transacting parties than Williamson believes. What accounts for much of the difference between firms and markets, Granovetter contends, is the higher density of relations inside firms than across organizational borders.

In discussing hierarchy and embeddedness as solutions to opportunism, Williamson and Granovetter are asking how the interests of transacting parties are brought into alignment and kept there. We can productively investigate opportunism, guile, malfeasance, and devices to control them by shifting our focus to examining the problem of moral hazard and how insurers, a group that has specialized in controlling moral hazard, have dealt with these problems (Heimer 1985b). Insurers manage moral hazard, which is essentially a behaviorally based and very reactive risk, in two distinct forms: as the subject of some lines of insurance and as a residual component of every insurance contract. Whenever an insurance policy covers the actions of parties other than the policyholder, moral hazard in effect becomes a subject of insurance. Thus, when marine contracts cover the behavior of stevedores or the captain and crew of the ship, insurers must concern themselves with opportunism and deceit and all the complications of how social ties sometimes increase trustworthiness and sometimes instead merely encourage collective rather than individual malfeasance. Similar arguments can be made about surety and fidelity bonds, covering the performance and the honesty of policyholders and their employees, as well as about other lines of insurance. Further, because policyholders' incentives change (sometimes dramatically if they are dishonest, sometimes only marginally) when an insurance contract covers some of their losses, moral hazard is a residual component of every insurance contract.

Because moral hazard is so central to the accurate prediction of losses and therefore to setting premiums at a level sufficient to cover expected losses, insurers have devised a variety of strategies to predict and control the effects of moral hazard. They use rating and underwriting techniques to predict where dishonesty and nonperformance are especially likely to be problems, refusing insurance in some instances and adjusting premiums in others. Insurers also create communities of fate with their policyholders through deductibles, co-insurance, and requirements to "sue and labor"; alter contractual arrangements to take account of the social distance between the policyholder and the actor who might prevent or cause the loss; make arrangements to have neutral third parties track compliance with key agreements so that policyholders cannot sacrifice loss prevention to production when the two conflict; and update insurance contracts reasonably often so policyholder interests are not deeply altered by a divergence between insured value and market value.

These contractual mechanisms take account of the hard economic facts (for example, divergence between market and insured values, conflict between devoting resources to production and using them on loss prevention). But they also attend to the sorts of social ties that Granovetter discusses. Because coworkers and employees are likely to have strong ties with the policyholder, they may share a policyholder's short-term priorities. For instance, a factory owner (the policyholder) and factory employees may share a concern with productivity, particularly if workers are paid on a piece-rate system, and agree that water pressure should be diverted temporarily from sprinklers to production. (Turning off the sprinklers to increase water pressure, and then forgetting to turn them back on again, was once an important contributor to large fire losses.) A third-party inspector is less likely to have strong ties to the policyholder and its employees, and so less likely to collude with them in choosing production at the expense of safety.

Or to take another example, the social distance between policyholder and the person who might control loss-causing events sometimes works to the benefit of insurers. Captains told to scuttle their ships sometimes performed the necessary acts sufficiently close to shore that they and the crew could escape safely (although their crime was more likely to be detected). But sometimes social distance works against insurers. Even when a policyholder is interested in preventing losses, the policyholder's employees may care little about whether the insurance premiums rise after losses. Employees are, after all, only very indirectly affected by any incentives the insurer may offer. On net balance, when there is considerable social distance (as measured by organizational boundaries, division of labor and specialization, or levels of hierarchy inside an organization) between the policyholder and the actor closest to loss-causing events, human behavior becomes more similar to other "hazards" and losses from human action are no more predictable than any other "accidents."

This suggests that there are multiple methods of solving the sort of problem that concerns Granovetter and Williamson. Under some circumstances, opportunism, moral hazard, and outright fraud can be controlled by bringing transactions inside the firm. But dense social ties, Granovetter contends, may be more important than authority in encouraging people to take account of the interests of those with whom they have made agreements, and so embeddedness may be the key to controlling self-interested behavior. (Of course embeddedness also facilitates collusion.) To hierarchy and embeddedness, we would add a third mechanism for reducing the costs of malfeasance and opportunism. People will sometimes opt for indemnity when they cannot do much else to secure the outcome they most desire.

What is missing from these accounts is an analysis of social forms as creators and reinforcers of social ties. For instance, in choosing hierarchy over market—that is, in choosing "make" over "buy"—a firm not only gets some authority over the production but begins the process of creating the social ties that might make producers responsive to the needs and interests of others in the firm (sometimes to the benefit and sometimes to the detriment of the employer). We need to ask, then, how different ways of solving problems of uncertainty—whether about the future needs of a firm, physical hazards, or the motives and capacities of other people—bring with them different possibilities for social ties. Some social technologies create and support social relationships while others make them irrelevant or difficult to maintain. Discussing the demise of the mutual aid tradition of American fraternal associations, Beito makes just this point: "Much was lost in this exchange [of formal insurance for mutual aid] that transcended economics. The old relationships of fraternity, reciprocity, and autonomy were replaced with paternalism and dependency. The decline of mutual aid networks of neighbors and friends opened the door to impersonal bureaucracies of outsiders" (1994:59).[5]

In *Bowling Alone*, Putnam makes a similar argument about the substitution of financial for social capital in politics, which has made party politics more efficient but has transformed citizens from active participants into disengaged consumers (2000:31–47). When expressive forms (such as letter writing) supplant collaborative forms (such as attending a meeting or serving on a committee), ties between citizens are less likely to be formed. I argue that insurance tends to have this same effect of undermining social ties by making relationships irrelevant. In short, an insistence on more insurance leads to a replacement of *ensuring* (making an outcome more likely) by *insuring* (indemnifying against losses). This substitution of insuring for ensuring arises in part from the techniques of formal insurance. (See O'Malley 2000 for a similar argument contrasting risk and uncertainty.) Equally important, however, is focus on the narrower interest of the insurer in avoiding liability for losses rather than on the broader interest of the insured in accomplishing some set of organizational goals. In replacing states or organizations as purveyors of regulations, insurance may avoid the stalemate of political controversy, but it does so at the cost of substituting narrow regulatory goals for broader ones. Government by the insurers for the insurers is not an inspiring alternative to government by the people for the people.

Embeddedness at the Organizational and
Institutional Levels

The thrust of Granovetter's argument is that when ties between business partners go beyond mere business, so that business is intertwined with other aspects of social life, business transactions are more reliable. People choose as business partners those whom they know and trust from other interactions, those who will be willing to bear some costs to maintain a tie because they have more at stake than the value of a single deal. Those who have multiple ties with the person or firm awarding the contract will then be more likely to be awarded contracts than those lacking such ties.

Granovetter's argument is about ties between particular people. But ties also develop between organizations, and although we might not expect ties between organizations to have all of the effects of ties between people, organizations are not completely interchangeable as interaction partners.[6] Organizations have reputations. Thus one university may be thought of as a "party school" and another as having an excellent chemistry department. Sometimes assessments are made and promulgated by rating bodies or news organizations or other media. Organizations evaluate each other's reliability and the quality of each other's performances. And organizations can even be said to have ties of loyalty to one another, for instance preferentially looking to each other as clients or customers, suppliers of goods and services, as labor markets, and even as suppliers of good ideas about how to do things.[7] Such assessments and feelings are ultimately lodged in the individuals associated with organizations and may even be primarily *about* the individuals in other organizations, but these assessments also are passed on in organizational culture and organizational routines. Because loyalty and collusion are partly organizational-level phenomena, we should be looking not just at social relations between individuals but also at ties between organizations. People may be embedded in social relations, but some of those social relations occur in organizations and create ties among organizations as well as among individuals.

If predictability is increased by interacting with known interaction partners with whom a person shares a rich history, part of that predictability comes from knowing how to accomplish tasks together. When parents are loyal to their child's school, then, this can be explained partly by their knowing and trusting the teachers and parents associated with that school, but also by their having mastered the role of "parent of Montessori preschooler" or "parent of public highschooler." And if my employer and support staff urge a person to use a particular travel agent, express mail service, caterer, or photocopying service, that is partly because they have worked out favorable payment schemes with the suppliers of those services but also because they have become comfortable interacting with known persons at those organizations, using known forms, following known routines, and the like.

What this suggests, though, is that some of the value of embeddedness comes not from the social ties between individuals or groups of people, but from the familiarity of routine. And that in turn suggests that we should be sensitive to the benefits of embeddedness above the individual level and even beyond the organizational level. Institutional embeddedness, the tendency of particular types of organizations to employ particular types of solutions to problems they encounter repeatedly, may increase predictability as well. Once organizations have settled on a common method for accomplishing some task, an insistence on employing an unusual solution may seem perverse, even suspect. As the institutionalized solution method for risk management, formal commercial insurance has just this advantage over informal methods.

The Institutionalization of Insurance and the Displacement of Informal Risk Management

Formal insurance is now employed, even mandated, by organizations as a solution to a variety of problems of uncertainty and unreliability that were once managed in other ways. No doubt much insurance is purchased for this reason, although it would be difficult to determine either how much or what alternative forms of risk management have been displaced. As Supple notes in a brief introductory chapter on the history of insurance, "the basic structure of insurance history . . . has been fashioned by [insurance's] business records" (1984:2), and it is therefore extremely difficult to offer evidence about such matters as archaic forms of risk management and other matters that the insurers did not trouble themselves to document.

Whether or not those purchasing real estate would wish to buy title insurance becomes irrelevant when mortgage companies make title insurance a condition of securing a mortgage. When people have information about the last five owners of a piece of property, they might well conclude that title insurance was unnecessary but for the mortgage company's requirement that they purchase it. Mortgage companies also insist on fire insurance to cover the property, sometimes going so far as to fold all insurance premiums and taxes into the monthly mortgage payment to ensure that insurance is not allowed to lapse. Mortgage companies may also insist, insofar as they have a legal right to insist, that property owners have life insurance policies.

Examples of such ties between insurance and acquisition of other goods and services abound. Most fundamentally, some forms of insurance have become compulsory. Hansell (1996) lists seven forms of insurance that are compulsory for those engaged in particular activities in the United Kingdom. Motor insurance has been compulsory since 1930; insurance to cover the liability of nuclear reactors since 1965; employers' liability insurance since 1969; insurance for horse-riding establishments since 1970; insurance to cover oil pollution by shippers since 1971; and professional indemnity insurance to cover the practice of solicitors since 1976 and insurance brokers since 1977. Other forms of insurance, such as court and government bonds of various sorts, may not be legally required for all people occupying a particular status but nevertheless can be legally required of some. In the United States, where mandates would come mostly from states rather than the federal government, auto insurance of some form or other is now compulsory in many states, and most states that have not mandated auto insurance have passed laws requiring drivers to furnish evidence of their financial responsibility (Dorfman 1994:245–46). Public officials holding a wide variety of positions in many different layers of government are also required to post bonds guaranteeing their performance, and bonds are often required for the operation of many types of businesses and trades ranging from the manufacture of liquor and tobacco to working as a plumber or electrician (Dorfman 1994:174).

Legally mandated insurance is only the tip of the iceberg, though. Beyond such legally mandated insurance, Hansell (1996) notes, many other forms of insurance are routinely required by private parties as part of the process of making a contract. That such requirements for insurance are not legally mandated may matter little if requirements for insurance are thoroughly institutionalized, for instance by inclusion in lists of standard practices for particular kinds of organizations, in the rules of professional associations, and the like. Hansell's discussion of marine insurance illustrates this sort of institutionalization of insurance requirements:

> The great majority of international commercial transactions are financed by the banks or similar institutions. Those lending money will normally insist that the venture is covered by marine insurance. Indeed, it is customary for the marine insurance policy to be considered one of the "documents of title" that must be produced before banks will discount the bills of exchange through which most international trading is

financed. The insurance policy is lodged with the bank as *collateral security* against the money advanced. (1996:32)

Similar hints about the thorough institutionalization of insurance requirements occur in his discussions of life insurance as mortgage protection policies (42), life insurance policies as security for loans (48), how the need for pollution insurance is "well appreciated" (95) even though only oil pollution insurance is legally required, which forms of insurance are "assignable" (because they are essentially forms of property) to other parties (170–72).

If life insurance and fire insurance are commonly required in connection with an application for a home mortgage, it may matter little that they are not *legally* required. This is especially true in the United States where the regulations for the government-run secondary mortgage market (Fannie Mae and Freddie Mac) have strongly shaped the rules for the entire secondary mortgage market (Carruthers and Stinchcombe 1999). When some form of insurance is legally required for a substantial portion of a market, in effect it becomes a requirement for the rest.

Large or otherwise important employers can similarly make some form of insurance a requirement for an entire occupation or profession. For instance, because hospitals require insurance for midwives attending hospital births, malpractice insurance is now essential for the practice of midwifery whether or not a midwife might wish to have a hospital-based practice. And when American physicians claim to be giving up certain specialties or refusing to perform particular procedures because of insurance costs, this tells us that insurance has become an institutionalized part of the practice of medicine in the United States. Moreover, it reminds us that activities can be regulated by being excluded. Fine-grained protocols are only half of the regulatory story; the other half is sorting activities into two groups, those that are insurable, and so subject to detailed rules, and those that are uninsurable and therefore often discouraged if not proscribed. To be uninsurable is to be suspect—undisciplined by reputable systems of standards and regulations, such activities are tainted as too dangerous to be part of normal social life.

But insurance penetrates even more deeply than this, and is built into many contracts in ways that make insurance contracts and insurance fees impossible to avoid. Car rental fees include some insurance coverage and additional insurance is offered at exorbitant rates. If one is an American citizen, employment in Australia is conditional on evidence that one has arranged for health insurance (countries with national health insurance are likely to have treaties with Australia providing coverage for their citizens residing in each other's countries). Some kinds of employment require the purchase of malpractice or other liability insurance.

Purchase of insurance may once have signaled that one was a particularly careful or responsible person (see Baker, chapter 2 this volume, on various meanings of responsibility in this context). But over the years, insurance has become a minimum requirement. The purchase of an insurance policy now signals only conformity rather than exemplary care, and anyone who has not purchased insurance is considered deviant, careless, or negligent. As ties between insurers and other organizations have become stronger, insurance has become a necessity for participation in the core economic and social activities of contemporary life.

What should not be overlooked here is the role of insurers as extralegal regulators. In requiring insurance coverage as a condition for operating a business, owning a home, driving a car, holding office, or engaging in any number of other activities, governments, employers, banks, and other organizations are also requiring policyholders to follow insurers' rules. But unlike government regulations, insurers' rules are not established after public debate, periods for comment and revision, or votes by an elected body. They also are not easily contested. Concealed by several layers of organizational routines, they typically are not immediately recognized as insurance rules because they masquerade as the rules of the organizations in which they are implemented alongside other truly indigenous organizational routines and standard operating procedures.

Competing Forms of Embeddedness: Parallels to Industry Concentration

Although insurance may have become a necessity in contemporary life, it is mainly formal insurance policies, not other forms of risk management, that have increased in importance. Although in the past many of the risks now handled by insurers were managed informally, such devices tend not to be acceptable substitutes as far as lenders, clients, employers, and the like are concerned. The guarantee of a personal surety that a person will perform contracted labor will not be satisfactory to others whose own contracts depend on the fulfillment of an antecedent contract.

The crowding out of informal forms of insurance by formal ones is similar to increasing concentration of an industry. As the market share of one firm or a small number of firms increases, the choices for consumers decrease. We usually discuss decreased competition and decreased consumer choice in commercially available options, but the concentration of an industry may also affect the availability of noncommercial options. Presumably the mechanism would be somewhat different. Rather than a decrease in the number of commercial suppliers of a product and consequent increases in price and decreases in variability of the product, we would instead be looking for some mechanism that made noncommercial substitutes less viable options than previously. The institutional level embeddedness discussed above is just such a mechanism. When other businesses refuse to accept noncommercial forms of insurance, such noncommercial forms are driven from the market just as surely as they would be in a price war, leaving the terrain open to the domination of formal insurers.

In effect, different forms of embeddedness are in competition. Forms of embeddedness that rely on ties between individuals are supplanted by forms of embeddedness constructed around ties between the organizationally based guarantees of reliability. When one way of doing things becomes "normal," other ways become "deviant" and suspect. Formal organizations rarely support alternative ways of doing things once one or a few become standard practice.[8] For instance, once universities accepted the Scholastic Aptitude Test (SAT) as a measure of a student's ability to do college-level work, it became harder for students to gain admission without having taken it.[9] Once formal credit ratings became the accepted measures of a person's creditworthiness, it became harder for potential borrowers to secure loans without the backing of a credit rating bureau. Organizations typically are unwilling to go to the trouble of assessing information supplied by nonstandard channels, and organizations grow up to mimic the standard forms for those who have chosen some other route. For instance, curriculum suppliers and consulting organizations offer home-schooling families the service of keeping their children's records in a form that will facilitate reentry into the public schools or admission to the university (Stevens 2001).

In addition to bearing higher transaction costs to bring themselves into some semblance of compliance with organizational expectations, though, such "deviants" also may be regarded with suspicion. What really accounts for a family's decision to home-school their child? Did the child have serious behavior problems? Why did a couple borrow money from a friend rather than seeking a regular mortgage? Was their credit rating so bad that they were unable to qualify? Or was the informal loan a handy way for the lender to dispose of illicitly gained cash? Lest this seem too far-fetched, we should recall that insurers were once unwilling to insure businesses owned by married women. If a business was listed in a woman's name, they reasoned, surely this must mean that the woman's husband had some reason not to list himself as the owner (Heimer 1982).

As some ways of doing things become the preferred mode, nonstandard modes cease to exist. Even those who might prefer an alternative mode of accomplishing something, or who for some reason cannot do it in the standard way, find it difficult or impossible to use an alternative. Loans from family members or friends may become less common now that bank loans have become the standard method of borrowing. And those who seek loans from nonprofits find that they use the same standards and procedures as the commercial lenders (Moulton 2000).[10] Running a tab at the local store may be less common now that so many people use credit cards. Asking a friend, colleague, or fellow church member to act as a personal surety would be regarded as rather odd in these days of formal insurance. Of course people still have friends and friends still help each other out, but some kinds of services are no longer part of the "routine" of friendship.

To understand how and when this substitution of organizational embeddedness comes about, we must examine the mechanisms by which the substitution is made. What accounts for organizational preferences for formal insurance as a risk-management device? I argue that at least three factors account for the preference. First, we should not ignore the very significant differences in the resource base of formal insurers compared with individuals and families. Insofar as people or organizations wish to be "made whole" after experiencing a loss, an organization with substantial reserves is a better bet (at least since governments have started regulating insurer reserves) than almost any person. And this disparity between organizations and individuals as guarantors has been exacerbated by the practices of courts. In their sympathy for people asked to make up for the deficiencies of those for whom they have generously served as personal sureties, courts have treated personal sureties as "favorites of the court," lightening their burden whenever possible (Heimer 1985b). For these reasons, the advent of corporate suretyship essentially "rendered private suretyship obsolete" (Hansell 1996:63).

Second, the very diversity of alternative forms of risk management makes for difficulties in the routines of organizations. When banks develop routines for processing mortgage applications, deviations from their routines become costly and bank personnel, schooled in the routines, may not know how to assess substitutes for formal insurance. The easiest solution is simply not to accept the alternatives and to make purchase of title and fire insurance a requirement for acquisition of a mortgage. Well aware that individuals may have difficulty paying their hospital bills, hospitals often insist that arrangements for payment be made before treatment is given. But hospital clerks have no way of assessing statements that a relative will pay the bill or verifying that a person has sufficient income from employment to cover the expense. Insisting on evidence of insurance coverage is the simpler and safer alternative (from an organizational perspective) as long as there is no competitive disadvantage from taking this position. As long as consumers are in a relatively weak bargaining position and other organizations follow suit in refusing to accept alternative forms of risk management, an organization has little to lose and much to gain by requiring that customers or clients have insurance coverage. Routinization has much to recommend it. And in general, such a position carries the additional benefit of screening out less "desirable people" (that is, the poor, the homeless, ex-convicts, or former bankrupts).

Organizations might favor insurers over informal risk-management devices for a third reason. Although a relative or friend might have some reason to collude in misrepresenting a person's financial circumstances or in agreeing to function as a guarantor (perhaps never imagining that they would ever really be asked to make good on their promises), a formal insurer has less interest in misrepresenting the situation and more experience in correctly assessing it. Thus institutional embedding becomes attractive in comparison with individual embedding because social relations between individuals increase the potential for collusive deception at the same time and by the same mechanism that they increase the predictability and trustworthiness of people. The question is essentially with whom a person is keeping trust. Collusion against an organization can occur at the same time as one keeps faith with one's partners in deception. In addition, the regulation of insurance companies offers other organizations some assurance that an insurer would have the reserves to make good on its promises (for example, to repay the bank in the event that a building covered by a mortgage was lost to fire) when an individual guarantor might not. Because they are subject to rules about how to operate their business, insurers might be regarded as more reliable guarantors than individuals. Shapiro (1987) points to the fragility of impersonal trust, based as it is on a hierarchy of guarantees and regulation. What makes each level seem reliable is that there is a higher level overseeing it. And although such an edifice is precarious and offers ample opportunity for dishonesty, it may seem less precarious and less prone to simple incompetence than a hierarchy of trust relations based only on individual guarantees.

Exceptions and Countertrends

We should be careful not to overstate the point. To argue that formal insurance has displaced many other forms of risk management does not mean that *no* substitutes exist, that insurance is *always* a prerequisite for access to other goods and services, or that the regulatory reach of insurance governs all aspects of contemporary life equally. A consideration of exceptions and countertrends will add nuance to the argument without challenging its core assertions, at least as they apply to developed economies.

The infrastructural support for insurance provided by stable governments is easy to overlook. As is the case with many economic phenomena that have come to seem "natural," insurance in fact flourishes only where contracts are enforceable. Ironically, effective management of some categories of risk and uncertainty depends on relative certainty about others. Where the state institutions are absent or too weak to enforce contracts, other risk-management devices continue to flourish. During periods of civil war or in countries where organized crime continually challenges states, we would not expect these arguments about governance by insurers to hold. Thus we would not expect the reach of insurance regulation to extend into the daily life of war-torn countries like Congo. Nor would we expect much government by insurance in Mafia-dominated areas of southern Italy (Gambetta 1988).

By controlling violence and the disorder it brings and by enforcing contracts, states may increase the pervasiveness of government by insurance. But states are also an alternative source of regulation, and in that sense they compete with insurance. Insurers may simply fill a regulatory void, bringing order to a field in which other regulators have shown little interest; or they may regulate at the invitation of the state, in an arrangement that resembles the hiring of contractors to supply services that the state does not itself wish to supply; or they may enter the political fray, actively opposing state attempts to regulate, particularly when citizen interest or outrage encourages states to enter areas previously left to insurers.

Each of these patterns can be seen in the regulation of health care in the United States (see Starr 1982; *Journal of Health Politics, Policy, and Law* 1993a, 1993b; Ruggie 1996). Starting in the colonial period, health professionals sought limited state intervention by asking state governments to protect the monopolies of physicians through licensure. Later Blue Cross and Blue Shield, the big third-party health insurers set the standards and governed the provision of health care with a few specialized areas (for example, state mental health facilities and veterans' hospitals) governed by the state. With the birth of Medicare and Medicaid, state competition for governance of health care increased, but at the same time health maintenance organizations (HMOs) introduced a tightly regulated form of governance by insurers. Even in this system of shared governance, though, both insurers and the state subscribe to a single set of standards articulated by such groups as the Joint Commission on Accreditation of Health Care Organizations (JCAHO). During Clinton's first term as president, insurers fought vigorously to retain their role as the regulators of health care, successfully stalling a major overhaul of American health care.

We might also expect to find other risk-management tools flourishing in the backwaters inhabited by those rejected by insurers. Although formal insurance may be the risk-management method of choice among those who have choices, informal methods may not have been crowded out among those prevented from choosing insurance solutions. If we take the relationship between mortgage lenders and insurers (title, homeowners, fire, and now private mortgage insurance) as an example, it seems likely that the cozy relationship between these two institutions does not extend into the subprime mortgage market. Online loan originators and subprime lenders may have more relaxed standards about insurance and credit ratings. According to some accounts, subprime lenders (such as the Money Store and Green Tree Financial) "use predatory tactics to lure and take advantage of consumers" (Aggie Brose of Pittsburgh Community Reinvestment Group, quoted in McNulty 1998). In one study, the number of loans offered by subprime lenders to black borrowers rose by 31 percent during a period when all loans to black borrowers increased by only 7 percent.[11] Another source claimed that subprime lending grew by 39 percent in 1997 when all mortgages grew by only 8 percent (Lubove 1998:50; see Canner, Passmore, and Laderman 1999 for similar figures). "Lending to folks with blemished credit reports is still a growth business," the author concluded (Lubove 1998:50).

One explanation for this rapid growth is that when Fannie Mae and Freddie Mac raised the credit ratings required for their loans, many borrowers were forced into the subprime market. What seems to many lenders a very risky business (bankruptcy rates are high and even the most optimistic acknowledge that controlling risk is a big problem) seems to others an opportunity. In these markets, success cannot hinge on offering loans only to those with good credit ratings or adequate insurance coverage. Instead, lenders use other strategies: high interest rates and relentless attention to collection. One lender states his company's objective this way: "Our goal is to make sure that if our customers are only going to make one payment a month, it's ours" (Lubove 1998:50). Those who lack the "calling card" of a good credit rating or the guarantees offered by insurers may still be able to get loans, but they do not get them because they can offer informal substitutes for insurance or a good credit rating. Instead, the cost is typically a considerably higher interest rate and a short leash.

These pieces offer a salutary reminder that we need to consider the distance spanned by insurers' regulatory power not as two categories but as a continuous variable. The regulatory shadow of formal insurance, like the shadow cast by law (Mnookin and Kornhauser 1979), varies from one location to another. The shadow surely fades as we move, in the banking world, from those seeking loans in the primary market, who are expected to have insurance; to those who do not quite meet the requirements of the primary mortgage market and so are required to purchase private mortgage insurance (as Witt 1999 notes is the case for 40 percent of new homeowners) or who arrange for asset integrated mortgages (Jud and Winkler 1995); to those seeking loans from nonprofit lenders, who still follow standard practices in regard to collateral and insurance (Moulton 2000); to the subprime lenders, who do not insist on insurance but simply charge higher prices. We would expect the same fading of insurance's shadow in other fields as we move along a continuum from thoroughly reputable mainstream activities and people to those perceived as more marginal. To judge the degree of insurance influence as a regulator, then, we would need to examine the full continuum.

Risk depends on more than just qualities of character and questions about prudence, though. It also depends on the extent to which an activity is itself orderly, predictable, and routinized. Again, bank lending and the use lenders make of insurance is instructive. Generally, banks and the federal regulators who oversee their activities monitor loan standards and quality, worrying that loan standards are too loose (and that banking institutions will be threatened if too many borrowers default) or too tight (depressing the economy by restricting the funds available to borrowers) (Hyndman 1996; Nadler 1994; Weinberg 1995). Insurance makes lending safer (although Weinberg 1995 worries that the existence of credit insurance will result in a loosening of standards), and thus loans made to people or businesses with insurance or good collateral are seen as higher quality loans.

But the interest expressed by bankers in whether their borrowers have insurance varies a good deal. In some fields, loan officers are urged to make insurance coverage a condition for the loan; in others they are not. Industry publications about the conditions under which loans should be given offer a hint about why this might be the case. Where property is an important component of the value of an enterprise, lenders exhibit the same concern with insurance as is seen in mortgage lending. In discussing lending to shipowners, for instance, Wood (1995) not only lists the various forms of insurance the shipowner should carry (hull and machinery, war risk, loss of hire, mortgagee's interest, protection and indemnity), but also urges that the bank monitor the vessel's insurance. Where the issue is performance, bonds may be required, but the bonding company will have first call on assets so that it can step in and meet contractual obligations (for example, in plumbing, heating, and air conditioning contractors; see Masters and Strischek 1991); lenders are therefore more interested in whether "keyman insurance" has been purchased and assigned to the lender. The same argument holds for architectural and engineering firms, but here lenders also want borrowers to have general and professional liability insurance (Koch and Williams 1990).

Banks lending to owners of frame and print shops, in contrast, are not cautioned about insurance. Instead they are reminded about the risks of damage to fragile products, the risk of obsolescence in an industry bound up with taste and style, and the industry's sensitivity to recession. Framing is a volatile industry with relatively low entry costs and no licensing requirements; success depends as much on taste and style as on training and standards. Under such conditions, industry-specific insurance regulations are unlikely to have been formulated and insisting on insurance as a precondition for a loan would do little to govern borrowers. Only when activities are orderly and predictable or when property values are especially high will government through insurance be very effective.

Finally, in considering the influence of insurers' regulatory efforts, we should heed the reminder of new institutionalists (whose work is summarized in note 8) that the effects of institutions often are more symbolic than instrumental. A widespread consensus that insurance regulations should be built into the standard operating procedures of the organizations does not mean the rules will be scrupulously followed. When ceremonial purposes are especially important (because, for example, one group of organizations is more powerful than others [Heimer 1985a]), the instrumental effects of regulations may be rather modest. In contrast, behavior decoupled from formal rules is of less importance when powerful actors within an organization are made into allies and given a hand in deciding how to adapt general principles (those articulated by insurers) to take account of local conditions (Heimer 1996, 1999). Insurers have been a powerful force in the governance of hospitals precisely because they allied themselves with physicians and made sure it was in physicians' interest to customize and enforce insurance regulations. Even regulation by stealth works better with local agents.

Insurer Moral Hazard: Does Governing *through* Insurance Mean Governing *for* Insurance?

Why, one might ask, is the decline of noncommercial informal insurance so crucial? To understand the social costs of the displacement of alternative forms of risk management, we need to look more carefully at the logic of control that is so central to insurance technology. Because policyholders have some control over losses, losses cannot be treated as fully accidental and the elegant simplicity of a risk-spreading technology has had to be cluttered up with regulatory complexity. But the regulatory complexity has been one sided, devoted entirely to the purpose of controlling policyholders. What about the parallel problem of controlling insurers? The absence of checks on the self-interested behavior of insurers, a key point of difference between formal and informal insurance, raises questions about whose welfare is being optimized when societies are governed through insurance. Does governing *through* insurance also mean governing *for* insurance?

Insurers were concerned about the problem of moral hazard long before it was taken up and popularized by economists. Although insurance has been designed primarily to cover other hazards (factors that increase the chances of a loss), insurers have been aware that the likelihood of loss is also much affected by moral hazards. Although economists have not followed insurance practice here, insurers distinguish "moral" hazards, essentially unchangeable factors such as honest (or dishonest) character that are not under the control of the policyholder, from "morale" hazards, motivational factors that are much more subject to manipulation. They have argued that moral hazards are properly managed by underwriting, that is by careful screening to eliminate those of unsound character from the pool, while morale hazards are properly managed by the design of contracts to offer incentives for loss prevention and honesty. Moral and morale hazards are serious problems in insurance because when insurers make contracts to compensate policyholders for some of the losses they experience, policyholder incentives shift. Because they no longer bear the full burden of losses, policyholders are somewhat less motivated to prevent losses. And when the insured property is worth less than its insured value, a policyholder will gain (financially at least) by destroying the property in order to collect the insurance money. Insurers have developed a wide variety of devices to manage these problems, ranging from deductibles to clauses requiring marine crews and property owners to "sue and labor" to minimize insurance losses (Heimer 1985b).

What is usually neglected in discussions of moral hazard is any acknowledgment that insurers too are affected by moral hazard (but see Baker 1996). Once a bargain has been struck, both insurer and policyholder experience a shift in their interest in lving up to the bargain. The insured may be less interested in preventing losses, but the insurer becomes less interested in repaying losses. Rather than taking policyholder claims as truth, insurers send out investigators to determine whether losses really arose from accidents, estimate the value of the damage experienced by the policyholder, and verify that the damaged or destroyed property really was as described in the insurance contract. Insurance adjusters are motivated to minimize their employers' losses, and they may not always be recruited primarily for their honesty.

Insurer moral hazard takes another form as well. Both policyholders and insurers have more interest in forming some contracts than others. Insurers are intensely aware that policyholder interest in entering insurance contracts varies directly with the likelihood that a policyholder will experience a loss. Policyholders who are ill or likely to become ill are especially eager to buy health insurance; businesses with high rates of "shrinkage" are especially likely to seek fidelity bonds and insurance to cover shoplifting losses. Insurers are constantly on guard against such adverse selection. Less is made of parallel selection processes by insurers. Insurer interest in entering insurance contracts varies inversely with the likelihood that the policyholder (and so eventually the insurer) will experience a loss. Health insurers commonly refuse insurance to people who have AIDS or a history of cancer. Fidelity bonds may exclude coverage of employees with criminal records.

Because offering coverage to such policyholders is likely to reduce insurer profits, and may raise premiums so that good risks forgo insurance, insurers devise intricate procedures to help them exclude the very policyholders most in need of insurance. As a device for spreading unexpected losses over a large group, insurance works best when the risk pool is both large and diverse. But insurers are able to offer more attractive premium rates and contract conditions to policyholders by decreasing the diversity of the insurance pool—that is, by excluding those most likely to experience losses. Such an arrangement, particularly when coupled with experience rating (in which a policyholder's premiums are adjusted over the years to reflect information about its own loss records), offers incentives for policyholders to prevent or minimize losses. But it also runs counter to the underlying purpose of insurance.

If we regard it as unscrupulous for policyholders to misuse insurance contracts, we should take a similarly dim view of insurers who do likewise. The extreme cases are insurance companies who simply do not pay losses to which policyholders are entitled, force policyholders into expensive litigation to collect, or cancel policies if policyholders insist on pursuing payment. But if insurers begin to behave more like investors than insurers, for instance devoting their energies to reaping profits from invested premiums rather than to developing ways of insuring those who most need coverage, we should regard this, too, as a serious moral hazard problem. Given their power as regulators, it is even more important for insurers to act like "good" insurers than for policyholders to behave like "good" policyholders. What's good for Aetna (or State Farm or Prudential or any number of insurers) may not be what's good for the country.

Inequalities in Access to Risk Management

Most analyses give a benign gloss to insurer selection techniques. For instance they show how insurers can decrease the effects of adverse selection by offering insurance on the basis of group membership. Because most people join a group (as when they accept employment) primarily for reasons other than access to insurance, insurers can assume that the pool will include good as well as bad insurance risks. In fact, insofar as one has to be competent, healthy, and honest in order to join the group, those controlling access to the group almost certainly do a good job of prescreening for insurers and supplying them with a better-than-average pool of policyholders.

But who is it that cannot secure insurance when it is offered to preexisting groups in preference to single individuals? Individuals who, for whatever reason, are not connected to large organizations (to employers, employee groups and professional associations, some voluntary associations) are unable to purchase insurance. Organizational embeddedness is the key here. Organizations have ties to one another, and individuals get access to goods such as insurance through their ties to organizations (Stinchcombe 1984).[12] An individual's embeddedness is irrelevant if it is not the right sort of embeddedness. Ties to other individuals or to community groups are not relevant except under particular circumstances. A person may have friendships galore, participate actively in the local PTA, attend religious services faithfully, and even have a job, but may still be unable to secure some kinds of insurance. Health insurance may only be available through "good jobs" with relatively large employers.

Risks have always been unequally distributed and harder to manage for those at the bottom of the heap. But changes in the business of insurance have made the situation of those at the bottom (in the United States and other developed societies) somewhat worse. As insurance has become the standard and preferred method of risk management, the displacement of nonmarket forms disproportionately harms those who have neither the security net of insurance nor the security net of traditional institutions.

In addition, with the increasing embeddedness of insurance, access to insurance becomes more important as a gatekeeper. Those who are denied insurance coverage are now more likely also to be denied access to other goods and services. For instance, people with AIDS are likely to be denied health insurance and life insurance. But whatever their income and employment situation, these same people may have difficulty securing home mortgages because they are unable to purchase life insurance, and may be unable to get medical care in an emergency because they lack insurance and are unable to offer other assurance that the bills will be paid.

Less formalized risk-management devices have often been especially associated with immigrant and laboring communities. The "friendly societies" of immigrant communities in the United States helped poor families arrange burial expenses that they might not ordinarily have been able to afford. Such groups sometimes grew into life insurance companies. The rotating savings and credit associations written about by Geertz (1962), Akerloff (1983), and most recently by Biggart (2000) similarly flourished within ethnically homogeneous groups, sometimes embedded in larger multi-ethnic societies. Such devices are excellent illustrations of what Granovetter (1985) means by embeddedness—people who could make use of such devices have strong and diverse ties with others in their community. These ties are the "stuff" that makes rudimentary insurance pools or lending organizations possible. Noting that in general life is more precarious in low-income countries, Besley (1995) suggests that nonmarket institutions for risk sharing and credit function effectively as cushions where market institutions would fail.[13] But these nonmarket institutions that flourish because of their comparative advantage in monitoring and enforcement tend to disappear as capital markets develop.[14] Besley attributes their disappearance partly to the scale economies available to market institutions, but also adds that "they use certain information structures and enforcement technologies that are eroded by the transformation to a modern economy" (121). Very likely the "erosion" of these information structures and enforcement technologies is hastened by market institutions' refusal to recognize and inability to use the information produced by such technologies. Standardization and routinization make institutions less flexible users of nonstandard information. As long as profits remain high, hegemonic insurers can dictate the terms of participation, and even more than other governing bodies they can afford to ignore those they exclude.

But note that such traditional, nonmarket risk-management devices were not primarily aimed at smoothing access to the resources of major organizations. A rotating credit association did not help one secure additional funding from a bank, and participation in the friendly society was not a first step in an application for a mortgage. But if these informal insurance mechanisms were not designed to facilitate access to the resources of other groups, participation in them rather than in more formal risk management or credit devices probably did not hinder access. Until the links between insurance and other organizations were forged, insurance coverage did not have much effect on access to other resources. Participation in nonmarket risk sharing clearly was not a prerequisite. A good reputation in one's community was probably as important in getting a loan or business contract as having access to insurance. While personal references are still sought for a variety of purposes (job applications, for instance), they cannot carry the same meaning that they did when recommenders and employers were at least known to one another by reputation.

The combination of insurer moral hazard and the increasing embeddedness of insurance thus may make some risk-management problems more intractable in societies with strong insurers, which have driven out less formal kinds of embedding, than in those societies in which informal risk management, with a different balance of incentives and different ties to individuals and organizations, exists side by side with formal insurance. It is different to be uninsurable when the safety net of nonmarket solutions is robust than when it has unraveled. When nonmarket institutions are robust, accepting risk means communal sharing of risk; without those alternatives, accepting risk means going it alone.

In concluding their book on risk and culture, Douglas and Wildavsky comment that "[i]f the selection of risk is a matter of social organization, the management of risk is an organizational problem. Since we do not know what risks we incur, our responsibility is to create resilience in our institutions" (1982:198). One might argue that a minimum condition for such institutional resilience would be the existence of a host of alternative risk-management devices rather than just the single alternative of formal insurance.

NOTES

This essay benefited enormously from comments from Tom Baker, Martha McCluskey, and other participants at the University of Connecticut School of Law conference on "Insurance, Risk and Responsibility." I am especially grateful for the superb research assistance of Barry Cohen and for Arthur Stinchcombe's capacity to give insightful comments after several decades of hearing about this topic. Address comments to author at Department of Sociology, Northwestern University, 1810 Chicago Ave., Evanston, IL 60208. Email: c-heimer@northwestern.edu.
1. Baker (chapter 2 this volume) contrasts the forms of insurance that would be

available to protect two fictitious couples, one working class and the other professional. Taking into account mandated basic social insurance financed through payroll taxes, insurance provided through employers, insurance purchased on the private market, and means-tested noncontributory safety nets, Baker lists sixteen forms of insurance that would protect professional couples but only nine (and these much stingier) forms that would cushion working class couples.

2. One correlate of difficulty buying fire insurance is how many agents live in the area. Because agents are mostly white, they do not live in predominantly minority areas, and those who do live in predominantly minority areas therefore have difficulty purchasing fire insurance (Schultz 1997).

3. Although insurers (both private and governmental) may be becoming more "selective," it is also clear that some of the decline in insurance coverage is arising from the decisions of individuals not to purchase insurance. For instance, according to a recent *New York Times* article, 5 to 6 million of the 43.4 million Americans who do not have health insurance "have family incomes exceeding $75,000 a year and can usually afford the insurance that, for any number of reasons, they do without" (Kilborn 1999:A14). It also seems that some of this decline in insurance occurred during what others have characterized as the "more insurance for more people" period. A recent study found that "the number of American households owning any type of life insurance has declined considerably, from 83 percent in 1976 to 74 percent in 1998" (Business Wire 1988).

4. The essays by Clark, McCluskey, and Simon (chapters 4, 7, and 8, respectively, this volume) also note the moral valence of risk and insurance.

5. These concerns are expressed by insiders as well as by outside observers. In comparing the Mennonites, who formed extensive enterprises for mutual aid, and the Brethren, an otherwise similar group who did not develop intradenominational organizations for mutual aid, Holt (1998) notes that the Brethren worried that formalizing mutual aid would erode informal support among members.

6. See Laumann, Galaskiewicz, and Marsden 1978 and Galaskiewicz 1985 on organizational networks.

7. Rosenbaum and Kariya (1989) discuss what is probably an extreme case of the loyalty of organizations to each other, namely, the commitments of Japanese firms to hire the graduates of particular schools.

8. This phenomenon is discussed in a more general form in the sociological literature on institutionalization. Among the "new institutionalists" in sociology, institutions are conceived primarily as solutions to problems of legitimacy. Institutionalists argue that much of what transpires in organizations occurs not because it increases efficiency or reduces transaction costs, but because it confers legitimacy and smooths interactions among organizations (Meyer and Rowan 1977; DiMaggio and Powell 1983, 1991). In adopting an institutionalized practice, an organization signals its willingness to play by the rules endorsed by other actors in its environment. It claims membership in a world in which organizations doing roughly the same thing agree on a core set of rules that make the game "fair" and a style of interaction with regulators, suppliers, customers, and other publics. How deeply the adoption of any institutionalized policy shapes organizational activity is another matter, though, and institutionalists differentiate instrumental from symbolic effects. For discussions of the process of institutionalization in specific fields, see DiMaggio (1991) on art museums, Edelman (1990) on fair employment practices, and Heimer on insurance (1985a) and health care (1996, 1999).

9. See the recent paper by Schwartz (1999) on test coaching for the SATs. Schwartz notes that "[f]or college officials seeking to distinguish thousands of students from different backgrounds and high schools of varying quality, and different

curriculums and grading policies, the S.A.T.'s do provide a common currency—whatever their actual predictive power" (1999:51). As a former Dartmouth admissions officer commented, "Deep down, admissions officers don't want S.A.T. scores to count that much, but the fact is they do" (Schwartz 1999:51, citing Michele Hernandez).

10. Moulton (2000) finds that commercial banks and nonprofit lenders often form partnerships with commercial banks sending the nonprofits the clients they have turned down and nonprofits returning their "graduates." But, interestingly, rather than applying their own standards, nonprofits adopt the practices and standards of the commercial banks. In effect, nonprofits are gatekeepers: "micro-lending in the US is being transformed into a disciplining mechanism that produces 'good borrowers' for conventional lenders" (15). In contrast to the risk-sharing or monitoring mechanisms employed by rotating savings and credit associations (Biggart 2000), these nonprofits instead bear the burden of higher risk while a more acceptable information base is being accumulated. But the isomorphism Moulton describes means a propagation of "the very model that contributed to the neglect of the poor, minorities and women in the first place" (23–24). It also means that there are even fewer options for those who cannot meet the standards of conventional lenders, now embraced by nonprofits as well.

11. As far as I can tell these figures are all about home mortgages and are fully comparable. But one should be skeptical. The data come from the 1997 Summary of Mortgage Lending in Allegheny County and were reported in the *Pittsburgh Post Gazette* (McNulty 1998).

12. Note the catch-22 aspect of access to insurance. Although insurers are gatekeepers who screen people for participation in core activities, the converse is also true: people gain access to insurance through other large organizations, particularly employers.

13. Besley (1995) also suggests that a blurring of the distinction between credit and insurance is common in these nonmarket institutions.

14. In a study of low-income countries, Morduch (1999) agrees that formal arrangements do tend to crowd out informal insurance, but suggests that the informal arrangements may be relatively weak and in any case may retard economic development and social mobility. Morduch suggests that other policies might help poor families; he does not propose that they be forced to rely only on what market institutions currently offer them.

REFERENCES

Akerloff, George. 1983. "Loyalty Filters." *American Economic Review* 73:54–63.

Baker, Tom. 1996. "On the Genealogy of Moral Hazard." *Texas Law Review* 75: 237–92.

Beito, David. 1994. "Thy Brother's Keeper: The Mutual Aid Tradition of American Fraternal Orders." *Policy Review* 70 (fall): 55–59.

Besley, Timothy. 1995. "Nonmarket Institutions for Credit and Risk Sharing in Low-Income Countries." *Journal of Economic Perspectives* 9 (3): 115–27.

Biggart, Nicole. 2000. "Banking on Each Other: The Situational Logic of Rotating Savings and Credit Associations." Paper read at the American Sociological Association Annual Meeting. August 2000, Washington, D.C.

Business Wire, Inc. 1998. "New Roper Starch Study Reveals One In Four Households Has No Life Insurance." October 28, 1998 (http://www.businesswire.com).

Canner, Glenn B., Wayne Passmore, Elizabeth Laderman. 1999. "The Role of Specialized Lenders in Extending Mortgages to Lower-Income and Minority Homebuyers." *Federal Reserve Bulletin* (November): 709–23.

Carruthers, Bruce G., and Arthur L. Stinchcombe. 1999. "The Social Structure of Liquidity: Flexibility, Markets, and States." *Theory and Society* 28:353–82.

DiMaggio, Paul J. 1991. "Constructing an Organizational Field as a Professional Project: U.S. Art Museums, 1920–1940." In *The New Institutionalism in Organizational Analysis,* ed. W. W. Powell and P. J. DiMaggio. Chicago: University of Chicago Press.

DiMaggio, Paul J., and Walter W. Powell. 1983. "Iron Cage Revisited: Institutional Isomorphism and Collective Rationality in Organizational Fields." *American Sociological Review* 48:147–60.

———. 1991. "Introduction." In *The New Institutionalism in Organizational Analysis,* ed. W. W. Powell and P. J. DiMaggio. Chicago: University of Chicago Press.

Dorfman, Mark S. 1994. *Introduction to Risk Management and Insurance.* 5th ed. Englewood Cliffs, N.J.: Prentice-Hall.

Douglas, Mary, and Aaron Wildavsky. 1982. *Risk and Culture: An Essay on the Selection of Technical and Environmental Dangers.* Berkeley: University of California Press.

Edelman, Lauren B. 1990. "Legal Environments and Organizational Governance: The Expansion of Due Process in the American Workplace." *American Journal of Sociology* 95:1401–40.

Galaskiewicz, Joseph. 1985. "Interorganizational Relations." *Annual Review of Sociology* 11:281–304.

Gambetta, Diego. 1988. "Mafia: The Price of Distrust." In *Trust: Making and Breaking Cooperative Relations,* ed. Diego Gambetta. Oxford: Basil Blackwell.

Geertz, Clifford. 1962. "The Rotating Credit Association: A 'Middle Rung' in Development." *Economic Development and Cultural Change* 10 (April): 241–63.

Granovetter, Mark. 1985. "Economic Action and Social Structure: The Problem of Embeddedness." *American Journal of Sociology* 91:481–510.

Hansell, D. S. 1996. *Introduction to Insurance.* London: LLP.

Heimer, Carol A. 1982. "The Racial and Organizational Origins of Insurance Redlining." *Journal of Intergroup Relations* 10 (3): 42–60.

———. 1985a. "Allocating Information Costs in a Negotiated Information Order: Interorganizational Constraints on Decision Making in Norwegian Oil Insurance." *Administrative Science Quarterly* 30:395–417.

———. 1985b. *Reactive Risk and Rational Action: Managing Moral Hazard in Insurance Contracts.* Berkeley: University of California Press.

———. 1996. "Explaining Variation in the Impact of Law: Organizations, Institutions, and Professions." *Studies in Law, Politics and Society* 15:29–59.

———. 1999. "Competing Institutions: Law, Medicine, and Family in Neonatal Intensive Care." *Law and Society Review* 33:17–66.

Holt, Steven. 1998. "Formal Mutual Aid Structures among American Mennonites and Brethren: Assimilation and Reconstructed Ethnicity." *Journal of American Ethnic History* 17 (3): 71–86.

Hyndman, Carl. 1996. "FDIC Survey Targets Deteriorating Loan Standards." *Commercial Lending Review* 11 (2): 61–66.

Journal of Health Politics, Policy, and Law. 1993a. Special Issue: Health Care Reform, Part 1. *Journal of Health Politics, Policy, and Law* 18 (2).

———. 1993b. Special Issue: Health Care Reform, Part 2. *Journal of Health Politics, Policy, and Law* 18 (3).

Jud, G. Donald, and Daniel Winkler. 1995. "An Evaluation of the Asset Integrated Mortgage." *Real Estate Issues* 2 (1): 30–32.

Kilborn, Peter T. 1999. "Uninsured in U.S. Spans Many Groups" *New York Times,* 26 February, A1, A14.

Koch, Timothy, and Mark Williams. 1990. "Lending to Architectural and Engineering Firms." *Journal of Commercial Bank Lending* (November): 34–44.

Laumann, Edward O., Joseph Galaskiewicz, and Peter V. Marsden. 1978. "Community Structure as Interorganizational Linkages." *Annual Review of Sociology* 4:455–84.

Lubove, Seth. 1998. "Willing Lender of Last Resort." *Forbes,* 16 November, 50.

Masters, James, and Dev Strischek. 1991. "Lending to Plumbing, Heating, and Air Conditioning Contractors." *Journal of Commercial Bank Lending* (February): 37–53.

McNulty, Timothy. 1998. "More Blacks Get Mortgage Loans: Up 7% in County '96 to '97; Denials Down 9%." *Pittsburgh Post Gazette,* 22 December, B7.

Meyer, John W., and Brian Rowan. 1977. "Institutionalized Organizations: Formal Structure as Myth and Ceremony." *American Journal of Sociology* 83:340–63.

Mnookin, Robert H., and Lewis Kornhauser. 1979. "Bargaining in the Shadow of the Law: The Case of Divorce." *Yale Law Journal* 88:950–97.

Morduch, Jonathan. 1999. "Between the State and the Market: Can Informal Insurance Patch the Safety Net?" *World Bank Research Observer* 14 (2): 187–207.

Moulton, Lynne. 2000. "Who Gets Credit? A Cross-Sectional Analysis of Money Lending Decision-making in the United States." Paper read at the American Sociological Association Annual Meeting. August 2000, Washington, D.C.

Nadler, Paul. 1994. "Why Are We Compromising Credit Standards Again?" *Commercial Lending Review* 9 (3): 57–62.

O'Malley, Pat. 2000. "Uncertain Subjects: Risks, Liberalism and Contract." *Economy and Society* 29 (4): 460–84.

Putnam, Robert D. 2000. *Bowling Alone: The Collapse and Revival of American Community.* New York: Simon and Schuster.

Rosenbaum, James E., and Takehiko Kariya. 1989. "From High School to Work: Market and Institutional Mechanisms in Japan." *American Journal of Sociology* 94:1334–65.

Ruggie, Mary. 1996. *Realignments in the Welfare State: Health Policy in the U.S., Britain, and Canada.* New York: Columbia University Press.

Schultz, Jay D. 1997. "Homeowners Insurance Availability and Agent Location."

In *Insurance Redlining: Divestment, Reinvestment, and the Evolving Role of Financial Institutions,* ed. Gregory D. Squires. Washington, D.C.: Urban Institute Press.

Schwartz, Tony. 1999. "The Test under Stress." *New York Times Magazine,* 10 January, 30–35, 51, 56, 63.

Shapiro, Susan P. 1987. "The Social Control of Impersonal Trust." *American Journal of Sociology* 23 (3): 623–58.

Squires, Gregory D., ed. 1997. *Insurance Redlining: Divestment, Reinvestment, and the Evolving Role of Financial Institutions.* Washington, D.C.: Urban Institute Press.

Starr, Paul. 1982. *The Social Transformation of American Medicine.* New York: Basic Books.

Stevens, Mitchell L. 2001. *Kingdom of Children: Culture and Controversy in the Home Schooling Movement.* Princeton: Princeton University Press.

Stinchcombe, Arthur L. 1984. "Third Party Buying: The Trend and the Consequences." *Social Forces* 62 (4): 861–84.

Strischek, Dev, and Debbie Bankston. 1990. "Lending to Framing and Print Shops." *Journal of Commercial Bank Lending* (October): 16–32.

Supple, Barry. 1984. "Insurance in British History." In *The Historian and the Business of Insurance,* ed. O. M. Westall. Manchester: Manchester University Press.

Weinberg, John. 1995. "Cycles in Lending Standards?" *Economic Quarterly* 81 (3): 1–18.

Williamson, Oliver. 1975. *Markets and Hierarchies.* New York: Free Press.

———. 1981. "The Economics of Organization: The Transaction Cost Approach." *American Journal of Sociology* 87:548–77.

Witt, Brian. 1999. "Get Ready for New PMI Laws." *Credit Union Magazine* 65 (5): 27–28.

Wood, Geore. 1995. "Lending to Shipowners." *Journal of Commercial Bank Lending* 77 (12): 2531.

Rhetoric of Risk and the Redistribution of Social Insurance

MARTHA MCCLUSKEY

The twentieth century was the "insurance age," according to a leading insurance scholar writing in its midst, a time of faith in the possibilities for security through rational risk control (Kimball 1960). But the turn to the twenty-first century seems to have brought an age of risk. Now, many people seem more willing to trust their future to the champions of chance of the stock market—or to lotteries and casinos—than to the grand social insurance schemes developed in the early decades of the last century, like workers compensation and social security. Images of risk taking as the ticket to success saturate contemporary society, from neoliberal (free-market) ideology in politics and economics to the extreme sports fad in popular culture (Simon, chapter 8 this volume). A comment from the *Economist* expresses the conventional wisdom: "It is no coincidence that free-market economies, which encourage personal risk-taking, have outlived centrally planned ones, which do not" (*Economist* 1994:21).

But something is missing from this story of a change from security to risk. By focusing on the choice between the two, we obscure how policies that *embrace* risk always also *redistribute* risk. The problem—for society as a whole and for insurance in particular—is not *how much* risk versus security is good policy, but *whose* risk and *whose* security is good policy.

First, the recent romance with risk reveals a double standard: celebration of risk taking depends on who gets the risk; condemnation of risk avoiding depends on who gets the security. Recent neoliberal political efforts to replace government security with market risk aim not to reduce social insurance as much as to redistribute it toward employers (and capital owners in general) and away from workers. I explore this double standard of risk embracing, and the redistribution of security it facilitates, in the specific context of recent reforms of workers compensation insurance in the United States.

Second, this double standard of risk privileges security for employers on the theory that too much risk bearing is harmful for those whose interests are most closely connected to society as a whole. In the prevailing neoliberal ideology, new conditions of global market interdependence make protections for capital owners, not workers, most beneficial. In this view, by reducing security in social insurance programs like workers compensation in favor of policies supporting investors, we can better promote market growth that will bring the most security to workers and others in the long run. I explore two examples of neoliberal policies that offer new "social insurance" to wealthy capital interests to show how this redistribution of security instead has tended to exacerbate insecurity for most workers.

Third, a close examination of the neoliberal rhetoric favoring risk over security shows that this distinction is fundamentally a social and political construction. The labels "risk" and "security" do not objectively describe discrete policy choices, but instead serve to prescribe a vision of community based on moral judgments about who deserves the costs and who deserves the benefits of social interdependence.

Redistributing Security in Workers Compensation

Most states adopted workers compensation in the early twentieth century, during a period of reform activity directed at protecting workers against the harsh effects of market risk taking (Moss 1996). Before workers compensation, the nineteenth-century tort system had barred most workers from recovering damages for work injuries through fault-based employer defenses that held workers largely responsible for their losses (Eastman 1910). Workers compensation replaced the right of employees to sue employers in tort with the right to limited no-fault compensation through mandatory employer-based insurance against accidental work injury.

Some early-twentieth-century century promoters of social insurance imagined workers compensation as a model that would bring protection against a wide range of risks of life to many American workers and their families (Rubinow 1913). The origin and staying power of workers compensation has long been explained in terms of the virtues of its risk-spreading approach compared to the risk-targeting approach of the previous tort system. In the traditional theory, by making the price of the product "bear the blood of the working man," workers compensation encourages consumers seeking lower-priced goods to create market pressures for safer production (Somers and Somers 1954). Second, in the conventional wisdom, workers compensation saves costs compared to the tort system by providing benefits that are more predictable and cheaper to administer than fault-based tort damages (Dewees, Duff, and Trebilcock 1996).

But in the last decades of the twentieth century, the predominant neoliberal ideology has stressed the virtues of replacing government protection with free-market risk. By the 1990s, workers compensation had come to stand for the problems, not the possibilities, of social insurance. Nonetheless, this change in vision of workers compensation is not so much a shift from risk spreading to risk-embracing as a shift in security from workers to employers.

Against Security in Workers Compensation Reforms

Since the late 1980s, most states have dramatically revised their workers compensation laws to impose new substantive and procedural limits on benefit claims (McCluskey 1998). Following these reforms, the amount of benefits received by injured workers plummeted for the first sustained period since at least the 1930s (Burton et al. 1997). For example, the nationwide amounts employers (and their insurers) paid out in disability benefits (cash awards compensating income lost due to work-related disability) dropped 32.8 percent from 1991 to 1994 (id.). Many reports of the reforms' effects tell stories of seriously injured workers whose inability to get timely or adequate compensation has taken them from middle-class stability to financial ruin (Fricker 1997; Ellenberger 1999; Consumer Reports 2000).

Supporters of these reforms argued that benefit reductions would "restore balance" because the previous period of expansion had pushed the system too far in the direction of security for injured workers (Alliance of American Insurers 1990). In 1972, a bipartisan commission appointed by President Nixon to study workers compensation found serious inadequacies in state benefit levels and recommended raising benefit amounts and lifting barriers to compensating many work-related illnesses and injuries (National Commission on State Workmen's Compensation Laws 1972; Burton 1994). Over the next decade, many states did expand compensation, though these changes nationwide fell significantly short of the commission's recommended benefit improvements. By the mid-1980s, employers and insurers in many states were complaining that excessive benefits had led to "skyrocketing" insurance costs (McCluskey 1998).

Advocates of these restrictive reforms stressed two general problems with expanded protection against the risks of work accidents. First, they claimed this security shielded workers from responsibility for reducing the costs of work injuries, thereby increasing society's overall risk from work accidents. This is the problem of moral hazard: the tendency of those who are protected from the costs of a loss to take less care to prevent those costs (Baker 1996; Heimer 1985). As evidence of such cost-increasing incentives, reform advocates pointed to data showing that benefit costs rose at a faster rate than statutory benefit increases during the expansionary period (Moore and Viscusi 1990). In their view, broad no-fault compensation allowed workers to bring claims for injuries and illnesses not caused by work (aging, sports activities, or preexisting illnesses) and for wage losses caused by factors other than injuries or illnesses (like plant closings, lack of skill, or poor motivation). Reformers argued that less security against work injury costs would better reduce those costs by reducing incentives for bringing fraudulent, or at least questionable, injury claims.

The second reason reformers gave for reducing security is that the goal of protecting injured workers against work injury costs can only be reached at the cost of increased productivity. As one insurance executive warned, "[S]ociety must weigh the compensation that will be paid to a worker . . . against the economic loss that will be sustained if a business moves out of the state—or out of the country" (Burke 1992). In this view, if employers spend less on mandatory workers compensation benefits, in the long run they will produce more jobs and more affordable consumer goods. By individually shouldering more of the unavoidable costs of work injuries, workers will have more resources to better avoid or insure themselves against these costs. In the standard neoliberal theory (also used to support efforts to privatize social security and Medicare) the market, rather than government mandated programs, can best protect workers at the least cost.

Rhetoric of Risk in Impairment Reforms

One of the major reform provisions, the change to an impairment-based approach to permanent disability benefits, provides an example of the double standard in the recent turn toward embracing risk. Workers compensation provides temporary benefits to replace income lost during recovery from an injury or illness; after no further recovery is expected, workers with long-term injuries and illnesses may seek permanent disability benefits to replace either *partial* or *total* loss of earnings, depending on the severity of the disability. Permanent partial disability benefits have been the most costly and most controversial part of the workers compensation system (Burton 1997; Oxfeld 1998).

States traditionally have used an impairment-based approach to fix the amount of disability benefits for certain "scheduled" permanent injuries—primarily traumatic injuries to extremities (Pryor 1990). For example, permanent loss of use of an arm in New York is compensated according to a set schedule of 312 weeks of benefits (based on a weekly benefit of two-thirds of lost income up to the maximum cap). Other permanent disabilities, such as back injuries or respiratory illnesses, typically have been compensated based on actual or predicted lost wages—the degree to which the injury reduces the worker's wage-earning capacity.

As part of their 1990s political campaign against high workers compensation costs, business and insurer groups have advocated that states expand this impairment approach by using ratings devised by the American Medical Association (AMA) in its *Guides to the Evaluation of Permanent Impairment* to determine benefit levels for a wide range of permanent injuries (Fletcher 1996). These ratings purport to measure an injured workers' medical condition alone, in contrast to wage-loss approaches to disability, which consider the economic impact of the medical condition by looking at factors such as age, occupation, skills, education, and labor market conditions. The *Guides* provide a system for translating measurements of certain bodily limitations into measurements of a person's overall functional loss. For example, the *Guides* specify that persons with 50 percent impairment of normal hand function have a 27 percent "whole-person" impairment—regardless of the extent to which the impairment actually affects any particular person's job performance (American Medical Association 1993).

A number of states have responded to this reform campaign by using the AMA impairment ratings as the sole factor, or as a more important factor, in determining certain permanent disability awards (McCluskey 1998) In addition, a number of states have used the ratings to set threshold requirements for obtaining certain kinds of permanent benefits (McCluskey 1998).

With impairment-rating reforms, seriously injured workers take on the risk that their particular impairment will produce greater economic loss than the norm assumed in the rating system. In the classic (though hardly typical) example, if a bank president loses a finger from a work accident, but is not incapacitated from her job as a result, she will get the same compensation as a pianist with a similar injury whose career is destroyed. In contrast, the wage-loss approach to disability protects (to some extent) against the chance that particular labor market conditions or characteristics of the worker will result in severe income loss from an impairment that might not similarly disable workers with different skills, education, ages, or geographic locations.

Moreover, these impairment-rating reforms increase the risk of work accidents for many workers because the AMA *Guides,* and the state reforms that adopt them, set the impairment ratings to underestimate the economic impact of injuries for many workers (Spieler 1995). For example, several recent state reforms require injured workers to have a whole-person impairment rating of 50 percent or more to qualify for permanent *total* disability benefits (McCluskey 1998). Yet a 50 percent impairment rating is set high enough to exclude the vast majority of permanently injured workers with no wage income. For example, a permanent neurologic impairment that leaves an injured worker in a "state of semicoma with complete dependency and subsistence by artificial medical means" only receives a rating of 30–49 percent whole-person impairment under the AMA *Guides* (American Medical Association 1993:4/142, table 4). Similarly, several states have enacted reforms excluding permanently injured workers with impairment ratings below 15 or 20 percent from qualifying for permanent *partial* disability benefits (McCluskey 1998). But in a study of the impact of this reform in Texas, more than one-third of injured workers with impairments rated less than 15 percent suffered a *total* loss of wage earnings for at least several years after their injury (Research & Oversight Council on Workers' Compensation 1996). The *Guides* offer no data or explanation to support the numbers in their ratings.

Moral Hazard

Nonetheless, advocates of impairment reforms justify this increase in workers' risk, first, on the ground that it reduces moral hazard. Because the wage-loss approach protects against economic loss, it creates incentives for workers to increase that loss: they get paid for not working. In contrast, business groups argued that the fixed payments of the impairment approach will "reduce a workers' incentive to stay off the job to increase the benefits received for his or her injury" (Fletcher 1996).

But the recent political attention to the deterrence value of risk bearing is one sided. The impairment-rating reforms shift rather than reduce the moral hazard problem, because these changes shift rather than reduce insurance against the economic impact of work injuries. Instead of bearing the risk that a compensable work accident will result in a worker's long-term economic incapacity, employers (through their insurers) pay a fixed amount per impairment regardless of the actual economic impact.

As a result of this "insurance," impairment-rating reforms reduce incentives for employers or insurers to return that injured worker to work. For example, under the impairment approach employers (and insurers) will have fewer incentives to keep workers' jobs available during the recovery period; to make accommodations that would allow permanently injured workers to safely return to work; to encourage claimants' loyalty and motivation by paying initial benefits promptly, fairly, and respectfully; or to ensure maximum medical recovery by facilitating prompt and high-quality medical care.

Furthermore, the impairment-rating reforms increase employers' and insurers' opportunities for moral hazard because the ratings particularly underestimate the economic impact of impairments for many of the workers for whom work injuries are most costly. As a result, these reforms reduce employers' and insurers' incentives for improving safety and reemployment precisely where this deterrence might produce the most societal cost savings. The reforms shift the economic risk of work injuries particularly to workers who have the least education, most investment in a particular occupation, and fewest marketable skills. In the study of Texas' impairment-rating system, almost two-thirds of injured workers with less than an eighth-grade education or older than fifty-five remained unemployed for at least several years despite receiving an impairment rating of under 15 percent (Research & Oversight Council on Workers' Compensation 1996). For example, following Kentucky's adoption of the impairment-rating system for awarding disability benefits, a fifty-seven-year-old coal miner with a high school degree received a 10 percent impairment rating for a work-related back injury, making him eligible for benefits of $58 a week for eight years (Garrett 1998). He probably would have received about $400 a week for life under the old wage-loss system because his particular skills, age, and the local labor market made obtaining alternative employment unlikely (Garrett 1998).

Lost Productivity

Reformers' second justification for the impairment-rating change is that spreading the risk of economic harm to employers is costly, aside from deterrence concerns. A lobbyist for the Ohio Manufacturers Association defended an impairment-rating proposal by explaining, "Workers' comp was never supposed to compensate somebody because they never got more than an eighth-grade education" (Goel 1995). Reform advocates claimed that to avoid making workers compensation a general welfare system, disability compensation should be limited to the effects of physical impairment alone, without considering age, education, or other labor market factors affecting earnings capacity (*Major Workers' Comp Reform Package under Consideration by State Legislature* 1997). A leading workers compensation expert, Richard Victor, explained the problem of providing security against these combined risk factors by saying, "Fundamentally, it comes down to whether you want a custom-tailored suit or a ready-made suit"; more accurate measurements are "expensive and slow" (Fletcher 1996:21). This explanation suggests that protection against standardized impairment ratings' risk of inadequacy is a luxury that workers generally cannot afford.

Proponents of the impairment approach assume that the nonmedical factors contributing to disability have effects that are particularly variable and therefore especially costly to insure. By basing disability benefit amounts on fixed medical measurements and by minimizing adjudicators' discretionary adjustments for particular economic circumstances, the impairment-rating reforms in theory allow employers and insurers to plan more easily for the costs of that disability. Reform advocates suggested that the cost savings of a more predictable system would benefit workers and society in general by strengthening the compensation system as well as fostering a more competitive business climate.

In addition, reformers argued that the greater simplicity and certainty of the standardized impairment ratings would reduce claims conflicts that delay compensation and divert resources from benefits payment. An insurance industry lobbyist explained, "States using the AMA Guides have been able to reduce litigation and related friction expenses (especially disability evaluations performed for this purpose) because the Guides provide an objective and uniform methodology" (Oxfeld 1998). Reform advocates contended that workers' gains from the wage-loss system's more accurate "fit" between disability benefits and actual economic loss are outweighed by the attorneys costs they incur in trying to prove their exact loss (Fletcher 1996).

But again, these arguments about the advantages of risk bearing do not represent a turn away from valuing security as much as a turn toward valuing security for employers (and insurers). The cost-savings rationale for accepting the lesser protection of standardized impairment ratings is really a rationale for shifting the benefits of custom-fitting protection from workers to employers (and insurers).

The wage-loss approach to calculating disability gives employers and insurers the higher risks of a "ready-to-wear suit." According to the traditional theory of workers compensation, in return for protection against tort damages, employers sacrificed the security of the tort system's individualized inquiry into exact causes of a worker's loss and accepted the standardized alternative of broad no-fault compensation of economic loss. As a result, employers and insurers assume the risk that actual costs will not closely fit their budgeted amounts and that high economic losses will require belt-tightening or changes in business plans (though this risk of variability remains less than under the tort system). Although many employers reduce their workers-compensation risk by purchasing outside insurance protection, generally they can expect that insurers will pass on at least some of the costs of this variability in premium charges (see, e.g., Fletcher 1991).

The arguments in favor of impairment-rating reforms rest on the assumption that, when it comes to employers and insurers, more *customized* protection will save money. By trimming down disability benefits to eliminate nonmedical reasons for wage loss (like lack of education or old age), the impairment-rating approach secures employers and insurers against the vagaries of workers' conditions, freeing up resources for other productive ends. But this increased predictability for employers and insurers reduces predictability for workers and their families. Under the new impairment-rating systems, workers' actual economic losses will be more variable and disruptive. By providing benefits ill fitted to injured workers' particular labor market situations, the impairment approach is likely to force many seriously injured workers and their families to make costly adjustments to cope with sudden, dramatic income loss.

This instability from more unpredictable losses can reduce productivity by workers and their families, just as it does for employers and insurers. The need to alleviate an immediate financial crisis caused by inadequate benefits may prevent injured workers from keeping or making investments critical to sustaining themselves and their families in the long run. For example, one seriously injured construction worker without a high school degree received a low rating under his state's new impairment system, entitling him to a settlement of only $7,400; under his state's previous wage-loss system, he could have received about $73,000 (Ellenberger 1999). In the previous wage-loss system, many injured workers with poor labor market prospects used such substantial settlements to start their own businesses or to return to school. In the new system, the injured construction worker lost his home, destroyed his credit rating, and struggled to survive on a low-waged job delivering pizza (Ellenberger 1999).

Furthermore, the impairment-based reforms do not *reduce* costly friction associated with the uncertainty of measuring economic loss; instead, they simply *shift* the costs of uncertainty to workers. Workers can no longer expect disability benefits to protect against their particular economic risks after an injury, but instead may have to spend more time and energy coping with a financial crisis and seeking alternative assistance from family or government. While employers and insurers may be less likely to dispute the narrower impairment-based benefits, workers probably will have to overcome other costly barriers to income replacement.

For example, in a case involving the wage-loss approach to compensation, an insurer denied a claim for disability benefits on the theory that a Florida construction worker with a serious leg injury, a tenth-grade education, and a family to support could obtain alternative work if he tried hard enough (*Consumer Reports* 2000). A judge overturned the insurer's denial after five years of litigation, but two days before that favorable ruling the worker committed suicide after financial destitution led him to despair (Miller 1998). An impairment approach might have reduced the insurer's questions about his benefit amount, thereby avoiding the prolonged litigation, but the low benefits he could anticipate under that approach probably would not have substantially reduced the claimant's stressful uncertainty about his future.

Redistributing Social Solidarity in Workers Compensation

As the example of impairment-rating reforms shows, reducing social insurance for workers tends to increase a form of social insurance for employers and insurers. This increased protection for employers brings the typical problems of security: moral hazard and constraints on others' productivity. Yet the workers-compensation reform campaign presented these problems for employers' and insurers' security as potential virtues. In their reasoning, employers' and insurers' freedom from personal responsibility reduces friction and promotes productivity, while the friction and lost productivity caused by spreading risks to workers increases their personal responsibility.

What makes greater security for workers an unaffordable and often hazardous luxury, while greater security for employers and insurers is a necessary and often beneficial foundation for healthy economic growth? First, reformers assumed that efforts to hold employers and insurers personally responsible for reducing work accident costs will be futile or even harmful. In their view, when the wage-loss approach to disability benefits forces employers and insurers to bear more of the risk of economic harm for work injuries, employers and insurers will not reduce those costs by increasing safety or reemployment of injured workers. Instead, they will reduce costs by aggressively resisting claims. Accordingly, increasing employers' and insurers' risk bearing only creates more, or different, moral hazard as employers (and their insurers) seek new ways to spread the increased risk to others.

Second, the arguments of reformers assumed that if employers and in-surers have to bear the uncontrollable risks of economic effects of work ac-cidents under a wage-loss approach, they will not simply absorb the costs in isolation from the rest of society. Instead, reform advocates assumed em-ployers' and insurers' costs will affect others, as reduced productivity and profits hurt jobs, the supply and price of products, and the economy in gen-eral.

And just as reformers assumed that the costs of risk to business inter-ests will spread to workers and to society in general, they assumed the ad-vantages from employers' and insurers' security will spread to benefit oth-ers. In this view, even if some workers and their families face more risk and disruption in the short term from the impairment-rating revisions, em-ployers' and insurers' increased predictability and stability will lead to more jobs and economic growth that will offset workers' losses in the long run.

These assumptions of shared costs and shared benefits reveal a strong vision of social solidarity, where workers and others feel the pain of busi-ness owners and reap their gain. In contrast, reformers have an individual-istic view of workers' interests. Reform advocates tended to assume that the benefits of increased security to *workers* under the wage-loss system would *not* trickle down to provide gains for employers and on the rest of so-ciety. Instead, reform discussions often presented these gains as a selfish and even fraudulent personal enrichment of workers (and their lawyers and doctors) at the expense of others.

Similarly, the reform arguments assumed the costs of risk to workers will be theirs (or their families') alone to either reduce or absorb. Proponents of impairment reforms treated the possibility of financial pressures, insta-bility, and reduced productivity likely to result from workers' increased risk bearing as personal problems that will have little effect on employers or the rest of society. While employers' and insurers' difficulties coping with the costs of risk bearing deserve sympathy and support, in this view, the difficulties faced by workers demand sacrifice, self-reliance, and tough choices.

For example, a medical expert speaking on occupational safety criti-cized the expansion of workers compensation to pay for wages lost due to cumulative trauma disorders such as carpal tunnel syndrome (Louis 1998). He contended that disabling pain from repetitive motions in computer or assembly line work is a personal problem undeserving of workers compen-sation benefits or regulatory protection. In his view, the loss of income from such strain is caused by the workers' individual physical, mental, and moral weaknesses, and by their choice of an occupation unsuited to their abilities (Louis 1998). But his emphasis on workers' "individual responsibility" for their risk accompanied an implicit assumption of *social* responsibility for alleviating *employers'* risks. He assumed that employers deserve the protection of "custom-fitted" workers who can adapt to the demands of job, regardless of the costs. He suggested that protecting *workers* from certain occupational injury costs fosters self-serving dependence, while protecting *employers* from these costs promotes an ethic of self-sufficiency.

In another example of one-sided individualism, Sebastian Junger, author of a best-selling story of danger and death in the swordfishing industry, wrote in a *New York Times* op-ed essay that "we need people who are willing to . . . work in jobs that kill people with relentless regularity" (Junger 1997). Junger romantically recalled how his own hazardous work as an arborist rewarded him with relatively high wages and feelings of power. But when he seriously injured himself with a chain saw, he was pleased to be a well-educated worker able to quit and find safer, more vicarious, ways of appreciating risk. He acknowledged that most workers in high-risk jobs have few alternatives and receive few rewards—often ending up facing financial hardship and unemployment, if not death, for their courage. He concluded that the socially useful suffering of these risk takers can help his more privileged peers gain "perspective" on their own thrill seeking.

Junger captures not just the neoliberal romance with personal risk bearing, but also its covert—and skewed—ideal of social solidarity. He treats the costs of workers' risk bearing as a matter of personal choice or fate. In his vision, it is up to individual workers, not employers or government, to accept or escape the tragic consequences of occupational hazards to human life and limb. In contrast, he assumes that workers, and society in general, must protect employers from the costs of reducing these risks. Capital owners' interest in being free from responsibility for avoiding work hazards is not their personal problem, to be resolved by heroic acceptance of lost profits or by careful choice of business. Instead, he identifies employers' dependence on risk spreading as society's gain: it is "we," not them, who need "relentless killing" to make money. In contrast, it is "them"—those with little education and few resources—not his imagined "we" who are left to personally bear the price. Indeed, Junger constructs the losses from occupational risk taking as a beneficial source of moral inspiration for his peers privileged enough to flee such grave responsibility.

This unequal approach to personal responsibility recalls the prevailing approach to work accidents in the nineteenth-century tort system. Then, the defense of contributory negligence insulated employers from liability if more careful or motivated workers could have prevented the accident, and the defense of assumption of risk barred recovery for workers deemed to have chosen the job despite its hazards. Nineteenth-century courts sometimes rationalized such strict individual responsibility for workers on the theory that the corresponding social protection for employers would benefit the rest of society in the form of broader economic development (Friedman and Ladinsky 1967). Supporters of the change to workers compensation countered this theory by arguing that increased social responsibility for workers' losses would benefit the public by relieving the burden on charities from impoverished families and by protecting labor resources necessary for robust economic growth (Eastman 1910; Moss 1996).

Promoting New Insecurity with New Social Insurance for Capital

The increased embrace of worker security in the shift from nineteenth-century tort law to workers compensation reflected twentieth-century policymakers' increased recognition of workers' interests as integral to societal interests. The recent scaling back of workers compensation and other forms of social insurance marks a turn toward a different vision that identifies the interests of employers with the interests of the whole.

In the prevailing neoliberal ideology, this new social solidarity directed toward capital interests reflects a new global economic reality that has made older theories of social insurance obsolete (Yergin and Stanislaw 1998). In this view, employers who once might have absorbed or prevented more of the costs of work accidents now have to meet the demands of heightened global competition, some of it from nations where employers have much less responsibility for avoiding or compensating occupational health and safety risks (Greider 2000). Investors who once might have accepted lower profits (or longer-term profits) allowing safety investments and better benefits for workers now have greater opportunities, and greater market pressures, to match the larger and faster returns available in emerging markets where workers are forced by poverty and repressive regimes to work under harsher conditions (Greider 1997).[1] Politicians who may once have identified with the security interests of workers and middle-class families now face pressure to shift more of their allegiance to the wealthy campaign financiers who control their political future (Clawson, Neustadtl, and Weller 1998; Greider 1992; Sanger 1999b), or to the globally mobile capital interests who control the future of their local economies (Page 2000). As a result of this perceived enhanced solidarity with global capital (Kristoff and WuDunn 1999), neoliberal doctrine presents enhanced security for employers and capital owners as the best route to security for workers and others (Yergin and Stanislaw 1998).

But neoliberalism's double standard of risk taking helps *create* the disproportionate capital power that makes this one-sided social solidarity seem necessary and natural. Workers and their families become more dependent on global capital market gains for their security when alternative sources of protection—such as government-provided social insurance benefits and labor protections—become weaker. In addition, the rest of society becomes more vulnerable to global capital market losses when increased security for employers and wealthy investors brings increased social responsibility for their risk taking.

Moreover, rhetoric promoting market risk taking has supported new affirmative forms of social insurance for global investors, not just reforms of workers compensation and other social insurance programs for workers. But, following the classic moral hazard analysis, this new social insurance gives wealthy capital owners incentives to take greater risks, which in turn makes it likely they will demand further protection from the consequences of that risk taking. As a result, this new shift toward capital security will not necessarily make up for the loss of workers' security produced by neoliberal social insurance reforms, but instead will often reinforce and intensify new conditions of insecurity for most of society.

One dramatic new social insurance program developed during the 1980s and 1990s came from the International Monetary Fund (IMF) (Hahnel 1999). When large commercial bankers faced losses from risky loans in the Latin American debt crisis of 1982, the IMF expanded its involvement in regulating and insuring international investment risks (Pastor 1993). The IMF socializes global investors' losses by offering below-market, taxpayer-backed loans to enable governments to maintain currency values and debt payments (Hahnel 1999).

For example, private foreign investors flocked to Mexico during the early 1990s to earn quick returns of 80–100 one hundred percent, taking advantage of that country's new risk-embracing policies that had deregulated financial markets, privatized government industries, and liberalized international trade and investment policies (Greider 1997). When the Mexican economic bubble burst in 1994, the IMF (led by the United States) provided a $50 billion bailout package that protected many of these high-flying investors from the risk of severe losses (Greider 1997). In the late 1990s, the IMF spearheaded more than $150 billion in funding to prop up collapsing investments in Indonesia, Thailand, South Korea, and Russia (Sanger 1998a), as well as a $41.5 billion loan to Brazil (Sanger 1998b).

Many policymakers and pundits acknowledge that the IMF's protection from losses from risky investments creates moral hazard by encouraging careless investment that will exacerbate risks of further economic collapse (see, e.g., Weinstein 1998). But, in the prevailing wisdom, the need for social solidarity in the face of global economic risk taking often precludes personal responsibility from global investors (Fischer 1999). In the international financial crises of the late 1990s, media reports and policy analysts justified public protection on the ground that global investors' losses were "contagious," like infectious disease or fires, bound to spread beyond individual risk takers (Sanger 1997, 1999a, 1998b; Kristoff and Wyatt 1999).

This reasoning circuitously promises that when taxpayers buy more insurance (more IMF protection) for wealthy global speculators, they will also insure *themselves* against the global upheaval that results from the irresponsible risk taking this insurance in turn produces. For example, *New York Times* columnist and author Thomas Friedman projects a scenario where a world without IMF bailouts leads to catastrophe: he imagines economic collapse sparking racist rioting in Southeast Asia that causes governments to impose martial law, in turn provoking threats of Chinese military action; South Korean mobs ransacking U.S. corporations and the U.S. Embassy; and the Russian government auctioning off nuclear technology and uranium to the highest bidder under pressure from legions of unemployed or unpaid workers (Friedman 1998). Friedman sums up his point with the quip, "How's that for a moral hazard!" (1998:C1).

Friedman's narrative turns the American taxpayers from *insurers* socializing global investors' losses into *insureds* who receive the IMF's protection from global chaos in solidarity with wealthy investors. Friedman obscures the IMF's risk spreading from the wealthy to taxpayers as a whole by focusing instead on risk spreading from desperate foreign masses, ignoring the question whether the IMF's protection of global speculators from the social and political consequences of their profit-seeking might contribute to those globe-spreading losses. In another example, President Clinton defended his support for the IMF bailout of Brazil's debts by asserting, "A strong Brazil makes for a strong United States" (Sanger 1998b), masking his policy of solidarity with wealthy global investors with rhetoric of international solidarity between the American public and the Brazilian public.

But increased *social* responsibility for risks to global investors has helped increase *individual* responsibility for workers, making this new global solidarity one sided. As investors spread more of their risk to the IMF, the IMF faces more pressure to control this risk. The IMF has sought to reduce the risks of global investment not by regulating investors' risk taking, but by imposing regulatory controls that help investors further shift their risks to others. The IMF plays a major role in constructing and enforcing the neoliberal double standard of risk taking by conditioning its loans—used to repay foreign investors—on plans for fiscal austerity and "structural adjustment" (Schydlowsky 1995; Hahnel 1999). These policies aim to increase investor security by (among other things) reducing government spending on social insurance for workers, families, retirees, and others dependent on labor income or government assistance. For example, the IMF's 1998 bailout of Brazil was conditioned on cutbacks in Brazil's pension system for state workers (Schemo 1998a). In turn, as the IMF's risk-reduction policies make many developing nations safer for global capital, nations with stronger social insurance systems for workers are likely to face additional competitive pressure to reduce their own protections.

In a second example of new domestic social insurance skewed toward wealthy investors, the U.S. Federal Reserve Bank has increased its protection for creditors and employers by shifting its policy emphasis further away from reducing unemployment toward reducing inflation (Bluestone and Harrison 2000). Under Paul Volker's leadership from 1979 to 1988, and continuing since then under Alan Greenspan, the Federal Reserve generally has pursued a tight money policy aimed at insuring capital owners—especially large banks and bondholders—against the risk that economic growth will lead to rising wages and consumer prices that will erode the value of their loans. This tight money policy spreads to others some of the risks from precipitous economic growth that would otherwise fall on capital lenders. When the Federal Reserve intervenes to raise interest rates in overheated economies, wealthy bondholders gain while consumers lose cheaper access to home mortgages and consumer credit, more businesses and farmers lose access to capital for production, and workers lose jobs and wages as employers restrict demand for labor (Grabel 1993).

Again, neoliberal theory predicts that the gains to creditors from that risk-spreading monetary policy will trickle down to benefit society in general in the long run as consumer prices fall and savings increases, bringing the economy back into "balance." However, this socialized responsibility for creditors' losses instead can produce moral hazard that will have the opposite effect—allowing wealthy lenders to spread more risks to others and to retain more gains from any ensuing economic growth, at least under some conditions (Greider 1987). For example, the high interest rates of the Volker era contributed to pressures for increased borrowing, thereby increasing much of society's dependence on creditors for continued financial

security (Greider 1987, quoting Sonnino 1986). With this heightened dependence on debt, society has become even more vulnerable to creditors'
increased risk taking, as creditors have more power to pass on risks of inflation to borrowers in the form of higher interest rates. In turn, this increased risk-spreading power has also increased wealthy creditors' power to
keep a greater share of their gains to themselves.

For example, as higher real interest rates during the Volker era suppressed wage growth and contributed to job insecurity (Greider 1987),[2]
many middle-class families relied on borrowing to maintain their assets
and living standards[3] (Crotty 1993; Greider 1987) and businesses relied in
part on consumer debt to maintain demand for goods and services (Greider
1987; Bluestone and Harrison 2000). Total home mortgage and consumer
installment debt rose more than 400 percent between 1980 and 1992 (in un-
adjusted dollars) (Sullivan, Warren, and Westbrook 2000, citing Bureau of
Census 1997), and from 1980 to 1994, household debt increased from 65 to
81 percent of total income (Sullivan, Warren, and Westbrook 2000, citing
Canner and Luckett 1991 and Canner, Kennickell, and Luckett 1995). During the Reagan and Bush administrations of the 1980s, the federal government racked up enormous federal deficits (Crotty 1993; Bluestone and Harrison 2000), partly in an attempt to counter the dampening effects of
monetary restrictions on the economy. Corporate debt similarly skyrock-
eted during the 1980s, in part because tax breaks stimulating supply-side
growth combined with high interest rates encouraged risky financing
(Crotty 1993; Greider 1987).[4] In addition, the Federal Reserve's policy favoring high interest rates inflated the value of the dollar relative to foreign
currencies, thereby dramatically increasing imports relative to exports and
encouraging a shift in manufacturing investment to other countries (Gordon 1996; Crotty 1993). Not only did this increased trade deficit further increase job insecurity in some sectors of the economy,[5] but it also changed
the United States from a net international creditor in the early 1980s to a
net international debtor owing about $440 billion to foreign creditors by the
end of the decade (Crotty 1993).

This major increase in societal dependence on borrowing has given
wealthy lenders additional power to demand further protections from inflation risks. For example, in his 1992 election campaign, President Clinton
supported a program of "Putting People First," which aimed to benefit the
middle class and poor through new public investments in job creation, job
training, education, and universal health insurance (Woodward 1994). He
withdrew much of his spending plans, however, when economic advisors
warned that bondholders would react by raising interest rates, thereby can-

celing the benefits of his economic stimulus plan because of the economy's heavy dependence on debt (Woodward 1994).

By the time of the 2000 presidential election, large government deficits had become large expected surpluses, and the candidates for both major parties made reduction of accumulated national debt a high priority. Even most Democratic leaders offered only modest proposals for spending any surplus on investments that would provide security for workers, the middle class, or the poor (Reich 2000b; Judis 2000; Meyerson 2000). In the conventional political wisdom, plans for major spending to benefit the middle class are constrained by the need to continue to maintain wealthy investors' "confidence" by further protecting them from risks of wage increases and threats to the value of the dollar (Page 2000).

In short, neoliberal policies aimed at protecting the wealthiest investors have not produced a new balance where capital owners' security provides stable ground for worker security. Instead, increased social responsibility for the risks of wealthy investors has helped redirect economic growth to foster both greater market risk and decreased government protection for a substantial number of Americans (Greider 1987; Reich 2000a). Real hourly wages fell by an average of 10 percent from 1973 to 1995; median family income rose only 4 percent during that period, despite a large increase in the number of hours worked to produce that income (Bluestone and Harrison 2000). After 1983, the least wealthy four-fifths of Americans received no gain in wealth from economic growth, even though their wealth had increased substantially during the growth of the 1960s and early 1970s (Bluestone and Harrison 2000). Indeed, the least wealthy 40 percent of U.S. families faced a substantial decline in net worth (including home ownership) through the 1980s and early 1990s (Keister 2000). In contrast, the richest 1 percent of wealth owners received two-thirds of the gains in financial wealth to American households during the 1980s (Wolff 1995).

Protection against inflation and against global risks for capital does not seem to have produced a substantial boost in spending power for many Americans: from 1973 to 1993, "the time necessary for a worker paid the average hourly wage to earn the average household's yearly expenses has grown forty-three percent" (Henwood 1993). Consumer interest rates remain at historically high rates, despite dramatic drops in inflation and despite other regulatory changes protecting creditors against risk: while banks' rates for borrowing fell from 13.4 percent to 3.5 percent between 1980 and 1992, average credit card interest rose slightly from 17.3 percent to 17.8 percent (Sullivan, Warren, and Westbrook 2000). Consumer bankruptcy rates among middle-class Americans surged from the 1980s through the 1990s and, in 1998, national aggregate savings rates were negative for the first time since the Depression era (Sullivan, Warren, and Westbrook 2000).

By 1998, inequality of U.S. family incomes was the highest since such data began being calculated in 1947, up substantially from the 1980s (Henwood 2000). And when the expanding economy began to push wages up during the late 1990s, a series of interest rate hikes by the Federal Reserve succeeded in keeping wage growth small while spurring further growth in stock market returns (Uchitelle 2000; Berenson 2000; Heilbrun 2000). And even though more workers and households are sharing in the stock market boom, 86 percent of stock market gains during the period 1989–98 went to the richest 10 percent of households (Hahnel 1998).

Embracing Subordination in the Guise of "Risk"

The problem with risk embracing as a characterization of the times is not only that the purported neoliberal move from security to risk is one sided. More fundamentally, the risk-embracing picture exaggerates security and risk as self-evident opposites. In fact, the distinction between seeking security and taking risks is subject to interpretation: the same behavior may be described as either or both depending on social context and political purpose.

Consider the greeting-card saying Jonathan Simon quotes at the beginning of chapter 8 of this volume: "The Loftier Your Goals, the Higher Your Risk, the Greater Your Glory." For most readers, that message of self-assured individualism probably calls to mind images of mountain climbers and Internet entrepreneurs rather than, for instance, workers compensation claimants, undocumented Mexican immigrants, or welfare recipients. But that is not as much because of differences in the riskiness of the actions involved but because of the differences in social status—often influenced by race, class, and gender identity—of the actors.

Returning to the example of workers compensation, the clerical worker with carpal tunnel syndrome who perseveres in bringing a contested disability claim is not likely to be hailed for her tenacity, rebelliousness, or high standards. Instead, prevailing popular culture and policy experts are more likely to portray her pursuit of compensation and her concern for health as selfish greed, or as irrational and irresponsible malingering.

For another example, border-crossing undocumented immigrants who defy heavily armed government authority in pursuit of personal economic gain could, in theory, personify the virtues of neoliberal risk taking. However, in mainstream U.S. politics and culture, even if immigrants' pursuit of gain in the global market requires entrepreneurial, antibureaucratic nerviness, their behavior is typically understood instead as base reckless-ness; not as self-reliant glory seeking but as parasitic evasion of responsi-bility. As one anti-immigration activist explained, "hundreds of millions of people have chosen to seek safer havens elsewhere rather than seek indige-nous solutions of their society's problems" (Pelto 1998:B5).

Similarly, consider the welfare recipient who refuses to give up her child, to get married, or to accept low-wage work, and instead aspires to stay on government aid to support her dreams of higher education, motherhood, and long-term independence. She is more likely to be condemned for being dependent and insolent than celebrated for setting lofty goals and for seek-ing individual freedom. The message of "work-first" policies included in re-cent welfare reforms is not to hold out for the best job or to pursue the "glory" of a better life for self and family, but to be grateful for any job (or for any bill-paying husband) (DeParle 1997). Mothers without well-paying jobs or well-paid husbands tend to be shamed for their irrationality and self-indulgence, not honored for shouldering the hard work of single parenting in high-risk circumstances.

While some risk takers are condemned both for their rash ambition and their careful concern for protection, others are glorified for embracing risk and security at the same time. Global securities traders, like former Trea-sury Secretary and investment banker Robert Rubin, exemplify both gutsy speculation and prudent calculation as they pursue high profits in newly deregulated markets (see, e.g., Weisberg 1998). International business deal-ers demonstrate free-market daring even while conducting their exploits under protection of bodyguards and armored cars in countries plagued by violence and corruption (Schemo 1998b). Ads for sport-utility vehicles en-courage affluent consumers to display their success by combining rugged adventure seeking with protective fortification (Bradsher 2000).

Furthermore, while the pursuit of protection by some—immigrants, welfare mothers, workers compensation claimants—is portrayed as a sign of irresponsible government dependence, the achievement of protection by others may be portrayed as productive market risk taking. The multina-tional corporations that represent the triumph of free-market risk taking in-herently depend on socialized risk spreading for their success. Limits on li-ability, which define the corporate form of doing business, are a form of government insurance through which the risks of capital ownership are spread to consumers, workers, citizens, and others (Baker 1996). This risk protection provides predictability and flexibility that facilitates rational in-vestment and promotes economic development, in the conventional wisdom. Yet in the prevailing view, this corporate legal structure has come to be an integral part of market risk taking, not an instance of government protectionism.

The neoliberal condemnation of certain people as both risk takers and risk avoiders represents not a value system in which risk outweighs security, but a value system in which both risk and security are constructed as reasonable and productive for some persons but unreasonable and destructive for others. The problem with the risk-embracing rhetoric that characterizes prevailing neoliberal policies is not that it fosters excessive individual responsibility at the expense of social protection. Instead, the problem is how neoliberal policy distributes risk and security: whose individual risk taking and social risk spreading is deemed to further the interests of the broader community? The most consistent message of the neoliberal system is not the embrace of individual risk but the embrace of a vision of community that subordinates the interests of the majority of people to the interests of a few.

NOTES

Thanks to Carl Nightingale and Lance Liebman for comments on drafts, and to participants in the New England Insurance and Society Study Group and the University of Connecticut conference on Insurance, Risk and Responsibility—Toward a New Paradigm. Portions of this essay were published in "Whose Risk, Whose Security," *American Prospect* 11, no. 6 (January 31, 2000): 38, and are reprinted by permission from *The American Prospect*, 5 Broad Street, Boston, MA 02109; all rights reserved.

1. For example, investors financing U.S. factories face competing choices from foreign stock markets with annual returns averaging 21 percent in Hong Kong, 28 percent in Argentina, and 18 percent in India, compared to closer to 11 percent in the United States and Germany (Greider 1987:235).

2. During the Volcker era, the share of the U.S. income produced by wages shrank to the lowest level since 1929; from 1979 to 1983, personal income from interest grew by 70 percent, compared to a 33-percent increase in wage income (Greider 1987:578–79). The tight money policies of the early 1980s particularly hurt organized labor, so that when the economy picked up again, labor was unable to bargain for a share of the gains (Greider 1987:585–87).

3. Consumer credit "exploded" beginning in the early 1980s as the credit industry took advantage of inflation-fighting interest rates and the related abolition of usury restrictions to expand marketing of debt (Sullivan, Warren, and Westbrook 2000:249).

4. However, this debt primarily went to finance buyouts and speculation rather than job-creating production, again contributing to the dependence on lenders and the weakened bargaining power of most workers (Crotty 1993). "In 1984, for instance, American business accumulated a staggering $140 billion in new debt that was devoted solely to finance corporate mergers and take-overs. It did not build any new factories" (Greider 1987:658).

5. The high dollar particularly hurt the high-waged, heavily unionized manufacturing industries like auto makers by encouraging a shift in production to other countries (Greider 1987, citing testimony by Lee Iococca before the House Banking Committee, April 28, 1983).

REFERENCES

Alliance of American Insurers. 1990. *Workers Compensation in a New Decade: Restoring the Balance.* Schaumberg, Ill.: Alliance of American Insurers.

American Medical Association. 1993. *Guides to the Evaluation of Permanent Impairment.* 4th ed. Chicago: American Medical Association.

Baker, Tom. 1996. "The Genealogy of Moral Hazard." *Texas Law Review* 75: 237–92.

Berenson, Alex. 2000. "Stocks Post Big Gain on Report that Shows Slowing Economy." *New York Times,* 3 June, C1.

Bluestone, Barry, and Bennett Harrison. 2000. *Growing Prosperity: The Battle for Growth with Equity in the 21st Century.* Boston: Houghton Mifflin.

Bradsher, Keith. 2000. "G. M. Has High Hopes for Vehicle Truly Meant for Road Warriors." *New York Times,* 6 August, 1.

Bureau of the Census. 1997. *Statistical Abstract of the United States.* Washington, D.C.: Government Printing Office.

Burke, James M. 1992. "Comp System Needs Intensive Care." *Business Insurance,* 19 October, 34.

Burton, John F., Jr. 1994. "Observations: The Twentieth Anniversary of the National Commission on State Workmen's Compensation Laws: A Symposium." In *Workers' Compensation Year Book,* ed. J. F. Burton Jr. and Timothy Schmidle. Horsham, Penn.: LRP Publications.

———. 1997. "Permanent Partial Disability Benefits: The Data." *Workers' Compensation Monitor* 10 (May/June): 1.

Burton, John F., Jr., et al. 1997. "Workers' Compensation Benefits Continue to Decline." *Workers' Compensation Monitor* 10 (July/August): 1.

Canner, Glenn B., and Charles A. Luckett. 1991. "Payment of Household Debts." *Federal Reserve Bulletin* 77:218.

Canner, Glenn B., Arthur B. Kennickell, and Charles A. Luckett. 1995. "Household Sector Borrowing and the Burden of Debt." *Federal Reserve Bulletin* 81:323.

Clawson, Dan, Alan Neustadtl, and Mark Weller. 1998. *Dollars and Votes: How Business Campaign Contributions Subvert Democracy.* Philadelphia: Temple University Press.

Consumer Reports. 2000."Workers Comp: Falling Down on the Job." February, 28–33.

Crotty, James. 1993. "The Rise and Fall of the Keynesian Revolution in the Age of the Global Marketplace." In *Creating a New World Economy: Forces of Change and Plans for Action,* ed. G. Epstein, J. Graham, and J. Nembhard. Philadelphia: Temple University Press.

DeParle, Jason. 1997. "U.S. Welfare System Dies as State Programs Emerge." *New York Times*, 30 June, A1.

Dewees, Don, David Duff, and Michael Trebilcock. 1996. *Exploring the Domain of Accident Law: Taking the Facts Seriously.* New York: Oxford University Press.

Eastman, Crystal. [1910] 1969. *Work-Accidents and the Law.* Reprint, New York: Arno Press.

Economist. 1994. "Prevention versus Cure." 3 December, Insurance Survey section, 21.

Ellenberger, James. 1999. "The Battle Over Workers' Compensation." *Working USA* (September/October): 23–37.

Fischer, Stanley. 1999. "On the Need for an International Lender of Last Resort." <http://www.imf.org/external/np/speeches/1999/010399.HTM>.

Fletcher, Meg. 1991. "Large Deductible Plans Grow Popular; Employers Attracted to Self-Insurance Alternative." *Business Insurance*, 16 September, 36.

———. 1996. "Permanent Partial Disability Benefits Are Focus of Growing Debate in States." *Business Insurance*, 4 November, 21.

Fricker, Mary. 1997. "Insult to Injury: Workers' Comp (Special Report)." *Santa Clara Press Democrat*, 7–10 December, 1–14.

Friedman, Lawrence M., and Jack Ladinsky. 1967. "Social Change and the Law of Industrial Accidents." *Columbia Law Review* 67:50–82.

Friedman, Thomas L. 1998. "Trash the I. M. F.!" *New York Times*, 13 June, C1.

Garrett, Robert T. 1998. "Debating Workers' Comp." *Louisville Courier-Journal*, 30 August, A1.

Goel, Vindu P. 1995. "Business Groups Begin Attack on Reform." *Cleveland Plain Dealer*, 10 September, H1.

Gordon, David. 1996. *Fat and Mean: The Corporate Squeeze of Working Americans and the Myth of Managerial "Downsizing."* New York: Free Press.

Grabel, Ilene. 1993. "Crossing Borders: A Case for Cooperation in International Financial Markets." In *Creating a New World Economy: Forces of Change and Plans for Action,* ed. G. Epstein, J. Graham, and J.Nembhard. Philadelphia: Temple University Press.

Greider, William. 1987. *Secrets of the Temple: How the Federal Reserve Runs the Country.* New York: Simon and Schuster.

———. 1992. *Who Will Tell the People: The Betrayal of American Democracy.* New York: Simon and Schuster.

———. 1997. *One World Ready or Not: The Manic Logic of Global Capitalism.* New York: Simon and Schuster.

———. 2000. "Global Agenda: International Trade Regulations." *Nation*, 31 January, 11.

Hahnel, Robin. 1998. "Capitalist Globalism in Crisis, Part I: Boom and Bust." *Z Magazine* 11:46–52.

———. 1999. "Capitalist Globalism in Crisis, Part III: Understanding the IMF." *Z Magazine* 12:47–54.

Heilbrunn, Jacob. 2000. "The Economy: Sacrificing Workers in War on Inflation." *Los Angeles Times*, 28 May, M1.

Heimer, Carol. 1985. *Reactive Risk and Rational Action: Managing Moral Hazard in Insurance Contracts.* Berkeley: University of California Press.

Henwood, Doug. 1993. "Money." *Left Business Observer* 60:6.

———. 2000. "Boom for Whom?" *Left Business Observer* 93:4, 7.

Judis, John B. 2000. "Embarrassment of Riches." *American Prospect* 11:10–11.

Junger, Sebastian. 1997. "Danger as a Way of Life." *New York Times,* 13 July, 17.

Keister, Lisa A. 2000. *Wealth in America: Trends in Wealth Inequality.* Cambridge: Cambridge University Press.

Kimball, Spencer L. 1960. *Insurance and Public Policy.* Ann Arbor: University of Michigan Press.

Kristoff, Nicholas D., and Sheryl WuDunn. 1999. "Of World Markets, None an Island." *New York Times,* 17 February, A1.

Kristoff, Nicholas D., and Edward Wyatt. 1999. "Global Contagion: A Narrative, Part 1: Who Went Under in the World's Sea of Cash." *New York Times,* 15 February, A1.

Louis, Dean. 1998. Comments as member of panel on "Ergonomics, Repetitive Trauma Disorders, and OSHA Standards." 22d Annual Symposium on Workers' Compensation, 21 July, at Dearborn, Michigan.

"Major Workers' Comp Reform Package under Consideration by State Legislature." 1997. *Ohio Worker's Comp Advisor* 7:3.

McCluskey, Martha T. 1998. "Illusion of Efficiency in Workers' Compensation "Reform." *Rutgers Law Review* 50:657–941.

Meyerson, Harold. 2000. "Bill & Al's Excellent Adventure." *Los Angeles Weekly,* 28 January, 30.

Miller, Carol Marbin. 1998. *Broward Daily Business Review,* 11 December, A5.

Moore, Michael J., and W. Kip Viscusi. 1990. *Compensation Mechanisms for Job Risks.* Princeton: Princeton University Press.

Moss, David A. 1996. *Socializing Security: Progressive-Era Economists and the Origins of American Social Policy.* Cambridge: Harvard University Press.

National Commission on State Workmen's Compensation Laws. 1972. *Report of the National Commission on State Workmen's Compensation Laws.* Washington, D.C.: Government Printing Office.

Oxfeld, Eric J. 1998. "Prepared Statement of UWC—Strategic Services on Unemployment & Workers' Compensation." Before the House Education and the Workforce Committee, Subcommittee on Workforce Protections. U.S. Congress. 24 March.

Page, Susan. 2000. "When it Comes to Economics, the Differences are Hard to Find." *USA Today,* 26 June, A1.

Pastor, Manuel, Jr. 1993. "The Latin American Debt Crisis." In *Creating a New World Economy: Forces of Change and Plans for Action,* ed. G. Epstein, J. Graham, and J. Nembhard. Philadelphia: Temple University Press.

Pelto, Richard. 1998. "Population Pressures—True Cause of Growth: Influx of Immigrants." Letter to the editor. *Seattle Times,* 4 August, B5.

Pryor, Ellen Smith. 1990. "Compensation and a Consequential Model of Loss." *Tulane Law Review* 64:783–856.

Reich, Robert B. 2000a. "The Great Divide." *American Prospect* 11:56.

———. 2000b. "Is Scrooge a Democrat Now?" *American Prospect* 11:96.

Research and Oversight Council on Workers' Compensation. 1996. *An Analysis of Texas Workers with Permanent Impairments*.
<http://www.roc.capnet.state.tx.us/impair.htm>.

Rubinow, I. M. 1913. *Social Insurance: With Special Reference to American Conditions*. New York: Holt.

Sanger, David E. 1997. "Case No. 3; Asian Illness Threatens World Organs." *New York Times*, 22 November, D1.

———. 1998a. "Domino Theory." *New York Times*, 2 August, §4, 1.

———. 1998b. "Brazil Gets $41.5 Billion to Prop Up Economy." *International Herald Tribune* (Neuilly-sur-Seine, France), 18 November, 1.

———. 1999a. "Why Couldn't Anyone Keep Brazil from Burning?" *New York Times*, 7 February, §3, 4.

———. 1999b. "Markets are Freer than Politicians." *New York Times*, 21 February, §4, 5.

Schemo, Diana Jean. 1998a. "Brazilian Economic Plan Encounters Some Naysayers." *New York Times*, 30 October, C3.

———. 1998b. "Risking Life, Limb and Capital: US Companies Operate in Colombia, But Very Carefully." *New York Times*, 6 November, C1.

Schydlowsky, Daniel M., ed. 1995. *Structural Adjustment: Retrospect and Prospect*. Westport, Conn: Praeger.

Somers, Herman Miles, and Anne Ramsay Somers. 1954. *Workmen's Compensation: Prevention, Insurance and Rehabilitation of Occupational Disability*. New York: John Wiley.

Sonnino, Edward, 1986. "Fed Tightness Boosts Borrowing." *Wall Street Journal*, 21 February.

Spieler, Emily. 1995. "Assessing Fairness in Workers' Compensation Reform: A Commentary on the 1995 West Virginia Workers' Compensation Legislation." *West Virginia Law Review* 98:23–170.

Sullivan, Teresa A., Elizabeth Warren, and Jay Lawrence Westbrook. 2000. *The Fragile Middle Class: Americans in Debt*. New Haven: Yale University Press.

Uchitelle, Louis. 2000. "May's Labor Data Indicate Economy Could be Slowing." *New York Times*, 3 June, A6.

Weinstein, Michael M. 1998. "When Lending Money Just Isn't Enough; Critics Seek a New Role for the I. M. F. as Recent Bailout Programs Fall Short." *New York Times*, 30 September, C1.

Weisberg, Jacob. 1998. "Keeping the Boom from Busting." *New York Times*, 19 July, §6 (Magazine), 24.

Wolff, Edward N. 1995. *Top Heavy: A Study of the Increasing Inequality of Wealth in America*. New York: New Press.

Woodward, Bob. 1994. *The Agenda: Inside the Clinton White House*. New York: Simon and Schuster.

Yergin, Daniel, and Joseph Stanislaw. 1998. *The Commanding Heights: The Battle between Government and the Marketplace That Is Remaking the Modern World*. New York: Simon and Schuster.

PART TWO

Risk(s) beyond Insurance

The essays in the second part of the book examine the embrace of risk as it is playing out in fields beyond insurance, including popular culture, environmental regulation, and the practice of professionals. As these essays reflect, concern with risk has moved well beyond the insurance trade. Because insurance never exists in a vacuum, these other institutions and practices are bound to be turned back on insurance institutions. Indeed, the embrace of risk these essays describe may be helping to naturalize the "de-socializing" of risk explored in the book's first part.

Like the earlier ones, the following essays help us see that risk is not an objective essence representing the same value for all people at all times. Instead, risk is a socially constructed concept—the product of specific organizational and institutional dynamics. At the same time, however, risk is an interpretive grid that we use to create our organizations and institutions. Once called into existence, a risk has the potential to reshape how we know and act.

Chapter Eight

In "Taking Risks: Extreme Sports and the Transformation of Risk in Advanced Liberal Societies," Jonathan Simon begins by analyzing risk and security in the context of extreme sports. Focusing on mountain climbing, he investigates how ideologies of risk taking and responsibility are disseminated and constructed through popular culture. Simon identifies "summiteering" and "mountaineering" as two competing approaches to risk. Summiteering focuses on reaching the summit and embodies the embrace of risk as "a nostalgic return to capitalism in the eras before regulation, welfare, and insurance." Mountaineering focuses on the personal skills and social relations necessary to survive and thrive in mountain environments.

For Simon, popular culture does not merely reflect larger political rationalities. It is also an important force in shaping individual attitudes about new forms of governance and risk taking. On the one hand, participation in and discussion about these activities showcase the new attitude toward risk being promoted by both business and government. In this regard, mountain climbing is a thinly disguised celebration of market triumph and, thus, reflects and promotes the distributional inequities explored by Heimer and McCluskey, respectively, in chapters 6 and 7. On the other hand, however, these activities may provide real opportunities to develop and rehearse skills, mentalities, and communities that will be useful to people who are being handed more responsibility whether they like it or not.

Chapter Nine

In "At Risk of Madness," Nikolas Rose explores a very different embrace of risk, that of "psy-professionals" (Rose's general term for the array of professionals and para-professionals who wield expertise and power in modern mental health systems). Rose undertakes what he calls a "diagnostic" approach to risk, exploring how risk has emerged in psychiatry, what consequences accompany governing madness through risk, what new "technologies of power and relations of authority" have arisen, and what ethical issues are raised by the heightened relation of psychiatry and risk.

In the process, Rose considers the role of tort liability and the management of risk and responsibility, and contends that "the shadow of the law" significantly shapes mental health workers' professional conduct. Rose argues that contemporary psychiatry confines patients not so much to cure them but more "for the secure containment of risk." Thus, like McCluskey, Rose focuses on the relationship between risk and security. As before, the question is whose risk and whose security: patients, the community, and/or the mental health workers themselves? Rose cautions that sometimes risk assessments are used more to protect the mental health workers from liability than to accurately predict the future behavior of the patient. As Rose's essay illustrates, the "embrace of risk" means more than the celebration of risk taking that Simon emphasizes. It also means the adoption of risk as a framework for understanding a problem like madness or, as the next essay will illustrate, crime.

Chapter Ten

In "The Policing of Risk," Richard Ericson and Kevin Haggerty examine police as agents of a risk society. In their recent book *Policing the Risk Society*, Ericson and Haggerty showed that police increasingly function as knowledge collectors for insurance companies and other private and governmental systems of risk assessment and distribution. In this essay they extend that work by exploring how policing risk entails population management well beyond crime control per se.

In the language of economic sociology developed by Heimer in chapter 6, risk management has led policing, like insurance, to become increasingly institutionally embedded. This embeddedness means that external institutions affect how the police investigate crime and classify data. Indeed, the "risk knowledge" requirements of other institutions often determine whether an incident requires police action. Like Rose and Heimer, Ericson and Haggerty raise questions about the potential consequences of risk management. For example, the recently developed "closed box" classification system of police reporting threatens a significant risk: constricting the space for creative problem solving in crime investigations and analyses. Closed-box classification questions may promote efficiency and thoroughness, but also may close off the possibility of alternative theories that are not conveniently encoded on the report forms. Just as "governing through crime" may exploit the public's fear of crime, it also may promote nuances and varieties of crime that are not easily classifiable on police documentation records.

Chapter Eleven

Finally, in "The Return of Descartes' Malicious Demon: An Outline of a Philosophy of Precaution," François Ewald revisits the historical dynamic he first explored in his influential *L'Etat Providence* (1986). That work documented a shift from a nineteenth-century approach to risk, characterized by ideas of providence and individual responsibility, to a twentieth-century approach characterized by ideas of prevention and solidarity. In this essay, he implicitly questions his earlier sense that these two governmental rationalities fit neatly into historical periods. He also identifies an emerging third approach to risk that is characterized by ideas of safety and precaution.

Ewald's essay continues a dialogue with Urich Beck. In an essay published in English just before the English translation of *Risikogesellchaft* (*Risk Society*), Beck described his "decisive" idea about "risk society" as addressing the impact of late modernity on the social compact that Ewald described in *L'Etat Providence* (Beck 1992:100–101). As Beck described, there are no insurance institutions that can address the "worst imaginable accident" that is possible because of any number of late-twentieth-century technical developments: nuclear power, bio-engineering, chemical production, ecological destruction. These are risks that are "beyond insurance," not in a normative sense, but rather in the sense that insurance institutions cannot spread or contain them.

Ewald argues that the "precautionary principle" emerged in international law in the late 1980s and 1990s precisely from the social developments Beck described in *Risikogesellchaft* in 1986. As Ewald describes, the precautionary principle reflects the social fact that, because of these developments, "[t]he problem is no longer so much to multiply the responsibility for risk and to organize the solvency of those who are liable through insurance, but rather to prevent certain risks from being taken."

Themes and Connections

This book reminds us that insurance is not a one-way monologue, dictating objective truths about spreading loss, embracing risk, and attitudes about individual and social responsibility. Instead, insurance forms and technologies are affected by how other institutions formulate and manage risk taking and loss spreading. Each of these essays investigates how governing through risk is in the process of reconfiguration. Clearly, insurance institutions, whose forms of risk spreading helped define the major twentieth-century century models of risk governing, are central to this reconfiguration. However, these essays illustrate that insurance is not the only institution concerned with risk. The discourse of risk permeates extreme sports, mental health care, law enforcement institutions, and environmental and tort liability.

Some of the essays suggest alternative possibilities—for example, that risk produces social opportunities as much as it valorizes individual responsibility and self-reliance. Similar to Deborah Stone's assertion in chapter 3 that expanding insurance creates moral opportunities, Jonathan Simon's discussion of mountaineering ethics reminds us that embracing risk does not have to be only about myopic or selfish individual achievement, but can also be about community and solidarity. Through everyday practices that seem far removed from insurance and governance, we construct new ways that affect how we perceive risk and responsibility.

None of these chapters offers a comprehensive blueprint of risk ideology. Instead, each illuminates a particular example of how risk thinking permeates contemporary Western culture. Extolling risk taking in popular culture—along with increased risk management in psychiatry, policing, and tort litigation—help to make certain attitudes about risk seem to be a matter of common sense. While mountain climbing may not usually be thought of in the context of the political arena, its discourses of risk and responsibility may accustom consumers of mountain climbing (climbers, or "vicarious" risk takers who read about climbing in books, magazines, web sites) to the more politicized types of risk thinking that characterize neoliberal governance.

Each of the essays also investigates the theme of risk(s) beyond insurance, including how insurance technologies and imaginaries govern risk outside insurance institutions. They prompt us to think about what role other institutions and practices play in producing technologies and imaginaries for dealing with risk, some of which may influence insurance. For example, the discourses of "governing through crime" and "governing through madness" affect how insurance institutions react to crime and mental health issues, while at the same time insurance institutions affect both specialized professionals and the popular media conceive of crime and madness.

These essays further push at the relationship between risk and security. For example, governing crime and governing madness each employ risk-management techniques to exploit public fears of crime and madness and corresponding desire for security. Ultimately, we must always ask who risk assessment provides security for, or, as McCluskey illustrated in chapter 7, security *from*. As these essays illustrate, risk and security are not binary oppositions to be contrasted. Instead, they form part of an ambiguous and complex ideology that runs through contemporary society, from popular culture to international policy.

In addition, references to tort liability permeate the essays, illustrating the active role of law in the sociology of risk and responsibility. For example, Simon discusses whether or not climbers should be able to sue mountain managers who prohibit climbers from altering the landscape to make climbing "safer." Rose considers how mental health workers have altered their diagnoses and risk management procedures in the wake of tort judgments deeming mental health workers liable if they should have foreseen harm to an identifiable victim. In a more abstract sense, Ewald suggests that defective products legal doctrines play a role in the shift to the age of precaution.

Finally, each essay explores how risk taking in everyday life affects emerging governmental rationalities. Discourses of mountain climbing, madness, and crime do not merely reflect larger rationalities of governance, but actively participate in their construction. Perhaps most significant, these essays illustrate that there is no one "correct" way to perceive risk and responsibility. As Ewald points out, there is nothing natural or necessary about our era of "precaution." A sociology of risk and insurance invites an interdisciplinary discussion and debate about the complex relation between risk, responsibility, insurance, and governance.

REFERENCE

Beck, Urich. 1992. "From Industrial Society to the Risk Society: Questions of Survival, Social Structure and Ecological Englightenment." *Theory, Culture and Society* 9: 97–123.

Taking Risks: Extreme Sports and the Embrace of Risk in Advanced Liberal Societies

JONATHAN SIMON

> Climbing mountains will never be a safe, predictable, rule-bound enterprise. This is an activity that idealizes risk taking; its most celebrated figures have always been those who stick their necks out the farthest and manage to get away with it. (John Krakauer, *Into Thin Air*)

> RISK: The Loftier Your Goals, The Higher Your Risk, the Greater Your Glory.[1]

In the industrial world of the twentieth century, reducing risks to life and limb and distributing the economic costs of risks was a primary concern of government. Under this approach to governing risk, sometimes referred to as the "social welfare state," public welfare was largely defined as shifting risks from the level of individuals, firms, families, and communities to society, which was meant to be accomplished through the state and its agencies directly or through law governing the practices of large corporations with the market power to recycle risk across the great ocean of consumers, workers, investors. In many postindustrial democracies, the social insurance systems such as unemployment insurance, old-age pensions, and victim-oriented tort liability rules serve as familiar parts of economic security for most people (Rose 1996). The form and scope of these tactics have been, of course, the subject of an endless variation and debate, yet we can speak of a more general imperative to control and spread risks—or as Baker and Simon put it in the introduction to this volume, "the principle of more insurance for more people."

Increasingly a new rationality of government is emerging that emphasizes the link between risk and the well-being of both individuals and society (Rose 1999). Individuals rather than collective bodies should assume re-

sponsibility for and control over risks. This emerging rationality of governance, sometimes described as "advanced liberalism" (Rose 1996, 1999),
"neoliberalism," or "post-Keynsianism" (O'Malley and Palmer 1996) encourages individuals, families, and firms to assume more risk. With risk,
according to this logic, will come more self-consciousness of risk taking,
more rewards, and more responsibility. This mandate to disaggregate risk
and its rediscovery of the political subjectivity behind risk taking is evident
across the spectrum of public policy from proposals for educational vouch-
ers to health care tax credits, as well as in the end of income support entitlements for parents of children and the transfer of publicly owned subsidized
housing for the poor to the real estate market through subsidized loans to
the poor. What is at stake here is less an abandonment of risk as a constitutive problem of government than a transformation of the relationships risk
creates.

   If the primary rationale of governing risk in the social welfare era was
spreading loss over larger and larger pools of people, the rationale now
emerging emphasizes disaggregating risk pools and placing more responsibility on individuals for bearing the risks of their life. While the political
Right has generally eagerly endorsed this shift, an increasing number of liberal policy thinkers have also moved in this direction, including among others Anthony Giddens in the United Kingdom (1999) and Bruce Ackerman
and Anne Alstott (1999) in the United States.[2]

   The disaggregating principle is illustrated in the 1996 law "reforming"
the federal system of income support for families with children. The former
Aid to Families with Dependent Children, repealed in 1996, provided a legal right to relief (although with wide variance in the substantive reality of
a subsistence income) based on a social status applied universally on the basis of belonging to the national population (although with significant state
variation). It was replaced by Temporary Assistance for Needy Families,
which by its very title implies there is a limit to socializing the risk of
poverty. The complex new law bristles with measures to make the individual more responsible for her fate, including work requirements and ultimately a five-year lifetime limit to government assistance. The much larger
population drawing income from the private labor market has also experienced a similar shift of risk and responsibility to individuals, albeit with far
less fanfare, through the wholesale transfer of benefits like heath insurance
and pensions from full coverage of provider defined care and defined benefit retirement plans to managed care plans and defined contribution retirement plans.[3]

   Beginning in the late nineteenth century, emergent discourses about the collective effects of work accidents, unemployment, and other "social" problems facilitated the growing social welfare approach to governing risk (Simon 1995, 1998). These discourses helped make the social logic of risk more visible by linking it to narratives of individual carnage and calamity. The law of employer responsibility remained formally hostile to the idea that employers were responsible for insuring their employees against loss due to the negligence of their fellow workers, or from the inherent risks of the employment. But increasingly juries, trial judges, and eventually appellate judges came to recognize the relative inevitability of accidents in the great industrial enterprises like railroads and steel manufacture, and the injustice of expecting individuals to make meaningful bargains over this kind of risk. Over time, decisionmakers who refused to recognize this logic were marginalized (Simon 1995). By the Great Depression the modern infrastructure for aggregating risk—private insurance on life, health, automobile and property, and social insurance systems like workers compensation—were in place.

At the turn of the twenty-first century, aggregation remains a large part of our law and our public risk culture, but it is increasingly undermined by a number of discourses that have become more influential than they were a generation ago. Perhaps the most prominent of these new risk discourses is the reinvigorated form of market economics that has become a common language of policy discussion in the political center. In finance economics theory, profit is a direct product of risk.[4] While the stock market itself was once seen as too risky for most working and middle-class people to invest their savings, today many retirement plans require individuals to choose among stocks, bonds, and other investment instruments. The popular perception of the stock market has been improved by the long period of growth in the share prices of many U.S. equities that has overshadowed past periods of catastrophic loss. However, it is difficult to believe stocks would be so central to contemporary visions of responsible economic behavior were they not commensurate with the valorization of risk taking in pursuit of reward.[5] Since the 1980s the normality of accepting increasingly extreme financial risks, even beyond those of the stock market, has been reinforced through the popularization of instruments with considerably more risk than ordinary equities, like junk bonds and derivatives.

The embrace of risk is also the message of a new and far more populist discourse thriving in postindustrial societies (at least the affluent ones)—namely, extreme sports and its close cousin adventure travel, both of which have rapidly become a major part of the huge recreation market.[6] Trekking through the Himalayas, skiing across the North Pole, and canoeing down the Amazon, or at least fantasizing about doing these things, has produced a burgeoning market for books, equipment, travel, and expertise. The marketing of these opportunities emphasizes the direct experience of risk in varying degrees, as it does in other activities like climbing, big-wave surfing, white-water rafting, helicopter skiing,[7] transocean solo yachting, and sports car racing, which have drawn unprecedented numbers of participants and even more onlookers (Cahill 1998; Tierney 1998). In these activities, risk taking is not simply an irreducible by-product of pleasurable actions, but in some respects the very source of pleasure. An even larger market exists for those whose taste for risk is limited to books, films, and magazines that depict risk taking and the clothes, equipment, and skills training necessary to pursue it.

Mountain climbing is perhaps the best known and most symbolically resonant of all the extreme sports. A recognized sport since the eighteenth century, climbing was long celebrated in its own literature. It is only in recent years that the sport has begun to attract large numbers of participants and a huge number of interested nonparticipants. The potential scope of this audience became evident after the death of eleven climbers on Mt. Everest in May of 1996.[8] The tragedy received unprecedented coverage from the mainstream media. Jon Krakauer's powerful first-person account, *Into Thin Air*, became a runaway bestseller and has been followed by several films and additional books by other survivors of the expedition. Remarkably, the Everest tragedy, rather than generating a backlash against the excesses of embracing risk, has only served to encourage more attention to and participation in extreme sports (Tierney 1998). In this essay, I offer a preliminary examination of the relationship between new governmental rationalities that urge the embrace of risk (as both life choice and public policy) and the discourses of extreme sports by examining aspects of the contemporary boom in climbing.[9]

It is important to attend to the specificities of these activities and discourses. In one sense, the discourses function in an ideological context as they recognize and misrecognize class-based differences in risk taking and its consequences. But they also function as resources for self-fashioning (Greenblatt 1980). In that sense they provide practical experiences, ideas, and narratives around which new kinds of subjectivity are being created and popularized. Even for those who read about or watch extreme sports, these activities produce a series of compelling images that tend to valorize precisely those attributes of subjects most valorized by advanced liberalism (Rose 1999). These discourses are, however, not simply an advertisement for the dominant ideology but a contested site for shaping subjectivities appropriate to the new forms of governance and the new status of risk taking. They provide, as it were, access to and a view of certain kinds of mentalities, skills, relationships, and objectives.

I begin with some further elaboration on the Mt. Everest calamity. Some of the most important features of climbing and its relevance to our current period of transformation in the governance of risk are evident in that tragedy and the publicity surrounding it. Next I offer a preliminary discussion of two different strands of the climbing experience as represented in popular culture. The first aspect, which dominates media presentation of climbing (and other extreme sports), is what I call "summiteering." This approach, rehearsed in a growing number of books, films, and magazine articles, portrays climbing as a powerfully redemptive symbol of personal triumph over adversity.

In summiteering, climbing is little more than a nostalgic invocation of capitalism in the eras before regulation, welfare, progressive income taxation, and insurance complicated the relationship between risk and reward. Climbing as a sport in practice often reduces to the goal of getting to the summit (preferably first, fastest, or with the greatest display of fitness by, for example, proceeding without oxygen in a high-altitude assent). The focus on the summit allows climbing to serve as an especially apt metaphor for embracing risk in a way that bungee jumping, extreme skiing, or sky diving (all variations on falling fast) do not.[10] Not surprisingly, climbing has become something of a cult sport among some corporate executives and wealthy financiers, who are the major customers for the very high end of the adventure travel market like Himalayan climbs or deep ocean sailing. *Forbes, Business Week,* and other popular business magazines regularly feature articles and columns on climbing, extreme sports, and adventure traveling.

The second aspect, which is subordinated by the mass media in its coverage of climbing but celebrated in the literature of climbing, can be called "mountaineering." Most climbers consider themselves mountaineers in the technical sense of persons competent in traversing mountainous wilderness areas, which includes the techniques of climbing (placing protection devices, using rope belays, alpine rescue, and so on), but also knowledge of plant and wild life, emergency medicine, and stream crossing.[11] I want to plumb a somewhat deeper meaning of that term, developed by many writers on climbing, in which mountaineering has an ethical and communitarian ethos in addition to its technical expertise. Mountaineering, in this broad sense, valorizes the act of "summiting" but also other aspects of life on the mountain, including confronting extremes of weather, self-reliance in extreme conditions, exposure (in climbing discourse, the immediate proximity to a fearsome drop-off), and especially the close work with partners sharing in the pleasures and dangers of the experience. Mountaineering narratives also embrace risk, but in more complex and nuanced ways than summiteering. Although much of the mountaineering ethic is anarchist in the classic sense that it eschews formal law, participants have long assumed the force of norms and debated precisely what principles should govern risk takers in their interactions with each other and with nature.

Climbers as a community have been writing and reading about each other for centuries and few would suffer to be called summiteers without objection. In this essay, however, I force the point a bit in order to contrast clearly the choices for responding to the current reconfiguration of the governance of risk that lie within close proximity to each other. Summiteering, whatever the intentions of writers on climbing, tends to highlight raw competition and struggle, while shadowing the conditions under which risk taking is carried out and individual effort supported. Mountaineering offers at least some preliminary clues as to how a deliberative public discourse about risk can be produced which empowers individuals and communities to respond to the risk that is often involuntarily imposed on them.

Calamity on Everest

In 1996 there were thirty separate expeditions on Everest including eight commercial ventures (Krakauer 1997). The two largest operations, Adventures Consultants from New Zealand and Mountain Madness from Seattle, each brought more than a dozen paying customers along with professional guides and Sherpas to Everest's slopes.[12] Rob Hall of Adventure Consultants, who would later die during the catastrophic summit attempt, charged what was then the highest rate in the business—sixty-five thousand dollars per person—but still placed an astonishing thirty-nine clients on the top of Everest during the period 1990–95. Competing guide Scott Fischer of Mountain Madness, who also died during the expedition, was making his first commercial foray on Everest during the fatal season. His tent at base camp was marked by a huge banner advertising Starbucks Coffee. Both outfits served a largely wealthy and corporate clientele mostly from the United States, Japan, Australia, and Western Europe.

Media attention directed at Everest climbing had been growing rapidly, and 1996 marked a new peak of that interest. In addition to the usual magazines that specialize in climbing, the 1996 season was also the subject of interest on the parts of ABC television, an IMAX film crew, and many web sites. This media attention was fed in part by the intense competition among commercial expedition outfitters, especially Hall and Fischer. John Krakauer was on the climb as a reporter for *Outside Magazine*, one of the strongest competitors in the busy market for adventure writing and gear advertising magazines. Indeed, reflecting its own status as a marketing gateway for the adventure community, *Outside* negotiated openly for a steep discount predicated on the value of the publicity a favorable Krakauer story would bring. Krakauer turned out to be only one among several expedition clients looking to write articles or a book about their experience, a number that grew after the disaster sparked enormous public interest. Writer Sandy Pittman, for example, had already arranged with NBC to provide coverage of the climb for that network's web page when she joined Rob Hall's expedition.

Late in the afternoon of 10 May 1996, summit day for both the Hall and Fischer expeditions (along with assorted others on the mountain), a disastrous storm on the upper reaches of Everest caught dozens of climbers in the late descent from the summit resulting in nine deaths, including head guides Hall and Fischer, other guides, Sherpas, and clients.[13] Many others found themselves struggling for survival. Everest is far from being the most technically difficult mountain to climb, but it is considered one of the most dangerous. The major dangers include insufficient oxygen—which can lead to severe edema, or swelling, of the pulmonary tissue or the brain, or can produce delusional behavior likely to be fatal when combined with the extreme exposure,[14]—and of course sudden changes in the weather. The deaths on Everest in May of 1996 were the result of these and a number of other such factors that occur frequently in high-altitude climbing. There was a dramatic alteration in the weather from clear skies and tolerable winds to blinding snow and hurricane-force winds; many members of both teams began their descent far later then is considered safe and after their own "turn around" times; several of the lead guides were climbing without oxygen, a factor intended to increase their prestige as climbers but likely to increase the risk of severe oxygen depletion of the blood stream and the poor judgment that can result. Finally, the intense competition between Hall and Fischer may have increased their willingness to take more risks.

The media treatment of the Everest disaster illustrates the media's role in producing images of climbing and other extreme sports. The 1996 expedition season was already being covered by a number of web sites, including those belonging to network television. Once the disaster struck, coverage spread quickly to mainstream news coverage media. Several months later John Krakauer published his first-person account in *Outside Magazine* (which sold out the issue). His story was retold in his best-selling book and a made for television movie. Nearly a dozen other books about the fateful expedition have been published, some of them by other survivors, and several films released. The publicity also encouraged a general increase in books and movies about Everest.

The 1996 Everest calamity provides a starting point for analyzing the significance of extreme sports. Here I briefly address three questions. First, what does the public interest in Everest climbing suggest about the changing construction of risk as a problem for government? Second, what kinds of skills, capacities, and mentalities relevant to the control of risk are promoted by participating in recreation like climbing or even in the discourse surrounding it? Third, how is the climbing community changing as the social prestige of extreme sports rises?

1. Despite some early criticism, the public reaction to the story of the deaths on Everest was not one of horror and condemnation, but fascination and sympathy. And the intensive media coverage it received has only added to the public interest in other adventure experiences. There has been no sustained demand to prohibit or even regulate such risk-taking activity. Everest expeditions are monitored by several well-financed web sites devoted to constant coverage of the latest developments from Everest or other prestigious climbing destinations.[15]

The public attraction to those who face death while climbing to the world's highest point for largely personal reasons contrasts sharply with the growing perception in affluent postindustrial societies like the United States that casualties suffered in the line of duty to the collective are almost intolerable. Consider the apparent transformation of attitude regarding military deaths, long celebrated as among the most honorable ways to die; it now seems almost unacceptable to late modern publics. In the United States, Japan, and much of Europe, political leaders now operate on the assumption that military actions must be nearly casualty free, a calculation responsible for the troubled peace-keeping missions in Somalia and the Balkans during the 1990s. That climbing now supplies some of our most compelling narratives of loss and sacrifice suggests that very different relationships and forms of subjectivity are being valorized.

2. To the much smaller but growing number of people who actually participate in climbing and other extreme sports, the valorization of a sport like climbing introduces new forms of prestige into fields of competition that they have often already succeeded at. At a cost-per-person of sixty-five thousand dollars, the Everest market is literally the peak of a large and

thriving market for adventure that includes far less dangerous activities like mountain biking, trekking, ocean kayaking, and long-distance yacht touring. These opportunities, heavily advertised and reported in magazines like *Outside* and *Men's Journal*, offer heightened adventure experiences and heightened risks to affluent and physically fit customers.

John Krakauer's brief profiles of his fellow clients of Adventure Consultants provides a glimpse into the sort of persons who are both interested in climbing Everest and can afford it:

- Leo Kasischke was a fifty-three-year-old lawyer from the suburbs of Detroit.
- Yasuko Namba (who died on the mountain) was a personnel manager for Federal Express in Tokyo. At forty-seven, Namba was the oldest woman and the first Japanese woman to summit Everest. The Japanese media covered her climb extensively.
- Seaborn Beck Weathers, a forty-nine-year-old Dallas pathologist, became famous walking into the high camp on the South Col of Everest, after being left for dead overnight in a near whiteout several yards from a nine-thousand-foot drop.[16]
- Stuart Hutchison was a thirty-four-year-old cardiologist from Canada.
- John Taske was a fifty-six-year-old anesthesiologist from Australia.
- Frank Fishbeck was a fifty-three-year-old publisher from Hong Kong.
- Doug Hansen (who died on the mountain) might have served as a poster boy for embracing risk had he made it back alive from his successful summit bid. The forty-six-year-old postal worker from Seattle moonlighted as a construction worker to pay for his second try at Everest. (Krakauer 1997:88–90)[17]

High status and affluence are obviously important. With the exception of Hansen, and perhaps Krakauer himself (at that time), all of them were affluent professionals or business managers of the sort that have prospered in the conditions of the liberalized and global economy of the 1990s. These people have the economic resources to afford such an exotic adventure and the global knowledge base to have imagined it. Perhaps most important, they all operate in fields in which risk taking in a remote and spectacular environment can provide the material for constructing personal reputation and status. Law and medicine are both fields where personal character is assumed to be part of professional excellence. The courage and discipline it takes to get up and down Everest are strong enough to sound in any field where these attributes are valued. Publishing and marketing global business services are fields where personal popularity and wide networks contacts are essential. Climbing Everest is material for a lifetime of conversation at dinner parties and creates an instant global network of fellow Everest enthusiasts.

3. The growth of interest in climbing has been seen as a decidedly mixed blessing by the core members of the more traditional climbing culture. The revenues generated by commercial tours, gear sales, and media coverage allow more climbers to win endorsements and employment opportunities that allow them to climb professionally. For others the opening of climbing to a much larger audience of less committed enthusiasts risks diluting or even destroying the special features of climbing as a largely self-regulating community.

This critique, in which Krakauer is an articulate participant, points to a different model of climbing from the life-style investment picture drawn by the adventure market. Although other more traditionally structured expeditions also suffered fatalities that season on Everest, Krakauer argues that in the attempt of which he was a part there was a confusion of roles members were expected to play—a confusion brought about by the commercialization of the climbing experience. In traditional climbing culture differences in skill and leadership ability are recognized but each member of a climbing party is considered equal to the others in their responsibility to take personal care and protect the well-being of all the others on the expedition. But the commercialization of climbing creates norms usually associated with high-end consumer goods and services, and even experienced climbers like Krakauer himself failed to provide needed support to others because they were playing out the roles of "customers." This shift in the self-perception of the clients was not matched by a parallel shift in the norms of climbers acting as paid expedition staff. Indeed, according to Krakauer's account, some guides took actions for their own personal achievement, for example, climbing without supplemental oxygen, rather than making the safety of the customers their first priority.[18]

Despite his success in summiting Everest and making it safely back to the high camp, Krakauer felt a loss in having become a client.

> During my thirty-four-year tenure as a climber, I'd found that the most rewarding aspects of mountaineering derive from the sport's emphasis on self-reliance, on making critical decisions and dealing with the consequences, on personal responsibility. When you sign on as a client, I discovered, you are forced to give up all of that and more.

For safety's sake, a responsible guide will always insist on calling the shots. . . .

Passivity on the part of the clients had thus been encouraged throughout our expedition. Sherpas put in the route, set up the camps, did the cooking, hauled the loads; we clients seldom carried more than daypacks stuffed with our personal gear. This conserved our energy and vastly increased our chances of getting up Everest, but I found it hugely unsatisfying. I felt at times as if I wasn't really climbing the mountain—that surrogates were doing it for me. (Krakauer 1998:219)

Krakauer's book is in many ways a jeremiad against the commercialization of climbing culture, but its mass popularity signals the power of that trend and may have contributed to it. For our purposes it is both the enormous attraction of extreme sports to a mass public and the sense of climbing as a historic community with its own moral and normative framework that must be kept in view to understand the salience of extreme sports to the moment of advanced liberalism. The extraordinary risk taking by people in the Himalayas and the responses to it in public culture raise questions about the place of risk in the reconstruction of authority. How does the public's fascination with these acts of voluntary risk taking reflect its expectations of the forms of social security—regulation, welfare, social insurance—developed by liberal governments in the twentieth century? What rewards explain the extraordinary prices individuals are willing to pay to take these risks? Do they find some skills or ways of looking at themselves and the world that make a difference in competing in the market or handling the risks redistributed back to them by the shift from fee-for-service medicine to managed care? Do the traditional climbing virtues point us to ways of understanding and governing risk independent of the dominant rationalities of government?

In seeking to answer these questions I delineate two different narratives about risk taking present in the contemporary discourses about climbing, although not often identified as such by those who produce such discourses. The first is risk taking as a model of pure competition unmediated by restraints of modern social arrangements. This aspect of climbing, "summiteering," is little more than a rationalization for the often unjustified and unfair inequalities in the distribution of risk within climbing, and provides a ready a metaphor for life under a postwelfare form of liberalism. The second, "mountaineering," is a model of risk taking as a means of access to certain skills, mentalities, and communities that are likely to be functional in the new political and economic terrain toward which many people in the affluent postindustrial West are moving (whether they like it or not).

Summiteering

I want to illustrate the main features of summiteering using Dick Bass and Frank Wells's 1986 book, *The Seven Summits* (with Rick Ridgeway), which is based on their true adventures as two successful fifty-something American chief executives who teamed up in the early 1980s to try and climb the tallest peak on each of the seven continents. This book is the foundation for a veritable flood of climbing adventure books that have come out since, and it inspired many readers to respond to their own midlife crises by climbing something. The abundance of such books in airport bookstores may be evidence of the interest in the business community. Amazon.com lists over 250 titles under mountain climbing, most published since 1995, including such titles as *The Climb of My Life; Dark Shadows Falling; Beyond Risk; Addicted to Danger: A Memoir about Affirming Life in the Face of Death; A Climb Up to Hell;*[19] *Climbing Back;*[20] *Facing the Extreme: One Woman's Story of True Courage, Death Defying Survival and Her Quest for the Summit;*[21] and *Beyond the Limits: A Woman's Triumph on Everest.*

Bass and Wells's "seven summits" project was the subject of extensive publicity including several books, a movie, and regular coverage in the media. Bass, a Texas entrepreneur who made money in the coal mining business and then developed the Snow Bird skiing resort in Utah, eventually became the first person to climb the seven mountains. The feat has been subsequently performed by many other wealthy amateurs and a few professional climbers.[22] Krakauer attributes a good deal of the commercialization of Everest directly to Bass's achievement.

> In 1985, the floodgates [to Everest] were flung wide open when Dick Bass, a wealthy 55-year-old Texan with limited climbing experience, was ushere d to the top of Everest by an extraordinary young climber named David Breashears. In bagging Everest Bass became the first person to ascend all of the so-called Seven Summits, a feat that earned him worldwide renown and spurred a swarm of other amateur climbers to follow in his guided boot prints. (Krakauer 1996:51)[23]

A life-long climber, Krakauer does not disguise a certain contempt for Bass and the project of the seven summits. He downgrades Bass's accomplishments because they were facilitated by the participation of top climbers who without a commercial relationship would never be climbing with Bass to begin with. The project itself is suspect not simply because of its self-promotional quality, climbing is full of that, but because as a problem to be solved it merits little attention from a purely climbing perspective. Bass himself is untroubled by the climbing ethos that haunts Krakauer. Indeed, he is of interest to us here because he self-consciously imagines his climbing project as one enmeshed in the experience of being governed and his resistance to it.

> With mountain climbing, I've discovered a tangible, short-term goal. It's me and the mountain, and that's it. There are no *bankers or regulatory officials* telling me what I can and can't do. It's just me and my own two feet, my own physical strength and my own mental resolve.
>   At the same time it's only rewarding if the mountain is a real one. Podunk hills don't count. I'm trying to make up for the frustration I face in the lowlands, and to do something that forces me to strain. There has to be a spirit of adventure to it, too, and an element of uncertainty and risk. Then when *I persevere and prevail* when I overcome and make it, I come back down to the *lowlands, back to the bankers and the regulatory officials,* and by golly I'm recharged and ready to take them all on. (Bass and Wells 1986:2; emphasis added)

One of the appeals of summiteering as a political subjectivity is that it is not limited to a narrow band of political philosophy. For most of the climbs, Bass teamed up with another fifty-something business man, Frank Wells, a lawyer and president of Warner Brothers Movies. Unlike Bass, a conservative who often in the book voices the view that self-help is the only kind of help, Well's was a liberal and a strong supporter of social welfare policies (Bass and Wells 1986:35). They argued occasionally about welfare policy and no effort is made in the book to resolve their differences. Instead the narrative celebrates their unity in personal philosophy despite politics. "If Frank Wells and Dick Bass had anything important in common it was their belief in following their hunches when a choice presented itself. When it came to decisions both men shunned a brooding analysis and preferred a quick, instinctual action. They took risks on visceral hunches. It was a modus operandi that had made their careers not only successful but also fun" (Bass and Wells 1986:36).

The fact that Bass and Wells (who went on to a very successful presidency of the Walt Disney Corporation) were both chief executives of businesses makes it tempting to cast the summiteering narrative as a classic bit of capitalist mythmaking in which real life captains of industry are shown to be worthy of their metaphoric predecessors who led trading voyages across the great oceans.[24] Their leadership role (largely making and spending other people's money) is validated by their ability to make and keep an absurd and bold promise. But the same features can be found in narratives of far less cartoonlike figures, including survivors of cancer, failed marriages, and traumatic and disabling injuries.

Here I want to point to several features of Bass and Wells's adventure and its narrative that stand out when the project is seen as primarily about sponsoring a certain kind of subjectivity, or more precisely a set of technologies of the self that promise a new subjectivity. In this perspective Bass and Wells have been highly successful in establishing not simply a climbing standard (the dubious seven summits) but a route to mastery in the world of the marketplace and the home that leads through the mountains.

Fetishization of the Summit

While Bass and Wells comment on the beauty and camaraderie that attend big mountain climbs, the ultimate payoff involves achieving the summit. Developing skill is regarded as an attractive feature of climbing but only insofar as it makes attaining the other summits more likely. Especially important is being the first to summit. But since virtually all of the highest mountains have been summited already, the quest for prestige moves toward narrower categories of self-identity: first woman, first Japanese woman, first Japanese woman over fifty, first breast cancer survivor, and so on. The spirit of Bass and Wells's seven summits is alive and well at the uppermost levels of professional climbing where highly publicized expeditions frequently string together arbitrary if independently worthy goals to establish some credible claim to being first. For example, a climbing expedition touted recently on a web site defined its objectives as an "attempt to measure by GPS the true height of Everest and then attempt to summit neighboring Lhotse and Nuptse, the first successful 'Everest Trilogy' by a single team in a single season" (http://www.mountainzone.com/99/).

Bass's version of climbing as summit collecting has a substantial resonance with more traditional climbing discourse. It is the rare story or book in climbing literature that celebrates an adventure that did not make the summit. From this perspective, the climbing adventure is just context for the redemptive possibility of reaching the summit.

Unmediated Adversity

The experience of climbing, and especially summiting, is framed as direct and unmediated by human relations. Although Bass and Wells acknowledge the tremendous importance of other climbers and facilitators in making the climbs possible, the ultimate triumph is singular and personal. Adversity is reduced to a singular and natural force with which negotiation and compromise are impossible. This reality is often explicitly set off against law and legal relations tainted with compromise and the need to recognize the claims of others.[25] Law is an especially salient example of what summiteers seek to escape in climbing. Lawyers and law bring complex entanglements with conflicting interests and authorities. Mountains are attractive because they call on people to act directly rather than through the law and because they appear to be relatively unregulated spaces (something that is becoming far less true).

This is also what allows survivors of abusive marriages and cancers to find in climbing a counterpoint to their experiences. The experience of radical threat in the domestic and health contexts is combined with the complexity of relationships, the vulnerabilities of being embodied, and dependence on various kinds of expertise. Climbing, in contrast, allows radical threat to be completely externalized. Traditional climbing culture also held law, in the sense of the positive law of the state, as something to be largely avoided. Thus we find Krakauer getting in a dig at lawyers that sounds a bit like Bass and company: "[T]hanks to the commercialization of Everest, the once hallowed peak has now even been dragged into the swamp of American jurisprudence. Having paid princely sums to be escorted up Everest, some climbers have then sued their guides after the summit eluded them" (Krakauer 1997:27–28).[26]

Many climbers contrast the ethos of personal injury plaintiffs and their lawyers with the self-reliant ethos of climbing, as in, for example, this letter to a climbing magazine written in response to an earlier letter suggesting law suits against public land managers:

> Liability of landowners and land managers is as great a threat to access as climbing fees or environmental concerns. The fear of lawsuits prompts numerous closures, especially of privately-owned crags. Although restrictions on bolting, trail use, etc. may alleviate impact concerns, the only protection against liability closures is the assertion that climbers take responsibility for their lives. We voluntarily engage in dangerous activity, and we must live with the consequences. . . . Perhaps Mr. Pickart is right in saying that he should have become a lawyer. He certainly has the requisite lack of ethics. Jason Blair, Blacksburg Va. (*Rock & Ice* 1995b:16)

There is an important tension hidden within this common rejection of law. Summiteers, like Bass, use law as a symbol for all forms of collective constraint impinging on their private freedom. Other climbers recognize the collective and community aspects of climbing and reject positive law in favor of norms arising from the climbing community itself. While formal law is mistrusted, the development of substantive norms regarding climbing culture is taken very seriously by climbers.

Summiting as Redemption

Summiteering narratives portray the reward of climbing through its ability to bring about personal growth in the individual who pursues it. Many such narratives involve a variant of the personal triumph genre in which a person subjected to some form of victimization or disability rediscovers himself or heals her wounds through confronting adversity in mountain climbing. In the hyperironic world of late modernity, mountains provide a source of meaning presumably unavailable from conventional sources like the labor market or marriage. Thus Stacy Allison (1993), the first American woman to summit Everest, contends that her successful climb helped to heal her wounds from an abusive marriage. She describes Everest as filling the vacuum of meaning in her life: "Climbing Everest was the only thing I had. Whether I was writing letters on team stationary or going running in a team T-shirt, the mountain on the team's logo gave me the only sense of purpose I had. I was going to Mount Everest—the highest mountain in the world. That *meant* something to people. It meant everything to me" (Allison 1993:126 [emphasis in original]).

The mountain is metamorphosed into a test that marks the participant as among an elect. Climbing, along with its technologies, skills, and companions, is ultimately just a right of passage. The triumph of Bass's "seven summits" did not so much stand for the possibility of developing climbing skills in middle age, but for the ability of even a middle-aged person to reach the summit (with plentiful assistance from paid expertise to help you up).

Summiteering, of course, is an incomplete culture. To get to the summit most of these adventurers relied on teams of professional climbers and Sherpas who have their own cultures. Yet part of what one might reject about summiteering is its very distancing of itself from these cultures. This does not mean that the others are ignored in the narrative. *Seven Summits* is full of heartwarming scenes around various campfires where Bass and Wells learn from and admire the climbers assisting them to the top. Yet ultimately summiteering highlights the individual on the summit as the primary meaning of the experience.

Mountaineering

It is difficult to know how many climbers are drawn to the summiteering aspect. Clearly, in the broader play of climbing as a symbol in the cultural struggle around risk, the features that I have described as summiteering figure prominently. From George Mallory who died on Everest in an unsuccessful 1924 summit attempt to Bass and Wells, there is a long history of celebrated risk takers who reach new summits or die trying.[27] Far less apparent is the complex discourse about risk that takes place within the climbing community. Indeed, what I call "mountaineering" is less a philosophy about risk taking than a set of debates within the climbing community. For those who pursue climbing as a way of entering this highly developed culture of risk taking, the features of climbing valorized in summiteering are not absent, but are part of a much more complex landscape.

For present purposes I describe this culture by summarizing some of the central debates about risk that emerge in reading the popular discourse of climbers in climbing magazines. Rather than a set of virtues, I will emphasize a set of problems raised by these discourses.

Risk and the Sublime

Just as summiteering seeks in risk taking a transformation that will allow an enduring transcendence, mountaineers also look to risk for psychological change. Rather than a test of personal worthiness, however, risk taking in mountaineering leads to a heightened psychological and physical experience. The personal gain here is not self-esteem but a permanent knowledge of what it is to feel so totally "wired" or "alive." Rather than the climb defining the climber as a particular kind of subject, it gives access to a particular experience of self and subjectivity that can be recaptured only fleetingly in the world of normal heights.

The Socially Constructed Nature of Risk

Summiteering tends to treat the risk of the climb as a wholly natural obstacle, the overcoming of which grants to the human climber a victory over an external reality with a fixed and constant meaning. Mountaineering, in contrast, produces a self-consciousness about the constructed nature of the risks involved in climbing. A major ongoing controversy within the climbing community concerns whether and how much to modify rock by chipping or sculpting it. Some purists argue that the rock should never be altered to make it more accessible. Others argue that at least some routes on key mountains should be altered to allow more climbers access to them. Noted Yosemite climber Ray Jardine, who did many famous first ascents in the 1970s, has recently advocated the prudent use of modifications as way of opening up climbing to more people:

> I don't see climbing as an elitist or spectator sport. I would hate to see it wind up like football where everyone sits around watching the pros. The bottom line is that establishing hard routes is not taking us into the future. Making routes of moderate difficulty in accessible and spectacular places will. . . . I'm not saying we should give everyone *carte blanche* to start modifying rock. Quite the contrary. We have to make a distinction between the visionary and the hacker. One is characterized by perception and motivated by love for the sacred stone; the other is motivated mainly by ego. (*Rock & Ice* 1995b:54, 56)

One aspect of this controversy involves whether or not to permit the placing of bolts into rock as a "bomb-proof"[28] security to which ropes can be attached to protect the climbers. Without such bolts, many popular routes would become limited to the most expert climbers. Yet bolts clearly alter the natural landscape in a permanent and visible manner. This debate combines questions of environmental protection with questions of safety, as well as the rights of first ascenders to establish the risk conditions on a particular climb. What is noteworthy about mountaineering as a discourse is its willingness to engage these complexities rather than reduce the climbing experience to simple abstractions. The ethics of "bolting" are discussed in a cartoon in the popular climbing magazine *Rock & Ice* (1995b:10):

> Ricky Rock Rat: It wasn't your Route, Dreg you had No right Retro-Bolting an established route.
>
> Dreg Vermin: The route is a 5.9 put up by a 5.12[29] climber.
>
> Ricky: Perhaps, but a climb is a statement, a work of art! You wouldn't embellish on the "Mona Lisa" to suit your own desires would you?
>
> Dreg: The route was bolted by an out-of-control ego with thoughtless selfishness. . . . This 5.9 climb was obviously not meant for a 5.9 climber, unless he has a death wish.
>
> Ricky: Hey, no one said you had to do the route. If you're not ready for it, leave it, but don't pull it down to your own abilities, it's not right.
>
> Dreg: Oh, Bull-@#*, its a terrible waste to have a climb that's only gonna get climbed once a decade! If you wanna prove you've got big balls, then put up a well protected route and solo[30] the thing!

This dialogue highlights several features of the debate that depart from the centrality of the individual in summiteering. One is the privilege accorded first ascenders. Somewhat like the rights of artists to control future alterations of their artwork, the first climber to put up a route has the right to name the route and to determine its relative degree of difficulty. Actions that permanently alter the difficulty of a route are highly controversial.

To see a climb as an artistic creation rather than a personal test of strength offers a very different model of the social product of risk taking and the possibilities of community around it. The ethical responsibilities of the risk taker are brought into direct focus. To oppose bolting and other mountain modifications is to insist that climbers limit themselves to routes they can handle given their current skill. Climbing in this perspective is a commitment to long-term development of skill, not a quest for immediate validation.

Risk, Rescue, and Responsibility

The other side of the risks undertaken in climbing is the problem of rescue. Accidents do not always mean death, but they can often involve disabling injuries that leave a climber dependent on others to undertake rescue. Within the mountaineering tradition there has been a consistent ethic that when rescue is possible it should be attempted. This ethic is being strained by the rapid growth of climbing and in particular by underprepared or underskilled climbers who get themselves in trouble and then impose risks on those who feel compelled to rescue them. This problem is also prompting increased formal government regulation of climbing. The National Park Service regularly rescues dozens of climbers a season at popular climbing sites like Mt. Ranier in Washington or Denali in Alaska. The use of helicopters and trained medical technicians to carry out such rescues costs thousands of dollars. With this increased government spending comes pressure to begin charging user fees and setting limits on who may climb. Both developments are repugnant to many in the mountaineering tradition, yet others recognize that the infusion of new climbers, many with a summiteering approach, makes regulation inevitable. Typical is a letter to the editor of a popular climbing magazine:

> Hooray for the Park Service for weighing charges against the ill prepared climbers rescued off of El Cap during the first storm of October. . . . My girlfriend spoke with the first party to reach Camp VI. It was well equipped and doing fine before seven other people reached the ledge. These irresponsible people put the first party in very serious jeopardy. They were very poorly equipped and should be charged for their rescue. . . . I mean, October, El-Cap, no rain gear? Come on! These people

make us all look bad in the eyes of land managers. Seth Leavens,
Yosemite, CA. (*Rock & Ice* 1995a:10)

But many climbers fear that increased government involvement will
lead to reduced access for all climbers. The freedom to make choices as individuals and small groups as to what risks to take is fundamental to mountaineering. Even many park rangers (many of whom are climbers) question
whether the government should deny access to those deemed insufficiently
prepared or skilled. As one ranger who regularly participates in rescues on
Denali in Alaska put it: "Everyone should have a right to face these challenges and risks" (Loso 1998:68). Government efforts to prevent the underprepared from climbing should be limited to education:

> Rather than expecting rangers to judge the preparedness of climbers, the
> best approach to minimizing rescues on Denali, and elsewhere, may be
> a more vigorous approach to climber education. This is particularly true
> for non-native English speakers. . . . English-speaking climbers have
> access to books, pamphlets, briefings, daily weather reports and the
> "war stories" that circulate within the climbing community, both on
> and off the mountain. (Loso 1998:68)

The National Park Service has taken to issuing pamphlets in multiple lan-
guages. Another recent innovation at Denali is a sixty-day preregistration
requirement designed to deter impulsive adventurers. "For those who go to
the mountains to get away from rules and bureaucracy, this seems an in-
fringement on climbers' rights. But it does allow time for registrants of all
backgrounds to thoroughly consider available information on these dangerous peaks" (Loso 1998:68).

The climbing community recognizes that public land managers are
friendlier to their culture of risk taking than many private landowners are
likely to be. The growing popularity of climbing has led to the development
of private facilities including a rapid proliferation of indoor climbing gyms
and commercially developed outdoor facilities on natural rock. Both face
huge liability exposure for injured climbers since the traditional mountaineering ethic against suing landowners for climbing injuries is unlikely
to hold in private facilities profiting from climbing. Owners have responded
by assuming much more control over who can climb and under what conditions. Developers of such facilities are naturally highly concerned with
installing protection and controlling protection placement by users. At
Seneca Falls Recreation Area, a private climbing site near Phoenix, paid professional climbers have placed bolts for a number of routes. The owners are
willing to let users place even more protection equipment but seek to mon-

itor their competence. As one of the managers of Seneca Falls put it: "We've taken the stance that we have to protect people even if they don't want to be protected" (*Rock & Ice* 1995a:10).

Normative Judgment and Community Standards of Risk

Michel Foucault identified "normalizing judgment," where one party observes and judges the performance of another in a manner systematically linked to training and rewards, as a key element of the disciplinary technologies of power that have transformed Western societies since the eighteenth century (Foucault 1977:177–84). In Foucault's account, such judgment is exercised within asymmetrical relations of power, as that between teacher and student, warden and prisoner, or doctor and patient. What is interesting about the use of this kind of critical discourse in climbing is that it is typically exercised on oneself, and across very equal relations of knowledge and power. For example, climbing journals regularly report on the deaths and injuries of climbers. These reports combine factual description with normative evaluation about the appropriateness of the risk taking involved. They often lead to dialogues in print. One letter writer to *Rock & Ice* responded to the climbing magazine's earlier report on a fatal accident in which the letter writer was involved along with a friend:

> I am upset with your misleading account of the death of my friend, Jim Klein. . . . Although Jim was killed by tons of falling ice, it was inac-´ curate to say that "It was a warm day to be climbing the south-facing route, with a high of 41 degrees in nearby Glenwood Springs." . . . This statement clearly says that we were being foolish and making poor judgments in our decision to climb that day. On the contrary. When we departed my house at 8 A.M., the thermometer read zero degrees. When we started hiking to the base of Glenwood Falls, the temperature was no warmer than 10 to 15 degrees, and the entire climb was in the shade. At the time of the accident, the upper half of the climb had been in the sun about 45 minutes and the temperature was probably in the 20s. . . . Jim and I had climbed Glenwood Falls many times, and in warmer conditions, without incident. We felt we were climbing as safely as was possible. . . . Brad Johnson, Vail, CO. (*Rock & Ice* 1995a:7)

The reports in climbing journals contrast with the modern approach to centralized expert control of information about risk. Here knowledge is gathered of individual misfortunes and archived in a way designed to shape future behavior. But here, unlike the panopticon, the knowledge is contestable and contested by the participants themselves. What emerges is less obedience than an evolving sense of normative obligation.

Climbing as Site for Developing Skills, Mentalities, and Communities Functional to a New Era in Governing Risk

The rise in popularity of climbing and other extreme sports opens a window on the conflicts and mentalities of risk in postindustrial societies. So far it is summiteering rather than mountaineering that has predominated. In drawing this sharp contrast I am concerned here not so much with real factions as I am with subtle but important differences in how risk is being embraced. For summiteering, risk is primarily a device for proving and redeeming the self. Mountains have no more intrinsic value in this discourse than charitable giving does under Calvinism. They are simply an opportunity to demonstrate one's belonging to the elect. Mountaineering, as a set of practices and discourses concerned with risk, offers some interesting clues as to the circumstances under which the embrace of risk may be empowering both to individuals and communities.

A useful analogy might be drawn to the context of work accidents in the nineteenth century (Simon 1995; Tomlins 1993; Witt 1998). No doubt motivations for risk taking at work, especially for those with the least bargaining power, are quite different from those involved in sport climbing. But here I am less concerned with the motivations that lead people to take risks and more with the effects of the discourses produced by risk taking on the larger cultural debate about risk.

Working in some industries in the nineteenth century, particularly railroads, involved risks just as extreme (by present standards) as mountain climbing. For most of that century the law set tough barriers against injured workers recovering for such injuries. Perhaps the most infamous feature of this regime was the fellow servant rule, which prevented a worker from recovering when the negligence that caused his injury was on the part of another employee of the company. In one of the most influential opinions in nineteenth-century American jurisprudence, Chief Justice Lemuel Shaw of the Massachusetts high court reasoned that workers in high-risk industries received a wage premium that compensated them for running the risks. He also assumed that workers were in the best place to observe and manage such risks: "The general rule, resulting from considerations as well of justice as of policy, is, that he who engages in the employment of another for the performance of specified duties and services, for compensation, takes upon himself the natural and ordinary risks and perils incident to the performance of such services, and in legal presumption the compensation is adjusted accordingly" (*Farwell* 1842:57).

Later generations came to see the logic of this position as highly contentious. Behind Shaw's blithe assurances about how risk operated in the
industrial workplace lurked the true surplus powerlessness of the working
classes (Tomlins 1993). In the late nineteeenth and early twentieth centuries, this regime of law was attacked and eventually replaced in favor of
system of strict liability and social insurance that we now recognize as
workers compensation. As I have argued elsewhere (Simon 1995), the success of workers compensation largely reflected the emerging consensus
that industrial risk operated beyond the level of individual skill or discipline and could best be addressed actuarially. Those supporting workers
compensation viewed the individual worker as having little real ability to
alter the likelihood of accidents. Control, if exercised at all, would have to
come from collectivist structures of government or cartelized industry.

John Witt (1998:1471) has recently argued that the long-running am-
bivalence of the labor movement toward workers compensation reflected
in part a strong cultural association espoused by skilled workers and many
nineteenth-century democratic thinkers between skillful risk taking, personal responsibility, and self-government. "Skilled workers and elites alike
argued that a worker's skill and his exercise of judgment and discretion over
work processes served an educative function, training citizens for the work
of self government by their participation in the governance of work processes." From this perspective, workers compensation was seen part of a
larger effort by management to eliminate worker control over the work process. Discretion, of course, need not mean risk of limb or life, but for many,
in fact, risk was an important part of the moralization of wage labor: "It was
the very 'pains' that work could and did inflict that preformed the morally
constitutive work of labor. '[B]y its perils, which demand continuous vigilance,' [one reformer argued] economic life developed critical moral and
mental faculties" (Witt 1998:1472).

Risk granted a kind of moral status empowering those who had only
their labor power to exchange to nonetheless view themselves as stake-
holders in the enterprise. Many within the skilled labor movement wanted
compensation for injuries, but in a way that would preserve workers' direct
relationship to risk and thus to control: "Thus, 'sore and sad' as American
Federation of Labor leader Samuel Gompers was as a result of the 'killing,
the maiming of so many of [his] fellow workers,' he sought to effect 'their
own emancipation through their own efforts.'" (Witt 1998:1498). Many saw
workers compensation as part of an effort to centralize expertise about
work risk in the hands of management.

This nineteenth-century embrace of risk among certain workers and unionists reflected a craft union ideology and a narrow focus on the circumstances of relatively elite skilled labor. For vast portions of the industrial working class given over to relentless deskilling, the appeal of discretion over organizing features of the work and the embrace of risk had little potential for expanding their real control over their lives or qualifying them for self-governance. In this sense it would be a mistake to read these remnants of an alternative approach to the risk of work accidents as a critique of the social insurance approach that came to dominate, beginning with workers compensation. At the same time, one can turn these limiting features around and explore which features of working class culture in that era created conditions under which this kind of embrace of risk was more than an example of false consciousness, and which features might be relevant to the increasing relevance of skill and risk in the new labor market.[31]

It would be interesting to explore what links if any might exist between the rise of American recreational mountaineering in the twentieth century and the decline of risk taking in skilled labor; there is clearly an analogy between the claims of citizenship through control of risk made by nineteenth-century skilled laborers and the claims of contemporary climbers to a moral and not just aesthetic value of climbing. For both, the possibility of real solidarity and effective will formation depend on a rich engagement with risk that in turn produces forms of knowledge and power that transcend the immediate circumstances of risk.

I close this essay by highlighting several features of mountaineering that might indeed lend themselves to the expansion not simply of individual self-esteem but collective self-government. These might be thought of as technologies of freedom.

Climbing and Literature

One such technology of freedom in climbing is writing. Over the last several centuries, the practice of mountaineering has produced a literature. This includes a long line of novels and memoirs by famous climbers recounting their legendary adventures on various peaks. Even more important is the remarkably strong tradition of ordinary climbers publishing narratives of successful first ascents and accounts of accidents and rescues that go back to the nineteenth century. Present-day accounts proliferate in climbing journals and the Internet. Unlike the novels, which often slip into celebrations of the self, this journalistic discourse is practical and technical. Narrative description of routes and accidents forms a critical part of climbing knowledge that informs decisions about when, where, and how to climb. It also models a kind of subjectivity that is analytic and reflective, which makes it possible to observe the climb from outside oneself and hence to evaluate one's performance.

Climbing and Community

Climbing can be a highly individualistic activity, even when done in groups. For the better part of any long climb, the climber clings inches from the face of the rock but far from any fellow climbers. However, for decades now, climbing has generated communities to share support, gear, and knowledge. Many towns near mountains have a "mountain rescue" group that maintains radios and equipment to respond to calls from or about fallen or stranded climbers. The largest of these maintain extensive networks and web sites. All of them participate in the above-described practice of collecting and publishing highly detailed descriptions of accidents and rescues. Thus mountaineering reproduces an experience of collective interests even while celebrating self-reliance. The rising popularity of climbing is stretching the capacity of these community resources to maintain a strong sense of normative integration, but it is also attracting considerably more investment into the production of climbing discourse through magazines, web sites, and climbing gyms.

Climbing as Jurisgenerative

While climbers often viscerally reject formal law (this seems to join summiteers with mountaineers), the climbing community is a classic example of what Robert Cover (1983) described as a *nomos*, a community bound by deep ethical commitments that serve as a source of normative lawmaking for the political community as a whole. As the examples described above suggest, climbing journals and organizations focus on normative evaluation and the creation of binding ethical obligations. While most of these are not enforced by formal organizations, they are often enforced by practices of confrontation and shaming (practices that have only been intensified by the Internet).

Climbers as a community find themselves facing a widening array of efforts to control and even ban the activity. Climbing on public land owned by the federal government is now being limited by environmental regulations. The U.S. Forest Service has formally banned "fixed anchors" in public lands designated "wilderness areas" (which include many popular climbing sites).[32] Without fixed protection, however, even the most careful climber faces a significant risk of falling. Low-impact protection, even properly placed, can "blow out" and result in an immediate fall to twice as far as the last protection (and if a chain of protection blows with the gathering force, a fatal disaster is highly likely).

Another challenge to climbing has come from Native American tribes who have acted to protect mountain sites of religious significance against what they perceive as the moral degradation of recreational climbing at those sites. A spectacular 1,270-foot rock tower in Wyoming, in English called "Devil's Tower," has been the center of a heated dispute between climbers and Native Americans who consider it a sacred place. Climbers in the area placed an intensive set of restrictions on climbing in an effort to achieve a compromise with the tribe, but a minority of climbers has openly flouted the ban.

These disputes may have a silver lining for all concerned—namely, bringing the climbing community with its distinct approach to embracing risk into discursive company (if not yet community) with groups like environmentalists and Native American tribes who hold other distinct and potentially productive approaches to risk. All of these groups have been marginal to the dominant twentieth-century social welfare approach to risk and to its official "free market" alternatives.[33] Conflict among them may be a first step toward hybridization and further innovation in approaches to managing risk.

Conclusion

Climbing is not likely to become a practical method for mass training in the new arts of self-government necessitated by postindustrial societies' shift of risk back to individuals.[34] It may provide a productive place, however, in which to explore the development of skills, mentalities, and communities appropriate to the risks that are being shifted to people.[35] Climbing may also provide useful analogies in those areas where paternalistic efforts to control risk have turned most coercive, such as drug law.[36] We need to develop arts of government beyond socializing risk and regulating conduct. That does not mean we should not remain skeptical of the ease with which some contemplate the risk-taking adventures of others, nor agree to taking major steps toward dismantling the forms of socialized risk that have successfully managed many of the gravest dangers of industrializing society. But neither should we be sanguine that the most pressing risk problems of our time can be solved by simply extending the scope of the same safety net. If there are risks that we cannot insure against, for example that we are miscalculating the dangers of genetically altered agriculture, it may be that climbing provides a model for empowering people to cope with such a risk environment. Practices of voluntary risk taking may be vulnerable to capture by out of control egos, and become little more than ideologies; but they are also productive of skills, mentalities, and strategies that make new solidarities, communities, and forms of governance possible.

NOTES

1. From the front of a greeting card distributed by Successories and distributed retail by Henderson Publishers. Thanks to Pat O'Malley who found this card and sent it to me.

2. Of course the political leadership of Tony Blair in the United Kingdom and formerly that of Bill Clinton in the United States parallels this new liberal approach to risk.

3. In other areas, to be sure, the attitude toward risk taking has been far more negative. Casual drug use was once being decriminalized as a private risk choice. That changed dramatically in the 1980s and 1990s as the federal government's longrunning war on drugs began targeting casual use for elimination through law enforcement and job-based drug testing. Casual sex among the young, tolerated to a large extent by government in the 1970s, and also thought to be a form of individual-level risk taking, has been problematized both by AIDS and the religious Right's moral campaign against permissiveness. Elsewhere I have been trying to reflect on the peculiar relationship between the decline of the risk spreading ideal and the emergence of an increasingly punitive approach to governing crime (Simon 2000).

4. Efforts to tell similar stories about the risks faced by workers became unconvincing by the early twentieth century (Simon 1995). By the end of the century, however, there was a significant decline in the standards of ex ante safety and ex post compensation for workers fueled largely by the success of economic narratives that blame excessive safety and security for lax work discipline and profitability in American business.

5. Other discourses have disappeared or ceased to be influential. For example, religion traditionally set limits to extreme risk taking either in gambling or other forms. While religion overall is enjoying a popularity surge at the beginning of the twenty-first century in the United States, it is not of the sort that earlier discouraged risk taking.

6. See the articles on adventure travel and extreme sports in *New York Times* 1998. The Travel Industry Association of America reported that 98 million Americans took an "adventure travel" trip in the last five years. Brian Alexander, "Making Sure Its an Excellent Adventure," id. at G4.

7. As the death of Sonny Bono in January of 1998 reminded us, off-trail skiing is highly dangerous. The danger is even greater in helicopter skiing, which transports you to an area unmanaged by any work force (which exist at ski areas) and which consequently raise the risks of injury and failure of timely rescue.

8. Interestingly, Everest and other particularly challenging mountains sparked interest in the past associated with the nationality of those making the first ascent of them. For example, the first ever known ascent of Everest, by Edmund Hillary and Tenzing Norgay, was met with considerable public interest in Great Britain and throughout the British commonwealth. Likewise the first known ascent of K2 by a French team was a source of enormous national pride in France. These occasions reveal how climbing can become a symbol of national triumph. One of the aspects that differentiates the new discourses of climbing is the focus on personal triumph rather than any national or collective meaning it might have.

9. Climbing and extreme sports are just one part of a field of new discources that articulate problems of risk and governance in the popular realm. Other examples include gambling, popular investing, and day trading.

10. It shares this quality with big-wave surfing and mountain biking.

11. This is becoming less true of the fastest growing part of climbing, known as "sport climbing," that is mostly done on indoor climbing walls or groomed outdoor cites. The goal is neither summiting or experiencing the mountains so much as the performance of fast and graceful moves in a competition setting.

12. Sherpas are the indigenous people of Nepal. Many of them are expert climbers, and guiding mountaineering expeditions has been a key part of their economy since Western adventure climbing in the Himalayas began in the 1920s. In many expeditions, commercial and otherwise, Sherpas have a complex role as both guide and servant. In the commercial expeditions, for example, both Western guides and Sherpas were responsible for aiding clients in climbing, but only Sherpas were expected to serve food and beverages. Some confusion as to these expectations of role was a factor in the Everest calamity of 1996.

13. Ironically there had been few deaths on Everest earlier in that climbing season, so that the total deaths for the year was not unusually high (Krakauer 1998:xv).

14. Picture how you would feel on a narrow path with sheer drops of thousands of feet in each direction. Now add a ice and slippery rocks to the path. While the climbing is not as challenging as many routes in the Unites States, the combination of factors makes it truly daunting.

15. Mountainzone.com picked up a lot of additional press coverage when it published news of the 1999 discovery of the frozen corpse of famed British climber George Mallory, who was last seen making a summit attempt with a companion in 1924. Mallory's famous answer to a reporter's question as to why he was trying to climb Everest ("because it is there") and mysterious disappearance captured public fascination with the mountain that presaged today's interest. This and other climbing web sites are discussed in Dizikes 1999.

16. After being abandoned for dead twice, Weathers was aided down the mountain and survived but lost all his fingers, his right forearm, and his nose to frostbite. Over the next two years he underwent multiple surgeries to create a functional hand out of his left palm. Doctors also constructed a new nose for him, replanting a portion of his ear cartilage on his forehead to grow, and then placing the new bridge under his skin.

17. Hansen was a single father who spent much of time at base camp writing faxes to his two children and to a grade school class in Kent, Washington, which had sold T-shirts to raise money for his trip. Rob Hall may have overridden his own mandatory turn-around time in order to help Hansen, whom he had persuaded to come back to Everest for one more attempt to the summit.

18. Krakauer in particular criticized Anatoli Boukreev, one of Scott Fischer's guides, who made the climb without oxygen and returned to the high camp while many of the clients were still on the mountain. Boukreev wrote his own book, *The Climb*, defending his role and attacking Krakauer for staying in his tent at the high camp and resting while rescue efforts were being mounted. Boukreev died on another Himalayan peak, K2, in January 1998.

19. Originally published in 1957 and now reissued.

20. Amazon.com's description is: "There is almost no limit to what we can accomplish except perhaps in our own minds. That is the message delivered to us by Mark Wellman. Crippled by a mountain-climbing accident, and perhaps further injured by his own impatient action, Mark was faced with seemingly insurmountable obstacles. But, finding strength and hope in his family and friends, he has in turn be-

come an inspiration to millions of people. Mark has designed equipment and developed programs to inspire and motivate others. *Climbing Back* is the story of Mark's struggle to survive a disabling accident, to become a park ranger and an accomplished wheelchair athlete, and ultimately to climb the sheer granite faces of El Capitan and Half Dome."

21. Amazon.com's description is: "Ruth Anne Kocour found herself in the middle of a brutal storm with 100-mph wind blasts and plummeting mercury. Problem was, she happened to be bivouacked halfway up North America's highest mountain, Alaska's 20,320-foot Mt. Denali (also known as Mt. McKinley). *Facing the Extreme* is her story of survival against the elements, a struggle that required every last bit of physical and mental endurance—not to mention alpine skills, resourcefulness, and luck. By the end of the storm, 11 climbers were dead. Kocour's gripping tale is one of the few of its kind written by a woman, a refreshing change of voice that reflects a changing demographic in the outdoors community."

22. Many serious climbers denigrate the seven summits concept because the particular mountains are not the seven highest mountains in the world (five of which are in Asia). Although some of the seven are considered extremely difficult (e.g., Everest and the Vincent Massif in Antarctica), there are many harder climbs around the globe.

23. Bass was the direct inspiration for Seaborn Beck Weathers, the Dallas pathologist who joined the Hall expedition.

24. Likewise climbers themselves often draw comparisons to the early capitalist adventurers who took to the sea in search of new markets or new routes to established markets despite the fact that the economic significance of their actions was marginal at best. While corporations have recently taken an interest in sponsoring climbing and other adventure expeditions, their goal is placing their image in the media and not discovering new routes or markets (Tierney 1988:22). The routes opened by extreme sports and adventures today, if any, lead through personal subjectivity to produce an altered relationship between self and power.

25. In the recent adventure movie *The Edge*, the character played by Anthony Hopkins, a billionaire named Charles, lost amidst stunning peaks in the Alaska wilderness, kills a huge bear in hand-to-hand combat. Afterward he tells his companion (and competitor) Bob: "All my life, I've always wanted to do something unequivocal." The unmediated confrontation provided by summiteering is especially contrasted with one's usual relationship with law. In *The Edge*, the character of Bob compliments the billionaire on killing the bear: "Six months ago, if Smokey here had reared his head, you would have called your lawyer."

26. In some cases it appears guides have reached the summit while leaving their clients below.

27. The 1996 tragedy helped spark historical interest in the first period of serious interest in climbing Everest and in George Mallory, the famed British climber who disappeared along with his climbing partner Sandy Irvine in 1924 near the summit. In 1999 an exploratory expedition climbed Everest in search of further evidence of Mallory and Irvine. They found Mallory's frozen body, photos of which were quickly circulated on the Internet and in the mainstream media. Two recent books (Hemmleb, Johnson, and Simonson 1999; Breashers and Salkeld 1999) explore Mallory's death and the early Everest climbing scene.

28. This is a climbing term for equipment that can withstand the weight of a climber falling from a significant height above it. Typically the lead climber is roped to those below her through a series of anchors designed to allow those below to break her fall by holding onto the rope (a technique called "belaying"). As she climbs, the lead climber places protection where appropriate to her skill and the circumstances. If she misses a hold and falls, and if those below are belaying correctly, her fall should

be no more than twice the distance above the last anchor. Some equipment is passively inserted into cracks in the rock. This is preferred because it does not mar the mountain but it is rarely as secure as a bolt placed in the mountain with the use of a drill and hammer.

29. The common scale used to rate difficulty in U.S. climbing. The 5 indicates technical climbing (4 is scrambling, 3 hiking, etc.). The 9 and 12 reflect the degree of difficulty and are inevitably subjective. The hardest routes currently being climbed are in the 5.14 to 5.15 range.

30. To "solo" means to climb without protection of any kind to break a fall.

31. In the Marxist sense of an ideology or identity that misrecognizes and disguises the conditions of oppression under which a person or class is living (Gabel 1975).

32. The ban has yet to take effect and is being litigated; climbing access groups are negotiating directly with environmental groups who support the ban (Berkheimer 1998:32).

33. In this sense they are all "sectarians" in Douglas and Wildavsky's (1982) typology of risk and organization.

34. Microscopic efforts to promote climbing as an enabling life experience have existed for years (see, e.g., Jerard 1998:24).

35. There is a growing social psychology of risk taking (see, e.g., Lyng 1990; Mitchell 1983) that I hope in future work to connect with the themes of this essay.

36. Drug use is a practice that bears some important comparisons to climbing. It is often about heightened experiences. It is often dangerous. It often invokes desires in others to repress and regulate it. During the 1960s and 1970s, a culture of drug taking grew up among younger Americans that bears some of the traits of the climbing community (writing, community, ethics). One effect of the war on drugs has been to raise the cost of sustaining such community, leading to a drug culture that is shallow, individualistic, and criminal. Likewise, the Internet, which is the subject of increasing calls for its regulation, shows some signs of generating the kinds of practices that in the climbing context support an embrace of risk (Froomkin 1996).

REFERENCES

Ackerman, Bruce, and Anne Alstott. 1999. *The Stakeholder Society.* New Haven: Yale University Press.

Allison, Stacy (with Peter Carlin). 1993. *Beyond the Limits: A Woman's Triumph on Everest.* Boston: Little, Brown.

Bass, Dick, and Frank Wells (with Rick Ridgeway). 1986. *Seven Summits.* New York: Warner Books.

Berkheimer, Priska. 1998. "Access: Fixed Anchor Ban Postponed." *Rock & Ice* 89 (December): 32.

Breashers, David, and Audrey Salkeld. 1999. *Last Climb: The Legendary Everest Expeditions of George Mallory.* Washington, D.C.: National Geographic.

Cahill, Tim. 1998. "Here, Sharky, Sharky." *Outside* 23 (August): 56.

Cover, Robert. 1983. "Nomos and Narrative." *Harvard Law Review* 97:4.

Dizikes, Peter. "Mountain Climbing as a Spectator Sport." *New York Times,* 6 May, D12.

Douglas, Mary, and Anson Wildavsky. 1982. *Risk and Culture: An Essay on the Se-*

lection of Technological and Environmental Dangers. Berkeley: University of California Press.

Farwell. 1842. Farwell v. Boston & Worcester Rail Road, 45 Mass. (Met.) 49.

Foucault, Michel. 1977. Discipline and Punish: The Birth of the Prison. New York: Pantheon.

Froomkin, A. Michael. 1996. "Flood Control on the Information Ocean: Living with Anonymity, Digital Cash, and Distributed Databases." Journal of Law and Commerce 15:395.

Gabel, Joseph. 1975. False Consciousness an Essay on Reification. New York: Harper and Row.

Giddens, Anthony. 1999. "Risk and Responsibility." Modern Law Review 62:1–10.

Greenblatt, Stephen. 1980. Renaissance Self Fashioning: From More to Shakespeare. Chicago: University of Chicago Press.

Hemmleb, Jochen, Larry A. Johnson, and Eric R. Simonson. 1999. Gosts of Everest: The Search for Mallory and Irvine. Seattle: The Mountaineers.

Irvine, Amy. 1994. "Perspective: Life by the Throat." Climbing, November/December.

Jerard, Christopher. 1998. "At Risk Youth Climb for Life." Rock & Ice 89 (December): 24.

Krakauer, John. 1998. Into Thin Air. New York: Anchor Editions.

Loso, Michael G. 1998. "Playing God on Denali." Rock & Ice 85 (May/June): 60–69.

Lyng, Stephen. 1990. "Edgework: A Social Psychological Analysis of Voluntary Risk Taking." American Journal of Sociology 95:851–56.

Mitchell, Richard. 1983. Mountain Experience: The Psychology and Sociology of Adventure. Chicago: University of Chicago Press.

New York Times. 1998. "Adventure Sports: A Special Section." 11 March.

Nicolson, Marjorie H. 1959. Mountain Gloom and Mountain Glory: The Development of the Aesthetics of the Infinite. Ithaca: Cornell University Press.

O'Malley, Pat, and Darren Palmer. 1996. "Post-Keynsian Policing." Economy and Society 25:137–53.

Potterfield, Peter, ed. 1996. In the Zone: Epic Survival Stories from the Mountaineering World. Seattle: The Mountaineers.

Roberts, David. 1991. The Mountain of My Fear, and Deborah: A Wilderness Narrative. Seattle: The Mountaineers. Originally published in 1968 and 1970, respectively.

Rock & Ice. 1995a. Letter to the editor. 66 (March/April): 10.

———. 1995b. Letter to the editor. 68 (July/August): 16.

Rose, Nikolas. 1996. "Governing 'Advanced' Liberal Democracies." In Foucault and Political Reason: Liberalism, Neo-Liberalism and Rationalities of Government, ed. A. Barry, T. Osborne, and N. Rose. Chicago: University of Chicago Press.

———. 1999. Powers of Freedom. Cambridge: Cambridge University Press.

Simon, Jonathan. 1987. "The Emergence of a Risk Society: Insurance, Law, and the State." *Socialist Review* 95:61–89.

———. 1995. "For the Government of its Servants: Law and Disciplinary Power in the Work Place, 1870–1906." *Studies in Law, Politics and Society* 13:105–36.

———. 1998. "Driving Governmentality: Automobile Accidents, Insurance, and the Challenge to the Social Order in the Inter-War Years, 1919–1941." *Connecticut Insurance Law Journal* 4:521–88.

———. 2000. "Megan's Law: Crime and Democracy in Late Modern America. *Law and Social Inquiry* 25:1111–50.

Tierney, John. 1998. "Explornography: The Vicarious Thrill of Exploring When There's Nothing Left to Explore." *New York Times Magazine,* 26 July, 18.

Tomlins, Christopher L. 1993. *Law, Labor, and Ideology in the Early American Republic.* New York: Cambridge University Press.

Witt, John Fabian. 1998. "The Transformation of Work and the Law of Workplace Accidents, 1842–1910." *Yale Law Journal* 107:1467.

NINE

At Risk of Madness

NIKOLAS ROSE

During the 1990s, the very idea of madness became inextricably linked with risk. A cascade of cases in which people with histories of mental health problems attacked, injured, or killed members of their families, psychiatrists, social workers, or members of the "general public" were reported by the mass media and became the subject of professional enquiry and public debate. In many of these cases it was claimed that mental health professionals were themselves culpable, for they appeared to have failed to recognize the danger posed by a patient or client who was living "in the community" or was about to be discharged from a mental health facility. While the evaluation of the potential harm that individuals posed to others on account of their mental condition had once been the task of a relatively small number of forensic psychiatrists who specialized in the assessment and treatment of mentally abnormal offenders, it now become central to the work of many, indeed all, mental health professionals. Proposals were urgently debated in various jurisdictions, and have already been implemented in some, to require risk assessments before patients are discharged from psychiatric hospitals; to assess and monitor risk in all cases dealt with by mental health professionals outside hospitals; to conduct psychiatric risk assessments on prisoners convicted of various offences such as pedophilia before discharge at the end of their sentence; and to introduce new provisions for the compulsory detention of those who were thought to pose a threat to others, not because of what they had done but because of who they were, because their very make up as a human being made them a threat to "the community."

Maybe there is nothing new or surprising about this association of mad-

ness with risk. Has not madness always been associated with unpre-
dictability, danger, hazard? Was not the mad person always thought to
be a potentially dangerous individual? And reciprocally, from the mid-
nineteenth century at least, was not the dangerous individual a person who
was, very likely, suffering from a form of madness (Foucault 1978). Perhaps
so. But the widespread and transnational displacement of the language of
dangerousness by that of risk suggests that something significant is indeed
occurring in the links between madness and danger and that this is bound
up with a more general reshaping, not only of the management of mental
health, but in rationalities and strategies of control.

From Dangerousness to Risk[1]

The debate about dangerousness recognized that, in practice, it
was difficult if not impossible to draw a sharp dividing line between those
mental patients who were and those who were not dangerous, and prediction was always uncertain. Nonetheless, until around the mid-1960s, it
seemed that the issue of dangerousness arose only in relation to a small minority of actual or potential patients or prisoners. Dangerousness was understood as an internal quality of a few pathological individuals—possibly
an organic defect—even though it was a quality that was difficult to explain, diagnose, or measure. Throughout the 1970s and 1980s, this understanding mutates: dangerousness becomes a matter of factors, of situations,
of statistical probabilities. By the 1990s, the organizing term of the debates
was no longer "dangerousness" but "risk" (Potts 1995; Grounds 1995). As
the British Journal of Psychiatry put it in 1997, in its special supplement on
assessing risk in the mentally disordered: "[T]here has been a sea change . . .
away from assessing dangerousness to assessing (and managing) risk" (Duggan 1997:1). And in the same publication, Snowden commences his paper
on practical aspects of clinical risk assessment and management by asserting that it "is debatable whether the notion of dangerousness now has any
utilitarian value for psychiatry . . . dangerousness is [nothing] more than an
adjective which has been elevated into a pseudoscientific construct whose
definitions [here he refers to Scott 1977; Walker 1978; and Home Office and
DHSS 1975] amount to little more than 'past harm predicts future behav-
iour.'" What does have such a value, however hard it is to assess, is risk.
Risk, apparently "does not contain pejorative connotations" and "invites
more objective and robust analysis" (1997:32).

But the embracing of risk by psychiatrists and other mental health professionals cannot be understood simply as the replacement of an unscien-
tific concept with a scientific one, or an ineffective strategy with an effec-

tive one. It indicates a subtle but very significant mutation in our way of understanding and responding to mental health problems. This shift in thinking owes something to the persistence, energy, and persuasiveness of a small number of researchers and campaigners. In the United States, the key figures were John Monahan and Herbert Steadman. Steadman's work in this area arose from the interest in protecting the civil rights of those with mental health problems, especially concerning excessive detention. It was argued then that while detention and involuntary treatment was justified in terms of danger of harm to self or others, mental health professionals were very bad at making accurate and reliable predictions of future behavior, and so were erring on the side of excessive caution leading to unwarranted detention. Steadman was among many who argued that assessments of dangerousness were inaccurate and unreliable, that psychiatrists tended to greatly overdiagnose offenders as dangerous, and that current psychiatric knowledge and procedures could provide no firm or legitimate basis for decisions about detention (Steadman and Cocozza 1974). Similarly, Monahan (1981) drew attention to the inaccuracy of clinical predictions of violent behavior, arguing that evidence from the best clinical research showed that psychiatrists and psychologists were accurate in no more than one out of three predictions of violent behavior over a several-year period, when their subjects were institutionalized populations with a history of violence and a mental illness diagnosis.

In subsequent years, in a number of very influential articles, Steadman, Monahan, and their colleagues outlined an alternative approach—one whose object was defined not in terms of dangerousness but risk, and which argued that mental health professionals should frame predictions of future violence in probabilistic terms. In 1993, in a paper entitled "From Dangerousness to Risk Assessment," they set out what they considered to be the key characteristics of the shift in thinking, communicating, and practicing. Risk assessment, they argued, differs from previous assessments in three ways. First, it is not about legal categorization but administrative decision-making. Second, it is not about binary distinctions but location on a continuum. Third, it does not identify something fixed, stable, inherent, and hence predictable to all futures, but implies continuous day-to-day risk management of the potentially risky person (Steadman et al. 1993; cf. Crichton 1995:29). In practice, to put it crudely, all psychiatric patients can and should be allocated to a level of risk, risk assessed and risk re-assessed, risk classified, risk managed, risk monitored: high risk, medium risk, low risk—but rarely no risk. And risk management should not be confined to the mentally disordered offender or to the question of whether a person should be detained in hospital or prison; it should extend over the everyday life of all "mental patients" and the everyday work of all psychiatric professionals.

During this period, many within the criminal justice system argued for a shift from "clinical" to "actuarial" methods in the prediction of future conduct (Floud and Young 1981; Morris and Miller 1985; Duckitt 1988; Gottfredson and Gottfredson 1988; cf. Pratt 1995). These proposals for a displacement of the diagnosis of dangerousness by an assessment of risk in the management of mental health were certainly consonant with such arguments. But these psychiatric arguments were to be so significant because of a more fundamental respatialization of control mechanisms, from the enclosed spaces of carceral institutions to the dispersed territory of "the community." With the emergence of community as the new territory upon which psychiatry must work, asylum walls no longer marked a simple and fixed distinction between those within and without the psychiatric system. A complex institutional topography of community had taken shape: outpatient clinics, open wards, day hospitals, sheltered housing, community psychiatric nurses, and so forth. The task for psychiatric professionals was now less therapeutic than administrative: administering problematic persons on this complex terrain in an attempt to control their future conduct.

It is through the notion of risk, and the techniques and practices to which it is connected, that care and control became inextricably linked in the community. Some British examples from the 1990s help make the point. The Care Programme Approach introduced by the Department of Health in 1991 required all patients referred to specialist psychiatric services to be assessed and allocated to one of three levels of care, an assessment that centrally involved a judgment about risk. The Mental Health (Patients in the Community) Act, which came into effect in 1996, introduced supervised discharge for some patients who have been detained in hospital for treatment under the provisions of the 1983 Mental Health Act: patients who are placed under supervised discharge "will have been assessed as presenting a substantial risk of serious harm to themselves or other people, or of being seriously exploited, if they do not receive suitable after-care." The risk assessment was to be carried out before a patient is discharged from hospital.[2] These risky persons, along with others who have not been detained in hospital and therefore cannot be subject to supervised discharge, were to be included in the supervision registers that, from April 1994, the Secretary of State for Health required to be established in England and Wales. These registers were to identify all patients in the care of the psychiatric services who "are, or are liable to be, at risk of committing serious violence or suicide, or of serious self neglect," whether they were existing patients or new patients to the psychiatric services (NHS Executive 1994). As the Special Working Party on Clinical Assessment and Management of Risk, set up by the Royal College of Psychiatrists, made clear in its report, risk assessment and risk management were to be "of the highest priority for the allocation of resources" (Royal College of Psychiatrists 1996:10): facilities, strategies, training, and interagency collaboration were all to be rethought in terms of the management of risk.

This was not merely an abstract or ideal program. In thousands of offices, team meetings, ward rounds, and case conferences, techniques were devised to identify levels of risk, signs of risk, indicators of risk, and the like; to measure risk levels; and to document risk levels in case notes and care plans. Training courses and materials were produced to educate mental health professionals in the characteristics of risk, its assessment, management, and the ethical and other issues that arise (Alberg, Hatfied, and Huxley 1996). Psychiatrists collaborated with a range of other mental health professionals, all of whom were now obliged to calculate risk and to manage individual patients or clients in the light of a calculation of their riskiness and in the name of risk reduction on the territory of the community. Who or what is it that is at risk of madness?

A Risk Society?

This pervasiveness of risk in contemporary culture has been extensively discussed by sociologists, historians, and cultural theorists. Many have been influenced by Ulrich Beck's claim that we live in "risk society," in which the process of modernization, in particular developments in science and technology, have displaced the belief in progress and the related concerns over the distribution of "goods" (wealth, health, life chances, and so forth) that characterised an earlier class society (Beck 1992). Risk society is saturated with fear and foreboding, and its political and governmental priorities are structured by concerns over the distribution of "bads" or dangers and attempts to avoid harm. From this perspective, risk thinking in mental health would be merely one aspect of the proliferation of risk within a general climate of fear and insecurity, which in turn is a symptom of a profound change in Western cosmologies arising from the modernization process. I think this notion of risk society, though suggestive, is misleading. It implies something homogenous and all embracing, an array of effects that are amenable to an epochal sociological explanation. But in fact, one finds not homogeneity but diversity, not effects of a general societal transition but attempts to grapple with difficulties and challenges arising in disparate problem spaces and sites. In these attempts, it is true, a motley array of ways of thinking and acting have come to reformulate themselves in vocabularies, techniques, and responsibilities of risk. But while these certainly have a family resemblance, they do not have a common origin or a common mode of functioning, far less a common set of consequences. Much of the vocabulary may be the same whether it applies to insurance against theft, assessment of pregnant women by midwives, or assessment of criminals by probation officers. But risk thinking is heterogeneous. It may be clinical, epidemiological, actuarial, forensic, probabilistic, and much else besides. So, rather than seeking some general explanation of the rise of risk thinking in mental health in epochal social or cultural shifts, I think it is more useful to be diagnostic: to ask where risk thinking has emerged (in which problem field?); how it has emerged (in relation to what knowledge and expertise?); and with what consequences (under new technologies of power and relations of authority, what new ethical dilemmas are generated?).

In undertaking this task, it is useful to begin by asking if risk thinking—as a style of thought—has any common characteristics. Across its various forms and calculative techniques, one feature stands out: risk thinking seeks to bring the future into the present and make it calculable (Hacking 1991). We could say that it tries to discipline uncertainty, in the sense of making uncertainty the topic of a branch of learning and instruction. And to discipline it in a second sense, by bringing uncertainty under control, making it orderly and docile. Risk thinking tames chance, fate, and uncertainty by a paradoxical move. By recognizing the impossibility of certainty about the future, it simultaneously makes this lack of certainty quantifiable in terms of probability. And once one has quantified the probability of a future event's occurring, decisions can be made and justified about what to do in the present, informed by what now seems to be secure, if probabilistic, knowledge about the future. Indeed, once it seems that today's decisions can be informed by calculations about tomorrow, we can demand that calculations about tomorrow should and must inform all decisions made today. The option of acting in the present in order to manage the future rapidly mutates into something like an obligation.

Some criminologists have argued that risk thinking is part of a new style of control. Feeley and Simon have suggested that a "new penology" is taking shape that is "markedly less concerned with responsibility, fault, moral sensibility, diagnosis, or intervention and treatment of the individual offender. Rather, it is concerned with techniques to identify, classify, and manage groupings sorted by dangerousness. The task is managerial not transformative. . . . It seeks to regulate levels of deviance, not intervene or respond to individual deviants or social malformations" (1992:452). Similarly Castel, speaking of psychiatry, has suggested that we inhabit a "post-disciplinary society": techniques of control seek to minimize direct therapeutic intervention upon individual pathological persons; instead control strategies attempt to reduce risk by anticipating "possible loci of dangerous irruptions through the identification of sites statistically locatable in relation to norms and means" (Castel 1981, translation quoted from Rabinow 1982:243). Interventions seek "the technical administration of differences"; they do not target persons, but populations at risk.

As we shall see presently, this analysis does pinpoint a change in practices of control, which certainly extends to the management of mental health and the role of mental health professionals. But this does not mean that either crime control or psychiatry have given up the clinical gaze of medicine or the individualizing gaze of the law to concentrate solely on regulatory strategies targeting groups. Probabilistic and actuarial styles of thought have supplemented and reshaped clinical and legal thinking, but they have not replaced them. Risk strategies may seek (actuarially) to reduce the risk to public safety (populations), but they do so by seeking to identify, classify, and if possible neutralize the riskiness of the individual pathological person. But very different logics of control are required when the sequestration of pathology, by enclosure in hospital or prison, is only a temporary option. Clinical reason in psychiatry may still focus on diagnosis and treatment of the pathological individual and his or her normalization. But this is now practised within wider networks of control, disseminated across the territory of the community. On this territory, ideas of cure or reform have given way to those of chronicity and coping. The troublesome individual appears in a different way against this background: as one who cannot lead a life; who is not attached to the normalizing practices of family, work, and consumption; who is not engaged in the arts of life-style maximization that now define an ordinary life. Institutions of enclosure are now only one moment in a wider network of control, in which a whole range of professionals attempt the impossible task of monitoring and managing a multitude of troubling, troubled, and troublesome individuals. Risk thinking establishes formats for assessing, communicating, deciding, and acting in these circumstances. However, it also generates and exacerbates the very fears it claims to secure against: a population suffused with fears about "the risk of risk." And it produces the paradox that probabilistic calculations about populations are used to make and justify administrative decisions about individuals that are inescapably determinist in their consequences.

Risk: A New Distribution

Psychiatry has long been an administrative as well as a clinical science. One only has to recall its role in relation to concerns about degeneration in the late-nineteenth century, in eugenic strategies over the first half of the twentieth century, in the programs of mental hygiene in the 1930s, and in the plans for a comprehensive, preventative health service in the 1950s and 1960s under the sign of community psychiatry. For twenty years the failures of community psychiatry were articulated in terms of the failure of its dream of comprehensive services for public mental health. The scandals of this era were the obverse of those of institutionalized psychiatry. Critics drew attention to the neglect, homelessness, and degradation that had been produced in the name of an unrealistic policy of reduction of hospitalization, which was, in any event, hampered by inadequate funding, incompetent management, and service rivalry. Newspaper headlines on the failures of community care focused on the despairing plight of former mental patients isolated in bedsit land, and on the vagrancy, homelessness, despair, and suicide among those who were sometimes called, after their Italian counterparts, the "abandoned ones."

The terms of this debate have shifted. The failures of psychiatry are now posed in terms of the failure of assessment, prediction, and management of risky individuals and the minimization of risk to the community. The responsibilities of almost all psychiatric professionals have come to be redefined in terms of the assessment of risk. As Duggan puts it, "While assessing dangerousness has been the province of the forensic psychiatrist, it is now clear that [risk assessment] is a skill which should be the concern of all mental health professionals" (1997:1). Through the generalization of the criterion of risk, all mental health professionals, to a greater or lesser extent, participate in the management of individuals across a complex institutional field comprising institutions of various levels of security, halfway houses of various types, day centers, drop-in centers, hospital hostels, clinics, sheltered housing, assertive outreach teams, and much more.

Upon this territory, it seems as if a new distribution of "the problem of mental health" is taking shape in terms of a distinction between low, medium, and high risk. It is, in fact, the problematization of high risk that has called this distribution into existence. In line with more general shifts away from the rationalities of solidarism and sociality, the work of public agencies and state institutions is increasingly residualized and focused on those who are most resistant to inclusion through the circuits of work, family, consumption, and community (I discuss this further in Rose 1999b).

In the zone of low risk, quasi-therapeutic techniques of control have proliferated across everyday life, regulating and reshaping individual conduct according to norms of autonomy, responsibility, competence, and self-fulfilment. Here one finds counseling, mediation, conciliation, cognitive therapies, behavioral techniques, and the like within the school, the factory, the training program for the unemployed, and in hospital clinics, tutors' studies, the work of health visitors and social workers, and in general practitioners' surgeries. These practices of control, usually entered into voluntarily, operate in a much broader therapeutic habitat: a culture in which radio, television, and cinema offer us psychologized images of ourselves, and in which a whole range of practices of life are shaped and organized in therapeutic terms.

In the zone of medium risk, state-funded facilities have been drastically reduced. There are public psychiatric wards, social workers, quasi-public provision from "voluntary agencies," and the like. Alongside this public provision, a private market has opened up for the management of acute mental health problems that do not appear to pose an immediate danger to others. The new private arrangements are supported by the growth of private health insurance and by the emergence of market-style arrangements in the purchase of care by publicly funded health services. And, in this zone of medium risk, mental health is increasingly governed through the family,[3] that is to say, through strategies that seek to enhance, intensify, and instrumentalize the apparently "natural" bonds of obligation between members of a domestic units. The self-governing family is urged, educated, and obliged to take upon itself the sociopolitical responsibility for managing its own mental health problems and its own problematic members.

Most important for present purposes is the role that mental health professionals have been given in the zone of high risk within an extending apparatus charged with the obligation (which it inevitably fails to live up to) of the continuous and unending management of permanently problematic persons in the name of community safety. It is here that the clinical language of diagnosis and treatment is increasingly replaced with the probabilistic language of risk assessment. And it is here that the professional vocation of therapy is replaced by that of administration. As psychiatry is urged to prioritize community protection, it is increasingly difficult to articulate its reciprocal obligations—for example, the obligation to protect those with mental health problems from the actual and symbolic violence they face at the hands of "the community," the obligation to enhance the powers of those who use psychiatry within the psychiatric system itself, and the obligation to deny the logic that equates difference with danger.

Forensic Psychiatry Today

From the mid-nineteenth to the mid-twentieth century, the primary role of forensic psychiatry was defined in relation to the criminal justice system (Bluglass 1990). It focused on the determination of the responsibility of the offender, although widening its remit to encompass advice to the courts as to sentence and treatment. In the 1960s and 1970s, forensic psychiatry established itself as a distinct discipline, responding to the increasing role of psychiatrists in treatment itself, in prisons, special hospitals, and other secure units for such offenders, and to the increasing demands for psychiatrists as experts witnesses in the courtroom and elsewhere in the criminal justice system. Its role changed most dramatically, however, with the rise of a new logic of community, where detention itself ceased to be the normal response to mental ill health and confinement in mental hospital is neither a necessary nor a sufficient condition for psychiatric treatment. Now, forensic expertise is deployed in assessing psychiatric patients' risk of future violence in order to make decisions as to their management in a diversified community mental health system. In this post-decarceration period, new rationales have emerged for confinement, and none is so compelling as that of security (Grounds, 1995).

Within the context of community, the logic of the trial process no longer dominates assessment practices in the same way: the question at issue is that of security, not culpability. Indeed, the different types of psychiatric institutions are virtually defined in terms of the needs of security rather than those of therapy or care. As the old mental hospitals are closed, a new approach to the confinement of the risky is beginning to take shape. In the United Kingdom, while the population of Special Hospitals has fallen from its peak in the early 1970s, Medium Secure Units have expanded. Compulsory admissions under the Mental Health Act have actually risen over the 1990s, and a number of acute wards in psychiatric hospitals have been re-locked and redesignated in security terms (Johnson et al. 1997). And, to those actually confined, one can add those restricted patients who have been released into the community on conditional discharge (Potts 1995). This enumeration does not of course include those who are detained in prison, though considered to be suffering from a "psychopathic disorder," because they are considered untreatable or because no psychiatric institution is willing to accept them.

The central rationale for confinement in psychiatry has changed: it is no longer primarily for purposes of cure or of care, but for the secure containment of risk (cf. Grounds 1995). Of course, this is sometimes a matter of the risks that a patient poses to herself, and not to others. But even so, admission to a psychiatric institution is often little more than a way of securing the most risky until their riskiness can be fully assessed and controlled. That is, if it ever can be. For those thought to pose risks to others, the specter of preventive detention reemerges. We have seen the birth of a new class of "monsters"—sexual predators, pedophiles, the incorrigibly antisocial—for whom a whole variety of paralegal forms of confinement are being devised.[4] We are familiar with the story of the apparently limitless increases in the populations of the asylums over the second half of the nineteenth century and the first half of the twentieth as they came to be used as receptacles for all manner of failed or anticitizens unable or unwilling to accept the obligations of civility. A new version of this history is now being played out in which quasi-psychiatric institutions seem to offer a solution to the problem of incapacitating those who may have committed no crime or have completed their sentence, but who seem to present a risk to the overriding political priority of the preservation of the security of "the public." Within this problem space, it seems that the constraints of rule of law can be waived in order to confine risky individuals not so much because of what they have done, but of what they are and what they might do.

Professionals of Risk

Robert Castel has argued that risk management—the identification, assessment, elimination, or reduction of the possibility of incurring misfortune or loss—has become an integral part of the professional responsibility of all those involved with psychiatry (Castel 1991). The management of risk does not take the form of a Big Brother society, where computers collate and interpret data from a variety of sources to identify risk levels and risk groups across a population, and engage in preventative targeting of particular sites and locales. Rather, it operates though transforming professional subjectivity. It is the individual professional who has to make the assessment and management of risk their central professional obligation. They have to assess the individual client in terms of the riskiness that he or she represents, to allocate each to a risk level, to put in place the appropriate administrative arrangements for the management of the individual in the light of the requirement to minimize risk, and to take responsibility—indeed blame—if an "untoward incident" occurs.

The nature of this blaming process varies from jurisdiction to jurisdiction. In the United States, in the *Tarasoff* case of 1976, the California Supreme Court was widely understood to have created a duty for mental health professionals to protect third parties against patients violence. Although there is disagreement about the precise scope of the duty, the case received great attention in the mental health community, in the United States and the United Kingdom. "According to the court," argued one British commentator, "this duty obtains 'once a therapist does in fact determine, or under applicable professional standards reasonably should have determined that a patient poses a serious danger of violence to others'" (Tarasoff, 1976:345, quoted in Borum 1996:945). In the United Kingdom, no such legal doctrine has been enunciated to date, and indeed, no action has been taken against any mental health professional following the enquiries into homicides committed by psychiatric patients discharged into the community. In this jurisdiction, psychiatrists are assured that the benchmark ruling remains that in the Bolam case (1957): "A doctor is not guilty of negligence if he has acted in accordance with a practice accepted as proper by a responsible body of medical men skilled in that particular art." Nonetheless, Harrison suggests that the publication of formal guidelines in various official policy documents have clarified standards of reasonable care, extended the boundaries of the duty of care, and created "a climate of expectation regarding standards of care and the obligations of mental health professionals in protecting the public from untoward incidents" (1997:38). In an increasingly litigious atmosphere, Harrison predicts that test cases will be brought against mental health professionals by patient's advocacy groups and suggests that "[m]ental health professionals are beginning to add an additional factor to their risk calculations when managing difficult patients: the assessment of risk (of a civil action) to themselves in the event of an untoward incident" (1997:37). It appears that it is no longer good enough for such a professional to say that behavior is difficult to predict and "accidents will happen." In different ways in different jurisdictions, every untoward incident can be seen as a failure of expertise: someone must be held accountable.[5]

This professional obligation to manage risk transforms the act of diagnosis. Previously, there was what might be described schematically as a kind of division of labor in the management of the psychiatric patient. Diagnosis and treatment was the responsibility of the doctor; day-to-day care and control was the responsibility of the nurse; assistance was the responsibility of the social worker. The clinical diagnosis by the psychiatrist was the fulcrum of this division of labor, even if, in the field of "the community," the actual management of the patient was to be undertaken by other experts and in other sites. The clinical diagnosis was a condition of entry to the domain of psychiatry: the diagnosis was not just classificatory but performative, in that it mandated a certain regime of drugs, detention, or referral to a particular specialist institution. One might, however, point to two correlated shifts in this situation.

First, the preeminent role of the psychiatrist is challenged. To quote Castel, "The site of diagnostic synthesis is no longer that of the concrete relationship with a sick person, but a relationship constituted among the different expert assessments which make up the patient's dossier" (Castel 1991:262). What is required is the classification of individuals in terms of likely future conduct, their riskiness to the community and themselves, and the identification of the steps necessary to manage that conduct. This judgment of riskiness is only partially conducted in medical terms. It entails a variety of other forms of expertise about such matters as employment history, family life, alcohol consumption, coping skills, capacity to cook, shop, and manage money as well as information on past conduct and dangerous behavior. While the psychiatrist may formally remain in charge of the case—although even this is in doubt with the nomination of "key workers" from other disciplines—the terms of psychiatric judgment are no longer clinical but "quotidian," concerned with the management of the everyday. While psychiatric diagnosis may still take place, the key judgment that must be made is a different one—what should be done with this person, should they be sent to this institution or to that, to this hostel or that sheltered housing scheme, back into the community or back into prison. As the logic of prediction comes to replace the logic of diagnosis, the claims of psychiatrists to a special and unique expertise at assessment are weakened. The demand for multidisciplinary teams emerges less out of the recognition of the diagnostic and curative significance of different sorts of clinical and social expertise than out of the attempt to answer the administrative question: what is to be done and how can we decide? Mental health professionals become, in certain fundamental senses, knowledge workers, engaged in the accumulation, calibration, classification, and interpretation and communication of information relevant to judgments about risk.

Second, the act of diagnosis itself changes. The new techniques of risk assessment involve a way of "individualizing" the patient that is rather different from that embodied in previous types of judgment. In official guidance notes concerning risk assessment, the diagnosis of the patient is often not mentioned. Instead, risk factors include not taking medication, previous records of violent or aggressive behavior, use of alcohol or illegal drugs, relations with other individuals, age, social isolation, place of residence, and self-neglect.[6] In assessing potentially violent patients, information thought to be relevant includes not only information from the treatment teams and the patient, but also from relatives, carers, friends, police, pro-

bation officers, housing departments, and social workers. Sometimes as-
sessors are advised that they should not overlook information from local
press reports and concerns voiced by neighbors, whatever the practical, ethical, and legal obligations relating to confidentiality. The criteria used for
assessing risk include the past history of the patient, self-reporting by the
patient at interview, observation of the behavior and mental state of the patient, discrepancies between what is reported and what is observed, the results of psychological and physiological tests, statistics derived from studies of related cases, and predication indicators derived from research, all
coming together in a "clinical judgment"—a balanced summary of prediction derived from knowledge of the individual, the present circumstances,
and what is known about the disorder.

The obligation to assess, evaluate, and minimize risk is significantly different from the obligation to care and control, or to diagnose and cure, or to
befriend and reintegrate. These new logics of individualization mandate
new forms of "team working" and are organized in the form of a range of new
devices for recording, monitoring, and evaluating. For the professionals
themselves, written and routinized assessment of risk performs an important function in a the context of new ways of regulating professional activity. In a situation where the outcome of a mental health assessment may be
an administrative decision to release a patient into the community, the risk
assessment may be used not so much to make accurate predictions as to ensure that the decision made was defensible if something should go wrong.
The psychiatrist must therefore reflect upon the present decisionmaking
from the perspective of the need to defend it in some public tribunal in the
future: were all relevant factors taken into account; were there sound reasons for the decision that can be adduced and justified; would any other competent professional in the same position have made a better decision; would
other colleagues consider the decisionmaking process as meeting standards
of good practice. Despite the shift in current regulatory regimes toward
market-based mechanisms, risk assessment thus takes its place within the
new modes that are emerging for the regulation of professional judgment.
Here professional practice is governed through enmeshing professionals in a
bureaucratic nexus of reports, forms, monitoring, evaluation, and audit, under the shadow of the law, thus governing them according to logics that are
not their own, in the interests of community protection.

Calculating Risk

In the United Kingdom, the psychiatric assessment of risk frequently involves the allocation of the assessed individual to a category that

is designated numerically: 1. low risk; 2. some risk; 3. high risk. But this categorization is seldom actuarial. That is to say, categorization is seldom a probabilistic prediction of future conduct calculated on the basis of comparison of the patient's scores on particular factors with statistical information on the association of such factors with future violence or danger to themselves or others. Mental health professionals in the United Kingdom tend to resist the use of numerical risk assessment schedules and classifications. They stress that assessment of risk is a clinical matter and must take place within a clinical assessment of mental disorder, and that the judgment can seldom be encapsulated by a single value on a scale, or a rating on a small number of factors. However, developments in the United States and Canada (and to some extent in Australia and New Zealand) suggest a gradual numericalization of judgments of risk. Why should this be?

It has been argued, I think convincingly, that professionals turn to the use of numbers, not when they are strong, but when they are weak (Porter 1996). Strong professionals, who are invested with public trust, have no need to justify their judgments in the supposed objectivity of numbers. Yet when under threat—when their powers and capacities are disputed by a distrustful alliance of politicians, professional rivals, academics, and public opinion—the lure of the number, the "power of the single figure," is hard to resist. It also represents a widely used professional device for "black boxing"—that is to say, rendering invisible and hence incontestable the complex array of judgments and decisions that go into a scale and a number (Hopwood 1988; Latour 1987).

I have already referred to the widespread doubts that have arisen, from the 1960s to the present, about the capacity of mental health professionals to make accurate assessments and predictions about the future conduct of their patients and clients. In the United States, as we have seen, the courtroom was a key site for the generation of such doubts. American laws on civil commitment and American criminal codes give a pivotal role to judgments about the risk of harm to others, but a succession of cases found the judgments of psychiatrists on this matter to be ill founded and inaccurate. To make matters worse, psychiatrists themselves acknowledged these doubts: while few confessed that they had nothing to contribute to legal decisions about patient's future behavior, most felt that they were being required to take responsibility for nonclinical judgments, assessments of the risks of future violent conduct in contexts where they themselves claimed no specific capacities. And these doubts were confirmed by research by psychiatrists themselves in the 1970s, so that when Monahan reviewed early studies of clinicians abilities to assess violence risk, he concluded that when clinicians predicted that a person would be violent, research indicated that they were accurate no more than one-third of the time (Monahan 1981). By 1993, Steadman and Monahan and their colleagues were happy to state bluntly "the criteria that clinicians say they are using to predict dangerousness do not appear to be the ones they use in practice (Steadman 1973), the accuracy of clinical predictions is poor (Cocozza and Steadman 1978), and the types of errors made are consistently ones of overpredicting dangerousness (Steadman and Morrissey 1981)" (Steadman et al. 1993:40; cf. Grisso and Tomkins 1996:928–29).

And yet, it appeared, however poor clinicians were at making such predictions, predictions were required of clinicians by the courts. Grisso and Tomkins cite the U.S. Supreme Court's decision in the *Barefoot* case (1993), where the court reasoned that where the need to assess future violence was a intrinsic element of the sentencing framework, as it was and remains in some states, someone was required to make the prediction, and that however unreliable clinicians' predictions were, they were still admissible. After all, the court explained, mental health professionals' predictions were "not always wrong . . . only most of the time" (*Barefoot* 1993:901, quoted in Grisso and Tomkins 1996:928). Given that over three hundred thousand people were, at that time in the United States, the subjects of involuntary civil commitment on grounds of dangerousness, it is not altogether surprising that a large program of research took shape that sought to reestablish the credentials of professionals, and that an appeal to the objectivity of numbers should have played a key role.

A variety of projects were initiated in the United States to try and provide professionals with a more defensible foundation for describing the possibilities of future risk of violence. Werner and his colleagues (1984) studied the factors that influenced psychiatrists' judgments of the likelihood of inpatient violence. Segal and colleagues (1988a, 1988b) studied clinician evaluation of emergency admission cases in California, correlating clinical judgments with observers' ratings on the TRIAD index (Three Ratings of Involuntary Admissibility). Lidz and Mulvey and their team trained researchers in speedwriting to record interviews between clinicians and patients admitted to a hospital psychiatric emergency clinic and compared these with clinicians ratings of current and chronic dangerousness and, in later research, compared nurses and psychiatrists assessments of potential patient violence with reports of violence committed by patients after release (see, e.g., Lidz et al. 1989; Lidz, Mulvey, and Gardner 1993). But the most significant of all the U.S. studies was undertaken by Monahan and Steadman and their colleagues in the John D. and Catherine T. MacArthur

Foundation's Research Network on Mental Health and the Law, created with a grant to the University of Virginia in 1988 to "build the empirical foundation for the next generation of mental health laws" (MacArthur 1998). And it adopted an actuarial approach.

Attempts to develop actuarial instruments for the assessment of risk in psychiatric patients, in particular risk of violence to others, go back at least to the early 1970s (attempts to develop actuarial risk assessment in criminal justice has, of course, a much longer history, cf. Pratt 1995). The MacArthur Risk Assessment Study is undoubtedly the most ambitious to date. It was initiated in 1989 and involved a prospective study of over one thousand discharged patients from psychiatric hospitals at three sites. The goal was to identify "cues" that could alert clinicians to future violent behavior. The research involved assessing each patient on dispositional or personal factors (personality, cognitive ability, . . .), historical or developmental factors (family history, psychiatric history, criminal history, . . .), contextual or situational factors (perceived stress, social support, means of violence, . . .), and clinical or symptom factors (delusions, hallucinations severity of symptoms, diagnosis, activities of daily living, substance use, treatment, . . .). A battery of tests were used: MADS (the Maudsley Assessment of Delusions Schedule), PCL (the Psychopathy Check List), BIS (the Barratt Impulsiveness Scale), the Novaco Anger Scale, the NEO-Five Factor Personality Inventory and the WAIS IQ test, together with other clinical assessments and interview schedules administered by clinicians and interviewers, patients self-reports, arrest records, and mental hospital records. Violence was assessed using another scale, and the study interviewed patients and "collaterals" (usually family members) five times over the first year after the patient's hospital release. It was accompanied by a further Community Violence Risk Study to enable comparisons of the rate of violence by former mental patients with those by other members of the community and assess whether different risk factors applied to former patients and others.

It is obvious that this was a remarkably expensive, laborious, and time consuming attempt to turn risk into numbers. The initial battery of tests alone, before being pared down, took between two and ten hours to complete with each subject. It would seem churlish not to welcome such concerted attempts to make predictions reliable, to avoid or minimize unnecessary detention or hazardous release.[7] It is undoubtedly the case that many of those who argue for standardization and objectification, for scales and numbers, do so because they believe that this would confer transparency upon a process often shrouded by professional discretion and open psychiatric assessments to scrutiny and challenge. Further, many argue that these studies will demonstrate objectively that the association between mental ill health and violence is much less than widely believed, and hence that the research will serve the function of public education, and contribute to the destigmatization necessary to gain political support for less carceral policies.[8] But, whatever their intentions, it is relevant to point to a number of other processes in play in such attempts to render risk measurable.

Theodore Porter's work is again helpful here (1996). For this was not simply an attempt to find an objective measure of risk, it was a complex and technical labour for the production of objectivity. Through this process, a whole variety of decisions and judgments—about what populations to choose, about how violence is to be defined, about what levels to choose as thresholds, about what measurements are practicable—are boxed up and rendered invisible within the final risk assessment instrument. For example, Steadman and his colleagues gave considerable attention to the issue of portability: they "wanted the set of risk factors that ultimately emerged from the research to be easily 'transported' into actual clinical practice" (Steadman et al. 1993:300). Practical, technical, and conceptual considerations thus form, as it were, the "positive unconscious" of the objectivity produced by the instrument itself. The very notion of the reasonable professional practice "that would be accepted by a responsible body of medical men skilled in that particular art" is transformed, and a new image begins to take shape of what it is to be a responsible mental health professional, an image cast in terms of the external logics of risk assessment and risk management. In the process, the discretion of mental health professionals, and their responsibility to their client and the community they serve, are both amplified and attenuated. Amplified in the sense that they are responsible for utilizing the decisionmaking technology appropriately according to normal and agreed professional standards. Attenuated in that it is dispersed and relocated in the technical capacity and objectivity of the risk assessment instrument.

Objectivity is relevant here in another sense, as objectivity versus subjectivity: a disciplining and standardization of the clinical gaze. As Monahan and Steadman put it: "If an actuarially valid array of risk markers for violence could be reliably identified, clinicians could be trained to incorporate these factors into their routine practice, and the accuracy of clinical predictions of violence among the mentally disordered would be commensurately increased" (Steadmann et al. 1993:13). Through the use of measures and scales, the gaze of the clinician will be standardized and turned into a uniform instrument of measurement. In the process, the craft-like or guildlike nature of the expertise of the mental health professional is deemphasized; it is displaced by a style of speaking truth that is formal, transparent, explicit, and justifiable, in the sense of being able to adduce reasons for judgments. This is to enhance the "objectivity effect" of the professional claim, and to increase its capacity to accrue conviction in a climate of doubt and criticism from those outside the field of knowledge itself. It is to help sustain the bureaucratic and political assertion of mental health professional that, potentially at least, they have the capacity to make objective, impersonal, and unbiased assessments.

Further, as Ericson and Haggerty have argued in relation to police work, "categories and classifications of risk communication and . . . the technologies for communicating knowledge [about risk] internally and externally" prospectively structure the actions and deliberations of psychiatric professionals (1997:33; I have drawn upon their arguments for what follows). To this extent, once stabilized in "communication formats"—more or less systematic rules for the organization and presentation of information and experience—risk classifications tend to become the means by which professionals think, act, and justify their actions. And the impact of studies such as those of Monahan and Steadman would be to shape communication formats themselves such that they embody the kinds of conceptions and calibrations of risk that are required by external authorities such as the courts. In that sense, the very clinical gaze of mental health professionals, and the nature of their encounter with clients or patients, is liable to be formatted by the demands and objectives of nonclinical authorities. Discretion thus shifts away from the individual clinician toward those who design the expert system for the calculation of risk. Ericson and Haggerty go so far as to argue that "[e]ven in medicine the doctor on the ground is a subordinate of expert systems and those who manage them. He or she is one of many contributors to the expert system of risk management that creates the patient's dossier, and therefore lose control over particular outcomes as well as over the progress of cases" (1997:37–38). The information so extracted, organized, and packaged is then communicated along channels, and with consequences, far removed from those of professional practice (cf. Castel 1991:281).

In a regime of risk, control is not merely a matter of repressing or containing those who are individually pathological; it is about the generation of "knowledge that allows selection of thresholds that define acceptable risks and on forms of inclusion and exclusion based on that knowledge" (Ericson and Haggerty 1997:41). In that context, a whole array of control agencies—police, social workers, doctors, psychiatrists, mental health professionals—become, at least in part, connected up with one another in circuits of surveillance and communication designed to minimize the riskiness of the most risky. They form a multiplicity of points for the collection, inscription, accumulation, and distribution of information relevant to the management of risk. Unsurprisingly, those who are most intensively the subjects of these risk regulation regimes are "the usual suspects"—the poor, the welfare recipients, the petty criminals, and, now, the users and survivors of psychiatry. The logics of risk thus locate the careers and identities of psychiatric patients firmly within a regime of perpetual surveillance that, however benign its intentions and objective its criteria, actually constitutes them all as actually or potentially "risky" individuals. The incompleteness, fragmentation, and failure of risk assessment and risk management is no threat to such logics, merely a perpetual incitement for the incessant improvement of systems, generation of more knowledge, invention of more techniques—all driven by the technological imperative to tame uncertainty and master hazard.

Steadman and his colleagues conclude their account by reflecting that "if the study is not successful, it will stand as testimony to the intractable difficulties clinicians face in assessing the likelihood of a behavior as complex and multi-determined as violence in a population as diverse and poorly understood as the mentally disordered" (Steadman et al. 1993:316). For the belief that it is possible to tame risk by actuarialism is ultimately related to a style of thought that is profoundly hostile to hazard, uncertainty, and chance. It is within such a style of thought that the tasks of objectivity are imposed upon the disciplines of mental health, for it appears that uncertainty can only be tamed by gridding the free and liberal space of community with surveillance, calculation, communication, and control.

Conclusion: Governing through Madness

Let me conclude by making three general points. The first concerns a new way of governing professional activity. Like budgets and audits, these new ways of working in terms of risk assessment and risk management strategies play a key role in shaping the conduct of mental health professionals, "governing at a distance" the very criteria and types of judgment that professionals are engaged in. It is, as we have seen, the shadow of the law—the concerns of the courts in the United States, for example, or the real or imagined fear of prosecution by patients, victims, or relatives in the United Kingdom—that shapes professional conduct, through the imperative to undertake the interminable tasks of inscription—information systems, registers, documentation, and the like—that are intrinsic to these new risk-based technologies. In the United Kingdom, the public inquiry, conducted in a quasi-legal manner, has become a routinized response to untoward incidents. The findings of these quasi-legal mechanisms, or rather their procedural recommendations that have little legal about them, have nonetheless played a key role in the elaboration and dissemination of a grid of obligations for risk assessment, risk management, and risk thinking that have enwrapped the professional judgment of all mental health professionals. It might be argued that professional participation in these practices is a necessary condition of a claim to expertise. But, inescapably, participation in the illusion of objective risk assessment gives credence to the "ideology of risk," to the prioritization of the demand for public protection over the duty of care owed to those with mental health problems, and to the myth that threats to public safety are increasing and that risk-based practice will actually enhance community security.[9]

The second point concerns trust in numbers. The increasing numericization of risk raises significant ethical issues (see Price 1997). Where are the authors of the assessment scales when things go wrong or when detention is challenged? What are the implications of transforming risk assessment from a matter of expert testimony to a "technical" issue? What are the consequences if risk assessments depend upon the interpretation by third parties of dubious "facts," about past actions, family circumstances, job stability, and so forth, accumulated in files and following patients over the years? Given that clinicians are not experts in the methodology and statistics "black boxed" within risk-assessment scales, the populations upon which they are standardized, the generalization from one population to another, the moral and social judgments involved in decisions as to what does or does not count as dangerous behavior in the populations on which the scales were developed, the "false positive rates," the effects of changes since the time the scales were constructed, the implications of national and cultural variation, what are the implications of their uncritical clinical acceptance of the "objectivity" of such scales? As Price puts it, "What, then, is the responsibility of the 'psy-practitioner?'" (Price 1997:3). Of course, those who promulgate the use of actuarial methods do not ignore these ethical issues. For example Steadman et al. (1993) acknowledge that an increase in predictive accuracy will not obviate the questions of social policy and professional ethics that arise when mental health professionals become embroiled in the use of the police power of the state. But the facticity conferred by scales and numbers, in which the decisions, calculations, techniques, and assumptions of the methods disappear into the apparent objectivity of the single number, not only serves to increase the appearance of

accuracy. It also serves to decrease contestability and to imply specious pre-
cision. And along with all these, a certain proportion of the responsibility
of the practitioner for his or her judgment and its consequences, a responsibility both to his or her patient, and to the community he or she serves, also
disappears into the numbers.

My final point concerns what one could call "governing through madness." I adapt this term from Jonathan Simon. Writing of the changing place
of the criminal law in strategies of governance, Simon has suggested that
advanced industrial democracies are increasingly governing themselves
through crime—that is to say, issues of crime and punishment have become
less about the punishment of the offender than about shaping the actions of
many other individuals in spaces, practices, and institutions far beyond the
criminal justice system (Simon 1996, 1997, 1998).[10] Further, while the rule
of law still makes crime primarily an offence against the crown or against
the state, the call for justice, and the call for control, is increasingly framed
in terms of the rights of the innocent victim and the security of the "general public," and hence it is organized in terms of an increasingly pervasive
"fear of crime." This fear is increased by an alliance of politicians vying for
office and seeking votes, by newspapers in search of stories and circulation,
and by victim groups transforming their undoubted injuries into an ethic of
ressentiment. As Wendy Brown has commented in another context, this
"produces an affect (rage, righteousness) that overwhelms the hurt; . . . produces a culprit responsible for the hurt; and . . . produces a site of revenge
to displace the hurt (a place to inflict hurt as the sufferer has been hurt"
(Brown 1995:68, paraphrasing Nietzsche's argument in *The Genealogy of
Morals* [see Nietzsche 1969]). And this call for justice and for control in the
name of the innocent victim and the "safety of the public" has the added
benefit of producing a good conscience for itself.

This new discourse has come to focus on a particular set of concerns
that lie at the crossover of psychiatry and penology. It has singled out for its
attention a new class of "monsters." These are sex offenders, pedophiles,
madmen or quasi-madmen on the loose, drug dealers, violent children, serial killers, and the like. If anything unifies these figures, it is their character as "predators"—they are those who, because of what they are, prey on
the innocent to satisfy their unnatural and rapacious desires. These monsters are not merely "abnormal." As Ian Hacking has argued, the notion of
the normal acquired its current sense in the early nineteenth century—the
notion that there were degrees of deviation from a norm, normal states and
deviant excesses. This idea was not part of the previous thought world,
which was peopled with "with monsters such as Caligula rather than devi-

ations from the mean" (Hacking 1991:162). Perhaps these monsters never disappeared from modern thought, but in criminology and psychiatry, the idea of norm and deviation ruled. Today the monstrous seems to have returned. It is the anomaly, the exception, not merely a deviation from the norm but a radically different nature, gross pathology, perhaps even evil. Rather than being structured by norms and deviations, our contemporary imagination is organized around "we, the public" and all that threatens us. Seductive fantasies of ideal communities within which individuals and families are free to live an untroubled life of freedom—understood as pursuit of contentment and life-style maximization—are troubled by the constant threat, somehow both inescapable and unjust, of predatory monsters. Risk assessment may be used in strategies of government that require the targeting of resources in residualized welfare systems focused only upon those in greatest need. But it is also used in strategies of government that valorize public opinion, in order to respond to the public demand that "something should be done about" the exceptional danger apparently posed by particularly dangerous individuals.

"Governing through madness" refers to the ways in which contemporary politics of mental health have come to be structured in terms of the questions of security and public safety. It is within this complex that the specter of the monstrous, and the demand for protection in the name of those who see themselves as potential victims, has forced a reorientation of psychiatry within strategies of control formulated in terms of risk. This is paradoxical. On the one hand, risk thinking actually blurs the distinction between the monstrous and the rest: it operates in terms of a continuum of risk. Yet on the other, as we have seen, risk thinking is quite amenable to the clinical and forensic identification of particular risky individuals. Hence these two ideas of risk are "translatable": they can live side by side in a relation of productive ambiguity. To satisfy the public and political demand for the identification of the potentially monstrous, psychiatric risk thinking has had to be turned once more to the problem of the identification of the exception, to preemptive intervention in the name of community safety, to renewed strategies for the exclusion of the incorrigibly risky and potentially monstrous person—incarceration without reform. Historical precedents would suggest that such strategies are unlikely to reduce the overall frequency of very rare incidents they seek to prevent, but that they are likely to result in threshold lowering and net widening, and the detention of many individuals who would otherwise be capable of leading lives that might be troublingly different but would pose no dangers to others.

Beyond its concentration on the exceptional, risk thinking transforms

the very activity of psychiatry, the conception of its civic role and professional responsibilities, and the public representation of madness itself—
not just as difference, but as a wholly negative focal point of risk. Madness comes to be emblematic of the threat posed to "the community" by a
permanently marginal, excluded, outcast, and largely unreformable sector
who require enduring management. All spaces of potential interpenetration
where these dangerous persons might come into contact with "normal"
members of the public are felt to be zones of risk—the shopping mall, the
car park, the railway station, the street. Calculated design, quasi-penal
rules against the habits of incivility such as loitering, consumption of alcohol, and smoking, and continual surveillance seeks to secure these risky
zones without saturating them with overtly coercive measures of control.[11]
In this new configuration, not only those with mental health problems, not
only psychiatric professionals, but "the community" itself is governed in
the name of the risks of madness. The critical questions here do not simply
concern the efficacy or otherwise of such a strategy. They should be directed toward the dream of contentment without risk to which this strategy is linked, the forms of life to which it is attached, the fears and anxieties
it produces and feeds off, and the hostility toward difference it engenders.

NOTES

        Versions of this essay were presented at the Conference of the Law and
Society Association, Glasgow, July 1996; the Cropwood Conference on "The Future
of Forensic Psychiatry," St. John's College, Cambridge, March 1997; the Sainsbury
Centre for Mental Health Summer School, Oxford, July 1997; and the 18th Annual
Congress of the Australian and New Zealand Association of Psychiatry, Psychology
and Law, Melbourne, April 1998. A brief outline of the argument was published as
"Living Dangerously: Risk Thinking and Risk Management in Mental Health
Care," *Mental Health Care* 1, no. 8 (1998): 263–66; and a slightly different version
was published as "Governing Risky Individuals: The Role of Psychiatry in New
Regimes of Control," *Psychiatry, Psychology and Law* 5, no. 2 (1998): 177–95.
        Thanks to those who have commented on the essay at different stages, in particular Tom Baker, Michael Cavadino, Pat O'Malley, John Pratt, Clifford Shearing,
Jonathan Simon, and Mariana Valverde. Thanks also to those who participated in a
workshop on risk assessment in Melbourne at the 18th Annual Congress of the
Australian and New Zealand Association of Psychiatry, Psychology and Law.
Jonathan Simon and John Pratt both kindly allowed me to look at unpublished manuscripts of their work in progress on current changes in penal regimes for "monstrous" individuals. Thanks also to Diana Rose for advice, to Maxine Thomas and
Cauline Brathwaite for finding me materials on local psychiatric policies and practices, and to Donald van Tol for his collaboration with me in research on the history of risk assessment. My argument is indebted to the ideas of Robert Castel and
Richard Ericson.

1. This is the title of Robert Castel's important paper on which I have here drawn (Castel 1991; see also Castel 1981).

2. Supplement to Code of Practice published August 1993 pursuant to Section 118 of the Mental Health Act 1983, dated February 1996.

3. I am grateful to John Pratt for stressing this aspect to me. I discuss "government through the family" in Rose 1999a.

4. This is an international phenomenon. In Victoria, Australia, in April 1990, the Community Protection Act was passed in order to legitimate detention of one individual, Garry David, who was considered to be dangerous but did not fall within the ambit of either criminal or mental health law (Greig 1997). In related quasi-psychiatric areas, notably "pedophilia," issues of preventive detention are being discussed in many national contexts: it appears that the conventions of "rule of law" must be waived for the protection of the community against a growing number of "predators" who do not conform to either legalistic or psychiatric models of subjectivity (see Pratt 2000; Simon 1998; Scheingold, Pershing and Olson 1994).

5. Clifford Shearing has pointed out to me that there is a long history of risk thinking in tort law. The history of the "reasonable care" argument in tort law, and the links between clinical and risk thinking in this domain, would repay analysis. In certain areas, such as private security, major changes in practice have been motivated, in part, by the increasing use of risk-based arguments in tort law by individuals and communities demanding better protection.

6. Camden and Islington Community Health Services Trust, Mental Health Services, Care Programme Approach, Guidelines for Use, October 1994.

7. Although some professionals continue to argue that the only reliable predictor of future violence requires little sophisticated research: it is evidence of past violence.

8. Initial results from the MacArthur study go some way toward supporting this view. They find that the population discharged from psychiatric hospital is heterogeneous, and that the prevalence of violence among those discharged is about the same as that among others living in their communities, except where substance abuse is involved. Substance abuse was linked to an increased prevalence of violence among all their sample—both those discharged from psychiatric hospital and others—but the prevalence was higher among those discharged from hospital for the first few months after discharge. Significantly, given the prevailing images of the types of crime committed by the "monstrous and murderous madman," the type and location of violence committed by people discharged from psychiatric hospital was very similar to that committed by others living in their community (MacArthur 1998).

9. Evidence from the United Kingdom indicates no increasing trend in any of the harms to which psychiatric and quasi-psychiatric risk management strategies are addressed. For example, the shift to "care in the community" has led to no increase in the numbers of homicides carried out by people with a psychiatric history, and the numbers of young children who are the victims of "sexual predators" are falling.

10. Simon is specifically discussing a law called "Megan's Law" named after the seven year old victim of rape and murder for which a previously convicted and released sex offender was charged, which was passed after a campaign led by the parents and framed in terms of the "betrayal of parents by a state unable to control predators and unwilling to empower citizens to protect themselves" (Simon, 1996: 21).

11. The classic discussions here are in Shearing and Stenning's discussion of Disney World (1984) and Davis's account of "Fortress L. A" (1990: chap. 4). I discuss this myself in chapter 7 of Rose 1999b.

REFERENCES

Alberg, C., Hatfied, B. and Huxley, P. 1996. *Learning Materials on Mental Health: Risk Assessment.* Manchester: University of Manchester.

Barefoot. 1993. Barefoot v. Estelle, 463 U.S. 880.

Beck, U. 1992. *Risk Society: Towards a New Modernity.* London: Sage.

Bluglass, R. 1990. "The Scope of Forensic Psychiatry." *Journal of Forensic Psychiatry* 1:5–9.

Bolam. 1957. Bolam v. Friern Hospital, 2 All E. R. 118; 1 W. L. R. 582.

Borum, R. 1996. "Improving the Clinical Practice of Violence Risk Assessment: Technology, Guidelines, and Training." *American Psychologist* 51 (9): 945–56.

Brown, W. 1995. *States of Injury: Power and Freedom in Late Modernity.* Princeton: Princeton University Press.

Castel, R. 1981. *La Gestion des risques: de l'anti-psychiatrie a l'apres-psychanalyse.* Paris: Edition de Minuit.

———. 1991. "From Dangerousness to Risk." In *The Foucault Effect: Studies in Governmentality,* ed. G. Burchell, C. Gordon, and P. Miller. Hemel Hempstead: Harvester Wheatsheaf.

Cocozza, J., and H. Steadman. 1976. "The Failure of Psychiatric Predictions of Dangerousness: Clear and Convincing Evidence." *Rutgers Law Review* 29:1084–1101.

Crichton, J. 1995. "The Prediction of Psychiatric Patient Violence." In *Psychiatric Patient Violence: Risk and Response,* ed. J. Crichton. London: Duckworth.

Davis, M. 1990. *City of Quartz: Excavating the Future in Los Angeles.* London: Verso,

Deleuze, G. 1995. "Postscript on Control Societies." In *Negotiations.* New York: Columbia University Press.

Duckitt, J. 1988. "The Prediction of Violence." *South African Journal of Psychology* 18:10–16.

Duggan, C. 1997. "Introduction." In *Assessing Risk in the Mentally Disordered,* ed. C. Duggan. Supplement 32 to the *British Journal of Psychiatry.* London: Royal College of Psychiatrists.

Ericson, R., and K. Haggerty. 1997. *Policing the Risk Society.* Toronto: University of Toronto Press.

Feeley, M., and J. Simon. 1992. "The New Penology: Notes on the Emerging Strategy of Corrections and Its Implications." *Criminology* 30 (4): 449–74.

Floud, J., and W. Young. 1981. *Dangerousness and Criminal Justice.* Cambridge: Cambridge University Press.

Foucault, M. 1978. "About the Concept of the 'Dangerous Individual' in 19th-Century Legal Psychiatry." Trans. A. Baudot and J. Couchman. *International Journal of Law and Psychiatry* 1:1–18.

Gottfredson, S., and D. Gottfredson. 1988. "Violence Prediction Methods: Statistical and Clinical Strategies." *Violence and Victims* 3:303–24.

Greig, D. 1997. "Shifting the Boundary between Psychiatry and Law." *Liberty: Journal of the Victorian Council of Civil Liberties,* February.

Grisso, T., and A. J. Tomkins. 1996. "Communicating Violence Risk Assessments." *American Psychologist* 51 (9): 928–30.

Grounds, A. 1995. "Risk Assessment and Management in a Clinical Context." In *Psychiatric Patient Violence: Risk and Response,* ed. J. Crichton. London: Duckworth.

Hacking, I. 1991. *The Taming of Chance.* Cambridge: Cambridge University Press.

Harrison, G. 1997. "Risk Assessment in a Climate of Litigation." In *Assessing Risk in the Mentally Disordered,* ed. C. Duggan. Supplement 32 to the *British Journal of Psychiatry.* London: Royal College of Psychiatrists.

Home Office and DHSS. 1975. Report of the Committee on Mentally Abnormal Offenders, Cmnd. 6244. London: HMSO.

Hopwood, A. 1988. "Accounting and the Domain of the Public: Some Observations on Current Developments." The Price Waterhouse Lecture on Accounting, University of Leeds, 1985. In *Accounting from the Outside.* London: Garland.

Johnson, S., et al. 1997. *London's Mental Health: The Report to the King's Fund London Commission.* London: King's Fund.

Latour, B. 1987. *Science in Action.* Milton Keynes: Open University Press.

Lidz, C., E. Mulvey, and W. Gardner. 1993. "The Accuracy of Predictions of Violence to Others." *Journal of the American Medical Association* 269:1007–11.

Lidz, C., E. Mulvey, P. Appelbaum, and S. Cleveland. 1989. "Commitment: The Consistency of Clinicians and the Use of Legal Standards." *American Journal of Psychiatry* 146:176–81.

MacArthur (1998) The MacArthur Research Network on Mental Health and the Law Web Site. <http://www.ness.sys.virginia.edu/macarthur/violence.html>

Monahan, J. 1981. *The Clinical Prediction of Violent Behavior.* Washington, D.C.: Government Printing Office.

Morris, N., and M. Miller. 1985. "Predictions of Dangerousness: An Argument for Limited Use." *Violence and Victims* 3:263–83.

NHS Executive. 1994. Guidance on the Discharge of Mentally Disordered People and their Continuing Care in the Community, HSG(94)27. London: Department of Health.

Nietzsche, F. 1969. *On the Genealogy of Morals.* Trans. W. Kaufmann and R. J. Hollindale. New York: Vintage.

Peay, J. 1994. "Mentally Disordered Offenders." In *The Oxford Handbook of Criminology,* ed. M. Maguire, R. Morgan, and R. Reiner. Oxford: Oxford University Press.

Porter, T. 1996. *Trust in Numbers: The Invention of Objectivity.* Princeton: Princeton University Press.

Potts, J. 1995. "Risk Assessment and Management: A Home Office Perspective." In *Psychiatric Patient Violence: Risk and Response,* ed. J. Crichton. London: Duckworth.

Pratt, J. 1995. "Dangerousness, Risk and Technologies of Power." *Australia and New Zealand Journal of Criminology* 28 (1): 3–31.

———. 2000. "Sex Crime and the New Punitiveness." *Behavioral Sciences and the Law* 18:135–51.

Price, R. 1997. "On the Risks of Risk Prediction." *Journal of Forensic Psychiatry* 8:1–4.

Rabinow, P. 1982. "Artificiality and Enlightenment: From Sociobiology to Biosociality." In *Incorporations,* ed. J. Crary and J. Winter. New York, Zone.

Rose, N. 1999a. *Governing the Soul: The Shaping of the Private Self.* 2d ed. London: Free Associations.

———. 1999b. *Powers of Freedom: Reframing Political Thought.* Cambridge: Cambridge University Press.

Royal College of Psychiatrists. 1996. *Assessment and Clinical Management of Risk of Harm to Other People.* London: Royal College of Psychiatrists.

Scheingold, S., J. Pershing, and T. Olson. 1994. "Sexual Violence, Victim Advocacy and Republican Criminology." *Law and Society Review* 28 (4): 729–63.

Scott, P. 1977. "Assessing Dangerousness in Criminals." *British Journal of Psychiatry* 131:127–42.

Segal, S. P., M. A.Watson, S. M. Goldfinger, and D. S. Averbuck. 1988a. "Civil Commitment in the Psychiatry Emergency Room. I: The Assessment of Dangerousness by Emergency Room Clinicians." *Archives of General Psychiatry* 45:748–52.

———. Averbuck. 1988b. "Civil Commitment in the Psychiatry Emergency Room. II: Mental Disorder Indicators and Three Dangerousness Criteria." *Archives of General Psychiatry* 45:753–58.

Shearing, C., and P. Stenning. 1984. "From the Panopticon to Disney World: The Development of Discipline." In *Perspectives in Criminal Law,* ed. A. Doob and E. Greenspan. Aurora, Ont.: Canada Law Books.

Simon, J. 1996. "Megan's Law: Governing through Crime in a Democratic Society." Unpublished manuscript, June 1996.

———. 1997. "Governing through Crime." In *The Crime Conundrum: Essays on Criminal Justice,* ed. L. Friedman and G. Fisher. Boulder, Colo.: Westview Press.

———. 1998. "Managing the Monstrous: Sex Offenders and the New Penology." *Psychology, Public Policy and Law* 4:1–16.

Snowden, P. 1997. "Practical Aspects of Clinical Risk Assessment and Management." In *Assessing Risk in the Mentally Disordered,* ed. C. Duggan. Supplement 32 to the *British Journal of Psychiatry.* London: Royal College of Psychiatrists.

Steadman, H. J. 1973. "Some Evidence on the Inadequacy of the Concept and Determination of Dangerousness in Psychiatry and Law." *Journal of Psychiatry and Law* 1:409–26.

Steadman, H. J., and J. Cocozza. 1974. *Careers of the Criminally Insane: Excessive Social Control of Deviance.* Lexington, Mass.: Heath.

Steadman, H. J., and J. P. Morrissey. 1981. "The Statistical Prediction of Violent Behavior: Measuring the Costs of a Public Protectionist versus a Civil Libertarian Model." *Law and Human Behavior* 5:263–74.

Steadman, H. J., J. Monahan, P. Clark Robbins, et al. 1993. "From Dangerousness to Risk Assessment: Implications for Appropriate Research Strategies." In *Mental Disorder and Crime,* ed. S. Hodgins. Newbury Park, CA: Sage.

Tarasoff. 1976. Tarasoff v. Regents of the University of California, 131 Cal. Rptr, 14, 551 P.2d 334.

Walker, N. 1978. "Dangerous People." *International Journal of Law and Psychiatry* 11:37–50.

Werner, P., T. Rose, J. Yesavage, and K. Seeman. 1984. "Psychiatrists' Judgements of Dangerousness in Patients on an Acute Care Unit." *American Journal of Psychiatry* 141:263–66.

T E N

The Policing of Risk

RICHARD V. ERICSON AND KEVIN D. HAGGERTY

Risk Communication

Risk refers to such external dangers as a natural disaster, technological catastrophe, and threatening behavior by human beings. The system for communicating risk—its people, rules, formats, and technologies—is a part of the social meaning of risk. That is, threats and dangers are recognized, responded to, and made real through the human invention and use of risk classifications and technologies.

Risk-communication systems are not simply conduits through which knowledge of risk is transferred. Rather, they have their own logics and autonomous processes. They are themselves the producers of new risks, because it is through them that risks are recognized, subject to calculation, and acted upon. They govern institutional relations, and they affect what individuals and organizations are able to accomplish.

Risk society is comprised of institutions that organize on the basis of knowledge of risk. These institutions expend a significant proportion of their resources on the production and distribution of knowledge of risk. This knowledge is used to manage populations, provide security, and take risks.

The Forms of Policing

The police are at the fulcrum of risk communication among institutions. They are first and foremost knowledge workers who think and act within the risk-communication systems of other institutions. An appreciation of the changing role of police within risk-communication systems can be gleaned from an examination of changes to their official forms for reporting occurrences. Changes to the occurrence report forms of a large urban police organization we studied illustrate the shift from an open narrative format to fixed-choice risk classifications.

Before 1939 the occurrence report was simply written on a blank sheet of paper. The reporting officer was required to compose a narrative of his investigation without the aid of any classification format. The first step in formalization of the occurrence report took place in 1939 (figure 1). The neophyte form was headed "Occurrence Report" and had spaces for the date, subject, occurrence number, file number, and inspector's signature indicating approval of the narrative. But the investigating police officer was still required to compose a narrative of the "once upon a time there was a theft" variety, as is illustrated by the narrative from 1939 reproduced in figure 1. This form remained in place until the 1960s.

Figure 2 reproduces the offence report as it appeared in 1964. Here we see the beginning of enclosed formatting. There are twenty-eight items in addition to the narrative. These relate to investigative details such as the victim's profile and how the crime was carried out. Apparently safecracking was a problem at the time, as it is given its own section. Vehicular information is also singled out as relevant to investigations. In addition, there are classifications related to the nascent effort to risk-manage police officers' activities and efficiency. For example, knowledge must be provided about how the matter came to police attention ("How Received: Radio, Station, Citizen, On View"), and about its disposition ("Case Declared: Unfounded, Cleared by Arrest, Cleared Otherwise, Inactive Not Cleared, Investigation Continuing"). The narrative space is now reduced to half the page.

Figure 3 reproduces the occurrence report in use in 1981. While officers could add a "continuation report" that included a space for a narrative, figure 3 is entirely formatted in fixed-closure terms. It calls for precise detail on the offence and when it occurred, and on the modus operandi ("M.O"). It requires a detailed population profiling of victims, and an even more detailed population profiling of accused persons, suspects, and missing-person "subjects." The population of vehicles is also subject to extensive classification and validation. The population of investigating police officers is profiled by recording how they were notified about the occurrence, how they processed the case—for instance, by applying for a warrant, issuing an appearance notice to the accused, serving a subpoena, issuing a victim services card, or entering information on the CPIC (Canadian Police Information Centre) national computerized police data system—and what the outcome of the case was. This profiling is also furthered by providing space

OCCURRENCE REPORT

City Police Headquarters
Province,   May 31st. 1939

Chief Constable

Subject: Re Theft of dresses   Occ.
                                      No._____
                                      File No._____

        I beg to report that on March 23rd, 1939, Mrs [Victim]
reported the theft of three dresses to the value of $5.94, from the
soft drink counter at Woolworth's Store, these dresses were taken on
Saturday the 11th of March.

        About a week after they were taken one of the dresses was
exchanged at the dress shop where they had been purchased by [the
Victim].

        On interviewing the Clerk that had sold the dresses I
learned that a girl from Woolworth's had exchanged this dress, I took
the Clerk to Woolworth's store and she pointed out [Miss X] who was
in charge of the soft drink counter as the girl that had exchanged
it.

        [Miss X] stated that on the date the dresses were stolen a
foreign woman who was described as about 35 to 40 yrs. old, dark
comp. slim build and wearing winter clothing had spoken to her, she
asked her for her address and she said that she would send her
something from the farm, a few days later this woman sent the dress
to her asking her to return it to the dress shop, get a refund of the
money and return it to her, she sent a letter with the parcel which
[Miss X] produced when she returned the dress, this letter was
destroyed when it served it's purpose and [Miss X] stated that she
was not sure of the name but it started with P and ended with uik,
this woman lived on a farm in the district.

        [Miss X] promised to get in touch with the police when she
saw this woman again in the City, she was discharged from Woolworth's
on account of this matter and stated that she did not get a chance to
see her again.

        As [the victim] called at this Office a few days ago, Miss
X was again interviewed and gave the same story as previously
mentioned, she is living above a store, 4th Ave. and 1st St. E., she
is working in the Restaurant on the corner of 6th Ave. and 4th St. E.

        Miss X appears very anxious to get this matter cleared and
if she ever sees this woman she will notify this Dept., Mr. Y was
looking after her interests in regard to this matter.

Examined and forwarded   Respectfully submitted,

.................................Inspector   Detective.

Figure 1. Police Occurrence Report Form, 1939

CASE NO.		

OFFENCE REPORT

1. OFFENCE				2. DIVISION	3. DATE AND TIME OF THIS REPORT	
4. PLACE OF OCCURRENCE					PATROL AREA	REPORT ZONE
5. TIME OF OCCURRENCE	DAY	DATE	MONTH	YEAR	HOUR	RELIEF
6. VICTIM (IF FIRM, NAME AND TYPE OF BUSINESS)				7. HOME ADDRESS		8. HOME PHONE
				9. BUSINESS ADDRESS		10. BUS. PHONE
11. DESCRIPTION OF VICTIM	SEX	AGE	RACE OR NATIONALITY	OCCUPATION		MARITAL STATUS
12. REPORTED BY (NAME AND RELATIONSHIP TO VICTIM)				ADDRESS		PHONE

13. TYPE OF PREMISES (PREMISES USED FOR)	14. HOW ATTACKED (HOW COMMITTED—ENTRANCE GAINED)
15. MEANS OF ATTACK (WEAPONS—TOOLS USED)	16. OBJECT OF ATTACK (MOTIVE—TYPE OF PROPERTY STOLEN)

17. SAFE ATTACKED YES ☐ NO ☐	EXPLOSIVES	TORCH	PUNCH	PEEL	WORKED COMB	CARRIED AWAY	OTHER (DESCRIBE)
18. TRADE MARKS							

19. DESC. OF VEHICLE USED	YEAR	MAKE	MODEL	COLOR	LICENSE	UNUSUAL FEATURES
20. DETAILS AND WITNESSES:						

21. REPORT BY				22. ACCOMPANIED BY	23. C.I.B. PERSONNEL IN ATTENDANCE	
24. HOW RECEIVED	RADIO	STATION	CITIZEN	ON VIEW DATE AND TIME REPORTED	APPROVED BY	
CASE DECLARED	UNFOUNDED	CLRD BY ARREST	CLRD OTHERWISE	IN-ACTIVE NOT CLRD	INVSTGN. CONT.	SIGNATURE
BULLENTIN NO.	CANCELLED	CIRCULAR NO.	CANCELLED	TABULATED		TYPED BY

Figure 2. Police Occurrence Report Form, 1964

for supervisory checks, including the warning "No approval unless all facts embodied. Approving officer will be held responsible."

By the early 1990s this process of the formalization of police reports had advanced to a "paperless" computerized occurrence report system. Officers are no longer required to fill out occurrence reports by hand, but rather do

Occurrence Report

Case No.

| | 1 ☐ Committed | 2 ☐ Attempted | 3 ☐ Conspiracy | |

OCCURRENCE

How Received	R ☐ Radio S ☐ Station V ☐ On View	Date & Time Reported to Invest.	Date & Time Report Submitted by Invest.
Type of Offence		Damage Value $	For Data Entry Use Only
Place of Occurrence	Zone	DAY .... DATE .... MONTH .... YEAR .... HOUR	

VICTIM

Victim(s)	LEGAL NAME		
Business Address		Phone	Postal Code	WEAPONS USED IN ATTACK:
Home Address		Phone	Postal Code	
Description of Victim	Sex	Age or Date of Birth	Race: W/C	Occupation	Marital Status	Drunk	Impaired	Sober
Reported by	Address		Phone

MO.

| Type of Premise or Location | Exact Location at Premise | How Attacked |
| Means of Attack (tool/weapon) | Object of Attack | Trademark/Type of Drug |

VEHICLE

C ☐ Crime Vehicle   S ☐ Stolen Vehicle   L ☐ Lost (for license plates and validation tags)

Type	01 ☐ Auto 02 ☐ Bus 03 ☐ Truck 04 ☐ M/Cycle 05 ☐ Snowmobile 06 ☐ Aircraft 07 ☐ Watercraft 08 ☐ Motorized Recreation 09 ☐ Trailer Recreation 10 ☐ Trailer Utility 11 ☐ Other 12 ☐ Lic. Plate 13 ☐ Val. tag 14 ☐ Motor 15 ☐ Transmission 16 ☐ Vin. plate
Year	Make	Model	Style	Color	License #	Province	Lic. Year	Value $
Vin #/Val tag # motor transm	Distinguishing Interior Features		
Exterior	Insurance Co.	Policy #

SUBJECT INFORMATION

C ☐ Charged S ☐ Suspected M ☐ Missing	C ☐ Charged S ☐ Suspected M ☐ Missing	C ☐ Charged S ☐ Suspected M ☐ Missing
Name # 1	Name # 2	Name # 3
Address	Address	Address
Postal Code	Phone	Postal Code	Phone	Postal Code	Phone
Sex	DOB	Ht.	Wt.	Race W/C	Sex	DOB	Ht.	Wt.	Race W/C	Sex	DOB	Ht.	Wt.	Race W/C
Eye	Hair	Occupation	Eye	Hair	Occupation	Eye	Hair	Occupation
Marks, Physical Peculiarities, Clothing	Marks, Physical Peculiarities, Clothing	Marks, Physical Peculiarities, Clothing
Alias or Nickname	Alias or Nickname	Alias or Nickname
Photo #	F.P.S. #	Photo #	F.P.S. #	Photo #	F.P.S. #
Charges	Charges	Charges
Relation to Victim	Fingerprint Date	Relation to Victim	Fingerprint Date	Relation to Victim	Fingerprint Date
App. Notice #	Appearance Date	App. Notice #	Appearance Date	App. Notice #	Appearance Date
Warrant Applied For ☐ Summons ☐ Arrested ☐	Warrant Applied For ☐ Summons ☐ Arrested ☐	Warrant Applied For ☐ Summons ☐ Arrested ☐

CONCLUSION

Report by	Reg. No.	Accompanied by Reg. No.	Zone	IDENT. SECTION		Reg. No.
Case Declared	U ☐ Unfounded C ☐ Cleared by Charge O ☐ Cleared Otherwise I ☐ Inactive A ☐ Investigation Continuing	C.P.I.C. ☐	Approved	Reg. #
DO YOU WISH TO SERVE THE CIVILIAN SUBPOENAS: ☐		
Victim Services Card Issued ☐	Assigned to Zone	No Approval unless all facts embodied. Approving Officer will be held Responsible.

Figure 3. Police Occurrence Report Form, 1981

so electronically using highly specific categories and codes. Fully printed out, the present occurrence report runs to twelve pages of fixed-choice classifications.

We interviewed a veteran member of this police organization and discussed the changes that had taken place over time in report formatting. He attributed the changes to the combined effects of computerization and the demand for knowledge from external institutions:

> When I joined, the [general occurrence] report was one 8.5 by 11 [page] that was folded into three, and the boxed information would then be on that much . . . and now we're up to twelve pages. . . . Computers are driving it. The fact that we *can* now collect vast amounts of data. . . . The more information you have, the more information people want, so you gather more, so they want more, and you just keep going and going and going.

The lengthening of a given police form and the proliferation of classifications within it has been accompanied by an enormous expansion in the number and nature of forms. For example, by 1992 the Royal Canadian Mounted Police (RCMP) had, because of the many federal, provincial, and municipal government jurisdictions and private sector institutions it served, approximately twenty-one hundred operational forms and a staff of six hundred full-time knowledge workers in a special "Informatics" division.

A single new reporting requirement can have a dramatic impact on police personnel allocation and resources. For example, in England and Wales there is a requirement that all police audiotape of interviews with suspects must be summarized on a standard form. The time devoted to this one knowledge-work requirement is estimated to be equal to the full-time efforts of fourteen hundred police officers, the equivalent of about 1 percent of the entire constabulary of England and Wales (Royal Commission on Criminal Justice 1993)!

Further appreciation of how the police have embraced risk can be gleaned from considering their reporting of vehicle collisions. In figure 4 we reproduce the 1991 Alberta Collision Report Form. This form requires the police to provide fine-grained detail on the background to the collision, the parties involved, the vehicles, the vehicle owners, and road and environmental conditions at the time. It comes with a forty-eight-page *Alberta Manual on Classification and Reporting of Vehicle Collisions*, which provides highly specific coding instructions for each category and classification on the form. The form and the manual together turn the investigating officer into, in effect, a social scientist field worker guided by fixed-choice criteria designed to facilitate systematic observation. Thus formatted, the officer is bound to report the collision within the constraints imposed by the risk-relevant criteria of external institutions. Every detail of context, people, vehicles, roads, and environments is registered and subsequently

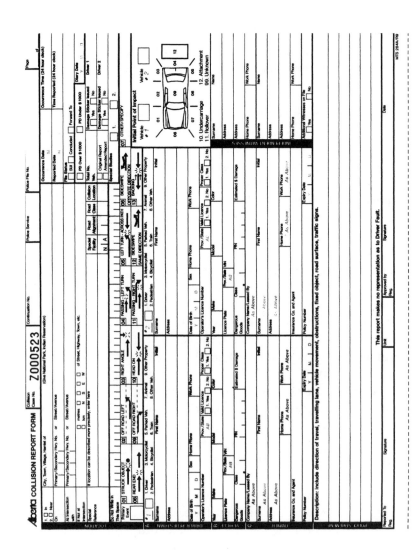

Fig. 4. Traffic Collision Report Form, 1991

Alberta COLLISION REPORT FORM   Collision Case No. **Z000523**   Police Service ___ Police File No. ___

Please Select One Item From Each Of The Sections Listed Below. (X)

Object Identification
1 2
- 01. Passenger Car
- 02. Pick-Up/Van <4500kg
- 03. Mini-Van/MPV
- 04. Truck >4500kg
- 05. Truck Tractor
- 06. Motorcycle/Scooter
- 07. Pedestrian
- 08. Bicycle
- 09. School Bus
- 10. Transit Bus
- 11. Intercity Bus
- 12. Other Bus
- 13. Fixed Object
- 14. Train
- 15. Animal
- 16. Motorhome
- 17. Construction Equipment
- 18. Emergency Vehicle
- 19. Farm Equipment
- 20. Off-Highway Vehicle
- 21. Motorized Snow Vehicle
- 22. Moped
- 98. Other/Specify
- 99. Unknown

Light Conditions (Choose one in A and one in B)

A
1 2
- 01. Daylight
- 02. Sunglare
- 03. Darkness
- 99. Unknown

B
1 2
- 01. No Artificial Light
- 02. Artificial Light
- 99. Unknown

Traffic Control Device
1 2
- 01. None Present
- 02. Traffic Signal/Lights
- 03. Stop Sign
- 04. Yield Sign
- 05. Merge Sign
- 06. Pedestrian Cross-Walk
- 07. School Bus
- 08. Lane Control Signal
- 09. RR Crossing
- 98. Other/Specify
- 99. Unknown

Contributing Road Condition
1 2
- 01. No Unusual Condition
- 02. Under Const./Maint.
- 03. Hole/Ruts/Bumps
- 04. Slippery When Wet
- 05. Oily Pavement
- 06. Soft/Sharp Shoulder
- 98. Other/Specify
- 99. Unknown

Environmental Condition
1 2
- 01. Clear
- 02. Raining
- 03. Hail/Sleet
- 04. Snow
- 05. Fog/Smog/Smoke/Dust
- 06. High Wind
- 98. Other/Specify
- 99. Unknown

Surface Condition
1 2
- 01. Dry
- 02. Wet
- 03. Slush/Snow/Ice
- 04. Loose Surface Mat.
- 05. Muddy
- 98. Other/Specify
- 99. Unknown

INSTRUCTIONS

This form is **NOT** to be used if there has been **A FATALITY OR INJURY, A HIT AND RUN CRASH, OR A CRASH INVOLVING A NATIONAL SAFETY CODE VEHICLE** (school bus, truck >4500 kg, truck tractor).

PLEASE HAVE YOUR DRIVER'S LICENCE, VEHICLE REGISTRATION, INSURANCE (PINK) CARD, AND THE VEHICLE WHICH WAS INVOLVED IN THE COLLISION WHEN REPORTING TO THE POLICE.

EACH DRIVER SHALL COMPLETE EITHER THE BLUE OR YELLOW SECTIONS OF THIS FORM ONLY.

A. DRIVER INFORMATION
   OPERATOR LICENCE NUMBER - This number should appear on the top portion of your
   Alberta Driver's Licence (Example: 123456-999):

B. VEHICLE INFORMATION
   Please take the following information from your vehicle registration documents:

   YEAR: Enter the year of vehicle using the last two digits only. ("86" for a 1986 vehicle)
   MAKE MODEL: EXAMPLE: Ford Bronco or Chev Camaro.
   COLOR: Enter the color(s) of the vehicle as per registration.
   LICENCE PLATE: This is the plate number on your vehicle.
   VIN: This is your vehicle identification number found on your vehicle registration.
   This number is a long one, please make sure you have copied it correctly.

C. WHO OWNS THIS VEHICLE?
   Please use your insurance pink card to assist you in completing the following:
   Owner Name and Address.
   Insurance Co./Agent:
   Write the name of the insurance company and the agent in this area.
   For example: XXX Insurance Inc., Protect Agencies Inc.
   Policy Number: Write the policy number from the area on the pink card.

D. Please select only ONE item from each of the sections listed: Check only the one which best describes.

♻ Printed on Recycled Paper

POLICE COPY

Fig. 4. *Continued*

risk profiled to ascertain the norm and the anomaly. That is, the job of the police, and of all other institutions connected with the collision event, is to ensure that the event is interpreted in terms of whether it is or is not a "normal accident," for a "normal accident" is no accident at all but, indeed, a collision.

Myriad institutions require knowledge of collisions as part of their risk-management systems, and they each influence the risk-communication format of this collision report. For example, the government motor vehicles registry requires risk knowledge regarding driver records, traffic engineering problems, collision prevention, and automobile industry compliance with safety standards. The automobile industry requires risk knowledge regarding the safety of its vehicles for compliance and product improvement. Insurance companies require risk knowledge to allocate liability in the particular case, develop risk ratings for drivers and vehicles in general, establish premium and deductible levels, establish levels of compensation, and undertake collision prevention initiatives. The criminal courts require risk knowledge if the collision results from a driving-related offense. Last and least, the police administration requires risk knowledge to measure the productivity records of its officers and to allocate resources.

The Police and Crime Risks

Risk communication is central to all aspects of police work. The police are not only involved in law enforcement, order maintenance, and social service, but in all of these roles they are also knowledge workers engaged in the production and distribution of knowledge of risk.

Risk-communication work certainly takes up a lot more police time and has greater salience than criminal law enforcement. For example, in an analysis of British Crime Survey data, Skogan (1990:9) found that the activity that required the most police time with citizens was the exchange of information, either citizens giving police noncrime related information (16 percent of contacts) or asking police for information (23 percent of contacts). Reporting crime accounted for only 18 percent of contacts.

It is extremely rare for a patrol officer to encounter a serious crime in progress (Clarke and Hough 1984). While patrol officers are proactive, it is mainly to obtain knowledge about possible suspects who appear out of place and time, or for regulatory matters such as traffic and liquor violations (Ericson 1982). Reactive calls for police services are also mainly about noncriminal matters. Up to 75 percent of calls for service are screened out without being forwarded to patrol officers for further action (Jorgensen 1981; Manning 1988). Even when there is a crime call, what operators define as serious crime is changed by officers to a minor incident or no crime in one-third to one-half of all instances (Comrie and Kings 1975; Ericson 1982; Manning 1988). What officers often find at the scene is not serious crime but a kaleidoscope of trouble that requires them to provide some combination of counsel, assistance, expertise, coercion, referral, and persuasion, and to make a report (Cumming, Cumming, and Edell 1965; Ericson 1982). For patrol officers, at least, direct involvement in crime work takes up as little as 3 percent of their working time (Comrie and Kings 1975; Ericson 1982).

There are, of course, criminal investigation specialists in police organizations—detectives—who devote all their time to crime work. However, detectives also spend relatively little time on direct criminal investigation. Draper (1978:31) estimated that only about 10 percent of the investigator's time was spent this way. Ericson (1993:45) found that detectives spent almost half their time in the office and that much more time was devoted to recording investigative activities than to actual investigation work.

On average, a patrol officer in Canada records one indictable crime occurrence a week, makes one indictable crime arrest every three weeks, and secures one indictable crime conviction every nine months (McMahon 1992). Even in New York City, which has an extraordinary high rate of serious crime, officers spend a relatively small amount of time dealing with crime and capturing criminals. Walsh (1986) found that among 156 patrol officers assigned to a high-crime area in New York City, 40 percent did not make a single felony arrest in a year and 69 percent made no more than three felony arrests in a year.

The police simply have an incapacity to do much about crime directly. This incapacity is related to the institution of privacy, which limits them in developing evidence to detect and solve cases (Stinchcombe 1963; Reiss 1987). They are also limited by their own resources and by a criminal justice system that is designed more to divert cases than to prosecute fully or heavily.

Attrition within the criminal justice is captured in figures 5 and 6. These data derive from the criminal statistics for England and Wales and 1994 British Crime Survey (Barclay, Tavaras, and Prout 1995). Figure 5 shows that for a range of crimes against individuals and their property—including criminal damage, theft of a motor vehicle, theft from a motor vehicle (including attempts), bicycle theft, domestic burglary, wounding, robbery, and theft from the person—less than half (47 percent) are reported to the police and only 27 percent are actually recorded by the police. Only 4.9 percent are cleared up by police after investigation. A mere 2.7 percent are

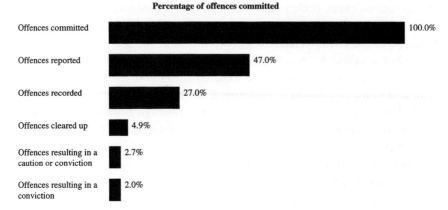

Fig. 5. Attrition within the Criminal Justice System: Crimes against Individuals and Their Property (criminal damage; theft of a motor vehicle; theft from a motor vehicle, including attempts; bicycle theft; domestic burglary; wounding; robbery; theft from the person)

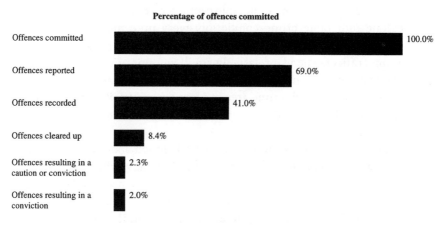

Fig. 6. Attrition within the Criminal Justice System: Domestic Burglary

cleared by either a police caution of the suspect or conviction of an offender, and 2.0 percent result in the conviction of an offender. Figure 6 shows that for domestic burglary, 69 percent are reported to the police but only 41 percent are actually recorded by them. Moreover, only 8.4 percent are cleared up by police after investigation, with 2.3 percent resulting in either a police caution of the suspect or conviction of an offender, and 2.0 percent resulting in the conviction of an offender.

Given such a low clearance rate for property crimes, the main task of the police is to provide good risk-management data for insurance purposes. The occurrence reports themselves are designed to suit the risk-knowledge requirements of insurance companies, and in many jurisdictions the insurance companies pay for the police reports they obtain. A police official engaged in negotiation with insurers over the change of occurrence reports said to us in interview, "Insurance companies now pay to get their form and so the form should look more like something they are buying rather than just a photocopy of something we are providing them—how to put it so that it could be more logical for insurance companies because they're actually the external customer."

In the management of property crime, the criminal law and its enforcement apparatus gives way to insurance law and its risk-management regime. Insurance law, embodied in property insurance contracts, provides a series of inducements for the householder or commercial property owner to become self-policing agents of preventive security. Premium levels, deductibles, exclusion, and policy limits all turn property holders into watchers as well as the watched, and the bearers of their own control. Insurance law steps in where criminal law is unable to meet the needs of the parties concerned, and the police become risk-knowledge brokers to the insurance system. As O'Malley (1991:172) remarks in analyzing this situation in the Australian context, "To protect its profits, especially against forms of moral hazard that are not prohibited under criminal law (and thus potentially subject to state policing), the insurance company must establish its own legal order within the framework of the insurance contract. The insurance contract (and more recently, the law of insurance contracts) establishes the coercive conditions for the operation of an enforcement network aimed at disciplining householders, in order to minimize the assumed moral hazard." A leading actuarial scientist in Canada described in an interview how, over the past fifteen years, this disciplining of property holders has intensified to the point where more and more responsibility for self-policing of risks resides with the individual insured:

> The whole idea of insurance works on the pooling of risk. . . . Those categories of the collective were very broad even fifteen years ago. . . . You'd have to have a couple of claims in a short period of time to see your premium change very much. Now it is going with the philosophy of the rest of society that you are responsible. . . . The whole concept of a pure accident is almost disappearing. There is no pure accident anymore. If you have a claim, you are partially at fault. And you need to change risk categories. . . . [This is a] move to more and more slicing and

TABLE I   Recorded Crime, Convictions, and Cautions: England and Wales, 1976, 1986, 1996

Year	Indictable Offenses Recorded by the Police	Clearance Rate %	Indictable Convictions	Indictable Cautions
1976	2,135,700	43	415,503	97,671
1986	3,847,410	32	384,000	137,000
1996	5,036,550	26	300,600	190,800

SOURCE: Adapted from Ashworth 2001. Data derived from Criminal Statistics, England and Wales 1976, 1986, 1996.

> individualization, and more and more passing the responsibility back to the claimant. If it goes too far people will say this isn't insurance anymore. . . . As soon as I have a claim my insurance goes up. So over the next six years I pay the claim. Well heck, I can run my bank account to do that.

One might think that while the police face major limitations in detecting crime, they can be efficient in taking cases to prosecution when they do manage to apprehend a suspect. However, even when suspects are apprehended and can be prosecuted, very often they are not (Royal Commission on Criminal Justice 1993:82; McConville 1993:86; Meehan 1993). Rather, there is an effort to "define deviance down" (Moynihan 1992) by diverting cases to other institutions such as families, schools, restorative justice facilities, and so on. For example, Ashworth (2001) records "the decline of English sentencing," as shown in table 1.

While there has been an almost 250 percent increase in indictable offenses recorded by the police between 1976 and 1996, the police clearance by arrest rate has decreased considerably from 43 percent in 1976 to 32 percent in 1986 to 26 percent in 1996. During the same period the absolute number of indictable convictions decreased from 415,503 in 1976 to 384,000 in 1986 and 300,600 in 1996. On the other hand the rate of police cautions rose considerably, from 97,681 in 1976 to 137,000 in 1986 and 190,800 in 1996.

Other data presented by Ashworth (2001) indicate that in 1996, 60 percent of all male juvenile offenders and 80 percent of all female juvenile offenders were cautioned by the police rather than prosecuted. Among males eighteen to twenty years old, 35 percent were cautioned, and for females in the same age range the cautionary rate was 50 percent. Male offenders twenty-one and older were subject to cautions rather than prosecution 26 percent of the time, while females over twenty-one were cautioned 44 percent of the time. Ashworth also observes that "these are only the options available to the police; it would be wrong to overlook the various forms of diversion employed by the tax authorities, Her Majesty's Customs, local councils, and the many inspectorates (health and safety, pollution, etc.) which have the power to prosecute."

The Police as Risk Communicators

Whether dealing with crime, vehicle collisions, regulatory matters, social service, or public order, the police operate as a center of calculation (Latour 1987) for the risk-communication systems of myriad institutions. As such, police mobilization is not only a matter of intervention in the lives of individual citizens, but is also reactive to institutional demands for knowledge of risk. They are required to intersect with, and broker knowledge to and from, a full range of institutions in the risk-communication network.

In large police organizations there is a coterie of specialists who manage the vast and complex systems of risk communication. For example, the aforementioned RCMP Informatics division with six hundred full-time personnel has a highly specialized division of labor to manage its risk-communication systems. There are telecommunications engineers, information technology specialists, and information system auditors. These risk-communication operators work within the framework of rules compiled in four thick manuals that total sixteen hundred pages. A lot of attention is focused on authorizing acceptable forms. This includes detection and elimination of "bootleg forms" developed by individual officers to meet their pragmatic needs but that do not fit the system's needs. It also includes policing the classifications used and narratives produced.

At each station level there are editorial control systems in place to patrol the facts. These systems detect any interpretive leakage that has occurred in spite of the use of closed formats. We observed a station-level operation in which patrol officers' reports were initially reviewed by their supervisor for completeness and accuracy. The supervisor would also assign a "diary date," usually set for two weeks after the initial review, for reviewing the file again. At the time of the second review the supervisor could keep the file open by assigning a new diary date, or close it. When a file was closed, the supervisor "scored" it in terms of fixed-choice classifications that satisfied various users within the police organization and in external institutions. An internal report on patrol supervisors' responsibilities estimated that 70–80 percent of their time was spent checking reports.

Once a supervisor completed the scoring, the file was passed on to a "reader" for further editorial scrutiny. The reader was a full-time police officer whose sole function was to review the files once again to ensure that everything was filled out completely and accurately, and that the scoring was correct. The reader functioned only as a data checker and could not, for example, reject a file and ask for further investigation. From the reader a file would go to a data entry clerk, who would again check the completeness of the file and competence of the scoring and seek clarification of any slippage.

In selected cases there was further cleansing of the data. For example, all sexual assault, domestic violence, and major crime files were sent to the second-in-command at the station for additional scrutiny. This officer also conducted random checks on other files. A police officer described this task as one that was "concerned with how the files are taken care of. He [the second-in-command] is also concerned on the administrative side with how the file is scored because if it is not scored properly then it is going to reflect back on him at audit time."

Some of the reports reviewed by the second-in-command had to be reviewed further by form managers at the division level. In such cases a form was filled out to flag the fact that a file needed further review and data cleansing. This was designed to ensure the appearance of uniform reporting across the police organization, especially in high-profile cases. A police officer observed that in such instances, "[y]our supervisor reads your work, the sergeant checks his work, staff sergeant looks after him, the commanding officer inspects all of it. Now it goes to another group of people and they inspect it. If they find anything they send it back. You have so many people checking up on what I do on the street it makes it kind of repetitive all of the time."

In addition to this complex system for case-by-case editing and data cleansing, this police organization had various communication format auditors. There were, for example, division-level auditing teams that spent a week in each station reviewing the quality of data entry. A division-level officer involved in this process said that the main task was a random audit of files "to make sure they have all the necessary information fields they're supposed to have, compared to the computer printout"; a 5 percent margin of error was allowed. The division also had file auditors in its field-support information unit, who on a three-year cycle audited every recordkeeper in every station. They served, in effect, as supervisors of station-level coders with respect to the reliability and validity of the coders' data collection.

Of course there are still murmurings among the police that information work as the means has become an end in itself, interfering with "crime fighting" as the "real" end of police work. But in the vast majority of cases information work is all there is to it. It is both the means and the end of police work, and the reason why there is such an obsession with the production of clean data.

Police Mobilization and Knowledge Production

The police think and act in relation to the communication formats of external institutions that demand knowledge of risk. As a result, they are mobilized not in terms of consensual order, as criminal law theory would suggest, but rather in terms of the different risk logics of the institutions with which they communicate. In this respect, something only becomes actionable as police work if it fits in the risk-knowledge requirements of external institutions.

This view of police-knowledge work differs sharply from existing research on police organizations that emphasizes how the police produce knowledge for their own *internal* management purposes. Researchers have focused on how line officers do their paperwork with an eye toward "covering ass" in their dealings with their supervisors (Manning 1980; Ericson 1982, 1993; Chatterton 1991). When studies go beyond the immediate gate-keeping aspects of street-level decisionmaking, they still remain within the police institution and examine only the internal flow of knowledge (Manning 1988; Chatterton 1989; Southgate and Mirless-Black 1991). Knowledge is rarely seen as moving beyond the police institution, only into it, across it, and up it. In this police-centered vision of knowledge work, the possibility of a communication environment outside the police institution is not even imagined. Chatterton even makes the extraordinary claim that the police "have not been information driven. On the contrary they have made information police property. They have interpreted it in accordance with their own interests and within their own cultural assumptions and typifications. Information has been used to achieve rather than to set objectives" (1991:8).

The focus on police mobilization as a response to external institutional demands for knowledge of risk is also contrary to the view that police work is of "low visibility." Because of their police-centric vision and their emphasis on knowledge reproduction and distribution for internal management purposes, researchers have emphasized secrecy and low visibility in police work. Following Goldstein's (1960) seminal formulation, researchers continue to contend that "most police decisions are virtually invisible or of low visibility" and that "[s]ecrecy is emphasized . . . . information is rarely shared" (Manning 1992:357, 370; see also Geller and Morris 1992; Chatterton 1983; Reiss 1982:146). To the contrary, in the context of demands from external institutions, the police engage in numerous kinds of institutionalized *publicity* that make their work an exercise in high visibility.

As risk communicators to various institutional audiences, the police not only distribute knowledge widely but also make their own actions highly visible in producing that knowledge. High visibility is augmented by auditing; computer terminals in police cars; surveillance cameras in patrol cars, police stations and mass private property sites; and electronic filing of occurrence reports. Every new technology for the surveillance of populations is also a technology for the surveillance of the population of police. As in other knowledge-based occupations, the police worker, in the very act of producing and distributing the knowledge needed to get the job done, also produces and distributes knowledge about his or her work (Ericson and Shearing 1986; Poster 1990, 1995).

Institutions beyond Criminal Justice

The risk-communication view of policing we are advancing here obviously de-centers the criminal law and criminal justice aspects of police work. Much of the demand from other institutions is for knowledge of risk that does not relate to crime (for example, vehicle collisions, missing person, unwell person, safety education in schools). Moreover, much of the knowledge about crime is produced for institutions other than criminal justice (for example, insurance, health, education, welfare). As documented earlier, the vast majority of cases are diverted away from the criminal justice institution, even when prosecution is possible. These cases are left to be handled by other institutions within their own risk-management systems, albeit with the aid of risk knowledge communicated by the police.

At the same time the criminal justice institution itself has moved in the direction of actuarial justice (Feeley and Simon 1994). There has been a proliferation of risk-assessment technologies to decide who to select for surveillance, arrest, bail, special prosecution, penal regimes, jury duty, victims programs, and so on (Royal Commission on Criminal Justice 1993; Ericson 1994b; Ericson and Haggerty 1997; Garland 1996, 1997; O'Malley 1998). The focus in criminal justice becomes the efficient production and distribution of risk knowledge for the management of populations of victims, informants, suspects, accused, and offenders.

In this context, the law of criminal procedure can be reread as providing the coercion necessary to meet the actuarial justice system's needs for knowledge of risk. The substantial erosion of rights of suspects in recent years (Royal Commission on Criminal Justice 1993; McConville and Bridges 1994), for example, can be understood as part of the wider decline of innocence (Ericson 1994a) in risk society, whereby the surveillance system's right to knowledge gains legal as well as pragmatic preference over individual due process rights that force the system to gather evidence un-aided. Compulsory DNA testing, erosion of the right to silence, and reduc-tion in accused rights to trial election options all signify the new emphasis on risk-knowledge production and control by policing authorities in risk so-ciety.

Compliance Law Enforcement within Private Policing Systems

External institutions have their own private policing systems that are based on preventative security arrangements and administrative compliance. These systems for policing risk are much more elaborate, and have greater technological and personnel resources, than the public police (Shearing and Stenning 1983; Shearing 1992; Johnston 1992, 1997; Loader 1999). A brief consideration of the private policing systems of retail stores and of insurance companies illustrates the policing of risk in conjunction with, and beyond, the public police (Haggerty and Ericson 1999, 2000).

In the city of Oxford, England, all downtown retail stores have full-time security officers. The security officers in each store are linked to their coun-terparts in other stores through a radio communication system that also is connected to the local police station. These security officers spend a good part of each day watching customers on surveillance cameras, and they use the video evidence from these cameras to proceed against shoplifters. In many cases the store goods are electronically tagged to trigger an alarm at the store entrance should a shoplifter proceed that far. The private security operatives and their surveillance cameras extend to the public streets out-side their stores, so that they also police the downtown public space during the hours of store opening. They do all the work of preventative security, public order policing, detection, apprehension, arrest, rights cautioning, production of evidence, and statement taking. The police only enter the picture when called upon to do so, and then only to refine the information on the offender and offense for brokerage to other institutions.

As introduced earlier, private insurance companies are a key institution of preventative security as they discipline property holders into being self-policing agents. There is no doubt that the retail security arrangements in Oxford described above are heavily influenced by insurance contract stipu-lations. Property insurance companies often undertake security inspec-tions, making every potential property crime victim also a *suspect*, that is, suspected of not doing enough to reduce the risk of loss. Moreover, every ac-tual property crime victim is also treated as an insurance *offender*. As an of-fender, she or he is likely to suffer one or more costly penalties on an escalating scale: higher premiums, higher deductible levels, more exclusion clauses, lower insurance limits, cancellation of the policy, and "redlining" as a bad risk to the point where no insurer can be found (Squires 1997).

Insurance fraud is typically dealt with by external compliance systems and very rarely dealt with by criminal prosecution (Ericson, Barry and Doyle 2000). There are many reasons why an insurance adjuster or investigator must tread lightly even when a fraudulent claim is suspected. First, there is often a great deal of ambiguity regarding the evidence for what is claimed. Exaggeration or soft fraud is easy to visualize but difficult to investigate and take action against. Second, in an industry where the operating philosophy is moral utilitarianism and therefore the supreme value is efficiency, it is often judged more expedient to make "nuisance payments" to claimants rather than investigate their suspected fraudulent claims. Furthermore, the loss can be absorbed in future higher premiums to the claimant and across the pool of insured persons. Third, and pervading the above considerations, is public relations. The claims process is also part of the sales process, since "all that an insurance company has to sell is its promise to pay" (Baker 1994:1401). Indeed, an insurance company may want to keep its dishonest customers because they continue to pay premiums that the company needs to invest and make profits. It is sometimes easier not to bite the hand that feeds, even if one's own hand is nibbled at from time to time.

There is an obvious tension, if not contradiction, in the compliance-oriented private policing of insurance relationships. On the one hand, as we have seen, anyone with a stake in a private property insurance relationship is contractually induced into participating in loss reduction, and penalized for failures. On the other hand a great deal of fraud and other loss through moral hazard is tolerated and even fostered in insurance relationships. As Garland (1997) observes, part of the responsibility of being *homo prudens* in risk society is to recognize which losses are not only inevitable but necessary for the smooth flow of social and economic life. Surveillance for preventive security has limits, as does law enforcement. "Precisely because crime occurs in the course of routine social and economic transactions, crime reducing intervention must seek to preserve 'normal life' and 'business as usual.' The characteristic modes of intervening involve the implantation of non-intrusive controls in the situation, or else attempts to modify the interests of the actors involved" (Garland 1997:87).

In compliance-oriented systems of risk management, such as insurance, the police are relegated to a secondary role as front-end suppliers of risk knowledge. They give insurance investigators routine and full access to police files, a legislated requirement in some insurance fields in Canada. They produce data on loss situations, and on people who create opportunities for loss, via occurrence and vehicle collision reports. Increasingly police involvement in this regard is minimized through self-reporting systems (for example, victim voice entry; self-report forms for minor vehicle collisions), or reports taken only by police clerical staff (for example, for thefts). In one large urban police organization we studied, one-quarter of complaints are recorded without even dispatching a patrol officer. As an officer from this organization explained, "People will call in the theft of an item. They know there isn't a hope in hell of finding it and they really don't have an interest in reporting it to the police, but they know they can't get their insurance claim until they do report it to the police. It's a paper exercise."

Governing through Crime

While the police can do little to control crime directly, and are primarily brokers of knowledge about crime and other risks to external institutions, they are nevertheless a central agency of government (Rose 1999). Indeed, their participation in the risk-communication systems of external institutions has made them part of those institutions and their modes of governance. Crime risk, and fear of it, has become the basis for police involvement in governance well beyond crime control itself. In addition to the governing of crime, there is governing through crime (Simon 1997). Crime risk, and fear of it, is the basis for proliferating surveillance systems in those public spaces and social institutions that the police still have jurisdiction over. Police involvement in public contact surveillance systems, public schools, watch programs, and missing persons registries are illustrative.

Census Taking

The "contact card" is the most pervasive device for police governance of populations. It is used to report police observations of people suspected of being out of place or associating with undesirables. Patrol officers are required to satisfy quotas for the submission of contact cards. The cards are sent to analysts who computerize the data and prepare and distribute profiles of suspect populations and their proper places.

Computer terminals in police vehicles permit the electronic entry of street-check information. This technological innovation has, along with increased quota expectations, encouraged greater numbers of random checks. In the eyes of police officers who have computer terminals, it has created the potential for more pervasive and systematic inspection of populations that appear out of place. As one patrol officer said:

> You can program into this machine a street check . . . whereas before I wouldn't have bothered filling out a form . . . because they were time consuming, a pain in the ass and nobody ever bothered to do anything with them. . . . What we are doing is a proactive patrol . . . go out in residential areas . . . and just write down anything suspicious. Vehicles, young fellow walking down the road at two o'clock in the morning. . . . [Computers] increase our street checks something like 700 percent. . . . [Previously] there was no way we could keep track of who was on the go. Now you do your street check, stop a specific car in a neighborhood at four o'clock in the morning and someone may find out that that night there was a specific break [burglary] or car broken into. You can go back and check this person and maybe they are responsible. The more people you know who are moving or who are on the go then the more people you are keeping track of. . . . We do the subdivision areas late at night and just kind of sneak around and park on the side of the road to see who is moving and do spot checks [on] who is driving or walking.

Another contact card system provides a means of tracing populations that reside in targeted residential areas. Inquiry forms are used to record systematic data on householders interviewed in connection with a crime or other risk in an area. In one police jurisdiction we studied, the attending officer was required to complete a form for each person in the household aged fourteen or older, which had spaces for, among other things, name, marital status, vehicle ownership, occupation and employer, name and address of ex-spouse, and number of persons living in adjacent houses (adult males, adult females, and children). The form included an admonition to the officer to "Be alert for spontaneous response." In light of the very low clearance rate in residential burglaries, police officers viewed this brand of police census taking as a tracking device for possible future use, rather than as a means of solving the crime that initiated the inquiry. As one interviewee remarked, "You have to check with neighbors on the left side and on the right and across the street. To some people that seems like a pain in the ass and you are not going to find anything, but we have found very often that you may be looking for the guy who is across the street down the road. And all of a sudden you have that in your computer."

School Programs

The police have a long history of serving as risk experts in schools. In particular they visit schools to provide instruction on traffic safety and personal security. Larger municipal police organizations usually have full-time officers dedicated to such education. Their role often extends to overseeing and evaluating school safety-patrol units.

Police education efforts in schools have broadened in recent years. Society's obsession with the risks of drugs has placed drug education on school curricula, and the police are brought in as experts. Some police organizations have full-time "drug awareness" officers who lecture in schools and elsewhere.

We studied a primary-school program staffed by four full-time police officers and a social worker who was also a police employee. The social worker was initially hired to help the police gain acceptance in the schools. The original justification of the program was the need for education about the risks of delinquent activity, especially the use of illegal drugs, but the program rapidly expanded into other areas. A person involved with the program explained the place of the educational component in relation to concerns about risk and security, exemplifying how crime is used as the basis for broader forms of governance:

> Drugs are the medium . . . but we've got programs that talk about self-esteem, problem solving, peer pressure. . . . [Drugs are] something that's in the news and in the media and all that kind of stuff, so it's a good way to catch kids' attention. . . . There's this concern in school about violence now. . . . And I predict that pretty soon the people that make the videos will pick up on that as a medium and develop some good programs to deal with it . . . [but] the underlying message is always the same . . . to get the students familiar with the officer who will be in the school. . . . The real thing that we're trying to do is to be accessible to the students and to the parents and the teachers. . . . A kid blows up . . . calm him down and get him back to the classroom. The teaching staff don't have time to do it.

"High needs" or high-risk schools were identified based on an epidemiological analysis of a whole range of population health problems such as truancy, poor nutrition, misbehavior at school, and crime. This selection of school organizations was followed by a selection, using the same criteria, of high-risk students. An official publication of the police organization was clear on this risk-management approach, stating that the program offered "outreach services to selected elementary schools . . . identifying children (primarily in grades 4, 5 and 6) who are experiencing problems, and assisting with the coordination of a multi-agency effort to help these children and their families."

High-risk children were identified by a wide range of informants. There was input from officials in health and welfare agencies, from teachers and school counselors, and from parents. Home visits were sometimes deemed necessary. The children themselves were primary informants, often relating problems that were not school-specific. A program official stressed that "students and their parents . . . can access the officer about anything they want. And they don't necessarily have to let the school know. We've got disclosures of sexual abuse, physical abuse from kids. And we've got parents coming seeking information on marriage separation, wife battering, husband battering. . . . The officers can make referrals to any community agency. . . . We advise the [school] principal that we've done that."

Members of the unit kept notes on potential high-risk children, and used a student-profile form to rate welfare history, school history, special problems, contact with other agencies, and family criminal history. The various knowledges were brought together at case conference sessions attended by the schools' police officer and staff as well as representatives of other agencies. Higher-risk students were identified and marked down for counseling by outside agencies or the school police officer. One such officer remarked that counseling was provided

> in the sense of trying to find out what the problem is. And then get the students and the family to the resource that can best deal with the problem. . . . There's some students that are more behavior problems. The student is taken out of class and actually spends some time with them [a police officer] one-on-one, playing board games. We've got some officers doing, building models with groups of kids . . . who have trouble interacting with their peers. . . . If these kids can be truly identified at the early stage, and if they can establish some sort of bond with a police officer, maybe they will think twice about the person they might be letting down if they go out and get in trouble.

The three dozen or so most risky individuals were placed in a risk-management system set up to track them throughout their school careers.

An official police statement on the program emphasized that "the officer's effectiveness is enhanced if he/she is viewed as being a member of the school staff." According to one police official, officers in the program were indeed viewed as school staff: "[officers are] part of the staff almost . . . get consulted . . . participate in the . . . school resource group . . . case conferencing . . . the problems can be academic behavior, whatever. . . . The officer might have a role to play, an equal role to play in the school. They really have worked their way into more of a, almost staff position, an extra resource. The resource just happens to wear a uniform and have a different viewpoint."

We also studied a high-school program that was staffed by twelve full-time uniformed officers and a sergeant who were stationed across the twelve largest high schools in the city. This program had many of the features of the primary-school program. There was extensive classroom instruction on crime, police, the law, driver education, bicycle safety, anger management, and suicide. In addition, the high-school police officers sought opportunities to integrate police instruction into courses in the academic curriculum. For example, a police traffic management specialist was brought into mathematics class to show how formulas and measurements were part of practical police work. In keeping with their strong sense of what counts in risk society, the program staff kept accurate records of all this activity. In a twelve-month period they recorded 812 presentations to a total of 27,009 students.

These presentations had several purposes and effects. They provided knowledge about legal institutions and processes, helped to promote the sensibility that the police are problem solvers, and stimulated new problems for them to solve. A program officer related that after recent presentations there were "now four people we've identified with suicidal problems in those classes and I helped to set straight."

The high-school officers worked to establish trusting relationships with individual students in the hope that those relationships would eventually pay off in the currency the police value most—risk-relevant knowledge. An officer described his risk-knowledge work in this way:

> I want to get involved with the new ones on a one-to-one basis so if they have a need then they'll come to me without being intimidated or scared, or [concerned] that I'm going to publicly announce what they come in to see me about. When they come in to see me I always have my window-blind down so nobody can see in. I have to give them that confidentiality when they're with me . . . there's always that stigma attached to [seeing me] . . . a student wants to see me behind [closed doors] in my office, confidential matters. I also provide that *service* to them. In fact, just this week I had one, was very startling actually. She had information on a major hydroponic operation in the city and we're dealing with that as an informant.

Crime Stoppers had a limited presence in the schools through wall posters. There was a desire by some, however, to have a full-time, student-based Crime Stoppers operation. Others argued that this approach would make the informant-centered nature of the police presence too obvious. A compromise was reached by setting up a school watch program, which one interviewee described as helping to

> make the students responsible for the security of their school. It's similar but not the same as Crime Stoppers. There's no reward for it. If there's something going on in the school that somebody sees, then they'll report it. There's going to be a box set up where they can put the information in a box, slide [us anonymous tips]. . . . So they will look after the security of the school. And then, if there's something that we can grab and run with it, that's what we'll do. We'll charge somebody or have it ground out for investigation if it's in the community.

The community policing ideal of making everyone responsible for his or her own security permeated the school program. School staff were regarded as security agents, as an embodiment of Sir Robert Peel's notion that "the police are the public and the public are the police." A school police officer said of school teachers, "They're security guards also, not just me . . . [and] I'm not just a uniform walking around here. . . . I am a staff member. We're all staff members. . . . I'm just like anybody else . . . we all deal with the same problems." This conception of security collaboration enabled the police to naturalize their role in the educational institution. A school police officer said that his ability to maintain security depended on his ability to blend into the school environment and thereby to cultivate informants: "[Cultivating informants] depends on how much visibility you have in the school, and I make a point of walking around, dropping in on classes just so they know I'm there. . . . Staff at the school I work with don't have a problem with that."

Watch Programs

Police-fostered watch programs have proliferated in myriad school, business, residential, and other public settings. These programs mobilize the inhabitants of local territories to become reflexive with respect to risks. Reflexivity is not only intended to prevent crime and capture criminals but also to help inhabitants confront their emotional responses to risk and to become responsible for governing their own territories. This sensibility is exemplified in a Block Watch brochure that says the program is designed to help people deal with their fears, as well as with crime, through intensive territorial surveillance that includes self-policing: "[Block Watch is] to deter *fear* and incidence of crime . . . through saturation . . . increase the identification and reporting of suspicious activities . . . [and] provide

neighborhood cohesiveness. . . . [G]etting to know your neighbors . . .
works best in low transient population communities. . . . [Block Watch re-
quires] an observant eye for any unusual activity and common sense precautions. . . . Crime prevention is not a series of lectures but a part of daily
life."

One large urban police organization we studied ensured that crime prevention, among other governmental tasks, was made part of daily life by introducing a computerized version of Block Watch. Known as the Personal
Computer Community Organization Prevention System, or PCCOPS, this
program is based on a computerized telephone dialing system that automatically sends out prerecorded messages to member residents. In a jurisdiction we studied, eight divisional police stations had acquired the system.
In one division there were approximately thirteen thousand residents and
fifteen hundred businesses in the contact databases. The program was
"mapped" onto neighborhood units of about three hundred telephone numbers in each unit. The system operated four lines, each capable of making
four calls at once, which allowed up to 320 three-minute calls to go out each
hour.

People who sign up for the program receive messages that begin, "It's
the City Police—Neighborhood Watch Computer—Dialed Alert Calling."
They receive "alert calls" regarding risks such as recent criminal acts,
threats posed by rabid animals, and lost children. They also receive "information calls" reminding them of their responsibility for managing their
own risks. Other functions include informing people about upcoming
Neighborhood Watch meetings and in some cases about inconveniences
such as public works programs.

PCCOPS exemplifies community policing as risk-communications
policing. A police officer told us that even though there were some cases in
which the program had led to the capture of criminal suspects, that function was not central to it: "You can't evaluate its effectiveness [in crime
prevention and detection]. . . . It's provided us a means of communicating
with the community on a regular basis without having to go and knock on
the door to do the town crier bit. We don't have the manpower to do the
town crier." A local government official who had become involved in developing the program said that it was, despite appearances, "still policing
. . . police and community policing community." He observed that crime
prevention was the best message to initially put forward in selling the program, but that in the long term the program could be used for governance
more broadly: "So I thought the best way of keeping people informed is
through a computer link-up. Rather than have the police force or myself,

whatever, these constant meetings, constant dropping-off of pamphlets, letters, it really is a waste of time and money and resources are limited. . . . So
you sort of involve yourself in community building, at the same time as
crime prevention."

The police viewed PCCOPS as a convenient tool for making some of
their routine tasks easier. When involved in direct, face-to-face relations
with the police, people can make annoying demands that are tangential or
irrelevant to the task at hand. It is far better, the police think, to avoid face-
to-face contact by relying on computer-assisted dialing systems such as PC-
COPS:

> [When you go door to door] and you tell them that little Johnny or Mary
> from next door is missing, they're concerned but they're going to say,
> "Are you going to my neighbor?" And you say "Yes." [They reply]
> "When you tell them could you also mention that their dog is awfully
> noisy at night?" This happens. So you go five minutes at every house be-
> cause you get twelve houses on one side of the street and you've used up
> an hour of your time. . . . I can record a message on the dialer and call
> sixty to eighty houses in that hour because they're not expecting to tell
> that machine about the barking dog next door, and it cascades. . . . I
> can't be rude. I'm there as a professional so [when] it's a two-way con-
> versation . . . I have to because its face to face, listen to whatever you're
> going to say to me.

Missing Persons

As suggested by the use of PCCOPS to trace the whereabouts of
"little Johnny or Mary," risk society hopes to keep track of everyone. People
who go missing even temporarily are registered, and the fact that they cannot be traced is in turn communicated to a variety of institutions. The police are at the fulcrum of the missing-persons knowledge system, once
again serving as key brokers of risk knowledge to other institutions, including knowledge of how to provide for one's own personal security well
beyond crime control per se.

Because the vast majority of missing persons are young people, many
police organizations coordinate their missing-persons systems through
their youth services division. An urban police organization we looked at received approximately thirty-two hundred missing-persons reports each
year, almost 85 percent of which concerned young people. It had a full-time
missing-persons coordinator who, according to his supervisor, "doesn't actually go out and search for people—he coordinates the files." Indeed, apart
from the rare occasion when foul play was suspected, or there was a request

for information from the voluntary organization Child Find, the unit did not actually investigate disappearances.

If the initial missing-person report mentions that the person might be at a certain location, the police will on occasion check it out. Otherwise, all that happens is that a form is completed and filed. There is such a large volume of missing-person cases from social service agencies and group homes for youths that their workers are bound by an agreement with the police not to report a missing-person case until eight hours have elapsed since the disappearance. An officer involved in administering the system said that this arrangement "saves some paper headaches for us." If the missing person has a record of disappearances, the responsibility for finding and dealing with the person is returned to the reporting agency. The officer also raised another point—police reluctance in some cases to simply return missing youths to the relatives or friends who report their disappearance: "We have one very vocal parent who would like us to drag his daughter back by her toenails, but I guess my fear is that she's being sexually abused at home. And here, we, the police, dragging them back to that situation. What we'll do is recommend that social services get involved, you know, crisis unit."

In missing-persons cases the police are almost exclusively risk-knowledge brokers. They enter missing-persons data into the CPIC system; check other institutional data systems to which they have access, such as those maintained by hospitals; notify school and welfare organizations and volunteer agencies such as Child Find; and, in some cases, distribute photographs of and notices about missing persons. Impelled by a risk-management sensibility, the goal of police knowledge workers in the missing persons field is to have no more than 3 percent of the year's missing persons still missing at the end of the year. This national standard is set by the RCMP.

The RCMP maintains a Missing Children's Registry staffed by police officers, a research analyst, and statistical analysts. The heavy reliance on statistical expertise emphasizes the fact that the registry's primary tasks are indeed registration and the associated risk profiling of youths who, however temporarily, cannot be accounted for.

Table 2 shows that the vast majority (74 percent) of unaccounted for young people were runaways. Abduction by strangers was very rare indeed. Only 78 of 59,135, or 0.1 percent, of recorded cases in 1991 were a result of "stranger abduction." And it must be noted, too, that the definition of "stranger" used by the registry included close relatives (such as grandparents, aunts, and uncles) and friends who did not have legal custody of the child! The available data do not indicate how many of the seventy-eight

TABLE 2   Missing Child Registry Cases, 1991

Reason	Cases Entered		Cases Removed	
	N	%	N	%
Stranger abduction	78	0.1	64	0.1
Accident	60	0.1	34	0.1
Wander off/Lost	783	1.3	746	1.4
Parental abduction	412	0.7	326	0.6
Runaway	43,786	74.0	40,426	74.1
Unknown	11,863	20.1	10,952	20.1
Other	2,153	3.7	1,967	3.6
Total	59,135	100.0	54,515	100.0

SOURCE: Adapted from Royal Canadian Mounted Police 1991.

stranger abductions were in fact abductions by relatives or friends, but it is reasonable to assume that most fell into that category. Clearly, stranger abductions were not a substantial problem for the authorities, although they have great symbolic importance in our society (Best 1990).

The police help foster this symbolic importance because it enables them to govern through crime. For example, in addition to routinely supplying news releases to the media, the registry cooperated with the producers of *Missing Treasures,* a "child find" version of police reality television (Fishman and Cavendar 1998). This show featured reenactments of high-profile, missing-child cases and solicited public assistance in supplying knowledge relevant to those cases. A police officer involved, talking after the termination of the show, commented:

> It's been a success in that it's brought forward the information to the public. I don't know of any particular case we can point to that we found the child because of that . . . [but it helps people to] realize that things like this happen and they have to have some protection for their children . . . tips for parents . . . keep the problem of missing children there in the forefront to the public so they don't forget about it.

At the symbolic level the police unite with other institutions in promoting the education of parents, who are expected to educate their children about the problem of stranger abductions. Thus, despite its own evidence, the 1991 *Annual Report on Canada's Missing Children* stresses the need to be eternally vigilant about the risk of stranger abductions:

> [B]ecause such high profile is given to any stranger abduction, the public's perception is that this phenomenon is common in Canada. This in fact is not the case. However, it is still prudent for parents to teach their children to be "street smart" and to be aware of the dangers of our

society. Street proofing of children is essential to preventing such tragedies. Many of Canada's police are actively involved in preventative policing and are able to provide tips on personal safety. It is important to remember that the legal definition of "stranger" is anyone who does not have custody of the child. Therefore, children who are taken by a grandparent, aunt, uncle, or friend of the family would be entered into CPIC under the category of stranger abduction.

Eternal vigilance is fostered by asking parents to include their children in special registration systems. One police organization we studied ran an "Operation Child Identification Program" in which detailed written descriptions, photographs, and fingerprints were placed on file. A brochure produced by a provincial solicitor general's office and distributed by police throughout the province urged parents to maintain their own home-based knowledge system for mapping and training their children: "Build a home information centre, which includes a map of your neighborhood and its play areas, and have your child identify where he will be at all times, and when he will return. . . . Maintain up-to-date records which include a recent photograph of your child, his height and weight, medical and dental histories, and if you wish, a video tape and fingerprint record." Parents are now also being encouraged to maintain a sample of their child's DNA for potential identification purposes.

A police officer we interviewed saw such urgings as part of the "continual reinforcement" needed to persuade parents to maintain good records. In her view, these records would be important in the event of an apparent missing-child case, because parents are usually in an "emotional state" at such times, which interferes with rational, efficient police work. In other words, families are to be like other institutions, providing data that are properly formatted and readily accessible: "They have that information just there, they can hand it to the officer, it saves a hell of a lot of time in the police officer trying to calm them down enough to ask questions so they can get the information from them—details and description. The person wants the policeman to get out right now and go out and find their kid."

Parents are not only to keep detailed records of their childrens' identities, they are also to remain perpetually reflexive with respect to risks. The aforementioned brochure stressed that the safety tips it offered "will not completely protect your child, however they will increase the level of awareness." Indeed, parents were made aware by the brochure of imagined negative consequences that lurked behind the most mundane aspects of a child's everyday life: "Avoid clothing and toys which personally display your child's name, because children are less likely to fear a stranger who knows their name . . . know all of your children's friends, their families and their phone numbers; insist that your child ask for permission to visit his friends . . . accompany your child on door-to-door activities, such as Halloween or school fund-raising."

As is suggested by the instruction to avoid labeling a child's property with his or her name lest it give dangerous strangers a way of becoming friendly with the child, many of the lessons in the brochure focused on communication. In the brochure, community policing as risk-communications policing extended into the home- and family-based education of the young. For example, children were expected to manipulate appearances and even lie in the interests of risk reduction. "When children are home alone, [they are] to tell phone callers that you are there, but you are busy, and cannot come to the phone, and that the caller should call back later." Like electronic home-security alarm systems, children were to be given a code that would help signal who were trusted insiders and who were to be excluded from contact: "[U]use a pre-selected code word with your child and those whom you may ask to give your child a ride; where necessary, change the code word with your child after it has been used for a period of time." No mention was made of the confusion that might ensue for a mother trying to remember the codes of the six children being picked up in her station wagon on the way to their Saturday morning hockey game. The parent was to know everything about the child's communications with other adults. In communications between children and adults who were not close family members, confidentiality was to be breached: "Some secrets—like surprise birthday presents—are fun, but a secret that another adult says only the two of you can know is not right—come and tell me."

The fear of child abduction has recently been extended literally to the cradle. An electronic ankle bracelet for infants, trademarked "Hugs," is being marketed to hospitals as

> a fully supervised and tamper-resistant protection system that automatically activates once secured around an infant's ankle or wrist. Staff is immediately alerted at a computer console of the newly activated tag, and can enter pertinent information such as names and medical conditions. Password authorization is needed to move infants out of the designated protection area and—if an infant is not readmitted within a predetermined time limit—an alarm will sound. An alarm also sounds if an infant with a Hugs tag is brought near an open door at the perimeter of the protected area without a password being entered. The display console will then show the identification of the infant and the exit door on a facility map. Alternatively, doors may also be fitted with magnetic

locks that are automatically activated. As well, Hugs can be configured to monitor the progress and direction of the abduction within the hospital. Weighing just 1/3 of an ounce, each ergonomically designed infant tag offers a number of other innovative features, including low-battery warning, the ability to easily interface with other devices such as CCTV cameras and paging systems and time and date stamping. (*Canadian Security* 1998)

Governing through Fear

All of these systems for governing through crime are based on governing through fear. Risk society is characterized by the marketing of (in)security. "In" or trendy security products are sold in the same way as other consumer products (Slater 1997; Loader 1999). The selling is facilitated by the reflexive awareness of insecurity that accompanies the probabilistic thinking of risk knowledge. And the more security products that are available, the more the signs of insecurity and the greater the fear. Fear ends up proving itself (Beck 1992). It is therefore understandable why some police organizations, such as the Thames Valley Police in England, now include a motto on the side of their vehicle that states their dedication to "Reducing Crime, Disorder and Fear."

NOTE

Unless indicated otherwise, the data reported in this essay derive from our research on the police and risk communication systems in Canada. This research is reported more fully in Ericson and Haggerty 1997. Earlier versions of this essay were presented by Richard Ericson at the Centre for Criminal Justice Studies, Faculty of Law, University of Leeds (Frank Dawtry Lecture); Centre for Criminological Research, Faculty of Law, Oxford University; Mannheim Centre for Criminal Justice, London School of Economics and Political Science; and the Insurance Law Center, School of Law, University of Connecticut. He thanks Adam Crawford, Roger Hood, Paul Rock, David Downes, and Tom Baker for organizing these talks, and all those present who responded critically. The authors also thank Andrew Ashworth for sharing data on trends in the criminal justice system of England and Wales, and Matthew Ericson for his observations on private policing in Oxford.

REFERENCES

Ashworth, Andrew. 2001. "The Decline of English Sentencing, and Other Stories." In *Punishment and Penal Systems in Western Countries*, ed. M. Tonry and R. Frase. New York: Oxford University Press.

Baker, Tom. 1994. "Constructing the Insurance Relationship: Sales Stories, Claims Stories, and Insurance Contract Damages." *Texas Law Review* 75:1395–1434.

Barclay, Gorden, Cynthia Tavaras, and Andrew Prout. 1995. *Information on the*

Criminal Justice System in England and Wales. London: Home Office Research and Statistics Department.

Beck, Ulrich. 1992. *Risk Society: Toward a New Modernity.* London: Sage

Best, Joel. 1990. *Threatened Children: Rhetoric and Concern About Child-Victims.* Chicago: University of Chicago Press.

Canadian Security. 1998. "The Importance of Hugs." November/December.

Chatterton, Michael. 1983. "Police Work and Assault Charges." In *Control in the Police Organization,* ed. M. Punch. Cambridge: MIT Press.

———. 1989. "Managing Paperwork." In *Police Research: Some Future Prospects,* ed. M. Weatheritt. Aldershot: Gower.

———. 1991. "Organizational Constraints on the Uses of Information Technology in Problem-Focused Area Policing." Paper read at the British Criminology Conference, July. York, England.

Clarke, Ronald, and Michael Hough. 1984. *The Effectiveness of the Police.* Home Office Research Unit. London: HMSO.

Comrie, M., and E. Kings. 1975. "Study of Urban Workloads: Final Report." London: Home Office Police Research Services Unit.

Cumming, E., I. Cumming, and L. Edell. 1965. "Policeman as Philosopher, Guide and Friend." *Social Problems* 12:276–86.

Draper, Hilary. 1978. *Private Police.* Harmondsworth: Penguin.

Ericson, Richard. 1982. *Reproducing Order: A Study of Police Patrol Work.* Toronto: University of Toronto Press.

———. 1993. *Making Crime: A Study of Detective Work.* 2d ed. Toronto: University of Toronto Press.

———. 1994a. "The Division of Expert Knowledge in Policing and Security." *British Journal of Sociology* 45:149–75.

———. 1994b. "The Royal Commission on Criminal Justice System Surveillance." In *Criminal Justice in Crisis,* ed. M. McConville and L. Bridges. Aldershot: Edward Elgar.

Ericson, Richard, and Kevin Haggerty. 1997. *Policing the Risk Society.* Toronto: University of Toronto Press; Oxford: Oxford University Press.

Ericson, Richard, and Clifford Shearing. 1986. "The Scientification of Police Work." In *The Knowledge Society: The Growing Impact of Scientific Knowledge on Social Relations,* ed. G. Böhme and N. Stehr. Dordrecht: Reidel.

Ericson, Richard, Dean Barry, and Aaron Doyle. 2000. "The Moral Hazards of Neo-Liberalism: Lessons from the Private Insurance Industry." *Economy and Society* 29:532–58.

Feeley, Malcolm, and Jonathan Simon. 1994. "Actuarial Justice: The Emerging New Criminal Law." In *The Futures of Criminology,* ed. D. Nelken. London: Sage.

Fishman, Mark, and Gray Cavender, eds., 1998. *Entertaining Crime: Television Reality Programs.* New York: Aldine de Gruyter.

Garland, David. 1996. "The Limits of the Sovereign State: Strategies of Crime Control in Contemporary Society." *British Journal of Criminology* 36:445–71.

———. 1997. "'Governmentality' and the Problem of Crime: Foucault, Criminology, Sociology." *Theoretical Criminology* 1:173–214.

Geller, William, and Norval Morris. 1992. "Relations between Federal and Local Police." In *Modern Policing*, ed. M. Tonry and N. Morris. Chicago: University of Chicago Press.

Goldstein, Joseph. 1960. "Police Discretion Not to Invoke the Criminal Process: Low Visibility Decisions in the Administration of Justice." *Yale Law Journal* 69:543–94.

Haggerty, Kevin, and Richard Ericson. 1999. "The Militarization of Policing in the Information Age." *Journal of Political and Military Sociology* 27:233–45.

———. 2000. "The Surveillant Assemblage." *British Journal of Sociology* 51:605–22.

Johnston, Lesley. 1992. *The Rebirth of Private Policing.* London: Routledge.

———. 1997. "Policing Communities of Risk." In *Policing Futures: The Police, Law Enforcement and the Twenty-First Century*, ed. P. Francis, P. Davies, and V. Jupp. Basingstoke: Macmillan.

Jorgensen, Birthe. 1981. "Transferring Trouble: The Initiation of Reactive Policing." *Canadian Journal of Criminology* 23: 257–78.

Latour, Bruno. 1987. *Science in Action.* Cambridge: Harvard University Press.

Loader, Ian. 1999. "Consumer Culture and the Commodification of Policing and Security." *Sociology* 33:373–92.

Manning, Peter. 1980. *The Narc's Game: Organizational and Informational Limits on Drug Law Enforcement.* Cambridge: MIT Press.

———. 1988. *Symbolic Communication: Signifying Calls and the Police Response.* Cambridge: MIT Press.

———. 1992. "Information Technology and the Police." In *Modern Policing*, ed. M. Tonry and N. Morris. Chicago: University of Chicago Press.

McConville, Michael. 1993. "An Error of Judgement." *Legal Action* (September).

McConville, Michael, and Lee Bridges, eds. 1994. *Criminal Justice in Crisis.* Aldershot: Edward Elgar.

McMahon, Maeve. 1992. *The Persistent Prison? Rethinking Decarceration and Penal Reform.* Toronto: University of Toronto Press.

Meehan, Albert. 1993. "Internal Police Records and the Control of Juveniles: Politics and Policing in a Suburban Town." *British Journal of Criminology* 33: 504–24.

Moynihan, Daniel. 1993. "Defining Deviance Down." *The American Scholar* 62: 17–30.

O'Malley, Pat. 1991. "Legal Networks and Domestic Security." *Studies in Law, Politics and Society* 11:171–90.

O'Malley, Pat., ed. 1998. *Crime and the Risk Society.* Aldershot: Dartmouth.

Poster, Mark. 1990. *The Mode of Information: Poststructuralism and Social Context.* Cambridge: Polity.

———. 1995. *The Second Media Age.* Cambridge: Polity.

Reiss, Albert. 1982. "Forecasting the Role of the Police and the Role of the Police in Social Forecasting." In *The Maintenance of Order in Society,* ed. R. Done-lan. Ottawa: Supply and Services Canada.

———. 1987. "The Legitimacy of Intrusion into Private Spaces." In *Private Polic-ing,* ed. C. Shearing and P. Stenning. Beverly Hills: Sage.

Rose, Nikolas. 1999. *Powers of Freedom.* Cambridge: Cambridge University Press.

Royal Canadian Mounted Police. 1991. *Annual Report on Canada's Missing Chil-dren.* Ottawa: Royal Canadian Mounted Police.

Royal Commission on Criminal Justice. 1993. *Report.* Cmnd. 2263. London: HMSO.

Shearing, Clifford. 1992. "The Relationship between Public and Private Policing." In *Modern Policing,* ed. M. Tonry and N. Morris. Chicago: University of Chi-cago Press.

Shearing, Clifford, and Philip Stenning. 1983. "Private Security: Implications for Social Control." *Social Problems* 30:493–506.

Simon, Jonathan. 1997. "Governing through Crime." In *The Crime Conundrum: Essays on Criminal Justice,* ed. G. Fisher and L. Friedman. Boulder: Westview.

Skogan, Wesley. 1990. *The Police and the Public in England and Wales: A British Crime Survey Report.* Home Office Research Study No. 117. London: HMSO.

Slater, Donald. 1997. *Consumer Culture and Modernity.* Cambridge: Polity Press.

Southgate, P., and C. Mirless-Black. 1991. *Traffic Policing in Changing Times.* Lon-don: HMSO.

Squires, Gregory, ed. 1997. *Insurance Redlining: Disinvestment, Reinvestment, and the Evolving Role of Financial Institutions.* Washington, D.C.: Urban In-stitute Press.

Stinchcombe, Arthur. 1963. "Institutions of Privacy in the Determination of Po-lice Administrative Practice." *American Journal of Sociology* 69:150–60.

Walsh, W. 1986. "Patrol Officer Arrest Rates: A Study of the Social Organization of Police Work." *Justice Quarterly* 2:271–90.

ELEVEN

The Return of Descartes's Malicious Demon: An Outline of a Philosophy of Precaution

FRANÇOIS EWALD (TRANSLATED BY STEPHEN UTZ)

We may be in the midst of a paradigm change concerning society's obligations for the physical security of its members and our shared political philosophy of security. The nineteenth century saw the dominance of a paradigm of responsibility. In the twentieth century this was fundamentally transformed: the prevailing paradigm was one of solidarity. Perhaps, at the beginning of a new century, we are seeing the birth of a new paradigm, one that has not yet found its true name, but whose arrival is presaged by various signs.

Where safety is concerned, rights and duties, legal and moral obligations are always issues; these fit together without necessarily overlapping. The paradigm of responsibility posits a certain economy of rights and duties in which the part played by moral obligations toward oneself and others is far greater than that of legal obligations. Implicit in the philosophy of liberalism, the paradigm of responsibility relies less on constraint than on freedom and individual will. Legal obligations with regard to others are summarized in the rule "do no harm to others." Virtue holds an important place here under the twofold guise of prudence (for oneself) and charity (for others).

By contrast, the paradigm of solidarity, which is associated with the welfare state, considerably extends the role of legal obligations, which here tend to overlap with moral obligations. Solidarity is accompanied by the multiplication of social rights and by the recognition of a sort of general right to indemnity for every mishap in life. This paradigm belongs to an era of scientific and technical utopia, in which society may have the possibility of controlling itself, where knowledge may have an indefinite priority over power. At its philosophical foundations, it is inseparable from the imperative of prevention: prevention of illnesses (with Pasteur's discoveries), prevention of crimes (with the system of social defense), prevention of accidents (with the sciences of safety), prevention of poverty and social insecurity (with social insurance).

The new paradigm of security calls forth a new economy of rights and duties. While the language of risk, against a background of scientific expertise, used to be sufficient to describe all types of insecurity, the new paradigm sees uncertainty reappear in the light of even newer science. It bears witness to a deeply disturbed relationship with a science that is consulted less for the knowledge it offers than for the doubt it insinuates. Moral obligations are swallowed up in public ethics, and the principle of responsibility is seen as a reflection of a brand-new notion of precaution.

The paradigm of responsibility is a paradigm of insurance—it assumes the logic of loss compensation. The paradigm of solidarity is also a paradigm of insurance, of universal and indeterminate insurance, of social and compulsory insurance. It is not so much concerned with voluntary and contractual forms of compensation as with the institution of pools of all kinds. The paradigm linked to the precautionary principle will undoubtedly remain a paradigm of insurance, but in a new shape that will have to integrate new cultural boundary conditions.

Responsibility

What characterizes the pattern of imposing liability and exacting damages that came to be known during the eighteenth and nineteenth centuries as "responsibility?"

A Political Strategy

We must first identify a broad public policy, an overall strategy of social control. Responsibility is based on the principle that "one person cannot transfer to another the burden of what happens to him." It is in direct opposition to the principle of assistance. Adolphe Thiers, reasserting the liberal credo that had been constantly repeated for a half-century, wrote in 1850 that "[t]he fundamental principle of any society is that each man is responsible for meeting his own needs and those of his family, out of resources that are acquired or transmitted. Without this principle, all activity would come to a halt since, if man could rely on work other than his own to survive, he would gladly leave to others the tasks and difficulties of life."

The formulation of this principle is linked to the advent of liberalism. It involved both making people provident, aware of the future, and preventing them from living solely in the present. The principle of responsibility reflects a view of humanity's relationship with nature, according to which everything that happens to a person must be considered a sanction, good or bad. Responsible for myself, I would not even know how to attribute to someone else a causal role in the obstacles I face. The responsibility for these obstacles, even if other causal factors contribute to them, is mine. It is I who was unable to take a particular element into account; it is I who did not understand the laws of nature or was unable to use them. In any case, and always without exception, *it is my fault.* I am the only target for attribution. "To err is human," as the saying goes. Accordingly, the principle of responsibility converts any mistake into a fault.

The principle of responsibility relies on a method of managing causality that makes it possible to devise self-regulation of conduct and activities. To the extent that one cannot lay one's own failures and sufferings off on someone else, failures and sufferings are able to become the indeterminate principle of their own remedy. The principle of responsibility, based on fault, thus serves as a universal converter of bad into good. But it is singularly demanding. Seen from this angle, security would not be a right, but merely a duty. For, on this philosophy, there is no room for the notion of victim. In this world, suffering a wrong gives you no right to anything (unless it results from the fault of someone else). And victims, whatever feelings of compassion and pity they may inspire, are always assumed to be the sole creators of their own destiny. The political principle of responsibility lies behind articles 1382 et seq. of the French Civil Code. It is precisely what these articles are intended to enforce. One might as well say that they were not intended to extend the reach of damages by increasing the possible number of responsible parties, but rather to limit them to the situation in which the injury suffered was due to the fault of another. A judge's task is to ensure that he maintains a delineation of fault that will uphold the sense of the general principle of responsibility.

The Virtues of Responsibility

The principle of responsibility and its legal sanctions aim to make man provident and prudent: provident as to the effect of fortune, prudent as to himself and the consequences of his actions. Fault by such logic is always a fault of prudence; it is the sanction for what one could or should have foreseen. A prudent and provident man has no excuse. To his own prudence he will not only owe his safety but also his capacity to associate with others to compensate for the effects of fate. If such a philosophy excludes any idea of insurance for responsibility, or even insurance for damages (long considered immoral as though encouraging crime, and thus prohibited), it evokes, on the other hand, the idea of self-insurance, on a strictly voluntary basis.

Fault is a philosophical principle for attributing liability, which should have the merit of combining harmoniously not only the three functions of sanction, prevention, and compensation, but also of integrating ethics, law, and politics. Thus the great legal commentator Jean-Etienne Labbé could write at the end of the nineteenth century, at a time when the mechanism of responsibility was already deeply shaken, that "[r]esponsibility is the most perfect regulator of human actions"(1885). This model no longer corresponds to our experience, and yet it is difficult not to feel its coherence and even its proximity. Its persistence as a model, or as a regulating principle, in the face of contrary social facts is nothing new. Since the time when it was first instituted, it has been contested by the developments of industrialization. The form of providence supports the formulation of articles 1382–86 of the French Civil Code as they were interpreted until the end of the nineteenth century. The legal notion of fault echoes that of providence: one can only reproach somebody for what he or she should have known. As seen in the jurisprudence of article 1382 of the French Civil Code, the reference to the diligence of a "prudent head of family" or to certain standards of professional conduct indicates that one can only be held responsible to the extent of the available knowledge, which varies depending on the activity. Doubt, uncertainty, or suspicion cannot make one responsible. Such emotions are more likely attributed either to chance, or to the prudence that each person owes to himself in the conduct of his life.

Providence is the great virtue of the nineteenth century. It is the foundation of responsibility in the conventional sense of the term, and it prohibits blaming another for what happens to you (except in the case that it is due to the fault of another). Indeed, when the term was coined in the nineteenth century, "responsibility" did not designate, as it does today, a general principle of blaming another for mishaps, but precisely the opposite. Responsibility as providence consisted of being aware of the risks to which one was subject because of the need to face up to them on one's own initiative. The world of providence is one in which one must recognize his or her weakness and fragility, subject to incessant reversals of fortune; it is a world of chance events. It is an unbalanced world where one knows oneself to be vulnerable and scarcely hopes to use science and engineering (which are not readily available) in order to rebalance one's relationship with nature. One must instead rely on cunning, intelligence, and calculations of probabilities, which teach that accidents do not happen without laws and that these laws are the foundations of opposed forces no one can face up to rationally. This is how insurance came to be promoted throughout the nineteenth century—as the institution of a rational providence. In the world of providence, one has no other resource than calculation and virtue. Faced with the accidents that one can hardly anticipate, the only possible tactic is to learn how to offset them. And insurance, which makes this possible, cannot be made compulsory, since that obligation would rule out the exercise of the virtue of providence.

Solidarity

The mechanism of responsibility was challenged, reformed, and replaced at the end of the nineteenth century, at least with respect to the coverage of certain types of events, by an arrangement based on solidarity. The major issue in all industrial societies was that of accidents at work and pensions. The mechanism of solidarity is not based on fault but on risk; its main instrument is insurance, rather than general legal rules for assigning liability.

Shift to Risk

The notion of risk, which makes its arrival in positive French Law in 1898 with the "professional risk" of the law on accidents at work, dated 9 April 1898, designates a way of envisaging the reparation which, without involving examination of the behavior of the worker or the boss, attributes them globally to the job and the firm. "All work has its risks; accidents are the sad but inevitable consequence of work itself" (Thoulon 1898). According to the principle of professional risk, the onus of accidents at work, whatever their cause, belongs to the firm, whether these accidents arise legally from a chance event or through the fault of the worker. Thus the result of the new law was to make the firm legally "responsible" not only for accidents resulting from personal imprudence or negligence, but also for those arising even when the firm has taken all precautions to avoid them, and those for which the worker is the cause (absent tortious intent on the worker's part).

The idea of professional risk thus divorces causality from attribution. The indifference of the latter in relation to the former is separated by the institution of a principle of attribution that no longer refers to the objective causality of damages. The rationality that underlies the notion of risk leads to a change in the legal allocation of damages, which is no longer in terms of "cause," but of "distribution"—distribution between profits and expenses of firms, or more generally, a socially constructed distribution of expenses. Risk only exists socially. Whether professional risk or social risk, it institutes a social contract between individuals.

The invention of professional risk and social risk consists of thinking through a principle of allocation that, freed from the old dependence on nature, finds its reference in a social relationship. This accounts for both the richness of the category and the difficulty of deploying it.

The idea of risk is linked with analyses of situations based on statistics and probabilities. Business risk, for example, characterizes a whole, the firm, which conserves its identity despite the variations that may affect its different parts. The regularity of risk is independent from the conduct of individuals. Their faults are factors of risk that do not affect the company's statistical reality. This is one of the principal benefits of the notion of responsibility: enabling the law to base itself on reparation of the actual fact of the accident, of the damage suffered, whatever the cause. While a principle of responsibility founded on an idea of cause implies a selective distribution of the costs, business risk, on the contrary, provides "solidarity." Solidarity of the boss and the worker in the context of the firm recognizes a species of business risk that can put an end to the antagonism of capital and labor that the law of responsibility fueled. Social solidarity, more generally, allocates risk by shifting the cost of accidents to the firm, thereby creating a new balance between rich and poor, producers and consumers.

A New Social Contract

The new solidaristic doctrine of spreading costs was to be articulated in eloquent terms by the reforming jurists of the end of the nineteenth century. Let's hear what they have to say. First, Raymond Saleilles:

> Modern life, more than ever, is a question of risks. Therefore, one takes action. An accident occurs, somebody must necessarily bear the consequences. This must be either the person who caused the accident or the victim. The issue is not of inflicting a penalty, but of knowing who must bear the loss, he who caused it or he who suffered it. Not the penal point of view but only the social point of view is at issue. Properly speaking, it is no longer a question of responsibility but a question of risks: who must bear them? Obviously, in reason and in justice, it must be he who in taking action has taken responsibility for the consequences of his deeds and his activity. . . . (1897:4)

This text is a testimony of the intellectual conversion that gave birth to the mechanism of solidarity. "Modern life," says Saleilles, "is more than ever a question of risks" (id). This is an acknowledgment that the real world is not one imagined by the drafters of the French Civil Code. Whatever diligence each person brings to his affairs, misfortune is not the exception but the rule. Injuries are "normal"—which does not mean they are inevitable. Social life is not naturally harmonious, but conflictual, prejudicial. When the "good head of family," who served as reference in defining fault, takes action, pursues his business, does his work, he "naturally" causes, without wishing to do so, injury to other good heads of family. The outcome is necessarily that the injuries must be objectified as "accidents" and no longer be considered faults. These are risks.

Another consequence: the problem of responsibility is no longer that of determining "who was at fault," but to whom the injury should be attributed, who should bear the loss caused by the injury. "Between two individuals, one of whom, even without being at fault, has caused a personal accident or a loss of property and the victim, who must bear the financial cost and, at the end of the day? On which asset-base must the final loss fall? That is the problem. The issue of fault has nothing to do with it" (Saleilles 1897:75).

Implicit in this approach is a problem of fairness in terms that are more economic than moral, causing the cost of damage to be borne by the victim or by another, in either case making one or the other "responsible." Spreading risks means judging who must bear them, not in terms of the moral responsibility, which is irrelevant here, but in terms of a "social fairness" to be constructed. The source and foundation of responsibility are displaced from the individual onto society: one is responsible not because one is free by nature and could therefore have acted differently, but because society judges it "fair" to make you responsible, that is to cause you to bear the financial cost of the injury, whether you are actor or victim.

Let us now hear the version of L. Josserand:

> The passer-by that I knocked down, the classmate that I injured, did not for their part commit any fault and yet today's doctrine declares them responsible for the accident, since it makes them bear the consequences. For, and this is an idea which, despite its evidence, is not sufficiently grasped, it is impossible to subtract the owner of the thing from the responsibility of injury without causing this same responsibility to be borne by the victim: Since the cause of the accident is unknown, some say, nobody must be responsible, since nobody is at fault. This reasoning is absolutely wrong: when an accident occurs, it is not possible for nobody to be responsible in the wide sense of the word, that is for nobody to bear the consequences of what happens: if the owner of the thing that caused the accident is not made to repair the damage, the victim

must of necessity be the one to bear it; the victim will incur the full responsibility for the accident, responsibility which is seen in the loss of
life or health, without compensation. Whatever the solution adopted,
there is always responsibility: the only question is that of knowing who
must assume it. In a nutshell: is there responsibility each time there is
final injury? (1897:107)

Can we be clearer on the transformations undergone by the notion of responsibility? Earlier, and always in common belief, responsibility was
thought an attribute of human nature. Responsibility has changed its
meaning. It is no longer the attribute of a subject, but rather a consequence
of a social fact. Responsibility, in a way, has become a relationship without
support.

There is no injury where loss is solely individual. All injury is social. A
distinction must be made between the injury suffered by an individual—
this is an affair of chance or mischance—and the loss linked to the injury
for which the attribution is always collective and social. In any case, society and the courts cause the cost of injury to be borne by someone, whether
this is the victim or another: they spread the risks. The notion of spreading
the risks implies that one conceives society not as an aggregation of individuals, who may be linked to each other by personal interest, but as a totality—the good and the bad of each individual dependent on everyone else.
This is true whether one conceives of society as a totality in which no individual is any longer a third party in relation to others, or whether one conceives of society in accordance with the principle of solidarity. We move
from an individualistic to a holistic perspective.

If injury is individual, it behooves society to spread the cost suitably,
and this necessarily disrupts what nature or fate has decided, throwing a
new light on the problem of justice. François Gény, another jurist from the
end of the nineteenth century, prophesied the continuation of the transformations that he witnessed:

One can imagine a social ideal which, without claiming to halt the
blows of fate or defy the decrees of providence, would aim to discover in
the nature of things, placed by God Himself at our disposal, the means
of sharing amongst all, in the form of an intelligently organized mutuality, the risks which incessantly threaten us as individuals. However,
and without speaking of the almost insurmountable difficulties, of the
prodigious organization required by the realization of such an ideal, one
easily glimpses the utopia and the danger of a system, which, firstly, in
order to remain loyal to its aim, should, by means of compensation, although necessarily imperfect, straighten out all inequalities, take into

consideration economic variations as well as material changes, share out the gains as well as the losses; which, secondly, however well-advised the application may be, will not fail to diminish the qualities of initiative, of diligence, of providence, which are among the conditions essential to the progress of humanity. (1902:817)

Here we have a description of the program of social security that took shape during the twentieth century, not only covering social risks (illness, old age, disability) but also in compensation for an ever more impressive number of accidental risks. It is a commonplace that, during the twentieth century, law and responsibility were transformed, bit by bit, into a legal system of compensation, based on risk and insurance. This is the case, on the one hand, for car accidents, but also for relief from natural disasters, for protection against assaults, and the consequences of crime and of injuries linked to defective products. Protection against sea pollution is also provided through these mechanisms, some of which must eventually be extended to land pollution. By way of responsibility, the twentieth century systematically thought compensation, so much so that today, in the early years of the twenty-first century, the victim of any sort of injury seems to be able to claim compensation, and the media are tempted to denounce the scandal as soon as they see what seems to be an unassimilated type of loss, as is still the case in France with medical accidents.

Prevention First

The paradigm of solidarity is not only a paradigm of compensation but also one of prevention. One forgets the extent that the paradigm has successfully distinguished the three problems of reparation, criminal sanction, and prevention. In fact, in the same way that compensation is no longer linked to the prudence or imprudence of individual conduct, prevention is objectified as a function now less of goodwill than of scientific know-how. The human being is no longer objectified as a free agent but rather as a link in a technical system in which faults are considered less as individual than organizational. We are all familiar with how the analysis of distinct systems has been swallowed up by this generalizing tendency.

Despite their separate spheres of application, compensation and prevention nevertheless derive from a single philosophical paradigm. The word *prevention* indeed took on its current meaning no longer a matter of reluctant reservation in the solidaristic environment as compulsory precaution, on the one hand, and as conduct bluntly designed to lower the probability of some unwanted happening on the other. In fact, the notion of prevention, applicable to Pasteur's discoveries on infection and their public health consequences, as well as to the efforts of engineers to reduce the probability of mechanical accidents, assumes and accompanies the promotion of the notion of risk and—what comes down to the same thing—of measurable risk. Prevention (the vocabulary of which henceforth replaced that of providence) presupposes science, technical control, the idea of possible understanding, and objective measurement of risks. Thus the problem is no longer that of compensating for practically inescapable losses but of reducing the probability of their occurrence.

The nineteenth century's dream of security is tied to a scientific utopia ever more capable of controlling risks. While one cannot eliminate risks altogether (there is never zero risk), they will have been reduced sufficiently to be able to be dealt with collectively: accidents are the by-product, necessary although always more marginalized, of scientific and technical progress. These are special or abnormal risks, the responsibility for which should be spread over the community. Our concept of assured public health and safety involves prevention, the dream of an ever more complete reduction of risk. It is not, at least not on purpose, a measure designed to take on all human misfortunes.

Prevention is an attitude which, by principle, relies on trust in science and its know-how. It presupposes the adjustment of knowledge and power, an ever-possible control of power by knowledge. Its utopia, the asymptote of a knowledge always in the process of mastering techniques and practices derived from them, will eventually reach its limit. One cannot foresee what one does not know, even less what one cannot know.

Safety

The second paradigm of solidarity, however, may be unraveling before our eyes as a result of three major issues, which are also the three principal foci of contemporary problems of safety. These issues are medical accidents, particularly the aspect of serial risk revealed by transfusions, grafts, and transplants; global threats to the environment; and products liability of manufacturers (innovation risk).

The Precautionary Principle

These three problematic areas have two characteristics in common. First, they emerged at roughly the same time, during the 1980s. Second, they were experienced as an ordeal of unexpected vulnerability, unsuspected by individuals in developed societies, who were lulled by the promise of an ever-safer world. We are seeing the return of disasters, the insistence on individual and collective injuries of unequalled magnitude, at least in peacetime. The nineteenth and twentieth centuries were obsessed with the problem of accidents (work-related or automotive); we are now rediscovering the existence of disaster, but with the difference that disasters are no longer, as before, attributed to God and Providence, but to human agency. It is in this deeply disrupted context that the precautionary principle now appears.

The category is henceforth part of positive law: international, European community, and municipal. First international: formulated at the time of agreements implemented, from the end of the 1980s, in order to combat the greenhouse effect and the hole in the ozone layer, in the context of the Brundtland Report on sustainable development (1987), the precautionary principle constitutes the tenth major principle recognized at the Rio Summit in 1992 (United Nations 1992). Here, precaution designates the attitude that consists of preventing serious or irreversible deterioration of the environment by a modification of the production, of the sale or use of products, of services or types of business, and this in accordance with a scientific and technical standard. Next the European community: the Maastricht Treaty specifies in article 130 R that "community policy on the environment" shall be based on the precautionary principle and on the principles that preventative action should be taken, that environmental damage should as a priority be rectified at source and that the polluter should pay. Finally, municipal law: since French parliamentaries have given a definition of the precautionary principle in the first article of the law, dated 2 February 1995, relating to the better protection of the environment, the precautionary principle, "in accordance with which the absence of certainty, taking into account the state of scientific and technical knowledge, must not postpone the adoption of effective and proportionate measures to prevent serious and irreversible damage to the environment at an economically acceptable cost," is specified as the first principle that should take precedence in policies for the protection of the environment.

From these different texts it is immediately evident that the precautionary principle does not seem to have a universal meaning: its field of jurisdiction is limited in principle to the area of the environment. But, make no mistake, to the extent that this represents a certain type of decision-making in situations of uncertainty, the application of the principle will cause it to be exported beyond its original territory. We have already seen that the Council of State put the principle to work in extending state responsibility in the blood transfusion crisis.*

Otherwise, it appears that the precautionary principle does not target all risk situations but only those marked by two principal features: a context of scientific uncertainty on the one hand and the possibility of serious and irreversible damage on the other. These two items are thoroughly problematic.

A New Balance

What does "grave and irreversible injury" mean? Any bodily wound, much less death, must constitute grave and irreversible injury for the person who suffers it, such that no economic compensation can ever make him or her whole again. In fact, the precautionary principle does not so much focus on individual injury, such as may be caused by an accident, as on collective "catastrophic" injury. Still, it may be impossible to exclude from the principle's sphere of application, for example, a physician's lack of "precaution" in treating a single patient. Beyond this, it is useful to distinguish between the severity of injuries, which determines their nature and extent, and their irreversibility.

If an irreversible injury is always a serious one, the converse is not true. Irreversibility focuses on transformations of nature, the balance between humanity and the environment, the introduction of a long-lasting result in the process of life on earth. Irreversibility should doubtless be understood to relate to a "goal of lasting development that purports to satisfy developmental needs of present generations without compromising the ability of future generations to respond to their own needs" (art. 1 of the French Law of 2 February 1995). It is concerned with halting any event that might interrupt the course of natural history, those "revolutions" of which Cuvier spoke. It is concerned with ensuring the continuity of the future with the past. The precautionary principle is counter-revolutionary. It aims to restrict innovation to a framework of unbroken progress.

But the precautionary principle does not proceed solely from a consideration of the nature and amplitude of injury that seems possible from our standpoint today. For this principle to apply, it must change our understanding of injury itself. Injury partakes of the irreparable, the irremediable, the incompensable, the unpardonable, the nonprescriptive. The appearance of the precautionary principle is registered in the context of victims who are no longer satisfied with compensation, no matter how large, but who are only satisfied when those responsible are held criminally liable.

This is certainly a modification of the solidaristic equation that took for granted that a risk was acceptable as long as it was reparable or repaired. This was the principle of the workers compensation law of 1898 (Thoulon 1898), and it was certainly behind awards indemnifying victims' costs for investigation of those responsible for their injuries. One could take a risk on the condition that one paid the price. This attitude, which presupposed that everything—gains as well as losses—had a price, was the principle of cost–benefit analysis, which legitimated entrepreneurial decisions. Was this not how the exercise of "objective responsibility" was justified, by internalizing "externalities" in the price of a product's production? The problems of decisionmaking, business activities, compensation, and responsibility henceforth became just economic problems. It was just a matter of adjusting the cost to the risk of the business enterprise.

The appearance of the precautionary principle no doubt marks the limit of this equation and its underlying logic. With the irreversible, we rediscover the irreparable. Not everything is a matter of economics. Not everything can be assessed a money equivalent. From now on, we no longer limit our attention to compensating, but are also concerned with preventing, forbidding, sanctioning, and punishing. A logic of responsibility returns alongside the solidaristic problematic of compensation.

The same idea underlies the apparently contradictory term *zero risk*. This involves not so much defining what an action without risk would be as asking what reason we have for running the risk—zero risk designates a risk that has a no price. Transformation, therefore, in our value systems and in our methods of valuation is beyond price. As such, it seems undeniable that the precautionary principle upsets certain postulates of an insurance-based society, which takes for granted that one can assign a price to anything, even the very notion of risk, the function of which is to attribute to a threat an objective value and price. In a way, the formula once used by Portalis to condemn life insurance again seems to fit: "People's lives," he said, "have no price" (1989). Except that under the precautionary principle the idea applies not only to human lives but also to the lives of animals (via the protection of the diversity of species) and to nature itself.

Of course, this does not mean that, in a precautionary society, all injury suddenly becomes irreparable and the logic of insurance and solidarity disappears. First, precautionary logic is limited to serious and irreversible injury that, in principle, limits the scope of cognizable injuries. Second, precautionary logic is, above all, a logic of decision applicable in situations of uncertainty, including that of remedying injuries.

The second element of a precautionary situation bears on the "absence of certainty taking into account the scientific and technical knowledge of the time," which is part of the French Law dated 2 February 1985. The formula defines the relationship between prevention and precaution: once there is certainty as to the consequences of an action, one remains with the logic of prevention, with all that this implies in conventional responsibility terms. The notion of precaution concerns a situation in which only a relationship of possibility, eventuality, plausibility, or probability between a cause and its effect can be envisaged. The hypothesis does not concern exactly an unknown cause, but rather a probable or suspected cause. This reference to scientific uncertainty is particularly disturbing.

Uncertainty does not solely concern the relationship of causality between an act and its consequences, but also the reality of injury and the measure of the risk of such injury. The precautionary hypothesis puts us in the presence of a risk that is neither measurable nor assessable—that is, essentially a nonrisk. While the logic of insurance and solidarity had reduced uncertainty to risk, in order to make the former systematically assessable, the logic of precaution leads us once again to distinguish between risk and uncertainty. Precautionary logic does not cover risk (which is covered by prevention); it applies to what is uncertain—that is, to what one can apprehend without being able to assess. Do the changes we currently observe in weather patterns constitute an irreversible interruption in the history of climates? Or are they only a deviation, the likes of which the earth has already seen on many occasions? Should we continue to use blood transfusions once we suspect that the blood contains the hepatitis virus—A, B, or C—of which one is not even capable of assessing the potential danger?

The precautionary hypothesis focuses on the uncertainty of the relationship of causality between an action and its effects. This implies that from now on, along with what one can learn from science, in a context that is always relative, it will also be necessary to take into account what one can only imagine, suspect, presume, or fear. The precautionary principle invites one to consider the worst hypothesis (defined as the "serious and irreversible" consequence) in any business decision. The precautionary principle requires an active use of doubt, in the sense Descartes made canonical in his *Meditations on First Philosophy*. Before any action, I must not only ask myself what I need to know and what I need to master, but also what I do not know, what I dread or suspect. I must, out of precaution, imagine the worst possible, the consequence that an infinitely deceptive malicious demon could have slipped into the folds of an apparently innocent enterprise.

From this point of view, the formulations that one gives of the precautionary principle do not, at least superficially, avoid self-contradiction: anticipating limits in the attitude of prudence to be adopted, either in terms of scientific-technical criteria in accordance with the formula adopted at the Rio Summit, which speaks of measures to be taken "in accordance with a scientific and technical approach," or in terms of more economic criteria if one follows the version of the French Law dated 2 January 1995, which speaks of "effective and proportionate measures at an economically acceptable cost." On the one hand, the decisionmaker is invited to expect the worst, the possible catastrophe, the irreparable; while, on the other, one finds that measures are to be taken only in a "scientific and technical" context—while, by principle, their validity is placed in suspense—or at "an economically acceptable cost"—just when one must envisage the non-assessable of the irreversible. This is no doubt explained by the fact that one wants to maintain a principle of economic and industrial development, which prohibits inaction in the face of uncertainty, at the same time as one seeks to limit as far as possible its harmful consequences. Hence the idea of "sustainable development."

The precautionary hypothesis, finally, introduces uncertainty in both decisions and sanctions, both a priori and a posteriori. A priori: to anticipate danger or avoid injury, as is the prudential intent of the statutes. Precaution designates, first and foremost, a logic of decision to act or not to act, to undertake or not to undertake. It complicates this by introducing the dimension of uncertainty, based on the worst hypothesis. Strictly speaking, it only makes sense before the decision is taken. And yet, to the extent that one cannot fail to call it into play, in the sanctioning of responsibilities, once injury occurs the principle will find itself applied a posteriori. And one can see what this implies: that the sanction escapes the reference to available knowledge, a standard of determined knowledge, whether one is judged not only by what one should know but also by what one should have or might have suspected. Here, precautionary logic, even if it extends the field of subjective responsibilities because it focuses on the act of decision, does not strictly speaking enter into the former logic of fault. The latter presupposes the existence of knowledge, which is absent here because one is *ex hypothesi* uncertain.

Verification of the observance of decisionmaking procedures takes on paramount importance, as should now be properly defined. Two contexts are to be taken into account: that where the injury is felt and that of the uncertainty of long-term causality. And one can hardly see how, under current law of responsibility, one could attribute to anyone an injury of unclear origin, except by employing new systems of causal analysis, vague logic, and other systems of probable causality, or by introducing a new law of proof, or by fixing responsibilities of principle to necessarily arbitrary foundations. The other context is that in which only with time does the causality of the injury become known and therefore assignable. What was only suspected now becomes progressively apparent. Under the old approach to responsibility, uncertainty of knowledge was innocence. The application of the precautionary principle gives a very different result: the uncertainty is not an excuse, but rather a reason for greater caution. The problem of responsibility therefore arises in a somewhat unusual fashion: while one cannot say that the risk was totally unknown since one might have or should have suspected it, sanctioning such "responsibility" can only lead to a considerable restriction of entrepreneurial effort.

A new dimension in the problematics of safety under the precautionary hypothesis is time. The uncertainty of precaution resides to a great extent in the temporal span between cause and manifestation of harmful effect; the delay can be considerable. The precautionary hypothesis goes with an awareness of a dilation of time, of a new understanding of the duration in causality of human actions. This is in stark contrast to any analysis that acknowledges the possibility of an "accident." Characterized precisely by the coincidence or the proximity of the cause and effect, an accident is conventionally defined by its sudden or instantaneous nature. Precautionary injury hardly has this nature; either time is needed for an injury to appear (cases of gradual pollution, climate changes), or it is only afterward that we understand that an effect resulted from a cause—a relationship that was, until then, unsuspected. The precautionary principle invites one to take account of considerably extended temporalities, which leads to the question of duration in the law of responsibility and of the very rationale of statutes of limitations. The principle specifies that "efficacious and proportionate" measures must be taken "without delay," which presupposes that in a way it is already too late. What is hoped for is most often just avoiding the exacerbation of an already bad situation.

The precautionary principle presupposes a new relationship with science and with knowledge. We knew all along that scientific knowledge was relative to a certain state of knowledge, that its validity was limited, that it behooved science to progress continually, and thus ceaselessly reform itself. But that is not exactly the case here. Within its domain of validity, science produces, if not definite certainties, at least an understanding of references, recognized by the scientific community. The precautionary principle invites one to anticipate what one does not yet know, to take into account doubtful hypotheses and simple suspicions. It invites one to take the most far-fetched forecasts seriously, predictions by prophets, whether true or false. We should remember the accusation made from Heidelberg by forty Nobel Prize winners against their "colleagues" meeting in Rio, at the time of the World Summit. The precautionary principle returns us to an epistemology of the relativity of scientific knowledge.

The ethics of precaution are both sophistic and skeptical. They are sophistic because they presuppose that any explanation is opposed by a countervailing explanation. To repeat the formula of Protagoras, man is the measure of all things, those he knows of as well as those he knows not (Plato 1991). Precautionary ethics are skeptical because one is invited to suspend judgment when faced with the assertions of science. For one must take all hypotheses into account, even and in particular the most dubious; one must be wide open to speculation, to the craziest imagined views. While the attitude of prevention presupposes a relationship with knowledge that guarantees the veracity of such knowledge, the precautionary hypothesis invites one to make the most deceptive malicious demon one's constant companion.

Marie-Angèle Sanson-Hermitte has already pointed out that the precautionary hypothesis compels one to take into account opinions that are acknowledged to be marginal and dissident within a scientific community (1996). Going into more depth, she calls attention to a disrupted relationship with science, such that we are now less interested in the confidence science provides than in the suspicions and doubts it can arouse both about what we know and what we do not know. With precaution, science becomes a principle of challenge. Science becomes a challenge to itself as well as to the many proofs that everyday life should not be the subject of permanent anxiety. Effectively, science today interests us less by producing new knowledge than introducing new doubts. Although we have scarcely recognized the change, certainty today is not procured so much by the conventional method of deduction as, rather like the Cartesian credo, by the logic of double negation: all that can be excluded is that anything should be excluded.

Development Risk

The extreme form of the precautionary idea is provided by the concept of risk of development that accentuates all the paradoxes and the difficulties. What is at stake is not suspicion but pure and simple ignorance. The question posed is whether one can permit a producer or a supplier, with objective responsibility for the consequences of product defects, to exonerate herself in the event that she could not have known the defect existed. Let us go further. The risk of development presupposes a product, affected by an undetectable and unforeseeable defect, which only becomes known after a certain span of time, and where the attribution to the product or to the producer presupposes a different level of science than that available to the producer. The most novel feature of the risk of development lies in the need to anticipate a transformation in knowledge, in awareness, in the very perception that transforms reality.

The concept of risk of development is new because it presupposes that we entertain a new relationship with science and engineering. Until now, we lived under the illusion that science might control itself. No doubt prudence was needed, but any advance in knowledge reduced uncertainty. In the field of engineering, the engineer's sciences seemed to possess a certain kind of power of infinite self-control. As new dangers were introduced, new possibilities of controlling and reducing them were provided. We lived as if a balance between knowledge and power were continually possible. Risk of development has become an issue for us because we are now aware both of the dynamism of science and of the essential relativity of knowledge. Thus, contemporary epistemologists teach us that science progresses less by the accumulation and extension of knowledge than by "paradigm shift." And we also move from one paradigm to another by the play of controversies and necessary conflicts, so that what is at stake is less the substitution of error for truth than the manipulation of power within the discipline. From this relativity of knowledge it can be deduced that, while scientific development always permits the discovery of new substances or new processes, it cannot do so without risk because no state of knowledge can claim a guaranteed mastery of itself. Science increases our powers and our capacities without reducing the uncertainty that it generates. We necessarily run the risk of the unforeseeable. In this rediscovered gap between power and knowledge, understanding and awareness, science and morals, we find the possibility and the necessity of a scientific ethic as well as the emergence of those previously unseen problems of decisionmaking and responsibility that we try to deal with by means of the precautionary principle.

In terms of responsibility, the novelty of the concept of risk of development lies in the fact that risk of development necessarily reveals itself after the fact, a posteriori. It does not take the form of risk objectively developed—when the risk becomes obvious, one has already left the context of precaution—but rather that of becoming aware that what one had believed to be of a certain nature was, in fact, of a different nature, foreign, even opposite. This aftereffect gives rise to a tragic or "dramatic" quality, as in the blood transfusion drama.

Now, the French legal tradition, at least since the Age of Enlightenment, was loath to accept these aftereffect problems. Since the Declaration of the Rights of Man and Citizen in 1789, the law of criminal responsibility has been founded on the nonretroactivity of the law. "Nobody can be punished except by virtue of a law established and promulgated prior to the offence and legally applied," specifies article 8 of the Declaration. The same standard is repeated in article 2 of the French Civil Code: "The Law only deals with the future; it cannot have a retroactive effect." The conventional principle of civil liability, formulated by article 1382 of the Civil Code, which introduced fault, took for granted that one could only be responsible for what one knew about; one could not be found responsible without an awareness of wrongdoing. Until then, one was judged and sanctioned for what one was expected to know, for what one should have known, this being necessarily defined in the context of a certain state of science and knowledge.

The question posed by the concept of risk of development is new in the sense that it involves imposing a sort of conflict of laws over time. Can one be fair in judging an act other than in accordance with the elements that accompanied awareness of it? Is it not unjust to judge an act from the perspective of another state of awareness than that under which it was carried out? Is it fair, even for purposes of compensation, to appraise an act in accordance with suspicions and doubts that one is only capable of having after the event?

With risk of development we rediscover the face of destiny, but with a difference: in the Old World, destiny wore the face of the gods, while for us it now has always and necessarily a human face. The face of tragedy belongs to the world of technology, to those situations in which, because of transformations in knowledge and in the very nature of things, the consumer discovers a sort of retroactive revelation, the evil that strikes at him. On the one hand, he experiences disappointment and misplaced trust—"it wasn't what I thought, what I expected, what I was told, promised"—and on the other hand, the awareness that industry sought something that not only he didn't want, couldn't want, but that he had done everything to avoid: "I didn't do that, I didn't want that, I couldn't want that." We now live in a new knowledge–power relationship and suffer the problems of responsibility that it poses, with an awareness that our societies are vulnerable to a new type of risk, a new awareness of tragedy.

The Return of Responsibility

In the now famous book by Hans Jonas, *The Imperative of Responsibility* (1984), one can find the philosophical bedrock of the precautionary principle. The importance of this book, written during the 1970s, lies in its highlighting the philosophical framework of contemporary ecological awareness. For Jonas, the history of humanity is marked by a clear division between the ancient and modern worlds. The human being's relationship with nature has reversed itself: while for a long time human being was *in* nature, as a part of nature, humans have now, thanks to science and technology, gained control of nature. The balance of powers has shifted to the benefit of humans, who now possess the capacity to destroy themselves and the nature surrounding them. It is from this considerable increase in power that is born responsibility in the sense given to it by Jonas. Man must be aware of his power as unlimited, sovereign, in the sense of an infinite capacity to produce effects that he could not anticipate with certainty and in the sense that he has no other master than himself. This is Jonas's first thesis: the world of ecology is a world of the most extreme responsibilities, a world in which humanity no longer has nature as guide, a world of radical uncertainty, therefore also of necessary decision.

The powers of modern man confer upon him an infinite responsibility. His nature is revealed in fear, a feeling that reveals the power of his new capacities. Temporality, within which is situated his action, dilates to encompass the whole history of humanity, past and future, but it must be acknowledged that his powers are such that they threaten the existence of life itself. Contemporary man is becoming aware of himself in the feeling of anguish before the possibilities of annihilation that he bears in himself: for the first time, he discovers in himself the power to commit suicide as a species. Faced with this possibility, and in order to overcome his anguish, modern man is on a quest to find the rules of a morality that will limit his powers: the ethics of responsibility. His enormous power needs holding.

The ethics of responsibility contain risk and uncertainty to the extent that modern man must take account in his actions of both their long-term consequences and their possibility of sweeping along with them, at least in certain cases, the worst—the catastrophe. Instead of the categorical Kantian categorical imperative, there should be substituted an imperative adapted to the new type of human action: "Act so that the effects of your action are compatible with the permanence of an authentically humane life on earth" (Jonas 1984:5). For while we have the right to risk our own lives, we do not have the right to risk the survival of humanity. This imperative is the basis of the precautionary principle: it invites us to measure each possible action against the principle of the worst scenario. Morality becomes a sort of negative morality: it is not so much turned toward the positive quest for the best as toward the avoidance of the worst. The uncertainty of long-term prognostics confers the nature of a wager on human action, which leads to questions such as: do I have the right to endanger the interests of others in my wager?

Contrary to the supreme good and eternal timelessness, the aim of responsibility is the perishable, the vulnerable. The new obligation, born from threat, focuses on the ethics of conservation, of preservation, of impediment. For we are living in an apocalyptic situation that presents as imminent a universal catastrophe due to the extreme power of our scientific, technical, and industrial civilization. It is necessary to "kiss the utopian ideal goodbye" and to denounce the psychological danger of the promise of prosperity. Given the warnings of the Rome Convention, Jonas was not afraid to affirm that "restriction, far less than growth, should become the watchword" (1984:190).

The appearance of a new word is never without significance. The nineteenth century invented "providence" and made it the highest of virtues. The twentieth century replaced "providence" with "prevention"—providence made compulsory for reasons of social security. Now we have "precaution." These overarching concepts represent three attitudes toward uncertainty. Providence is linked to the notions of fate, chance and misfortune, and hazard. It involves incorporating the future into the present, but on an individual scale and with the idea of a possible mastery of the event. Insurance has long been presented as the science of providence. The logic, essentially liberal, of individual providence was, at the end of the nineteenth century, a victim of the Pasteur–Léon Bourgeois association: Pasteur's discovery of infection showed that the well-being of each person did not depend solely on his own conduct but also on that of his neighbor. From that time it became possible, for reasons of public health, to impose, when faced with risks, certain behaviors that one can call by the name, new at the time with this meaning, of "prevention." Prevention is a rational approach to an evil that science can objectify and measure. Providence was contemporary with ignorance of the hazards of existence; prevention came with the certainties of science. It speaks the same language and beckons toward the reduction of risks and their probability. Prevention is a matter for experts who are confident in their knowledge. Precaution, such as we are seeing emerge today, focuses by contrast on uncertainty—the uncertainty of scientific knowledge itself.

The precautionary framework echoes ontological and epistemological conditions that are neither those that saw the emergence of providence, nor those which presuppose prevention. Precaution is not the result of an individualistic ontology such as providence. The threats that it involves are collective. It implies motivations that are not regional, but international. And it does not belong to the contemporary preventive dream of solidarism.

The recent formulation of the precautionary principle is doubtless linked to several factors. First of all, there is the awareness of the utopian nature, relative and limited, of the attitude of prevention. We are, in fact, seeing the proof that our societies and their members are threatened by risks that can be disastrous but are introduced by the very acts that sought to reduce these risks. The issue of medical accidents in the age of what Jean Hamburger has called the therapeutic revolution exemplifies this problematic. When our societies discover themselves, in accordance with the now-sacred term, to be "vulnerable," they experience a certain inseparability of good and evil, that, within the paradigm of prevention were thought to have been indefinitely separated. We are also aware of the relativity of scientific knowledge and the necessity for an ethics of science, and finally of our overweening power over knowledge that is nevertheless at the foundation of that power. Modern science no longer offers certain knowledge, as can be seen, for example, from the proliferation of ethics committees. Science now seeks its own legislation. It never ceases doubting the effects of its own development. The building of nuclear power stations demanded strict measures of prevention. This was the task of the engineers. The blood transfusion drama put a halt, if not to scientific knowledge itself, at least to the relationship we had with it. Regrettably, those responsible had been able to claim that they were only able to make decisions based on scientific certainty and had not adopted a precautionary attitude.

Precaution starts when decisions must be made by reason of and in the context of scientific uncertainty. Decisions are therefore made not in a context of certainty, nor even of available knowledge, but of doubt, suspicion, premonition, foreboding, challenge, mistrust, fear, and anxiety. There is to some extent a risk beyond risk, of which we do not have, nor cannot have, the knowledge or the measure. The concept of risk of development is found within the limit of this new figure of prudence. We have seen, in fact, that once we are aware of the existence of risk of development we can no longer plead for industry to put into circulation products offering total quality, since the precautionary attitude affirms that this is not possible. Precaution finds its condition of possibility in a sort of hiatus and time-shift between the requirements of action and the certainty of knowledge. It enters into a new modality of the relationship between knowledge and power. The age of precaution is one which reformulates the Cartesian demand for methodical doubt. Precaution results from an ethic of the necessary decision in a context of uncertainty. The appearance of the precautionary principle is a sign of the profound philosophical and sociological transformations that characterize our fin-de-siécle.

Precaution and the Risk Society

In the mid-1980s, Ulrich Beck published *Risk Society* (1992), a widely read book in which he demonstrated how contemporary societies re-volve around the notion of risk. He could not have known then that his hypotheses would be borne out by the appearance and future development of the precautionary principle.

In effect, the principle of precaution rounds out the agenda of the "risk society" in several ways. First of all, the principle of precaution appears as one of the primary instruments of "reflexive modernization" which, as Beck demonstrates, characterizes postmodernism. Through the notion of precaution, modern society thinks about its problems and questions its basic assumptions. More than ever, modern society finds itself cut off from the natural world, removed as it were from the scientific and technological project on which it is based. Precaution appears when scientific expertise comes up against its own limitations and forces the politician to make sovereign decisions, alone and without recourse to others. It can perhaps be said that, with the principle of precaution, the analysis made by Beck within a specific national context has become an international preoccupation. Indeed, the true sphere in which the principle of precaution applies is international law—environmental law, trade law, and government liability. Along with the principle of precaution, the notion of reflexive modernization has become a central preoccupation of the international community.

Through the notion of precaution, the experience of risk takes on three additional dimensions that build on the descriptions provided in *Risk Society*. First, the power dimension. The issues of liability and risk are linked to the phenomenal technological capabilities we have achieved. The industrial "will to power"—to borrow Nietzsche's famous formulation—is apparent in the proliferation of highly efficient technical systems. As this century comes to a close, industrial power is such that it no longer only causes accidents, but also catastrophes. We experience the industrial promise as fraught with the threat of disaster. When the multinational firms that manufacture genetically modified organisms (GMOs) state that, thanks to their efforts, world hunger will soon be eradicated and that environmental problems linked to intensive farming are already a thing of the past, the news sets off alarm bells. This is because such exploits are in fact tremendous displays of strength. Modern industrial power is a superpower of such might that the horizon of our accountability necessarily extends over the very long term. We are responsible for future generations. The Stoics, in an attempt to free man from worry, suggested that he draw a distinction between that which depends on us and that which does not, it being understood that we are only accountable for those things over which we have control. The problem with industrial power is that it appears that we no longer lack control over anything. Hence the boundless nature of liability that is so worrisome. It leaves no room for innocence, as we can see from the rarefaction in law of the notions of the fortuitous event and force majeure (or act of God). However, this sense of boundlessness is merely the reflection of our awareness of contemporary industrial power.

But as Beck points out, risk is also a social relationship. The notion of precaution also raises the issue of power relationships in a global society during an era of globalization. Specifically, the power of the industrial society is exercised through relations of power, which are fundamentally asymmetrical. Modern technologies create dependencies, not equality. The more technologically developed societies become, the less they seem capable of being governed by the contractual model. The asymmetrical relationship between employer and employee is epitomized by the notion of the employment contract, which organizes the employee's subordination and the apportioning liability for professional risks. The relationship between producer and consumer is also asymmetrical, as is the relationship between the professional and the layman, underpinning the right to consume. Today, questions of liability turn essentially on these asymmetries. It is this asymmetrical dimension, and the feeling of dependency to which it gives rise, that lie at the heart of precaution. Risk is not only a danger, it is a social relationship. It is the relationship between those who have technological power and those who benefit or perhaps suffer from it.

In addition to power in the relationship with nature and power in relationships between human beings, there is the third dimension of the experience of precaution: that of harm suffered. In the industrial society, it is believed that activity and business are impossible without risk. Risk is considered normal; it is not contested in and of itself. The only question is how to organize the apportioning of risk. We can't even conceive of the idea that the acceptability of an activity or business could hinge on its posing no risk for others, provided that we do not hold liable only those who suffer harm due to the risk, and that those who put others at risk be held responsible.

With precaution, we are witnessing a remarkable change in this schema. The problem is no longer so much to multiply the responsibility for risk and to organize the solvency of those who are liable through insurance, but rather to prevent certain risks from being taken. Not only is prevention taking precedence over compensation, we are also trying to anticipate and prevent risks whose existence has not been proven. There are two major reasons for this: one is that the nature of damages has changed from mere individual accidents to catastrophes, and the other is that there has been a reevaluation of the cost of risk. A perfect illustration of the new scale on which risk is measured: during World War I, a general could send three hundred thousand soldiers to their death in waves of fifteen, as in the battle of the Chemin des Dames. Today, the only acceptable war is the "zero risk" war. This is a peculiar transmutation of values. In the traditional cost–benefit trade-off, it was enough that the advantages sufficiently outweighed the risks for us to feel justified in taking action and thereby accepting the residual portion of the risk taken. Today, we tend to measure the risk on the basis of this residual portion: what is worth sacrificing for this? Are those who are unlucky enough to be among the victims of so much less value than the others? This is the method of valuation that lies behind the zero risk problematic.

Conclusion

1. If it appears that precaution results from an appropriate epistemologico-legal system, than it is worthwhile to distinguish providence and prevention, for precaution introduces a world that is neither that of responsibility nor of solidarity; it should be remembered that these three formations, far from being incompatible, are in fact complementary. We are not concerned with three worlds that succeed each other over time, each replacing another, but rather with three attitudes with regard to uncertainty, assessed and developed at three moments in time. They already existed before receiving the formalizations that have been seen over the last two centuries. We are concerned with three faces of prudence, to the extent that we interpret this notion in the sense that Aristotle gave it of behavior in the face of uncertainty. These three attitudes are not the only possible attitudes of prudence. Each has its field of competence and area of validity. For this reason, it is essential not to confuse them and to respect their spheres of influence and jurisdiction: while providence is always necessary, it is inadequate in order to confront these "global threats" that themselves relativize the attitude of prevention. Precaution condemns neither providence nor prevention. It only introduces another level of preoccupation in the conduct of humans in certain situations of uncertainty.

2. Precaution, properly understood, reintroduces the true, sovereign decision in public policy and in the practices of responsibility. Conventional law on responsibility does not so much sanction a decision well or badly taken as it does the disregard of available knowledge. The logics of fault and prevention presuppose that, in the spheres they govern, it is always possible to articulate a standard of conduct that everyone must observe. One incurs one's responsibility as soon as one does not respect the practical consequences of available knowledge, a standard that makes possible the formulation of sanctioned obligations. Precaution, which resituates us in a con-

text of uncertainty, reintroduces a pure logic of decision. And the rationality of the decision can no longer satisfy itself with the conventional cost–benefit balance, which is in principle unknown or at least dubious. It derives from logics that are, according to risk economists, irreducible to conventional utility functions. This has a twofold consequence: the decision still belongs to the politician rather than to the expert and is the result more of an ethic, of the respect of certain procedures, than of a morality linked to the application of a preexisting framework. It does not follow that scientific expertise is useless, but that it will not release the politician from the sovereignty of his or her decision.

3. Precaution, to a certain extent, brings us out of the age of insurance companies. It creates a world in which, in principle, compensation no longer has meaning, because the only rational attitude is to avoid the occurrence of a threat with irreversible consequences. Precaution is an attitude of protection rather than compensation. Concurrent with the growth of the theme of precaution, one can observe a great prudence from insurers as to the possibility of covering the corresponding losses. This is understandable: one is in the order of the unlimited (from the point of view of amounts), not only of the indefinite but also the undefinable (from the point of view of risk). But precaution does not itself disqualify the need for compensation once the threats at issue have consequences for individuals. From this point of view, precautionary logic accentuates the dissociation between responsibility and compensation that already characterized the face of solidarity. If the cause of injury is no longer revealed by, properly speaking, a logic of risk, the same can be said of compensation. Precautionary logic does, however, impose the construction of new outlines: contractual definition of the risks covered either by a limitation of the duration of claims periods, by fixing limits of coverage or by changing the size of ranges of mutualization. In this respect, the mechanism implemented in France in 1982 for the coverage of natural disasters provides an interesting model. It makes prevention into a political function; it institutes a mechanism for solidary compensation, at two levels, anticipating coverage if necessary from the state in the event of a superdisaster (Magnan 1995).

Responsibility, in the strict sense of the word, corresponds to providence and solidarity to prevention. Categories that were simultaneously moral, political, and economic, responsibility and solidarity described a form of social contract, a method of distribution of rights and obligations in society. The word is missing that would correspond to them within the precautionary paradigm. Maybe one can, while waiting for a better locution, speak of safety, inasmuch as the term describes, as in nuclear terms, a particularly strict safety requirement. And, in the long term, precaution demonstrates a sort of inflexion in our attitude with regard to risk. Fear, from which our societies had perhaps, in accordance with the progressive utopia of the twentieth century, believed they could free themselves, returns in a new form. Solidarity had almost made us riskophiles; now we are almost riskophobes, individually and collectively, and will likely remain so for some time.

The emergence of precaution accompanies the crisis of progress, a certain overvaluation of the past in relation to the future, the desire to limit the destructive effects of time, and perhaps also a new suspicion aroused on the human species and the rationality of its development. This occurs with the proviso that what is concerned is freedom, enterprise, innovation, their unwanted consequences, in the long term, on the scale of the species. Precaution is a way of raising, considerably, the price of innovation. The alert has been given by a succession of affairs in the sectors of the environment and public health. Damage, serious and irreversible, has been caused that now appears could have been avoided by the observation of a precautionary attitude. It is behind the crisis of confidence that means that the spirit of enterprise, of creation, and of innovation, even in this period of unemployment, is no longer valued as before, with a certain privilege being given to abstention. In the age of precaution, the value of enterprise depends less on the well-being that it procures than on the urgency and the degree of necessity for products that it makes available. We wondered, in a previous age, whether it was better to have a big enterprise or a small enterprise; now what counts is frugality. Paradoxically, at the dawn of the twenty-first century, value is no longer in abundance, but in scarcity. So be it; but if precaution is no doubt necessary, one can also fear the consequences of too great a precaution. Precaution demands regulation.

As we become aware that certain activities demand a precautionary attitude, and that precaution is being discovered as a principle of responsibility, we see the formulation of precautionary legislation. In fact, precaution may be the worst or the best of principles. As the saying goes: "When in doubt, do nothing." The danger of precaution is that it may result in inaction. There is another saying: "Too many cooks spoil the broth." The precautions to take in the context of a technologically developed society are no doubt necessary, but, they must remain "reasonable" to prevent them from leading to an exhaustion of innovation and therefore to a revolutionary change in society with even more unfortunate consequences. This is the difficult tight rope that we must tread in pursuit of the idea of sustainable development.

NOTES

An earlier version of this essay was published as "The Return of the Crafty Genius: An Outline of a Philosophy of Precaution," *Connecticut Insurance Law Journal* 6, no. 1 (1999): 47–80, and is reprinted by permission of the *Connecticut Insurance Law Journal.*

Editors' Note: France's tainted blood crisis received only cursory attention in the United States, and it is therefore helpful to include a brief explanation. In June 1985, Michel Garretta, then-director the of French National Blood Transfusion Center, ordered the normal distribution of nonheated blood products. Garretta decided that the widely accepted and American-pioneered heat treatment procedure that inactivated the AIDS virus in blood was unnecessary. This order was in direct conflict with the practices of other nations, including the United States and Canada. As a result of this order, French patients received untreated and untested blood for six months. In 1992, it was reported that about one-half of France's four thousand hemophiliac population had contracted the virus and more than 250 had already succumbed to it. A battle of who was to blame ensued—scientists pointed the finger at the politicians and the politicians at the scientists. And there were also those who claimed they were blameless. Georgina Dufoix, at that time the Social Affairs Minister, stated paradoxically that she was "responsible but not guilty." As one author noted, "[N]one individually were responsible; the system was assigned responsibility. And now they all claim that they were not at fault. The hemophiliacs are dead because they were not seen. As public technocracies spread, perhaps this is the sort of defendant we had better get used to." *Wall St. Journal* 1992; see generally Feldman 2000.

REFERENCES

Beck, Urlich. 1992. *Risk Society: Towards a New Modernity.* Translated by Mark Ritter. Beverly Hills: Sage.

Cuvier, Baron Georges. [1863] 1969. *The Animal Kingdom.* Reprint, New York: Kraus.

Descartes, Rene. *Meditations on First Philosophy.* [1641] 1992. Edited and translated by George Heffernan. South Bend, Ind.: University of Notre Dame Press.

Feldman, Eric A. 2000. "Blood Justice: Courts, Conflict and Compensation in Japan, France and the United States." *Law and Society Review* 34:651–702.

Gény, Francois. 1902. "Risque et responsabilite." *Revue Trimestrielle de droit civil.* Paris: Sirey.

Jonas, Hans. 1984. *The Imperative of Responsibility.* Translated by Hans Jonas, in collaboration with David Herr. Chicago: University of Chicago Press.

Josserand, Louis. 1897. *Responsabilite du fait des choses inanimees.* Paris: Libr. nouv. de droit et de jurisprudence, A. Rousseau.

Labbé, Jean Etienne. 1885. Paris: Sirey.

Mangan, Serge. 1995. "Catastrophe Insurance System in France." *Geneva Papers on Risk and Insurance* 20:474–80.

Plato. [n.d.] 1991. *Protagoras.* Translated by C. C. W. Taylor. Oxford: Clarendon Press.

Portalis, Jeane-Etienne Marie. 1989. In *Naissance du Code Civil, an X11— 1800–1804*. Paris: Flammarion.

Saleilles, Raymond. 1897. *Les Accidents de travail et la responsabilite civile*. Paris: A. Rousseau.

Sanson-Hermitte, Marie-Angèle. 1996. *Le sang et le droit: essai sur la transfusion sanguine*. Paris: Editions du Seil.

Thiers, Adolphe. 1850. *Rapport Au Nom De La Commission de l'assistance et de la prevoyance publiques* 6. Paris: Paulin, Lheureux.

Thoulon, Edouard. 1898. *La Responsabilite des accidents don't les ouvriers sont victimes dans leur travail*. Paris: Libr. nouv. de droit et de jurisprudence, A. Rousseau.

United Nations. 1992. U.N. Conference on Environment and Development, Rio de Janeiro. The Rio Declaration on Environment and Development, Principle 10. The Earth Summit, AGENDA 21, rio declaration, forest principles. New York.

Wall St. Journal. 1992. "Murder by Bureaucracy." *Wall St. J.*, 5 August. A14.

Index

ABC (television), 182
abortion, 40
accidents: assigning responsibility in, 279–81; automobile, 243–46, 281; climbing, 180, 182–86, 195–97; definitions of, 246, 284–86, 288; medical, 281–82, 294; nineteenth-century work, 198–99, 277. *See also* injuries; workers compensation insurance
accountability: distribution of, 39, 40–41, 47–48, 49n. 4; as requirement, 220
Ackerman, Bruce, 178
actuarial fairness principle, 73
actuarial justice: crime and, 254–55; example of, 9–10; in Friendly Societies, 99–101; paradigm of solidarity and, 278; in police reporting, 251–53, 261; in psychiatric risk assessment, 223–28, 229–30
adjusters, 137, 256
advanced liberalism, concept of, 17, 178. *See also* governmentality (governmental rationality); liberalism; neoliberalism
Adventure Consultants, 182, 185
adventure travel, 6, 179–81, 203n. 6. *See also* extreme sports; mountaineering; summiteering
adverse events: political construction of, 52–53; services to counter, 66–67; standard of care issues and, 63–64; in workers compensation, 68–69
adverse selection, effects of, 138
advertising and marketing: altruism message in, 57–58; of children's protective devices,

267–69; discourse fostered by, 55–56; helping emphasized in, 56–57, 75–76n. 1; sales and claims visions in, 9; vulnerability emphasized in, 55–56
AFDC (Aid to Families with Dependent Children), 59, 118, 178
AFL (American Federation of Labor), 199
agents, race of, 141n. 2
aging, changing expectations of, 66
Aharoni, Y., 113n. 8
AIDS, 138, 139, 203n. 3, 300n
Aid to Families with Dependent Children (AFDC), 59, 118, 178
AIG (company), 55–56
Akerloff, George, 139
Alberta Collision Report Form, 243, 244
Alberta Manual on Classification and Reporting of Vehicle Collisions, 243
Allison, Stacy, 192
Allstate Insurance Company, 8, 55
Alstott, Anne, 178
AMA (American Medical Association), 150–58
amazon.com, 188, 204–5n. 20, 205n. 21
American Federation of Labor (AFL), 199
American Medical Association (AMA), 150–58
American Psychiatric Association, 71
Amicable Society, 84–85, 91, 93
Aristotle, 297
Ashworth, Andrew, 250–51
assurance, use of term, 113n. 1. *See also* insurance